POLICY ANALYSIS
IN BELGIUM

International Library of Policy Analysis

Series editors: Iris Geva-May and Michael Howlett,
Simon Fraser University, Canada

This major new series brings together for the first time a detailed
examination of the theory and practice of policy analysis systems
at different levels of government and by non-governmental actors
in a specific country. It therefore provides a key addition to
research and teaching in comparative policy analysis and policy
studies more generally.

Each volume includes a history of the country's policy analysis which
offers a broad comparative overview with other countries as well as the
country in question. In doing so, the books in the series provide the
data and empirical case studies essential for instruction and for further
research in the area. They also include expert analysis of different
approaches to policy analysis and an assessment of their evolution and
operation.

Early volumes in the series will cover the following countries:

Australia • Brazil • China • Czech Republic • France • Germany •
India • Israel • Netherlands • New Zealand • Norway •
Russia • South Africa • Taiwan • UK • USA

and will build into an essential library of key reference works. The series
will be of interest to academics and students in public policy, public
administration and management, comparative politics and government,
public organisations and individual policy areas.
It will also interest people working in the countries in question
and internationally.

In association with the ICPA-Forum and *Journal of Comparative Policy Analysis.*
See more at http://goo.gl/raJUX

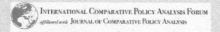 

POLICY ANALYSIS IN BELGIUM

Edited by Marleen Brans and David Aubin

International Library of Policy Analysis, Vol 10

First published in Great Britain in 2017 by

Policy Press
University of Bristol
1-9 Old Park Hill
Bristol BS2 8BB
UK
+44 (0)117 954 5940
pp-info@bristol.ac.uk
www.policypress.co.uk

North America office:
Policy Press
c/o The University of Chicago Press
1427 East 60th Street
Chicago, IL 60637, USA
t: +1 773 702 7700
f: +1 773 702 9756
sales@press.uchicago.edu
www.press.uchicago.edu

© Policy Press 2017

British Library Cataloguing in Publication Data
A catalogue record for this book is available from the British Library.

Library of Congress Cataloging-in-Publication Data
A catalog record for this book has been requested.

ISBN 978-1-4473-1725-8 hardcover
ISBN 978-1-4473-1726-5 ePdf

Cover design by Qube Design Associates, Bristol
Front cover: image kindly supplied by istock
Printed and bound in Great Britain by CPI Group (UK) Ltd, Croydon, CR0 4YY
Policy Press uses environmentally responsible print partners

Contents

List of tables and figures

Tables

Figures

List of abbreviations

ABSP	Belgian Francophone Political Science Association (*Association belge francophone de science politique*)
ABVV	Belgian Socialist Trade Union (*Algemeen Belgisch Vakverbond*)
ACLVB	Belgian Liberal Trade Union (*Algemene Centrale der Liberale Vakbonden van België*)
ACV-CSC	Christian Democrat Trade Union (*Confédération des syndicats chrétiens*)
ACW	Flemish Christian Workers' Movement (*Algemeen Christelijk Werkersverbond*)
APAO	Alternative policy advisory organisation
BBB	Better administrative policy (*Beter Bestuurlijk Beleid*)
BELSPO	Belgian Federal Science Policy Office
CAAD	Autonomous Advisory Cell for Sustainable Development
CBA	Cost-benefit analysis
CCATM	Consultative Commission on Town Planning and Mobility (*Commission consultative communale d'aménagement du territoire et de mobilité*)
CD&V	Flemish Christian Democrats (*Christen-Democratisch en Vlaams*)
CdH	Francophone Christian Democrats (*Centre démocrate humaniste*)
CDLD	Walloon Code for Local Democracy and Decentralisation (*Code wallon de la démocratie locale et de la décentralisation*)
CEDER	Study centre of the Flemish Christian Democrats
CEG	Study centre of the Francophone social-liberals (*Centre d'étude Jacques Georgin*)
CEGLG	Committee for Efficiency Gains in Local Government
CEPESS	Study centre of the Francophone Christian Democrats
CESW	Social and Economic Council of Wallonia (*Conseil économique et social de Wallonie*)
CJG	Study centre of the Francophone liberals (*Centre d'étude Jean Gol*)
CPDT	Permanent Conference for Territorial Development (*Commission permanente du développement territorial*)
CWATUP	Walloon Land Planning, Urbanism and Heritage Code (*Code wallon de l'aménagement du territoire de l'urbanisme et du patrimoine*)
CWEDD	Walloon Advisory Body for the Environment and Sustainability (*Conseil wallon pour l'environnement et de développement durable*)
DAV	Agency of Administrative Simplification (*Dienst Administratieve Vereenvoudiging*)
DéFI	Francophone Social-Liberal Party (formerly FDF)

Ecolo	Francophone Green Party
EFMN	European Foresight Monitoring Network
EIA	Environmental impact assessment
EP	European Parliament
EU	European Union
FAEA	Federal Advisory Committee for European Affairs
FDF	Front of Francophones (*Front des Francophones*)
FGTB-ABVV	Belgian Socialist Trade Union (*Fédération générale des travailleurs de Belgique*)
FPS	Federal public service
FRESH	Francophone Research Fund for Social Sciences and Humanities
F.R.S.-FNRS	Francophone National Research Fund
FTE	Full-time equivalent
FWA	Walloon Farmers' Federation (*Fédération wallonne de l'agriculture*)
GROEN	Flemish Green Party
IBSA	Brussels Institute for Statistics and Analysis (*Institut bruxellois de statistiques et d'analyse*)
IEV	Study centre of the Francophone Socialist Party (*Institut Emile Vandevelde*)
ILO	International Labour Organisation
IWEPS	Walloon Institute for Evaluation, Foresight and Statistics (*Institut wallon d'evaluation, de prospective et de statistiques*)
KU	Knowledge utilisation
MC	Ministerial cabinet
MCA	Multi-criteria analysis
MFWB	Ministry of the Federation Wallonia-Brussels (French Community)
MOC	Walloon Christian Workers' Movement (*Mouvement ouvrier chrétien*)
MP	Member of parliament
NDIIA	National Democratic Institute for International Affairs
NGO	Non-governmental organisation
NPM	New public management
NSVP	National Syndicate for Policy and Security Personnel (*Nationaal Syndicaat voor het politie- en veiligheidspersoneel*)
N-VA	Flemish Nationalist Party (*Nieuw-Vlaamse Alliantie*)
OECD	Organisation for Economic Co-operation and Development
OEJAJ	Observatory of Childhood, Youth and Youth Assistance (*Observatoire de l'enfance, de la jeunesse et de l'aide à la jeunesse*)
OPC	Observatory of Cultural Policies (*Observatoire des politiques culturelles*)
Open VLD	Flemish Liberal Party

PBO	Policy-oriented research
PCDR	Communal plan for rural development (*Plan communal de développement rural*)
PMB	Private members' bill
PMC	Policy and Management Cycle
PPBS	Planning-programming-budgeting system
PS	Francophone Socialist Party (*Parti socialiste*)
PST	Transversal strategic plan (*Plan stratégique transversal*)
PUMP	Public management programme
PVDA/PTB	Workers' Party of Belgium (*Partij van de Arbeid van België/Parti du Travail de Belgique*)
RIA	Regulatory impact analysis
RTBF	Belgian Francophone Radio and Television (*Radio-télévision belge de la Communauté française*)
RTL-TVI	Luxembourg Radio and Television (*Radio Télévision Luxembourg – Télévision indépendante*)
SELOR	Recruitment agency of the federal government
SERV	Flemish Social and Economic Council (*Sociaal-Economische Raad van Vlaanderen*)
SME	Small and medium-sized enterprise
sp.a	Flemish Social-Democratic Party (*Socialistische Partij Anders*)
SPW	Public Service of Wallonia (*Service public de Wallonie*)
SVR	Study centre of the Flemish government (*Studiedienst van de Vlaamse Regering*)
SWEP	Walloon Society of Evaluation and Foresight (*Société wallonne d'évaluation et de prospective*)
SWOT	Strengths, weaknesses, opportunities, threats
UCM	Union of the Small Businesses (*Union des classes moyennes*)
UN	United Nations
UNESCO	United Nations Educational, Scientific and Cultural Organisation
UNIZO	Flemish Organisation for the Self-Employed and SMEs (*Unie van Zelfstandige Ondernemers*)
UWE	Walloon Employers' Organisation (*Union wallonne des entreprises*)
VBO-FEB	Federation of Enterprises in Belgium (*Verbond van Belgische ondernemingen-Fédération des entreprises de Belgique*)
VEP	Flemish Evaluation Platform (*Vlaams Evaluatie Platform*)
VIONA	Flemish Interuniversity Research Network on Labour Market Monitoring (*Vlaams Interuniversitair Onderzoeksnetwerk Arbeids Marktrapportering*)
VIWTA	Flemish Institute for Research in Science and Technology Assessment (*Vlaams Instituut voor Wetenschappelijk en Technologisch Aspectenonderzoek*)

VOKA	Flemish Business Association (*Vlaams Netwerk van Ondernemingen*)
VPW	Dutch Political Science Association (*Vereniging voor de Politieke Wetenschappen*)
VRT	Flemish Radio and Television (*Vlaamse Radio- en Televisieomroep*)
VTB-VAB	Flemish Tourist and Drivers Union (*Vlaamse Touristenbond-Vlaamse Automobilistenbond*)
VTM	Flemish Television Company (*Vlaamse Televisie Maatschappij*)
VVSG	Association of the Flemish Municipalities (*Vereniging van Vlaamse Steden en Gemeenten*)
WWF	World Wide Fund for Nature

Notes on contributors

David Aubin graduated from Sciences Po Lyon (1996) and Université libre de Bruxelles (ULB, 1998), and holds a PhD in political science from Université catholique de Louvain (UCL, 2005). He is professor of political science at UCL where he teaches policy analysis, evaluation and sustainability. He is also involved in several training programmes for civil servants. Embedded in Belgian and European collaborative research projects, his research activities concern policy work, the comparative analysis of environmental policies, and regulatory policies, including the multi-level regulation of network industries. He was invited scholar at Université de Montréal, Katholieke Universiteit Leuven (KU Leuven) and University of Colorado Denver, and has published in journals such as *Policy Sciences*, *Journal of Public Policy*, and *Environment and Planning Part C*. He has also recently co-edited a book on multi-level regulation in the telecoms sector (Palgrave, 2014).

Benjamin Biard holds a Master's in political science from UCL. Since 2015, he has been an F.R.S.-FNRS research fellow at the Institute of Political Science Louvain-Europe. His main research interests include populism and the influence of populist parties on public policy and democracy. He is co-secretary of the Belgian Francophone Political Science Association (ABSP).

Nele Bossens studied history and public administration at KU Leuven and UCL. She was a researcher at the KU Leuven Public Governance Institute, where her areas of interest include diversity policy, the influence of particular interest groups on policy, and competing sources of policy advice. Since 2016, she has taught societal orientation at Atlas, Antwerp.

Marleen Brans (Lic. KU Leuven; MA Hull; PhD European University Institute) is professor of public policy and administration at the KU Leuven Public Governance Institute. Her research interests focus on the production and use of policy advice by academics, civil servants, personal advisors and strategic advisory bodies. She has published in journals such as *Public Administration*, *West-European Politics*, *Halduskultuur*, *Evidence & Policy*, *Policy and Society*, and the *Journal of Comparative Policy Analysis*. She has co-edited *The politics of Belgium* (Routledge, 2009) and *Rewards for high public office in Europe and the US* (Routledge, 2012). With Iris Geva-May and Michael Howlett she edited the *Handbook of comparative policy analysis* (Routledge, 2017). In addition, Marleen Brans is Vice-President of the International Public Policy Association and President of the Accreditation Committee of the European Association for Public Administration Accreditation.

Bart De Peuter (MA Political Sciences and European MA Public Administration) is senior researcher at the KU Leuven Public Governance Institute. His research interests and expertise comprise policy evaluation, monitoring, local government and intergovernmental relations, built up via 15 years of policy-relevant research projects. He combines research on policy evaluation with evaluation practice in different fields, provides professional training in evaluation and is member of the coordinating committee of the Flemish Evaluation Platform.

Christian de Visscher (PhD Political Science) held several positions in the Belgian civil service (both at the federal and at the regional level) before being appointed professor of public administration at UCL in 1998. He teaches public administration and public management both at Master's and PhD level and is also involved in the organisation of Executive Master's degrees for professional civil servants. Between 2010 and 2016, he chaired the Institute of Political Sciences Louvain-Europe at UCL. His research interests lie in the field of public sector management in Belgium and in Western Europe.

Lieven De Winter is senior professor at the UCL (where he is co-director of the *Pôle interuniversitaire sur l'opinion publique et la politique*). He obtained his PhD on the Belgian legislator at the European University Institute. His research interests include (the comparative analysis of) coalition formation, party and cabinet government, parliament, political parties, territorial identities and community conflicts, and electoral behaviour at the regional, national and European elections. As well as contributing to numerous articles in international journals, he is co-editor of *Puzzles of government formation: Coalition theory and deviant cases* (Routledge, 2011); *The politics of Belgium* (Routledge, 2009); *Elections: le reflux? Comportements et attitudes lors des élections en Belgique* (De Boeck, 2007); *Autonomist parties in Europe* (ICPS, 2006); *Mise à l'agenda politique en Belgique (1991-2000)* (Academia Press, 2005); and *Regionalist parties in Western Europe* (Routledge, 1998).

Catherine Fallon first trained as biochemical engineer (Massachusetts Institute of Technology, 1981) and worked in industry and at the European Commission before obtaining a PhD in political science at the Université de Liège (ULg, 2009). She is currently professor of policy analysis and evaluation at ULg and director of the SPIRAL research centre, and teaches public management and public policy. Her field of research is science and society, where she has studied the social and political aspects of environmental issues (soil/air pollution, treatment of radioactive wastes) and their impact on science policy in Belgium. She currently works on the governementality of new genetic tests in health policy, and the modalities of public participation and their impact on the decision-making process. She has published or co-edited several books about management reforms, public participation and risk management, as well as journal articles, notably in the *Journal of Risk Research* and *The Lancet*.

Ellen Fobé (MA Political Science, MA Public Management and Policy, KU Leuven) is a PhD candidate at the KU Leuven Public Governance Institute, where she has been working as a researcher since 2008. Her research interests include diverse types of policy work, policy advice, policy instruments, policy capacity and knowledge utilisation. She has conducted research on the Flemish strategic advisory system, and on the practice and use of policy-oriented foresight in Flanders (Belgium), within the framework of the Policy Research Centre Governmental Organisation. Her current research activities and PhD focus on the analytical capacity of policy workers in Belgium. She has published in journals such as *Evidence & Policy*, and *Policy and Society*.

Bert Fraussen is post-doctoral fellow and lecturer in the Research School of Social Sciences, at the Australian National University (ANU). He was awarded his PhD in political science from the University of Antwerp, where he has been guest lecturer and also holds an honorary position. His work, which focuses on the organisational development of interest groups and their interaction with policymakers, has appeared in *Public Administration, Policy Sciences, Political Studies* and the *Journal of European Public Policy*.

Athanassios Gouglas joined the KU Leuven Public Governance Institute research team in September 2013 just after his graduation from the Master's in European politics and policies. In the period 2004-12, as a civil servant and political adviser, he worked closely with policymakers in Greece and the EU on numerous bilateral cooperation projects. Since March 2014, he has been working on a PhD research project funded by the Research Foundation Flanders on the determinants of parliamentary turnover in Western Europe between 1945-2014.

Vincent Jacquet is a PhD candidate (FRESH F.R.S.-FNRS) in political science at UCL. He graduated in public administration from ULg. His research interests are participatory and deliberative democracy, political participation, local politics and democratic theory. He is currently working on a doctoral thesis on citizens' reluctance to take part in deliberative mini-publics and criminal juries, and has published several works on democratic innovations.

Sylke Jaspers has been a PhD candidate at the KU Leuven Public Governance Institute since 2015. She holds a Master's in political science from the Vrije Universiteit Brussel and an advanced Master's in European politics and policies from KU Leuven. In her PhD research, Sylke analyses the trade-offs between public values that citizen-volunteers and public professionals deal with when coproducing public services. In addition to co-production and public-service delivery, her main research interests lie in the field of participation, representation, ministerial cabinet systems, political advisers and (digital) innovation.

Michael Keating holds a BA from the University of Oxford and in 1975 was the first PhD graduate from what is now Glasgow Caledonian University. He is ESRC professor of politics at the Universities of Aberdeen and Edinburgh and Director of the Centre on Constitutional Change. He has held posts in the universities of Strathclyde and Western Ontario and from 2000 until 2010 he was Professor at the European University Institute in Florence. His research interests include European politics, nationalism, public policy, urban and regional politics and society, and social-science methodologies. His most recent book is *Rescaling Europe*, published by Oxford University Press in 2013.

Marine Kravagna holds a Master's in public administration from ULg (2014). Her research interests include the study of European institutions, democracy and local policy analysis, as well as language and politics. She has contributed to several scientific publications, notably as co-editor for a special issue in *Revue internationale de politique comparée*. She currently works at the Federal Public Service Foreign Affairs as attaché for European trade policy and the World Trade Organisation.

Justin Lawarée holds a Master's in public administration from UCL. From October 2010 to August 2011, he was a staff member of the Belgian Chamber of Representatives. Working as a research and teaching assistant at the UCL since September 2011, his PhD project examines the strategies used by policy entrepreneurs in Walloon innovation policies. His areas of research include policy entrepreneurship, policy innovation, regional policy and social network analysis.

Valérie Pattyn (PhD KU Leuven, MA Political Science, BA Educational Studies) is an assistant professor and teaches at Leiden University College The Hague. Her main areas of expertise are policy evaluation, evidence-based policy, and policy advice. She combines research on the institutionalisation of policy evaluation and evaluation-capacity building with applied evaluation studies in various policy fields. In addition, she is involved in research projects about policy advice production and use within and outside the civil service. Valérie is one of the co-chairs of the EGPA Study Group on Policy Design and Evaluation, member of the coordination committee of the Flemish Evaluation Assocation and of the Dutch Evaluation Society. She has published in journals such as *Evaluation, Journal of Comparative Policy Analysis, International Review of Administrative Sciences, Public Management Review*, and *Policy and Society*.

Maxime Petit Jean holds a Master's in public administration (ULg, 2010), a Master's in European politics and policies (KU Leuven, 2011) and a PhD in political and social sciences (UCL, 2016). His main research interests are public management reforms, policy advisory systems and policy-oriented futures studies.

Pauline Pirlot holds a Master's in political science from UCL (2013). She is currently a teaching assistant in political science at UCL and is studying for a PhD in European politics. Her main research interests concern the formulation of EU external policy in the context of fragmented international regimes, particularly in forestry.

Min Reuchamps (PhD) is Professor of Political Science at UCL. He graduated from ULg and Boston University. His teaching and research interests are federalism and multi-level governance and political sociology, as well as participatory and deliberative methods. He has recently published books on federalism and minority nations (Routledge, 2015) and on constitutional deliberative democracy in Europe (ECPR Press, 2016). He is the president of the ABSP.

Benoît Rihoux is Professor of Political Science at UCL, where he manages CESPOL (Centre for political science and comparative politics). He is involved in several research projects around his own topics of specialisation (political parties, social movements, organisational change) as well as around other themes that can be better comprehended through systematic comparison: crises, community conflicts, national and European policymaking, organisational innovation, natural resource management, and professional ethics. He has played a leading role in the development and dissemination of innovative comparative methods, in particular configurational comparative methods (CCMs) and QCA, applicable to many fields and research disciplines. He is the initiator and co-ordinator of the COMPASSS international network (www.compasss.org) and also steers broader initiatives around methodology in his role as joint Academic Convenor of the ECPR Methods School.

Silke Ruebens (MA Educational Sciences, MA Public Administration and Public Policy) was educational co-ordinator of the KU Leuven Master's programme in public administration and public policy and of the KU Leuven Master's in European politics and policies. She is an expert on curriculum development and the quality control of university education. She has also carried out research in the field of leadership.

Nathalie Schiffino (Lic. Public and International Affaires, MA Political Science, PhD Governement and Public Administration) is Professor of Political Science at UCL. Her research interests include democracy and policy analysis. She is co-director of civil-service training programmes on topics such as risk, policy analysis and policy evaluation. She has published in journals such as *Risk Analysis*, *Journal of Risk Research*, *International Review of Administrative Sciences*, and *West European Politics*. She is the author or co-author of several books published by Routledge (2003), Lexington (2006), and Peter Lang (2015). Her online course on political science was a finalist of the first-ever edX (Harvard and MIT) Prize for Exceptional Contributions in Online Teaching and Learning.

Dave Sinardet is a professor in the Department of Communication Studies at the Free University of Brussels. His research interests include federalism, nationalism, consociational democracy, political communication and multilingual democracy. He published on these themes in journals such as *Party Politics*, *Acta Politica*, *Governance*, *Pouvoirs*, *Regional and Federal Studies*, *West European Politics*, and *Government and Opposition*. He is also an expert on Belgian politics and particularly on Belgian constitutional reform. His PhD (University of Antwerp, 2007) dealt with how a public sphere functions in a federal multilingual country such as Belgium and more specifically analysed the Dutch-speaking and French-speaking media's role in the representation of Belgium's political language conflict.

Valérie Smet (MA Moral sciences, PhD Political Science) is a former researcher of Ghent University, who now works in educational management (quality assurance). Her research concentrates on social science–policy interaction as well as evidence-based (national and international) drug policy.

Jan Van Damme (PhD Political and Social Sciences) works as a city administrator in Hoeilaart, Belgium (Leisure & Welfare Unit), and has a consultancy firm, BOOM Policy Research. From 2007–2015, he was researcher and later post-doctoral fellow at the KU Leuven Public Governance Institute, where he co-ordinated the Flemish Policy Research Centre Governmental Organisation (2012–2015). His research interests include public consultation and participation, coproduction, democracy as well as specific policy domains such as youth and education policy. He obtained his PhD, titled 'Interactive policy planning: An analysis of the organisation and outcomes of interactive planning in two Flemish highly polluted "hot spots"' in 2012. He has published in international and national journals such as *Public Administration*, *Policy and Society*, and *Halduskultuur*. Prior to his academic career, he was active as a teacher, policy analyst and director of a non-governmental organisation.

Baldwin Van Gorp (PhD) is an associate professor of journalism and communications management at the Institute for Media Studies, KU Leuven. His research interests include the framing approach, journalism and public relations. On these topics he has published articles in several journals, such as *Journal of Communication*, *European Journal of Communication* and *Public Understanding of Science*.

Steven Van Hecke (PhD) is an assistant professor at the KU Leuven Public Governance Institute. Previously he was a senior research fellow at the University of Antwerp and a visiting fellow at the Robert Schuman Centre for Advanced Studies at the European University Institute. His research focuses on political parties and EU institutions. He has published in *Journal of Common Market Studies*, *Journal of European Public Policy*, *Regional and Federal Studies*, *Journal of International Iberian Studies* and *Journal of Contemporary European Research*. He is co-editor of *Readjusting the Council Presidency: Belgian leadership in the EU* (ASP Editions, 2011).

Ellen Wayenberg (PhD) is an associate professor at the Faculty of Economics and Business Administration, Ghent University, Belgium. She specialises in public policy and public administration with a specific interest in multi-level governance, intergovernmental relations and local government. She has published in various international journals including the *International Review of Administrative Sciences, Local Government Studies*, and *Urban Research and Practice,* and co-edited *Policy, Performance and Management in Governance and Intergovernmental Relations* (Edward Elgar, 2011) and *Governance and Intergovernmental Relations in the European Union and the United States, Theoretical Perspectives* (Edward Elgar, 2010). She is one of the co-chairs of the EGPA Study Group on Regional and Local Government, and is actively involved in COST Action IS1207: Local Public Sector Reforms: An International Comparison.

Wouter Wolfs is a PhD candidate at the KU Leuven Public Governance Institute, where he has been working as a research assistant since 2013. His research interests include Euroscepticism, the role of national parliaments in the EU, the organisation and management of the European Parliament, and parliamentary capacity-building. His PhD project deals with the finance regimes of European political parties.

Alex Wilson (PhD) is a policy analyst in the Members Research Services of the European Parliament, as well as associate research fellow at Vesalius College, part of the Free University of Brussels (VUB). Previously he worked as an assistant professor at the VUB and as a research fellow at the University of Aberdeen. Alex obtained a PhD on multi-level party politics in Italy and Spain at the European University Institute in 2009. His research has been published in leading international journals including the *European Journal of Political Research, West European Politics, Comparative European Politics*, and *Regional and Federal Studies.*

Acknowledgements

This volume is part of a collection that constitutes the stepping stone for a wide-ranging and ambitious comparison of policy analysis practice and the profession all over the world. This major project, which is expected to theoretically and empirically boost comparative policy analysis and policy sciences, was initiated by the two co-editors of the collection, Iris Geva-May and Michael Howlett. We are very grateful to them and committed to pushing their initiative forward and contributing to the expansion of policy analysis through the comparative study of policy analysis systems.

The production of this book relied on the mobilisation of policy analysis scholars and many colleagues in political studies, in both Belgium and abroad, who all shared their knowledge and skills in order to aid understanding of Belgium's idiosyncratic and divided political system, which is still an example of a pluri-national polity. In each chapter both Francophones and Flemish share their expertise in order to provide the reader with an unusual nation-wide view of policy work. Rather than arriving at a so-called Belgian policy analysis style, they refer to the real-world situation of at least three 'country' case studies. We wholeheartedly thank all the contributors for their willingness to collaborate on this project.

The editors are also very grateful to the thousands of civil servants, ministerial advisers and policy analysts outside government who agreed to the many requests for interviews and answered very long and detailed surveys. We also thank our senior colleagues, particularly Roger Depré, Rudolf Maes, and Geert Bouckaert, who brought to life the history of the discipline, which mainly remains an oral heritage in Belgium. Finally, we thank the publishing team at Policy Press for their precious professional guidance.

Editors' introduction to the series

Professor Iris Geva-May and Professor Michael Howlett, ILPA series editors

Policy analysis is a relatively new area of social scientific inquiry, owing its origins to developments in the US in the early 1960s. Its main rationale is systematic, evidence-based, transparent, efficient, and implementable policymaking. This component of policymaking is deemed key in democratic structures allowing for accountable public policies. From the US, policy analysis has spread to other countries, notably in Europe in the 1980s and 1990s and in Asia in the 1990s and 2000s. It has taken, respectively one to two more decades for programmes of public policy to be established in these regions preparing cadres for policy analysis as a profession. However, this movement has been accompanied by variations in the kinds of analysis undertaken as US-inspired analytical and evaluative techniques have been adapted to local traditions and circumstances, and new techniques shaped in these settings.

In the late 1990s this led to the development of the field of comparative policy analysis, pioneered by Iris Geva-May, who initiated and founded the Journal of Comparative Policy Analysis, and whose mission has been advanced with the support of editorial board members such as Laurence E. Lynn Jr., first co-editor, Peter deLeon, Duncan McRae, David Weimer, Beryl Radin, Frans van Nispen, Yukio Adachi, Claudia Scott, Allan Maslove and others in the US and elsewhere. While current studies have underlined differences and similarities in national approaches to policy analysis, the different national regimes which have developed over the past two to three decades have not been thoroughly explored and systematically evaluated in their entirety, examining both sub-national and non-executive governmental organisations as well as the non-governmental sector; nor have these prior studies allowed for either a longitudinal or a latitudinal comparison of similar policy analysis perceptions, applications, and themes across countries and time periods.

The International Library for Policy Analysis (ILPA) series fills this gap in the literature and empirics of the subject. It features edited volumes created by experts in each country, which inventory and analyse their respective policy analysis systems. To a certain extent the series replicates the template of *Policy Analysis in Canada* edited by Dobuzinskis, Howlett and Laycock (Toronto: University of Toronto Press, 2007).

Each ILPA volume surveys the state of the art of policy analysis in governmental and non-governmental organisations in each country using the common template derived from the Canadian collection in order to provide for each volume in the series comparability in terms of coverage and approach.

Each volume addresses questions such as: What do policy analysts do? What techniques and approaches do they use? What is their influence on policymaking in that country? Is there a policy analysis deficit? What norms and values guide the work done by policy analysts working in different institutional settings? Contributors focus on the sociology of policy analysis, demonstrating how analysts working in different organisations tend to have different interests and to utilise different techniques. The central theme of each volume includes historical works on the origins of policy analysis in the jurisdiction concerned, and then proceeds to investigate the nature and types, and quality, of policy analysis conducted by governments (including different levels and orders of government). It then moves on to examine the nature and kinds of policy analytical work and practices found in non-governmental actors such as think tanks, interest groups, business, labour, media, political parties, non-profits and others.

Each volume in the series aims to compare and analyse the significance of the different styles and approaches found in each country and organisation studied, and to understand the impact these differences have on the policy process.

Together, the volumes included in the ILPA series serve to provide the basic data and empirical case studies required for an international dialogue in the area of policy analysis, and an eye-opener on the nuances of policy analysis applications and implications in national and international jurisdictions. Each volume in the series is leading edge and has the promise to dominate its field and the textbook market for policy analysis in the country concerned, as well as being of broad comparative interest to markets in other countries.

The ILPA is published in association with the International Comparative Policy Analysis Forum, and the *Journal of Comparative Policy Analysis*, whose mission is to advance international comparative policy analytic studies. The editors of each volume are leading members of this network and are the best-known scholars in each respective country, as are the authors contributing to each volume in their particular domain. The book series as a whole provides learning insights for instruction and for further research in the area and constitutes a major addition to research and pedagogy in the field of comparative policy analysis and policy studies in general.

We welcome to the ILPA series Volume 10, *Policy Analysis in Belgium*, edited by Marleen Brans and David Aubin, and thank the editors and the authors for their outstanding contribution to this important encyclopedic database.

Iris Geva-May
Professor of Policy Studies, Baruch College at the City University of New York, Professor Emerita Simon Fraser University; Founding President and Editor-in-chief, International Comparative PolicyForum and *Journal of Comparative Policy Analysis*

Michael Howlett
Burnaby Mountain Professor, Department of Political Science, Simon Fraser University, and Yong Pung How Chair Professor, Lee Kuan Yew School of Public Policy, National University of Singapore

Introduction: policy analysis in Belgium – tradition, comparative features and trends

Marleen Brans and David Aubin

This book provides the first comprehensive examination of policy analysis in Belgium. At the domestic level, the book integrates knowledge about the science, art and craft of policy analysis at different levels of government and by all relevant policy actors that bear on the analysis of problems and on the search for solutions. For comparative purposes, the book's analysis of policy analysis at different levels in and outside government in Belgium highlights key comparative features of policy analysis in federal systems, in polities with a neo-corporatist consensus tradition in policymaking, and in countries with partitocratic features. The book also adds to a comparative understanding of how such international trends as the professionalisation of policy analysis, greater participation and coproduction are translated in specific contexts, as well as revealing whether there is any ground to claim that European member states are converging their policy-analytical styles under the pressures of Europeanisation.

The book brings together a number of invited experts as well as a number of early-career researchers who are currently engaged in policy-analytical research. For many of the chapters novel empirical data is gathered specifically for the purpose of the book, through surveys (on policy work and policy-analytical activities) and interviews with key players both within and outside government. Whenever possible, the editors of the book have strived to compose teams of contributors from both sides of the Dutch–French language border (from university research institutes in Flanders, Brussels and Wallonia), in order to prevent bias and to provide maximum coverage of the multi-level setting of policymaking in Belgium. As such, the book, by the very nature of the Belgian polity, is comparative to start with, and attempts to draw comparative conclusions on divergence and convergence of policy analysis within Belgium.

The book has several goals. *Policy analysis in Belgium* will be a work of reference for students and practitioners engaged in policy analysis, as well as for scholarly exchange. It can be used as a textbook in university curricula, and provides background material for open and in-house training on policy analysis to government and civil society actors. By highlighting the features of policy analysis that are typical for Belgium and its regions, as well as those features that might travel across jurisdictions, the book will also enhance the comparative understanding of policy analysis in both its theoretical and normative dimensions.

This introduction starts with what is understood by policy analysis in this book, and how policy analysis as a discipline and practice relates to other much-used concepts such as policy work, policy advice, policy evaluation and the like. Second, the introduction highlights the relatively young tradition of policy analysis as a discipline and recognized practice. Third, it puts policy analysis in Belgium in context and identifies those characteristics of the Belgian political system that are most likely to explain the way policy analysis is practised in Belgium and how it is put to use by different actors in the policy process. Fourth, the introduction addresses recent global trends that have emerged on the global meta-policy agenda and, we believe, affect the practice of policy analysis at different levels of government. The introduction concludes with an overview of the plan of the book.

Policy analysis defined

Following Dobuzinskis and colleagues (2007), this book defines policy analysis as applied social and scientific research as well as more implicit forms of practical knowledge. It is pursued by government officials and non-governmental organisations, is directed at designing, implementing and evaluating policies, and influences political decision makers' courses of action. Policy analysis in this volume is thus seen as the application of intellect to real-world public problems, both inside and outside government.

Following Lasswell's (1971) distinction of analysis *for* policy and analysis *of* policy, this book studies practices of analysis for policy in order to inform analysis of policy. One is reminded that analysis for policy refers to applied policy analysis, and encompasses both formal and informal professional practices that organisations and actors entertain to define a problem marked for government action, as well as to prescribe the measures to solve that problem by policy action or change. In this meaning, policy analysis relies on policy work by actors, encompassing the garnering of information, the demarcation of problem definitions, the design and comparison of policy instruments, and the evaluation of policies. The outcome of policy analysis is eventually policy advice, which in this book is understood as a recommendation or opinion for future courses of government action.

The editors of this book do not employ a strict normative understanding of what policy analysis should be in terms of analytical rigour and methods, and will not venture into textbook like prescriptions of best practice. The aim is to understand variations in professional practice, which in some cases may be very much based on the application of formal policy-analytical methods or on scientific research. In other cases, the policy work of actors may rely on less formal methods and practical knowledge, which is put to use to advise government on a course of action.

Policy analysis as analysis for policy directs the different chapters to empirically capture the professional dimension of policy analysis, or, put differently, the characteristics of policy work. For some of these chapters, the authors rely on surveys, specially designed for the book's data collection, and hence some chapters include data on the profile and skills of policy workers.

By an empirical study of applied policy analysis or policy work by different policy actors, the book also aims to make a significant contribution to the study of what Lasswell (1971) called the analysis *of* policy. Analysis of policy refers to the scholarly understanding of the way in which policies are made and what role policy actors play in the policy cycle. How does their policy-analytical work set the agenda, inform the search for solutions, support decision making, affect implementation, and eventually help to evaluate policies? This being said, the book's anchorage points for studying the bearing of actors' policy work on policymaking are not distinct stages of the policymaking process. While an understanding of policymaking as a process encompassing different stages may be a useful heuristic tool to map actors and their influence over policy choices, the stages model was not chosen for organising the book's chapters. Rather, inversely, the book focuses on the different actors inside and outside government and maps their professional practices of policy work in order then to consider what difference they make in the policy process. Some of these actors may put their policy work to use for agenda setting but not for policy evaluation, while others may have a more encompassing impact across different stages.

There is another reason to avoid using the cycle approach as an organising principle for the book. The policy cycle may have meaning to analysts of policy, but less so to analysts for policy. In many organisations, the policy cycle has no meaning and the level of specialisation is such that actual policy work is not organised along stages. It may be that in some administrations, policy work is organised along stages of the cycle, with, for instance, the presence of special evaluation units in policy departments. However, the majority of other actors do not organise their work along this logic, nor do they have the specialised skills or follow the procedures that would fit a stages approach.

The relatively young tradition of the discipline and practice of policy analysis in Belgium

Policy analysis in Belgium is a young academic discipline and constitutes a relatively weak institutionalised practice. Empirical research in the field is rather limited and unevenly distributed across Belgium. Only a handful of senior researchers, mainly in Flanders, explicitly research policy advisory systems, while substantive policy analysis is relatively better developed, on both sides of the language border. Recent empirical studies on policy advisory systems include the relationship between science and policymaking; bureaucratic policy work; the role of political advisors in ministerial cabinets; and the role of permanent advisory bodies. Substantive policy analysis is strong in such domains as education, environmental policy, social policy, urban planning and development studies, and at times includes research on particular policy-analytical methods, such as impact analysis, effect studies and scenario analysis. The contributors to this book integrate existing fragmented secondary knowledge with freshly collected insights to even out different states of knowledge across substantive policy domains, across the language border and across levels of government.

As a practice, policy analysis in Belgium is characterised by the rather weak and late institutionalisation in the working methods of Belgian governments. The initial enthusiasm for policy-analytical methods in the 1960s waned in the wake of the federalisation of Belgium. The consecutive state reforms that occupied the government(s)'s agenda from 1970 onwards explain the regional governments' preoccupation with building administrations, and the relatively poor attention paid to professionalising policymaking. Continual state reforms with an intermezzo of narrow public management reform slowed down the articulation of policyworkers' roles and policy-analytical procedures in the administrations.

Nowadays, the functions of policy adviser or policy worker are not recognised as specific categories. In the French-speaking federated entities, for instance, there is not so much of a tradition of generalist civil servants. Top civil servants, usually called 'top managers', are held to be devoted to management functions, organising and leading their department. They scarcely intervene in the content of policymaking. In the middle range of the civil service, professional positions are identified as jobs (*métiers*) (lawyer, economist, biologist, civil engineer, data manager and so on). In their recruitment policy, administrations search for specialised professionals more than generalists. Of course, these individuals in their daily work conduct policy work, but this activity is not always recognised as a function. The survey conducted for the redaction of this book will help in finding the places where policy work is conducted.

Characteristics of the Belgian polity

For contextualising and explaining policy analysis in Belgium, it is necessary to highlight a number of characteristics of the Belgian political system. Some of these features affect the nature of policy work, while others influence the way in which policy analysis is put to use in policymaking.

First, the Belgian polity should be understood as a federal system, where coalition governments emerge from proportional elections. Given the political cleavages in Belgium, and the fragmented party political landscape, federal government coalition formation is traditionally cumbersome. With five periods of more than 100 days each of government formation during the past 25 years, the country has a reputation for long government formations. The 2011 government formation process set a new record of more than 500 days of caretaker government before a coalition agreement was reached (Brans et al, 2016). At the level of regions, government formation is less difficult because there are no language borders to be crossed, and because the number of parties is smaller, but the importance of the coalition agreement achieved during negotiations has equal value. It very much demarcates and limits the policy space of the legislature. The coalition agreement is what holds governments together, setting constraints on the width of agenda setting during the legislatures. It is used to measure policy proposals, and in some administrations it is the formal starting point for government policy documents alongside which policy work is organised.

Second, the Belgian system is often described as a typical partitocracy, where political parties are the strongest players in the policymaking process (Swenden et al, 2006). The dominance of political parties involves many functions and dysfunctions in a polity that is highly fragmented along linguistic and ideological lines. Political parties not only assert their institutional position as gate keepers to the demands and interests of legislative and executive politics; they also play a dominant role in the policymaking process, by framing problems, ideologically promoting solutions, and negotiating compromises in the cumbersome formation and continuation of coalition government.

These partitocratic features extend to some degree also to the division of policy work between civil servants and the personal advisers of ministers. While bureaucratic policy capacity is traditionally weak, the personal staffs of ministers are large by international standards and dominant in policy formulation. Partitocracy may suggest another impact when studying policy analysis in Belgium. In the extreme, partitocracy may induce a logic of facts-free politics or a rejection of intellectualism in policymaking. At the very least, what counts as evidence in policymaking is constrained by the partitocratic rules of conduct.

Third, Belgium is a consensus democracy with neo-corporatist traits. This means that interest groups with strong representational monopolies possess access to the policymaking process. They have multiple opportunities to weigh on agenda setting, and to formulate and negotiate policy options, and some even play a role at the street level of policy implementation.

Fourth, Belgium is a complicated federation. Its federalism is bipolar and centrifugal, and may therefore engender sources of divergence in policy styles across the language border and across government levels. At the same time, policy actors outside government adapt their strategies following the rescaling of the state. This book considers whether there is evidence for the fragmentation of policy communities and advocacy strategies of actors outside government.

The Belgian federation is highly complex, and the book will not give a detailed account of policy work and policy advice for each single government. In fact, the country counts nine governments and parliaments: federal government, Flemish government, Walloon government, Brussels-Capital government, French Community government (or Federation Wallonia-Brussels), German Community government, government of the Common Community Commission, government of the Flemish Community Commission and government of the French Community Commission (for more information, see Deschouwer, 2009; Wayenberg et al, 2010; and Chapter Five of this book).

In this book, the study is limited to the federal government, Flanders, Wallonia and Federation Wallonia-Brussels (or French Community). These are the most important entities in terms of size, with the largest administrations. The German Community manages competencies and services for only about 77,000 inhabitants located in nine municipalities, and is characterised by much informality. The Brussels-Capital region could have been interesting, but it is extremely complex as it combines four governments sharing the regional and community competencies. In fact, no great differences between these two cases and the ones already considered in the book are expected. All of them share a common administrative tradition and have only incrementally diverged in 25 years, given their organisational autonomy and their attempts to demarcate themselves from the others.

Trends

While the comparative features of the Belgian polity and policymaking system are expected to matter for describing and explaining the production and use of policy analysis by the key actors in and outside governments, it is also true that policy analysis is not static, and is subject to a number of emerging trends that affect the practice of policymaking. In the different chapters, the contributors take stock of these trends and developments, and address the impacts these might have on the institutional structure of policy analysis, the strengthening of policy analysis capacity, and the transformation of policy analysis.

Europeanisation is a first such trend. The EU has a substantive impact on policymaking in Belgium. It not only affects the policy space of Belgian government, but is also a lever for the adoption of formal policy analysis and methods in the Belgian administrations: impact analysis, environmental effects reporting, fiscal effects measurement. Europeanisation has definitely contributed to the use of new policy-analytical tools in different regional governments, given the obligation of accountability for the use of agricultural and structural funds in the 1990s. The pressure of some directives (for example in telecoms, railways and water management) has also led to the creation of agencies that negotiate management plans with the government, which are evaluated on a regular basis. This culture of accountability in public administration has increased the use of policy evaluation, considered as a subtype of policy work. In this perspective, the Court of Audit (*Cour des Comptes/Rekenhof*) was reformed in 1998 and contributed to enhancing policy evaluation practices both at the federal and regional levels.

A second trend is public sector reform: New Public Management (NPM) reforms at the federal level have triggered the strengthening of policy-analytical capacity in the bureaucracy. This was the case with the Copernicus reform at the federal level, and with agencification in Flanders. NPM also gave root to a culture of formalisation of procedures and the measurement of outputs. NPM, together with Europeanisation, pressurised laggards in formal evaluation cultures to adopt practices of formalisation and objectification, on which a policy-analytical culture could later build. Although one may be critical of many aspects of NPM, one must credit the Belgian NPM variants of at least having led to an articulation of what policy analysis could entail, and set in motion a process towards the adoption of formal tools with a spillover function for policy analysis.

While the evidence needed to support NPM innovations may be restricted in scope, often only encompassing outputs, the evidence required by the so-called evidence-based movement – the third trend considered – is much bigger in scope. Having first focused on state reform, and second on managerial reform, most Belgian governments have embraced the evidence-based movement in both discourse and practice. They have indeed started to invest more in policy indicators and outcomes monitoring, and also in optimising the use of substantive policy research.

The fourth trend discerned is the increased attention to citizen coproduction: at several government levels, administrations experiment with new kinds of citizens' consultation and participation in policymaking beyond the ballot box, and beyond formally institutionalised procedures of hearings and appeals. Citizens too professionalise in terms their contacts with policymakers, in that they are increasingly involved in combining their experience-based expertise with sectoral expertise.

Together, these four trends seem to foster a culture of professionalising different kinds of policy-analytical work, particularly in government services, but also among organisations or citizens who seek to influence them. In the view of this book, this formalisation is no threat to the primacy of democratic politics in policymaking. Extending the evidence and consultation base of policy decisions is beneficial for greater transparency and accountability about policy choices that remain ultimately the responsibility of politics.

Structure of the book

This book consists of five parts. Part One deals with policy analysis as a profession in Belgium, and with professional practices in the use of policy-analytical methods. In Chapter One, Ellen Fobé and the book's editors define what they understand by policy analysis, policy work and policy advice. They also explain the methods that were used to collect data for the different chapters. Chapter One further identifies the policy-analytical capacities and resources among civil servants engaged in policy analysis. It shows that these resources are important but dispersed as career paths mainly encourage specialisation in substantive issues. In Belgium, policy analysis is still an emerging profession that is not recognised through explicit labels and job positions. Nevertheless, a variety of policy-analytical methods is frequently used in the Belgian administrations. In Chapter Two, Ellen Fobé and her co-authors delve more deeply in the development and application of these policy-analytical methods and tools within Belgium's federal and subnational administrations, against the background of common pressures towards Europeanisation, evidence-based policymaking and the professionalization of policy-analytical work. They demonstrate how these trends have influenced the institutionalisation of analytical practices and the creation of units and professional networks for policy analysis and evaluation.

Part Two of the book takes a more detailed look at policy analysis in government and in the legislature. It deals consecutively with policy analysis by ministerial advisors, civil servants in the central and regional government, local governments, the legislature and institutionalised advisory bodies. Belgium has a long tradition of engaging ministerial cabinets in policymaking. Through the activities they perform, ministerial cabinets have an enduring functionality in a polity characterised by fragile collation government and high pressures for political control. In Chapter Three, Marleen Brans and her co-authors zoom in on the policymaking functions of ministerial cabinets and the policy analytical roles of political advisers within them, as well as these advisers' relations to the civil service at the federal level. The role of ministerial cabinet advisers as dominant players in the policy process is confirmed by civil servants engaged in policy work in the different Belgian administrations. In Chapter Four, the editors of the book and Ellen Fobé present this finding and other survey results on in-house policy analysis by civil servants in the federal and regional administrations. Even if civil servants are not the only actors engaged in policy analysis, and external policy-analytical activities have their bearing on different stages of the policy process, the ultimate production of public policy remains located with the authoritative sphere of government. The chapter shows how civil servants in the Belgian administrations perform a number of core policy analytical tasks, how they garner and process information, and who they turn to for advice. It highlights how in-house policy analysis performs in the light of dimensions of professional policymaking. Particular points of attention are shown to be deficiencies in the outward- and forward-looking dimensions of policy analysis, as well as in its evidence base.

Chapter Five turns to policy analysis at the local level. Ellen Wayenberg and her co-authors explore whether local government in Belgium displays a specific style of policy analysis. To this end, they use a two-level comparative analysis to show which policymaking tools are currently in use at the local level and which ones are emerging. Chapter Six and Seven move the analysis away from executive government to focus on policy analysis in the legislature and in institutionalised advisory bodies. In Chapter Six, Lieven De Winter and Wouter Wolfs show that policy analysis in several Belgian parliaments remains weak in terms of resources and practice as a result of the partitocratic political context in which the assemblies operate. In Chapter Seven, Ellen Fobé and her co-authors focus on the role of institutionalised advisory bodies in Belgium, by investigating their origin, the nature of the expertise they bring to the policy process and the influence they have. They show how the Belgian institutionalised advisory system struggles with the competition of policy advice, with blending of expert advice with representative opinion, and with pressures for political control.

Part Three of the book moves the study on to the political dimensions of policy analysis performed by political parties and interest groups. As political parties are key players in Belgium's partitocracy, their involvement in policy analysis merits close inspection. In Chapter Eight, Valérie Pattyn and her co-authors investigate the organisational characteristics of party study centres, and delve more deeply into the nature, process and products of the policy advice they generate. They show how parties' study centres typically combine day-to-day policy-analytical support to politics for drafting bills and for answering parliamentary questions with studies on long-term developments and ideological positions.

Given the neo-corporatist traits of the Belgian polity, it is typical for the membership of institutionalised advisory bodies to include interest groups. While Chapter Seven concerns the advisory bodies in which interests are represented, Chapter Nine focuses on the policy-analytical capacity of interest groups themselves. Bert Fraussen and his co-authors examine the way in which both traditional and newer interest groups organise to acquire policy expertise, as well as the characteristics and dissemination of their policy advice. They show that while most groups consider policy influence as a very important objective, their investments in policy-analytical capacity varies considerably and is at times rather low.

Part Four of the book turns to policy analysis by the public, with Chapter Ten focusing on public consultation beyond the ballot box, and Chapter Eleven investigating the role of the media in policymaking. In Chapter Ten, Jan Van Damme and his co-authors look into the growth of diverse types of public inquiries and public consultation arrangements in policymaking that bring to the table individual members of the public who otherwise have no direct policy advisory role, given the predominance of neo-corporatist-style advisory bodies in Belgium. They show that the actual use of these mechanisms still remains limited. It appears that the current state of affairs in Belgium regarding public consultation and participation is still firmly embedded in an indirect democratic perspective, and that experiments with broader and more deliberative citizen participation are adapted to fit and not to challenge this perspective. In Chapter Eleven, Baldwin Van Gorp and Dave Sinardet explore the role of the media in policymaking. Although it is difficult to determine the direct impact of media on the policy process, they find that the role of the news media in Belgium is not limited to that of a conduit for policy actors, and show how they act as a contributor to the political and the policy process, both indirectly and directly.

Part Five, finally, deals with policy analysis by advocates and academics. In Chapter Twelve, Bert Fraussen and his co-authors discuss how think tanks in Belgium are relatively new players in the Belgian policy advisory system, with generally few resources for policy analysis. Their investigation confirms that think tanks are given a hard time getting a foot in the door and finding their place in Belgian policy networks. In Chapter Thirteen on policy analysis by academics, Valérie Smet and the editors of the book analyse the importance of research dissemination strategies and structural interfaces for the utilisation of policy-relevant research. Supplementing case-study research with survey data, their analysis confirms enduring mismatches between the communities of policymakers and policy-interested academics, while a descriptive analysis of the Belgian governments' financing of policy relevant research points at promising avenues for reconciling diverging expectations of both communities. The final chapter of the book deals with policy analysis instruction. Ellen Fobé and the editors of the book revisit the starting point in Chapter One. Comparatively speaking, policy analysis has no well-established tradition in Belgium, neither as a recognised professional practice nor as an academic discipline. In the past decade and a half, though, policy analysis instruction has taken a firmer root in social science education at universities and in permanent education. Given the importance of education and training in the development of professional practices, the fruits of these developments may be harvested in the not-too-distant future.

References

Brans, M., Pattyn, V. and Bouckaert, G. (2016) 'Taking care of policy in times of crisis: comparative lessons from Belgium's longest caretaker government', *Journal of Comparative Policy Analysis: Research and Practice*, art. no. 1080/13876988.2015.1104811. Published online 29 January.

Deschouwer, K. (2009) *The politics of Belgium. Governing a divided society*, Basingstoke: Palgrave Macmillan.

Dobuzinskis, L., Howlett, M. and Laycock, D. (eds) (2007) *Policy analysis in Canada: the state of the art*, Toronto: University of Toronto Press.

Lasswell, H.D. (1971) *A preview of policy sciences*, New York, NY: American Elsevier.

Swenden, W., Brans, M. and De Winter, L. (2006) 'The politics of Belgium: institutions and policy under bipolar and centrifugal federalism', *West European Politics*, 29(5): 863-73.

Wayenberg, E., De Rynck, F., Steyvers, K. and Pilet, J.-B. (2010) 'Belgium: a tale of regional divergence', in F. Hendriks, A. Lidstrom and J. Loughlin (eds) *The Oxford handbook of local and regional democracy in Europe*, Oxford: Oxford University Press, 71-95.

Part One
Policy styles and methods
in Belgium

ONE

The policy-analytical profession in Belgium

David Aubin, Marleen Brans and Ellen Fobé

This book provides a comprehensive examination of the practices of policy analysis in Belgium. It studies the professional practices that organisations and actors entertain to define a problem marked for government concern and to prescribe the measures to solve that problem by policy action or change. Rather than looking at the theories of the policy process (Sabatier and Weible, 2014), it examines what kind of analysis is provided by policy workers, in-house or external to government, as a source of advice for making and improving public policies.

Only recently has empirical research started to map who policy analysts are and what they do. This chapter defends the widely accepted view of policy analysis and aims to catch the full extent of activities conducted by policy analysts both inside and outside government. It relies on a review of literature about policy work, policy advice and policy analysis that denotes a common concern for the various forms of contribution to policy formulation.

Further, this chapter presents the methods used in the following chapters to locate policy analysts and describe their activities. While partly relying on secondary resources, the contributors to this book conducted original research that filled the gaps in knowledge about policy analysis in Belgium. Middle-ranking civil servants were surveyed in the federal and regional governments with the aim of describing in-house policy analysis. To complete the picture, the authors conducted more specific surveys into policy analysis by actors outside government, notably in the Belgian political parties, interest groups and think tanks, and conducted qualitative case studies, for example on local authorities.

The survey of in-house policy analysis helped identify the characteristics of the largest communities of policy analysts in Belgium. This chapter attempts to identify policy-analytical capacities and resources among middle-ranking civil servants. It shows that these resources are important but dispersed in the public organisations, as the career path mainly encourages specialisation in substantive issues. In Belgium, policy analysis is still an emerging profession that is not recognised through explicit labels and job positions.

Policy analysis in the literature on public policy

Policy analysis has different meanings. Since Lasswell (1971), two approaches are usually distinguished, the first being pure academic description and theory building about the policy process (Sabatier and Weible, 2014), and the second being an application of knowledge on policy for providing advice to the policymakers. There are many expressions that characterise this dichotomy: policy sciences versus policy analysis, and analysis of policy versus analysis for policy, among others. The two views of policy analysis are run by different groups of experts, the first mostly tied to academia, and the second usually associated with practitioners: the civil service, think tanks and consultancies.

The first view, analysis of policy, covers a wide array of theories that have the aim of depicting how policies are made, in order to improve knowledge, formulate predictions and ultimately train students of public affairs. These theories of the policy process offer different perspectives, from the policy cycle approach (Jones, 2001), public choice (Ostrom, 1999), new institutionalism (Pierson, 2004; Streeck and Thelen, 2005), policy networks (Atkinson and Coleman, 1992; Montpetit, 2003) and interpretive analysis (Hajer and Wagenaar, 2003; Zittoun, 2014) to more integrated theories such as the advocacy coalition framework (Sabatier and Jenkins-Smith, 1993) and the punctuated equilibrium (Baumgartner and Jones, 1993; Jones and Baumgartner, 2005), to name but a few. The main theories of the policy process are now widely accepted and have been tested in most policy sectors and many countries throughout the world. The findings are reported in the many public policy textbooks that are used for teaching (John, 1998; Dye, 2007; Dunn, 2008; Howlett et al, 2009; Cairney, 2011; Kraft and Furlong, 2012).

However, the more policy analysis develops as an academic discipline, the more it seems to have become distanced from the real world of public administration. Those who teach policy analysis to civil servants in continuous training programmes experience indifference and sometimes hostility. The holistic depictions of the many interactions within policy communities are politely viewed as brilliant intellectual constructions, but the audience does not feel concerned by the stories told. What they expect are recipes that help them succeed in their tasks.

The same goes for graduate students. Policy analysis offers a broad understanding of the policy process, but hardly provides answers to questions about the day-to-day activities of decision makers and policy workers, or the usual steps of policy formulation and decision making in students' own country or state (for an earlier account, see Hogwood and Gunn, 1984, p v). This observation calls for an in-depth study of the representations and beliefs of policy workers, notably civil servants, and a description of their everyday practice (Colebatch and Radin, 2006, p 225). It is time to reconcile both views of the policy process, the theory-driven one and the process-oriented one, in order to elaborate both better theories and provide solutions to practitioners.

Policy work, policy advice and policy analysis are loose concepts that characterise a common endeavour to better describe the machinery of the policy process, notably the activities of civil servants (Colebatch et al, 2010b; Page and Jenkins, 2005). They illustrate different perspectives put forward by different authors, but they are not contradictory. Their interest lies in the activities developed around the making of public policy and the concrete contribution of individuals or organisations predominantly to policy formulation, but also to other stages in the process of policymaking.

Policy work as an interpretive account of policy analysis

Policy work consists of providing analytical support to government for making intelligent choices for solving societal problems (Colebatch, 2006a). It is 'undertaken by any actor (individual or collective) that seeks to shape policy processes and outcomes' (Tenbensel, 2006, p 199): academics, think-tank employees, consultants, politicians, staff of political parties, interest group representatives, citizen activists, and so on. 'Policy work is how these participants bring their diverse forms of knowledge to bear on policy questions' (Colebatch et al, 2010b, p 12). Colebatch refuses to tighten the definition of policy work on the grounds that its content differs given the commonly held perspective on public policy: '[Our] thinking about policy activity draws on several distinct and potentially conflicting perspectives, and that what is seen as 'policy work' depends on the conceptualisation of the policy process' (Colebatch, 2006b). In the same way as Mintzberg described managerial work (Mintzberg, 1973), there is no single account of policy work, and each account reflects different contexts (Hoppe and Jeliazkova, 2006; Tao, 2006).

Policy work can be understood at least from three perspectives. First, public policy is perceived as a problem-solving approach led by government (for example, Dye, 2007). Colebatch calls this top-down view 'authoritative instrumentalism'. Political leaders make decisions that shape policies, and must be assisted in this task by a variety of 'policy advisers', seen as 'the functional experts in the field under review – medical scientists, social workers, marine ecologists, etc' (Colebatch et al, 2010b, p 13). Some experts are specialists in the preparation of the decision, the 'policy analyst' who 'speaks truth to power' (Wildavsky, 1979): 'The policy analyst was considered an expert adviser who clarifies the problem, identifies the alternative courses of action, and systematically determines the optimal response' (Colebatch et al, 2010b, p 13). In the US, schools of public policy were set up to train such experts, and most public policy textbooks reflect this perspective.

The second perspective, 'structured interaction', attests to the relational character of policymaking. The government is not alone in identifying public problems and selecting alternative courses of actions to resolve them. Many actors, from the public sector and civil society, participate and defend their own interests, values and interpretations of public problems. These interactions are not random and tend to stabilise over time within policy subsectors (Klijn and Koppenjan, 2016). These structured interactions are labelled as policy communities, policy networks or advocacy coalitions (Heclo, 1979; Sabatier and Jenkins-Smith, 1993; Rhodes, 1997; Richardson, 2000). 'In this framing, policy work is less about giving well-crafted advice to a decision-maker, more about the construction and maintenance of relations among stakeholders – the diplomacy of public authority' (Colebatch, 2006b, p 314). Policy is perceived as the construction or maintenance of relations among stakeholders rather than a rational response to objective public problems.

The third perspective is 'social construction', or the search for common understandings of the problem. Public policy is a common construction resulting from an interaction between stakeholders. It relates to the interpretive public policy field relying on discourse analysis (Fischer, 2003; Hajer and Wagenaar, 2003; Zittoun, 2014). The framing of problems carries with it the designation of target groups and the choice of policy instruments, and the activity of framing has more importance in creating sense and legitimising the actors' positions than actually solving problems. Actors gain meaning and resources around public recognition of the problem. They seek power and influence rather than effectiveness in problem solving.

According to Colebatch, different forms of knowledge and understandings of the process are produced and compete in different organisational locations: 'Policy workers are drawing on experience to determine which sort of knowledge will be most significant at any particular time, and need to be able to frame their argument in a way appropriate to the situation' (Colebatch, 2006b, p 317). Nevertheless, the question remains how civil servants actually behave in such an environment and how they cope with limited information and ambiguity.

In the real world, policy analysts conduct very different tasks, which renders it difficult to consider them as a professional community. Beryl Radin (2000) noticed that it is not clear what policy analysts actually do: research, educating the public, or lobbying for specific measures (see also Hird, 2005). The production of policy analysis is rather instrumental in providing arguments to politicians or top civil servants to support or resist programme proposals (Tao, 2006). For Radin, policy analysis has become the 'duelling swords' that policy actors use in negotiations (Radin, 2000). In addition, policy analysts are nowadays confronted with many types of client with competing perspectives and values (Radin, 2013). Obviously, this affects the kind of analysis conducted and the methods used in providing evidence to decision makers (see also Majone, 1989).

Policy analysis by middle-ranking civil servants

In their daily work, civil servants have considerable margins of manoeuvre when making public policy. They do not only advise executive politicians, but more than often truly take part in the decision-making process. Page and Jenkins have shown that middle-ranking officials are 'not simply concerned with subordinate "embellishment and detail" of issues settled at a higher level' (Page and Jenkins, 2005, p 15), but rather work with considerable discretion. Their instructions are 'rarely specific enough to guide with any precision the work they do' (Page and Jenkins, 2005, p 81). Ministers rarely give direct instructions, but tend to informally (and often orally) indicate the lines along which they would like their officials to work.

Also, civil servants are expected to determine when the minister should be involved: 'Policy bureaucrats at middle-levels are able to take general indicators of ministerial intent and work them into fairly specific proposals or options by using a variety of cues to estimate what the minister is likely to want' (Page and Jenkins, 2005, pp 148-9). As a consequence, middle managers are involved in broad cross-cutting issues, not only details (Page, 2012). Page and Jenkins further identify middle-ranking civil servants as important actors in the policy process whose precise roles are underestimated in public policy textbooks.

Policy analysis as the outcome of policy advisory systems

Michael Howlett retains a more instrumental view of policy advice and policy analysis that perceives public policy as a rational and authoritative choice and promotes the evidence-based policymaking movement (Nutley et al, 2007; Craft and Howlett, 2012). He endorses the definition of policy analysis as 'a method for structuring information and providing opportunities for the development of alternative choices for the policy-maker' (Gill and Saunders, 1992, pp 6-7; see also Howlett et al, 2014). Howlett's approach aims to locate and clarify the role of policy analysts in the policy process with an emphasis on the policy-analytical capacity of governments to design 'good' policies. The primary purpose of policy analysis is then to improve policy outcomes by the application of systematic analytical methodologies (Kohoutek et al, 2013, p 46).

Given a combination of patterns such as globalisation, accountability, managerialism and the emergence of 'wicked problems', the policy process has been deeply affected (Radin, 2000, 2013). Traditionally, policy advice was generated by bureaucratic officials located at the top of a public organisation to guide policymakers and support their decisions, but the monopoly of contemporary bureaucracies on expertise and policy advice has been increasingly contested by several stakeholders who participate in the policy process (Meltsner, 1976; Colebatch, 2006c; Brans et al, 2012). Nowadays, in order to understand one country's capacity to design 'good' public policies, one must consider the resources located outside government:

> [The] various advisors to government can be arrayed as actors within a complex system of internal and external sources of information who interact in various ways to provide the advice upon which decision-makers operate. (Howlett, 2013, p 5)

The policy advisory system constitutes such mapping, which varies across countries and exposes a variety of policy-analytical styles, that is, the kinds of analysis and techniques used in these systems (Mayer et al, 2004).

For policy formulation, governments rely on the policy-analytical capacity of the organisations within the advisory system. Policy-analytical capacity is the ability of organisations to carry out research and analysis of public policies. It refers to

> ... the amount of basic research a government can conduct or access, its ability to apply statistical methods, applied research methods, and advanced modelling techniques to this data and employ analytical techniques such as environmental scanning, trends analysis, and forecasting methods in order to gauge broad public opinion and attitudes, as well as those of interest groups and other major policy players, and to anticipate policy impacts. (Howlett, 2009, p 162)

In this view, policy analysis is more closely related to the applied use of social science methods to inform the policy process.

Different attempts to depict everyday work of policy advisors

The broad definition given to policy analysis reflects a lack of consensus between public policy scholars about the concepts of policy work, policy advice and policy analysis. A tentative classification in concentric circles would make policy work as the encompassing concept, comprising both policy advice and policy analysis, and policy analysis one particular kind of policy advice. As a consequence, policy analysis would be narrowed down to the application of social science methods for the provision of policy advice to policymakers. It would open the way to consider that not all policy advice relies on sound evidence, but also on experience, consultation of stakeholders, or strategic thinking given the background, experience and skills of policy advisers. Evidence-based policymaking is certainly more the exception than the rule (Nutley et al, 2007).

This hierarchical ordering of the concepts of policy work, policy advice and policy analysis is not faithful to the literature. First, policy work focuses more on the contribution to policy formulation than activities of implementation and control. 'Policy workers thus take part in defining social problems, clarifying public policy goals, identifying strategies for goal achievement, making recommendations of the most plausible solutions and possibly evaluating the effects of such solutions' (Kohoutek et al, 2013, p 34). Second, the nature of policy work depends on the epistemological position of the authors: '[Policy] is too ambiguous and contested to be defined in neutral ways' (Colebatch et al, 2010a, p 243).

In sum, this volume sticks to a broad definition of policy analysis that remains open to the different views about the job of making public policies.

Policy analysis as a profession

Policy analysis is not purely the ownership of analysts or in-house consultants, but part of the day-to-day activity of middle-ranking officials. Of course, policy analysis may be concentrated in internal think tanks or consulting offices, but it can also be dispersed among departments.

Policy work is not an activity that would be in the hands of specifically trained policy analysts:

> The overarching concept of policy work thus covers not only policy analysts in the traditional sense but also other professions such as lawyers, doctors, architects, etc. that utilise their expertise one way of another in order to participate in the making of what we call policy. (Kohoutek et al, 2013, p 32)

Behind the label of policy analyst stands an image of specialisation, of concentration of analytical skills and expertise on policymaking that is not a reliable account of everyday practice.

In the public administration literature, civil servants are usually perceived as specialists or generalists (Mayer et al, 2004; Lindquist and Desvaux, 2007). Specialists have an 'expertise on the specific technical issues pertinent to [the unit's] domain of expertise' (Lindquist and Desvaux, 2007, p 123). For example, the term specialist may refer to a civil engineer who maintains road infrastructure or a biologist who monitors the dispersion of invasive species. Generalists rely on capabilities 'to develop broader views on policy issues, to identify horizontal linkages across issues, and sometimes to develop more comprehensive as opposed to selective policy initiatives' (Lindquist and Desvaux, 2007, p 123). Process skills and system knowledge are usually associated with generalists.

According to Page and Jenkins (2005, p 148), middle-ranking officials in the United Kingdom are not subject specialists, but generalists who move regularly inside the administration and take up new tasks in a short period of time. Although they are expected to work on substantive issues, their expertise is not subject-based or technical. This conclusion certainly applies to the Westminster model of public administration, and to some other models too (for example, Germany – see Fleischer, 2009; Blum and Schubert, 2013), but not to all. Belgium, for example, gives preference to specialists. These civil servants are less mobile, and usually spend their whole career in a single department.

Generalists are expected to engage more in policy analysis and to use more formal analytical techniques than specialists. Policy analysis draws on the mastery of policy-analytical skills such as the ability to apply statistical methods and manage techniques such as environmental scanning, trends analysis and foresight, and also to engage in interactions with stakeholders, and communicate effectively with political executives.

Hence, policy analysis provides many analytical techniques, formal and less formal, to produce sound analysis to inform the decision-making process (Mayer et al, 2004; Colebatch et al, 2010b; Howlett, 2013, p 4). Formal techniques comprise quantitative methods (for example, surveys, cost-benefit analysis, multiple-criteria decision analysis), trend extrapolations (for example, causal models, logical frames, foresight or futures studies and impact analyses), and analysis of organisations (for example, SWOT [strengths, weaknesses, opportunities, threats], management games and decision tress), and are put forward in many 'toolkit' policy analysis textbooks (for example, Dunn, 2008; Weimer and Vining, 2010). These formal techniques are usually associated with 'evidence-based' policymaking (Cairney, 2016; Nutley et al, 2007).

However, the emphasis on formal techniques is somewhat exaggerated and underestimates the importance of procedural activities (Radin, 2013). Sources and types of used knowledge are diversified (Halligan, 1995). The study of policy work must emphasise the key activities of making, maintaining and coordinating the actors' interactions as well: 'Instead of finding rational solutions to policy problems, policy work is used for getting support for certain ideas and interests' (Kohoutek et al, 2013, p 34). It involves analysing the political and multi-actor context (for example, stakeholder analysis and Delphi methods) or attempting to 'make sense together' (for example, interviews, focus groups or brainstorming) (Hoppe, 1999). Experience-based expertise is quite often placed on equal footing with scientific analysis as relevant and valuable information to the policy process (Williams, 2010).

The use of formal analytical tools may be limited in both cases of generalists and specialists, as policy analysis remains 'more art than science' (Bardach, 2000, p xiv, cited in Prince, 2007, p 165). In Canada, both government and non-governmental analysts employ 'process-related tools more frequently than "substantive" content-related technical ones, reinforcing the procedural orientation in policy work identified in earlier studies' (Howlett et al, 2015, p 165). Process-related tasks take precedence over formal policy analysis in the community of policy advisers (Howlett et al, 2014, p 274; Craft, 2015).

The survey conducted in the different federal and regional governments in Belgium assesses the involvement of civil servants with a university degree in policy analysis and reveals their characteristics.

Method of enquiry on policy analysis in Belgium

Research on policy analysis is not an easy task when this activity is spread across a range of professions, public departments and private organisations. Initially, the contributors to this book relied on secondary sources for this national synthesis of policy analysis in Belgium, but they soon fell short of information and hence decided to engage in new original research. This section presents the methods they used for improving understandings of policy analysis in Belgium.

The authors of Chapters Three, Eight, Nine and Twelve conducted a series of targeted surveys to improve knowledge about policy analysis outside of government. They investigated ministerial cabinets, political parties, interest groups and think tanks, respectively. The results as well as the methods used are described in detail in each chapter. Several of these surveys replicated questions formulated initially in the in-house survey, described later on in this section. Chapter Five on local policy analysis applied qualitative case study as a method, looking at specific municipalities, while the remaining chapters relied on secondary sources of information. The latter was the method used for parliaments, formal advisory bodies, public consultation and the media, respectively, presented in Chapters Six, Seven, Ten and Eleven.

Regarding in-house policy analysis in Belgium, an original large-scale survey was conducted between the end of 2013 and mid–2015 both at the federal level and in the two main regions of the country. At the federal level, it targeted eight ministries or federal public services (*services publics fédéraux / Federale Overheidsdiensten,* or FPS): Economics, Finance, Justice, Foreign Affairs, Interior, Health, Defence and Social Security. In the regions of Flanders and Wallonia, both regional administrations, including the centralised departments and selected agencies, were studied. For Francophone Belgium, the Federation Wallonia-Brussels (or French Community), a federated entity distinct from Wallonia (or Walloon Region), was investigated too.[1]

In terms of content, this survey replicates most of the questionnaire used by Howlett and colleagues in Canada, but is partly adapted to national characteristics (Howlett and Newman, 2010; Howlett and Wellstead, 2012; Howlett et al, 2014). It includes about 30 questions (with variations between the levels of government) divided into four chapters: the nature of policy work, analytical techniques, advisory system in the sector and policy capacity.

An in-house version of LimeSurvey at KU Leuven was used for constructing the questionnaire and sending invitations to potential participants. It can also be noted that the survey was set up in both French and Dutch and sent out to each person individually. That is to say, respondents in the unilingual subnational entities received the survey either in French or Dutch, while respondents at the bilingual federal level were contacted in their mother tongue, based on the contact lists provided by each organisation.

The large-N electronic survey targeted Belgium's civil servants (N=2,717). The political advisors in the ministerial cabinets were not included. Given the fact that policy analyst is not a recognised profession or position in the Belgian administrations, it was not possible to operate with samples. Therefore, an online questionnaire was sent to civil servants holding a university degree, that is, the target population for the survey, as these individuals are assumed to take up positions in Belgian governmental organisations that relate to policy work and policy analysis. The group of civil servants to which invitations were eventually sent differed across levels of government, depending on the degree to which the heads of the departments or agencies were willing to accommodate the research team's request to provide them with the whole population of university graduated civil servants (operating in Belgium's governments at 'A level'). Sometimes, the contact lists provided by the organisations included a limited number of public servants, as those officials actually involved in policy analysis had already been selected.

Specifically, at the federal level, only the federal Interior department provided a full list of A level civil servants. Six other FPSs provided a select list of email addresses for A level civil servants (Finance, Justice, Defence, Economics, Social Security and Foreign Affairs), based on the assumption that these were the people the questionnaire was targeting. The selected population predominantly includes middle-ranking civil servants, working as *attachés*, advisers or advisers-general. But it equally pertains to a limited number of mandated top civil servants, such as administrator-generals at the N-1 level for some but not all departments (for example, Health, Interior and Social Affairs). It also needs to be noted that the FPS Health did not provide any contact details but dispersed the survey through its internal communication channel to all of its employees.

By contrast, at the regional level the Flemish government provided the contact details of a more focused subset of university-graduated civil servants, that is, those working at rank A1 and A2. Similar to the situation at the federal level, this select group of civil servants was assumed to be involved in policy-analytical work frequently and considered as the questionnaire's target group. These two ranks at the A level do not pertain to the mandated top civil servants in Flanders (A3 rank or N level), nor do they include high functional positions such as director-general. Rather, the selected population includes civil servants working as heads of unit, senior advisers, researchers or *attachés*.

In Francophone Belgium, then, the population is broader in comparison with those at the two other government levels. It includes all civil servants with a university degree without consideration of their function or rank, nor of their presumed involvement in policy-analytical work. In this regard, the population includes both middle-ranking civil servants as the top-level civil servants in both Wallonia and Federation Wallonia-Brussels.

The survey was sent to the population of each government level in several rounds between the end of 2013 and the middle of 2015. More precisely, the first round occurred between November and December 2013, when the survey was sent to the targeted civil servants in the Flemish central departments and agencies. The second round took place in October and November 2014 for the university employees of the Ministry of the Federation Wallonia-Brussels (MFWB) and the government agencies in Francophone Belgium. A third round of questionnaires was sent to the Public Service of Wallonia, that is the central departments of the Walloon Region (*Service public de Wallonie*, or SPW) and seven of the eight participating FPSs between February and March 2015, followed by a last round in June and July 2015 for the remaining FPS.

In total, the survey was sent to 7,560 people. The overall response rate to the survey is about 40% (see the details about the population and number of respondents in Appendix 1.1). At the federal level, the total number of civil servants contacted to complete the survey was 2,253. This number includes the six FPSs that provided a select list of email addresses, as well as the FPS Interior, which provided a complete list of university-level civil servants in the department. The total number of civil servants contacted in the latter department is therefore much higher compared with the other FPSs. Moreover, the total number of civil servants contacted within the FPS Health is unclear. The survey link was sent out indirectly, through the FPS's internal communication channel. A similar procedure was followed for the FPS Defence, although this department provided an approximate number of 340 military personnel contacted to complete the survey. The response rate for the federal level is about 38%, based on 858 responses. This is the total number of respondents (N=904) from which those in FPS Health (N=46) have been subtracted, as the population in that department is unknown.

In Flanders, the then 13 governmental departments and respective agencies made up 1,152 civil servants at A1 and A2 level contacted to participate in the survey. All of the centralised departments participated in the research, whereas several agencies did not. On contact by the research team, the heads of the agencies that opted not to participate often indicated that their agency did not carry out matters of policy formulation but was predominantly involved in policy implementation. In total, 499 Flemish government officials participated by (partially) completing the questionnaire. The response rate for Flanders is 43%.

In Francophone Belgium, then, 4,155 officials were contacted, that is, civil servants with a university degree regardless of their function or level. This included 2,893 civil servants within the centralised department (SPW) and respective agencies of Wallonia and 1,262 civil servants within the administrations of the Federation Wallonia-Brussels, including the single ministry (MFWB) and several agencies. Some agencies refused to participate in the research, but their absence does not affect the results as they involve few dozens of people and do not hold core policy competencies. Of 4,155 officials contacted in both Wallonia and Federation Wallonia-Brussels, 1,314 completed the survey fully or partially. Thus, the response rate for the entities of Wallonia and Federation Wallonia-Brussels is about 32%.[2] In terms of data analysis, the presentation of the results mainly relies on descriptive statistics using relative frequencies. The goal is to give a fair and easily accessible description of what Belgian civil servants do in a field that has never been comprehensively investigated until now.

Belgian civil servants' knowledge of policy analysis

This section presents the results of the survey of the federal and regional middle-ranking civil servants, and shows that considerable resources for policy analysis are present in the civil service, but dispersed among specialists of substantive issues. The policy-analytical resources located outside the Belgian government are discussed in the other chapters of this book.

The middle-ranking civil servants are 45 years old on average, with a population a bit younger in Flanders (43 years) than in the other governments (46 years). The variation in the age distribution is more clear-cut (see Figure 1.1). In Flanders, almost half of respondents (44%) are less than 40 years of age, against less than 30% at the federal level and in Francophone Belgium. These two governments account for a significant proportion of officials over 50 and 60. One can suppose that many of them are not much concerned by policy analysis as it was certainly not part of their initial training (see Chapter Fourteen), but their replacements will raise the issue of training for newcomers. In terms of gender, males are still overrepresented at this level of public service, except in Flanders. Women constitute a larger group of respondents in Flanders (50%) than in Francophone Belgium (45%) or at the federal level (40%).

Figure 1.1: Age distribution of civil servants in Belgium

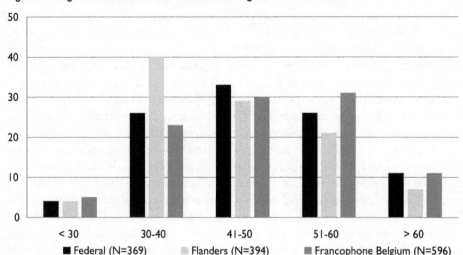

All the respondents hold at least a university degree given the initial definition of the survey population. Among them, the variation in the educational background is important, even if law, political science and social sciences score highest (see Table 1.1). About 20% of the respondents held a degree in political and social sciences, including in majors such as public administration, European or international studies and communication, the youngest having attended a public policy course (see Chapter Fourteen). At the federal level, where the FPS Justice and Interior are situated, there are comparatively more respondents with a law degree (31%) than in the regions (around 10%). Conversely, the number of civil servants with a degree in engineering or architecture is higher in the regional governments, which include policy sectors in which civil servants with such degrees are assumed to be employed regularly (such as spatial planning, housing, mobility, environment, energy and agriculture).

About a quarter of civil servants (20% in Flanders) find their first job in the federal or regional governments. Another 7% to 16% have moved from one government to another (see Table 1.2). This means that more than two thirds of them had prior work experience before joining the administration. Although their experience is diverse, about a third of this group worked in the private sector (that is, for a private company or as self-employed person), and a significant number in research institutions, notably in the federated entities. These figures indicate that joining the public service was not the first option for these respondents even if it is hard to know why they chose to take a new direction in their careers. It just appears that people are no longer novices when they decide to become civil servants.

Table 1.1: Educational background of Belgian civil servants

	Federal (N=480)	Flanders (N=494)	Francophone Belgium (N=780)
Humanities	80%	63%	61%
Law	31%	13%	10%
Political and social science	20%	21%	18%
Economics and management	15%	9%	16%
Arts, history, philosophy	8%	12%	9%
Psychology, education, teaching	6%	8%	8%
Exact/applied science	13%	31%	29%
Engineering, architecture	8%	13%	16%
Bioengineering	2%	11%	9%
Exact sciences	3%	7%	4%

Table 1.2: Prior professional experience of Belgian civil servants

	Federal (N=411)	Flanders (N=466)	Francophone Belgium (N=694)
Private sector	34%	32%	37%
Research institute	9%	20%	15%
Ministerial cabinet	9%	4%	9%
Other (sub)national government	7%	13%	16%
Civil society organisation	6%	8%	7%
Local government	5%	9%	6%
Political party	3%	1%	3%

In addition, a substantial proportion of civil servants has worked in politics, that is, as adviser to a minister, or as a member of parliament or a political party study centre. This result not only tells that becoming a member of a ministerial cabinet is an important step in a civil servant's career, but that many respondents have experience in politics and the policymaking process. Knowledge about the policy process is certainly present within departments, even if it is not concentrated in policy formulation units. The same conclusion can be drawn from the extent of experience in research, which is an indication of the capacity of departments to use formal analytical methods.

The Belgian administration has a career system where public servants have lifelong jobs and advance with merit and seniority. This explains the longevity of their positions (see Figure 1.2): 55% of the respondents in Flanders, 63% in Francophone Belgium and 70% at the federal level have spent more than 10 years in their current organisation.[3] Moreover, the survey results indicate that

Belgian civil servants rarely migrate from one policy sector to another and can be regarded as specialists in their own policy domain. Indeed, about three quarters have already acquired more than six years of professional experience in the policy sector in which they are currently employed. There are, however, substantial differences between the federal-level and the subnational governments. At the federal level, almost 90% of civil servants have been affiliated with their current policy sector for more than six years. This number is lower in Flanders (72%) and in Francophone Belgium (66%), where civil servants with less than two years of sector experience also make up about 10% of the total compared with 4% at the federal level. Internal mobility is very limited among the Belgian civil service, even if the younger regional administrations tend to make it easier.

Figure 1.2: Professional experience working for the government

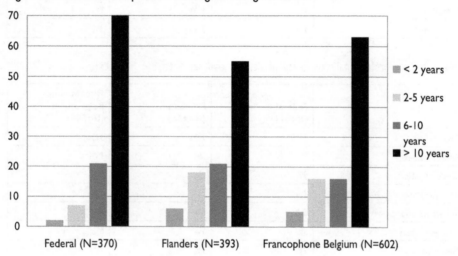

As for the respondents' participation in professional training, the results of the survey show, first, that a large number of respondents attended a public-policy-related course at least once during the past two years (see Table 1.3). The concern for public policies seems to be the highest in the Flemish government (79%), but also important at the federal level (56%). Civil servants in both Wallonia and Federation Wallonia-Brussels are less involved in such training, partly because of a focus on training in (public) management, but also due to the fact that these administrations do not reason so much in terms of public policy, but more in terms of strategies and politics (contrary to France where the term *politique publique* is officially used). However, this item in the table concerns policy issues in general and encompasses courses on the context and content of substantive public policies as well as conceptual public policy and policy evaluation courses.

Certified training is also popular, mainly at the federal level. It can be organised by the hierarchy or attended on a voluntary basis. A limited number of these training programmes include courses on policy analysis (see Chapter Fourteen). Also, it is notable that a substantial amount of civil servants (about 30% in the regions and again almost half at the federal level) were trained in analytical tools and methods. In addition to initial training, and prior work experience, there seems to be considerable resources in terms of policy analysis within the Belgian governments, even if they are unequally distributed. Attending conferences, workshops and seminars, or participating in study visits, is an alternative source of learning for a majority of respondents.

Table 1.3: Participation in training programmes (at least once in the past two years)

	Federal (N=370)	Flanders (N=397)	Francophone Belgium (N=608)
Policy issues	56%	79%	33%
Applying analytical tools	46%	29%	33%
Certified training programs	45%	28%	27%
Writing policy documents	38%	37%	25%
To solicit policy advice	21%	14%	15%

Although substantial numbers of civil servants participate in training programmes related to their policy-analytical work, they are not all overly satisfied by the offer. Almost 60% of the Flemish civil servants are satisfied by the training opportunities, as opposed to smaller numbers in the federal and Francophone Belgian governments (see Figure 1.3). In sum, it appears that the training

Figure 1.3: Sufficient training offer related to policy analysis

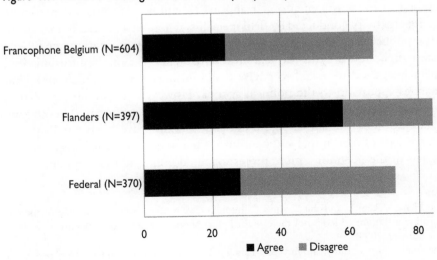

opportunities in terms of policy analysis are satisfying the demand in Flanders, but are lacking in the two other governments.

In terms of profile, there seem to be considerable resources available for practising policy analysis in-house, even if they are unevenly distributed between the different governments. The middle-ranking civil servants in the Flemish government, who are younger than their counterparts in other administrations, are also more satisfied about the public policy and analytical method courses on offer. At the same time, this regional government does not train either professional policy analysts (generalists) or experts in enquiries and design who would be more likely to move from one department to another. It appears that Belgian governments remain rather attached to a career system with low internal mobility, which encourages civil servants to become specialists of substantive policy issues rather than becoming pure policy analysts.

Conclusion: is policy work a profession in Belgium?

A broad conception of policy analysis is necessary to understand the involvement and contribution of every stakeholder in the policy formulation process. The concept of policy analysis has not been firmly established and is often used interchangeably with related concepts of policy work and policy advice. However, a large group of policy scholars appears to focus on the many contributions to policy formulation, leaving implementation to one side. An overly restrictive definition of policy analysis would reduce the concept to the mere use of social science methods and related formal analytical tools. It would narrow the lens so much that students would be at risk of missing most civil servants' contributions to policy formulation. In Belgium, indeed, only a few policy analysts use formal analytical tools as sources of advice (see Chapter Two).

In Belgian administrations, policy analyst is an emerging profession, not yet recognised in every organisation. It appears that policy analysis is a part-time professional activity conducted by field specialists whose first job it is to manage or monitor public programmes. Policy analysts in Belgian administrations are subject specialists first, and only in the second instance experts in policy formulation. As specialists, they are asked to advise decision makers when policy problems or changes appear on to the political agenda. However, this picture is relative, given the fair proportion of political and social scientists among middle-ranking bureaucrats. Since the late 1990s, these civil servants have been taught policy analysis as part of their initial and continuous training, which may create greater awareness of the need for a more professionalised policy advisory system.

Notes

[1] The Flemish Region and the Flemish Community were merged in one single government and administration, which is not the case for Francophone Belgian entities (Brans et al, 2006; Deschouwer, 2009).

[2] The combination of direct and indirect mailing in both governments renders complex the task of calculating separate response rates.

3   Civil service mobility in the regions is bigger than in the federal administrations. In Flanders this may be explained by the wholescale agencification of the Flemish administration in the mid-2000s.

References

Atkinson, M. and Coleman, W. (1992) 'Policy networks. Policy communities and the problems of governance', *Governance*, 5(2): 154-80.

Bardach, E. (2000) *A practical guide for policy analysis. The eightfold path to more effective problem solving*, New York, NY: Chatham House.

Baumgartner, F.R. and Jones, B.D. (1993) *Agendas and instability in american politics*, Chicago, IL: University of Chicago Press.

Blum, S. and Schubert, K. (ed) (2013) *Policy analysis in Germany*, Bristol: Policy Press.

Brans, M., De Peuter, B. and Ferraro, G. (2012) 'Public work old and new: challenges to bureaucratic policy work as a craft', paper presented at Organization Studies Summer Workshop, Rhodes, 24-26 May.

Brans, M., de Visscher, C. and Vancoppenolle, D. (2006) 'Administrative reform in Belgium: maintenance or modernization?', *West European Politics*, 29(5): 979-98.

Cairney, P. (2011) *Understanding public policy: theories and issues*, Basingstoke: Palgrave Macmillan.

Cairney, P. (2016) *The politics of evidence-based policy making*, Basingstoke: Palgrave Macmillan.

Colebatch, H.K. (2006a) 'Introduction', in H.K. Colebatch (ed) *The work of policy: an international survey*, Lanham, MD: Lexington Books, vii-xiii.

Colebatch, H.K. (2006b) 'What work makes policy?', *Policy Sciences*, 39(4): 309-21.

Colebatch, H.K. (2006c) *The work of policy: an international survey*, Lanham, MD: Lexington Books.

Colebatch, H.K., Hoppe, R. and Noordegraaf, M. (2010a) 'The lessons for policy work', in H.K. Colebatch, R. Hoppe and M. Noordegraaf (eds) *Working for policy*, Amsterdam: Amsterdam University Press, 227-45.

Colebatch, H.K., Hoppe, R. and Noordegraaf, M. (eds) (2010b) *Working for policy*, Amsterdam: Amsterdam University Press.

Craft, J. (2015) 'Conceptualizing the policy work of partisan advisers', *Policy Sciences*, 48(2): 135-58.

Craft, J. and Howlett, M. (2012) 'Policy formulation, governance shifts and policy influence: location and content in policy advisory systems', *Journal of Public Policy*, 32(2): 79-98.

Deschouwer, K. (2009) *The politics of Belgium. Governing a divided society*, Basingstoke: Palgrave Macmillan.

Dunn, W.N. (2008) *Public policy analysis, an introduction* (4th edn), Englewood Cliffs, NJ: Prentice-Hall.

Dye, T.R. (2007) *Understanding public policy* (12th edn), Englewood Cliffs, NJ: Prentice Hall.

Fischer, F. (2003) *Reframing public policy. Discursive politics and deliberative practices*, Oxford: Oxford University Press.

Fleischer, J. (2009) 'Power resources of parliamentary executives: policy advice in the UK and Germany', *West European Politics*, 32(1): 196-214.

Gill, J.I. and Saunders, L. (1992) 'Toward a definition of policy analysis', *New Directions for Institutional Research*, 76: 5-13.

Hajer, M.A. and Wagenaar, H. (ed) (2003) *Deliberative policy analysis. Understanding governance in the network society*, Cambridge: Cambridge University Press.

Halligan, J. (1995) 'Policy advice and the public service', in B.G. Peters and D.J. Savoie (eds) *Governance in a changing environment*, Montreal/Kingston: McGill-Queen's University Press, 138-172.

Heclo, H. (1979) 'Issue networks and the executive establishment', in A. King (ed) *The new American political system*, Washington, DC: American Enterprise Institute, 87-124.

Hird, J.A. (2005) *Power, knowledge and politics. Policy analysis in the States*, Washington DC: Georgetown University Press.

Hogwood, B.W. and Gunn, L.A. (1984) *Policy analysis for the real world*, Oxford: Oxford University Press.

Hoppe, R. (1999) 'Policy analysis, science and politics: from "speaking truth to power" to "making sense together"', *Science and Public Policy*, 26(3): 201-10.

Hoppe, R. and Jeliazkova, M. (2006) 'Policy work at the local level in the United States: whispers of rationality', in H.K. Colebatch (ed) *The work of policy: an international survey*, Lanham, MD: Lexington Books, 35-60.

Howlett, M. (2009) 'Policy analytical capacity and evidence-based policy-making: lessons from Canada', *Canadian Public Administration/Administration publique du Canada*, 52(2): 153-75.

Howlett, M. (2013) 'Policy work, policy advisory systems and politicization', *Central European Journal of Public Policy*, 7(1): 4-7.

Howlett, M. and Newman, J. (2010) 'Policy analysis and policy work in federal systems: policy advice and its contribution to evidence-based policy-making in multi-level governance systems', *Policy and Society*, 29: 123-36.

Howlett, M., Ramesh, M. and Perl, A. (2009) *Studying public policy, policy cycles and policy subsystems* (3rd edn), Toronto: Oxford University Press.

Howlett, M., Tan, S.L., Migone, A., Wellstead, A. and Evans, B. (2014) 'The distribution of analytical techniques in policy advisory systems: policy formulation and the tools of policy appraisal', *Public Policy and Administration*, 29(4): 271-91.

Howlett, M., Tan, S.L., Migone, A., Wellstead, A. and Evans, B. (2015) 'Policy formulation, policy advice policy appraisal: the distribution of analytical tools', in A.J. Jordan and J.R. Turnpenny (eds) *The tools of policy formulation. Actors, capacities, venues and effects*, Cheltenham: Edward Elgar, 163-83.

Howlett, M. and Wellstead, A.M. (2012) 'Professional policy work in federal states: institutional autonomy and Canadian policy analysis', *Canadian Public Administration/Administration publique du Canada*, 55(1): 53-68.

John, P. (1998) *Analysing public policy*, London/New York, NY: Continuum.

Jones, B.D. and Baumgartner, F.R. (2005) *The politics of attention: how government prioritizes problems*, Chicago, IL: University of Chicago Press.

Jones, C.O. (2001) *Introduction to the study of public policy* (4th edn), Orlando, FL: Harcourt College Pub.

Klijn, E.H. and Koppenjan, J. (2016) *Governance networks in the public sector*, Oxon: Routledge.

Kohoutek, J., Nekola, M. and Novotný, V. (2013) 'Conceptualizing policy work as activity and field of research', *Central European Journal of Public Policy*, 7(1): 28-59.

Kraft, M.E. and Furlong, S.R. (2012) *Public policy: politics, analysis, and alternatives* (4th edn), Washington, DC: CQ Press.

Lasswell, H.D. (1971) *A preview of policy sciences*, New York, NY: American Elsevier.

Lindquist, E. and Desvaux, J. (2007) 'Policy analysis and bureaucratic capacity: context, competencies, and strategies', in L. Dobuzinskis, M. Howlett and D. Laycock (eds) *Policy analysis in Canada: the state of the art*, Toronto: University of Toronto Press, 116-42.

Majone, G. (1989) *Evidence, argument, and persuasion in the policy process*, New Haven, CT/London: Yale University Press.

Mayer, I.S., van Daalen, C.E. and Bots, P.W.G. (2004) 'Perspectives on policy analysis: a framework for understanding and design', *International Journal of Technology, Policy and Management*, 4(1): 169-91.

Meltsner, A.J. (1976) *Policy analysts in the bureaucracy*, Berkeley, CA: University of California Press.

Mintzberg, H.J. (1973) *The nature of managerial work*, New York, NY: Harper and Row.

Montpetit, E. (2003) *Misplaced distrust: policy networks and the environment in France, the United States, and Canada*, Vancouver: UBC Press.

Nutley, S.M., Walter, I. and Davies, H.T.O. (eds) (2007) *Using evidence: how research can inform public services*, Bristol: Policy Press.

Ostrom, E. (1999) 'Institutional rational choice. An assessment of the institutional analysis and development framework', in P.A. Sabatier (ed) *Theories of the policy process*, Boulder, CO/Oxford: Westview Press, 35-71.

Page, E.C. (2012) *Policy without politicians: bureaucratic influence in comparative perspective*, Oxford: Oxford University Press.

Page, E.C. and Jenkins, B. (2005) *Policy bureaucracy: government with a cast of thousands*, Oxford: Oxford University Press.

Pierson, P. (2004) *Politics in time: history, institutions, and social analysis*, Princeton, NJ: Princeton University Press.

Prince, M.J. (2007) 'Soft craft, hard choices, altered context: reflections on twenty-five years of policy advice in Canada', in L. Dobuzinskis, M. Howlett and D. Laycock (eds) *Policy analysis in Canada: the state of the art*, Toronto: University of Toronto Press, 163-85.

Radin, B.A. (2000) *Beyond Machiavelli: policy analysis comes of age*, Washington, DC: Georgetown University Press.

Radin, B.A. (2013) 'Policy analyses reaches midlife', *Central European Journal of Public Policy*, 7(1): 8-27.

Rhodes, R.A.W. (1997) *Understanding governance: policy networks, governance, reflexivity and accountability*, Buckingham: Open University Press.

Richardson, J.J. (2000) 'Government, interest groups and policy change', *Political Studies*, 48(5): 1006-25.

Sabatier, P.A. and Jenkins-Smith, H. (1993) *Policy change and learning. An advocacy coalition approach*, Boulder, CO: Westview Press.

Sabatier, P.A. and Weible, C.M. (eds) (2014) *Theories of the policy process* (3rd edn), Boulder, CO/Oxford: Westview Press.

Streeck, W. and Thelen, K. (eds) (2005) *Beyond continuity: institutional change in advanced political economies*, Oxford: Oxford University Press.

Tao, J.L. (2006) 'Policy work at the local level in the United States: whispers of rationality', in H.K. Colebatch (ed) *The work of policy: an international survey*, Lanham, MD: Lexington Books, 181-98.

Tenbensel, T. (2006) 'Policy knowledge for policy work', in H.K. Colebatch (ed) *The work of policy: an international survey*, Lanham, MD: Lexington Books, 199-215.

Weimer, D.L. and Vining, A.R. (2010) *Policy analysis: concepts and practice* (5th edn), Englewood Cliffs, NJ: Prentice-Hall.

Williams, A. (2010) 'Is evidence-based policy-making possible?', in H.K. Colebatch, R. Hoppe and M. Noordegraaf (eds) *Working for policy*, Amsterdam: Amsterdam University Press, 195-210.

Zittoun, P. (2014) *The political process of policymaking: a pragmatic approach to public policy*, Basingstoke: Palgrave Macmillan.

Appendix

Table AI.I: Population of the Belgian in-house policy analysis survey

Organisation	Population	Distribution	Response rate
Federal government	2,253		38%*
FPS Finance	70	Direct mailing	
SPF Interior	1,230**	Direct mailing	
FPS Foreign Affairs	37	Direct mailing	
FPS Justice	59	Direct mailing	
FPS Economy	319	Direct mailing	
FPS Health	No data	Internal mailing	
FPS Defence	370***	Internal mailing	
FPS Social Security	168	Direct mailing	
Flanders	1,152		43%
General Governmental Policy	80	Direct mailing	
Public Affairs	88	Direct mailing	
Finance, Budget	23	Direct mailing	
International Affairs	59	Direct mailing	
Economics, Science, Innovation	38	Direct mailing	
Culture, Youth, Sports, Media	55	Direct mailing	
Work, Social Economy	45	Direct mailing	
Wellbeing, Health, Family	69	Direct mailing	
Education, Training	153	Direct mailing	
Agriculture, Fisheries	96	Direct mailing	
Environment, Nature, Energy	290	Direct mailing	
Mobility, Public Works	13	Direct mailing	
Spatial Planning, Public Housing	143	Direct mailing	
Francophone Belgium	4,155		32%
Walloon Region	2,893		
Public Service of Wallonia	1,957	Direct mailing	
Walloon Employment Agency	636	Internal mailing	
Walloon Agency for the Integration of Disabled Persons	116	Direct mailing	
Wallonia Export and Investment Agency	71	Direct mailing	
Walloon Housing Company	50	Direct mailing	
Walloon Institute for Evaluation, Foresight and Statistics	37	Internal mailing	
CRAC	26	Internal mailing	
Federation Wallonia-Brussels	1,262		
Ministry of Federation Wallonia-Brussels	1,205	Direct mailing	
Office of Birth and Childhood	31****	Internal mailing	
Broadcasting Authority	26	Direct mailing	

Notes:

★ The response rate does not take into account respondents linked to the FPS Health, of which the total number of officials to whom the survey was sent internally is unknown.

★★ Includes all civil servants with a university degree in this policy sector; no selection was made based on functional tasks relating to policy work by the FPS Interior itself.

★★★ Estimated number of military personnel included in the indirect mailing list, as indicated by liaison officer of ministry of Defence.

★★★★ Number of people involved in the policy work according to the director-general, who established the list. The number of employees with a university degree is, in this case, much higher.

TWO

Analytical techniques in Belgian policy analysis

Ellen Fobé, Bart De Peuter, Maxime Petit Jean and Valérie Pattyn

Policy analysis has long been recognised as a core function of modern bureaucracies (Lasswell, 1971; Meltsner, 1976; Brans et al, 2012). It consists of providing analytical support to government to make intelligent choices for solving societal problems (Colebatch, 2006). Policy analysis is not static, nor is the content of the civil servant's toolbox. The emergence and development in the use of specific analytical techniques (or 'formulation tools') is best understood against the background of important past and emerging trends that affect policymaking practice: the evidence-based movement; Europeanisation; and the professionalisation of policy analysis. While policy analysis is not confined to the governmental arena alone and involves the work of many actors, such as policy analysts situated in academia, think tanks, consultancy firms and specialists of organised interests outside government (Colebatch, 2006), this chapter is exclusively devoted to in-house policy analysis in Belgium. It explores in depth the development and application of policy-analytical techniques and methods within Belgium's federal and subnational administrations.

Considering that policy analysis is an emerging professional activity, the chapter has a twofold aim. First, it investigates to what extent trends and challenges to policy analysis have affected Belgian national and subnational governments with regard to the methods and techniques used in policy analysis; the institutionalisation of analytical practices within government; and the establishment of policy networks engaging civil servants, academics and private or non-profit actors in policy analysis. This discussion focuses on the development of two institutionalised practices symbolising a growing use of analytical techniques: regulatory impact analysis and policy-oriented futures studies. These can be considered as two meta-methods, in the sense that they both encompass a wide range of tools such as cost–benefit analysis, stakeholder analysis, SWOT (strengths, weaknesses, opportunities, threats) analysis, interviews and focus groups. Moreover, they can be applied to a broad array of policy sectors. Second, the chapter assesses at the individual level to what extent analytical techniques are used by Belgian civil servants. Based on a sample of civil servants (N=1,601), the use of a variety of well-known analytical techniques such as cost–benefit analysis, multi-criteria analysis, stakeholder analysis or benchmarking is investigated. The discussion finally focuses on an analysis of the use these techniques by individual civil servants across government levels and policy sectors. Policy analysis is in this sense approached from both an organisational and an individual perspective.

Definition of and trends in policy-analytical practice

This section outlines the importance of policy-analytical practices and provides a definition of policy-analytical techniques. It also reveals how internal and external pressures have triggered developments in policy analysis.

Defining policy-analytical techniques

Policy analysis is regarded as a core function of modern bureaucracies (Lasswell, 1971; Meltsner, 1976; Brans et al, 2012). It is not confined to individuals in governmental organisations alone. Rather, a high degree of policy analysis is situated outside of the government arena and carried out by organisations that are often closely linked to the public sphere (Colebatch, 2006; Radin, 2013). The non-governmental actors that engage in professional policy analysis are legion: particular interest groups such as trade unions, societal, environmental or consumer organisations and NGOs, think tanks, political parties, consultancies, universities, policy research centres and private companies (Dobuzinskis et al, 2007). Yet, the civil service remains a prime venue for policy analysis.

The deployment of policy-analytical techniques (Radin, 2013), often also referred to as policy-analytical methods (Dunn, 2004) or 'formulation tools' (Howlett et al, 2014), has been the topic of research and training since the 1950s (for an overview, see Radin, 2013). Various countries have also introduced sets of guidelines for the application of analytical techniques aimed at their integration and formalisation into government practices (Brans and Vancoppenolle, 2005; Nillson et al, 2008) in what can be seen as an attempt to further professionalise an aspect of policy work that over the years has already gained quite a lot of scholarly attention. Numerous textbooks indeed discuss in detail how to apply policy-analytical techniques. Examples of such policy formulation tools are cost-benefit analysis, scenario analysis, or gaming and decision trees – rooted in classical post-war planning and in modern operations research traditions (Wildavsky, 1979; Carley, 1983; Weimer and Vining, 1991; Bardach, 1996; Nagel, 1999); or stakeholder or Delphi analysis, designed to take into account more effectively the interests and knowledge held by stakeholders and other informed opinions (Rayens and Hahn, 2000; Linstone and Turoff, 2002; Bryson, 2004). These tools are applied for various reasons and purposes linked to policy formulation activities, such as understanding (complex) policy problems, assessing policy alternatives, and even identifying recommended policy responses (Dunn, 2004; Jordan et al, 2015).

The sheer number of analytical techniques that is currently available in policy analysis and the variety of purposes they serve renders it difficult to come up with a clear definition of the subject at hand. Turnpenny and colleagues (2015), drawing on Jenkins-Smith (1990), opted for a broad definition, viewing policy-analytical techniques as the particular means through which policy formulation activities are taken up and decision support is provided to policymakers:

> ... a technique, scheme, device or operation (including – but not limited to – those developed in the fields of economics, mathematics, statistics, computing, operations research and systems dynamics), which can be used to collect, condense and make sense of different kinds of policy relevant knowledge to perform some or all of the various inter-linked tasks of policy formulation. (Turnpenny et al, 2015, p 19)

Whereas in recent years there has been an increase in the number of techniques applied in policy analysis (see, for example, Radin , 2013), insight into how civil servants engage in policy analysis or to what extent they apply policy analytical techniques within particular policy settings remains relatively limited overall (Page and Jenkins, 2005; Colebatch and Radin, 2006; Howlett, 2009). Recent efforts to gather evidence on a large scale have complemented the available anecdotal case-study research on the policy-analytical activities of civil servants. These include studies in Canada (Howlett and Newman, 2010; Howlett et al, 2014), the Czech Republic (Vésely, 2013; Nekola, 2014), Australia (Carson and Wellstead, 2015) and Poland (Olejniczak et al, 2015). Equally, in Belgium, several large-scale surveys have been conducted to assess policy analysis by civil servants (for more details, see Chapter One). This chapter relies on the empirical evidence these surveys brought about to assess the extent to which policy-analytical techniques are deployed. Similarly, it builds on the main findings from past and recent qualitative research in Belgium regarding policy-analytical work (for example, Brans and Vancoppenolle, 2005; Varone et al, 2005; Destatte, 2006; Fobé and Brans, 2010, 2012, 2013; Pattyn, 2014, 2015; Pattyn and Brans, 2014; Vandoninck et al, 2016) to assess current developments and practices.

Trends in policy analytical practice

The emergence and development of policy-analytical practice within governments is characterised by three important developments. A first trend refers to the increased attention for evidence-based policy. A second development relates to the Europeanisation of policy issues, while a third trend includes the professionalization of practitioners of policy analysis. Policy analysis in Belgium can only be adequately understood by situating it against the background of these three interconnected trends, as discussed in this section.

Policy-analytical practice is, first, characterised by an increased attention for evidence. The trend toward evidence-based or evidence-informed policy is the result of technological advancements, the spread of democratic values in society and the growing complexity of policy problems, all of which have boosted awareness of knowledge production and management within governments and rendered policy-analytical practices more knowledge-intensive (Banks, 2009; Head, 2010). Policy issues have indeed become more enmeshed with one another, implying that many actors need to engage in vertical and horizontal cooperation to disentangle deadlocks and bottlenecks.

To address these issues, evidence seems indispensable for developing efficient and effective policy theories. The trend toward evidence-based policymaking is also the product of specific public sector drivers. More precisely, fiscal stress and value-for-money aspirations, as well as NPM reforms creating multiple steering and feedback lines, has gradually increased the need for evidence, including the production of measurable data on inputs, outputs and outcomes (Hood, 1991; Bouckaert and Auwers, 1999). Alternatively, increased awareness of evidence in policy has fostered a discussion on the issue of what constitutes knowledge, and on the quality standards for policy-relevant information. Advocates of a quantitative or qualitative approach, pertaining to different paradigms of positivism and constructivism, take up opposing views in this (Worthen et al, 2003).

A second trend that has had an impact on policy analysis within government is multi-level governance and specifically Europeanisation. The European Union has expanded its role in a large number of policy areas. It has demonstrated that it is a lever for formal policy-analytical practices and the deployment of analytical techniques in national governments and domestic administrations, in both a direct and an indirect way. The EU actively requires its member states to produce problem analyses and implementation reports, and to carry out monitoring and evaluation activities within several policy areas, often in return for subsidies (for example in the framework of the structural funds programme). The EU also influences national and regional policy practice, for example through monitoring the regulatory management capacities of several of its member states (OECD, s.d.; Radaelli, 2004, 2005). Similarly, via the process of information sharing and exchange, new techniques and methods introduced by the EU are over time often duplicated or transposed within the national and regional administrations, leading to the dissemination of benchmarking or cost-benefit analysis to name but two examples (European Commission, 2008; Cini and Perez-Solorzano Borragan, 2013).

The trends towards evidence-based policymaking and Europeanisation have led to a third important development in policy analytical practices. They have induced pressures for professionalising in-house policy analysis (Brans and Vancoppenolle, 2005). Changes to government structures, procedures, personnel and values are aimed at developing an infrastructure for better (that is, more effectively) tackling identified social problems. Aside from this, an increasing demand for more interactive policymaking processes has led to a higher degree of consultation of and participation by external actors, and/or individual citizens. Stakeholder management has become an integrated part of policy analysis.

Policy analytical practice in Belgium: techniques, organisations and networks

This section investigates the implications on the Belgian federal and regional administrations of the trends toward evidence-based policymaking, Europeanisation and professionalization of policy analysis. Three areas of impact are treated in more detail. First, the techniques used by civil servants in Belgium are discussed. The cases of RIA and policy-oriented futures studies are used to exemplify how policy analytical practices have developed. Second, the institutionalisation of policy analytical practices within the government is investigated by identifying policy units across the levels of government in Belgium that are assigned specific tasks of policy formulation, futures studies, monitoring and/or evaluation. Third, this section elaborates on the existence and maintenance of networks bringing together practitioners of policy analysis internal and external to the public sector.

The diffusion of policy-analytical techniques

Policy-analytical practices can be traced back to the 1960s in Belgium, with the implementation in some national ministries of performance-measurement activities linking for the first time financial information with objectives and policy programs (Bouckaert, 1995). Notably in 1968, a planning-programming-budgeting system was introduced via a pilot programme in the Ministry of Agriculture and the Ministry of Public Health, Family and Housing. Policymakers' attention for performance measurement had, however, faded by the end of the 1970s when the issue of decentralisation and state reform was given more prominence in the political debate. Other attempts to introduce specific budgetary tools were made in the late 1980s in response to financial strains and the need to balance the government's budget (Jacqmotte, 1970; Thijs and Van de Walle, 2005).

Belgium is a typical case of a country where the diffusion of policy-analytical practices and techniques has been fostered by new public management (NPM) ideas and European Union obligations (Pattyn, 2015). This especially applies to the Flemish public sector, which implemented an NPM-inspired reform framework in 2006. The reforms of 'Better Administrative Policy' (*Beter Bestuurlijk Beleid*) put policy formulation and evaluation practices in the spotlight and introduced new methods and tasks for *ex ante* analysis, as well as *ex post* and *in itinere* evaluation. A few years after the reforms, policy evaluation was gradually introduced across the Flemish public sector, although differences across policy sectors remain (Pattyn, 2014). The EU was a major catalyst for the promotion of evaluation regularity in Flanders. The introduction of evaluation requirements, linked to the receipt of funds, made several organisations develop evaluation routines; these were also applied to policy measures even though these were not subject to the same requirements (Pattyn and Brans, 2014). A similar situation existed at the federal level and in Wallonia and Federation Wallonia-Brussels, where Varone et al (2005) noted the key role of the EU structural funds programme in fostering evaluation practices in the administrations.

Currently, both at the federal and regional levels in Belgium, a number of *ex ante* 'tests' are deployed as standard practice in policy analysis. The formal implementation of impact assessments and regulatory impact analyses are strong cases in point. The use of these analytical techniques in Belgium mirrors a broadly developed practice of impact assessment at the EU level (Radaelli, 2005).[1]

Similarly, EU practices have also mobilised champions of policy-oriented futures studies at different policy levels in Belgium. The next sections will treat in more detail the institutionalisation of these two analytical practices, symbolising a growing use of policy analytical techniques in Belgium. They can be considered as two meta-methods, in the sense that they encompass a wide range of analytical techniques such as cost-benefit analysis, stakeholder analysis, SWOT analysis, interviews and focus groups (Radaelli, 2004; EFMN, 2009). Moreover, they can be applied to a broad array of policy sectors. The descriptions show that Belgium, generally speaking, is a latecomer in terms of adopting analytical practices and that their institutionalisation still faces some challenges. The quality of policy analytical practices often falls short of official guidelines; and policymakers are often only partially committed to using the results of policy analysis in support of their policy decisions (Varone et al, 2005; Fobé and Brans, 2013; Vandoninck et al, 2016).

Regulatory impact analysis

In Belgium at the federal level, a number of *ex ante* 'tests' have been developed as standard practice in policy analysis. This type of *ex ante* analysis is typically linked to the preparation of legislation or policy decisions. Examples are found in various policy sectors, such as poverty, sustainable development, local government, youth, small and medium-sized enterprises (SMEs) and gender policies. To cope with the increasing number of thematic tests, the former federal government decided in May 2013 to integrate them into the more generic tool of regulatory impact analysis (RIA). This meant that the federal thematic *ex ante* tests on administrative simplification (established in 2004) sustainable development (2007), gender (2007), SMEs (2008) and policy coherence for development aid (2013) were integrated in a framework for regulatory impact assessment (DAV, 2014). The federal RIA is mandatory for all draft legislation, ministerial and royal decrees, excluding draft legislation constituting the ratification of international treaties, intergovernmental agreements and auto-regulation regarding the federal government.

It is composed as a checklist, and covers 21 different themes, four of which are described in more depth (that is, the formerly separated tests, excluding administrative simplification). RIA is carried out at the sector level, by the policy unit proposing the draft legislation. The results of this *ex ante* evaluation are made accessible online (albeit after a policy proposal has been turned into legislation). They are also included in the parliamentary documents relating to the proposed legislation. It remains to be seen whether the integrated RIA at the federal level obtains its goal of raising awareness for assessing the impact of policy decisions, and whether it can overcome the difficulties encountered by the former separate tests, that is limitations to self-evaluation and poor quality control from the overseeing agency (Varone et al, 2005; OECD, 2015a).

A similar integrated procedure for *ex ante* evaluation of proposals for legislation exists in Wallonia, where it is mandatory in certain policy sectors such as environment, energy and agriculture. Rather than actively using the term RIA, the Walloon government refers to this set of tests as 'an examination of conformity of sustainable development goals' (Regional Law of 27 June 2013). More precisely, the *ex ante* evaluation investigates to what extent policy proposals are horizontally and vertically integrated (that is across sectors and levels of government), whether they take into account long-term effects across societal groups, and whether they allow for participation of stakeholders during different stages of the policy process. This 'examination of durability' is in fact considered a light version of the federal RIA. The appraisal is carried out by a central unit within government and its result is formulated as advice to the government. The examination is considered an internal document whose content is not made available to the public (SPW, 2014a). At the end of 2014, the total number of examinations provided to the government stood at 86 (SPW, 2014b).

Similar to the federal level, RIA has been introduced in Flanders following its promotion by supranational organisations like the Organisation for Economic Cooperation and Development and the EU (Radaelli, 2005; Radaelli and De Francesco, 2007; Hugé and Waas, 2011). Nowadays it is required for all drafts of regional laws and governmental acts that have a regulatory effect on citizens, private or non-profit organisations. RIA has developed into a standard procedure in policy analysis, specifically as regards the preparation of policy initiatives that are translated into regulation. It is a structured process resulting in a document that outlines the pros and cons of possible policy options by comparing expected direct and indirect effects. As is the case at the federal level and in Wallonia, its relevance and impact should, however, not be overestimated. While it is meant as a tool for supporting policymakers in their decisions, it quite often serves as a retrospective justification for decisions derived from political bargaining (Van Humbeeck, 2009; Fobé and Brans, 2013; Vandoninck et al, 2016). Indeed, it is quite often simply viewed as a box that needs ticking and as such it has limited influence on policy decisions. That said, RIA has introduced (or has at least the potential to do so) a way of analytical thinking in terms of policy alternatives and estimates regarding impact in several topical areas (see, for example, Hugé and Waas, 2011; Vandoninck et al, 2016).

Policy-oriented futures studies

A second type of meta-policy-analytical practice is the development of policy-oriented futures studies. This concept refers to 'studies of the future aimed at supporting the policy process' (van't Klooster, 2007, p 18) and differs from the more general concept of futures studies that includes studies carried out within a private sector context. After the Second World War, this practice became part of several European governments' economic planning policies. In comparison with neighbouring countries like France, Germany and the Netherlands, which boast an extensive futures tradition driven by both governmental and private actors,

Belgian policy-oriented futures is still a relatively new field of practice (EFMN, 2009; Fobé and Brans, 2010).

Nonetheless, futures studies in Belgium have gained more ground in the regions as a result of the increased devolution of powers from the Belgian federal entity, pertaining to such sectors as energy, housing, spatial planning, science and technology, and economics (Verlet and De Smedt, 2010). Not only are these policy areas rooted in long-term planning traditions, they are also covered by a wide range of futures studies at the European and international levels. Both factors seem to have contributed to increased awareness of long-term policymaking, and, as such, of policy-oriented futures studies at the subnational level in Belgium. This development took off in the 1980s in Wallonia through several large-scale futures studies that were carried out in light of the first Walloon regional policy plan in 1999, termed Contract for the Future of Wallonia (Destatte, 2006). In Flanders too, the turn of the century proved important in setting up government-wide future projects aimed at envisioning a normative, desirable future for the Flemish region (for example, the Vilvoorde Pact in 2001, or the Colourful Flanders project in 2002). It also brought about more projects and futures studies in sectoral departments (Verlet and De Smedt, 2010).

Contrary to RIA, policy-oriented futures studies are not mandatory for draft regional laws. Nor are there any fixed guidelines or general procedures for carrying out such *ex ante* analyses. Consequently, the policy-oriented futures studies conducted in Belgium are diverse in nature. Futures projects are often initiated in accordance with a sector's interests and needs and only occasionally with legal obligations. They typically deploy a variety of analytical techniques. Those most commonly applied for studying the future are creative techniques such as SWOT analysis, Delphi analysis, expert panels, brainstorming and scenario analysis. More formal, analytical techniques such as prognoses, projections and complex models, are also frequently used (Popper, 2008; EFMN, 2009; Verlet and De Smedt, 2010; Fobé and Brans, 2013; SVR, s.d.).

The influence of policy-oriented futures studies on policymaking remains relatively limited overall, as is the case with RIA. Several elements restricting the influence of foresight on decision makers stand out. Despite some exceptions, there is still relatively little interest from policymakers in using futures studies as a decision-support mechanism. Government-wide foresight activities are also often concerned with the identification of broad political orientations, without linking these much to day-to-day policy issues. This limits their relevance and reduces their applicability to policymakers. Other futures studies then, rather than being vague on desirable policy measures, are perceived as too prescriptive, constraining the flexibility and discretion of policymakers. And futures studies initiated by policy departments are found to suffer from a lack of coordination with the political principal or across other policy sectors. These constraints clearly curb the potential for the diffusion of policy-oriented futures studies and inhibit their influence on policies and decision makers (Fobé and Brans, 2012, 2013).[2]

The institutionalisation of policy-analytical practices

The trends in in-house policy analysis towards more evidence-based policies, Europeanisation and professionalization have led to the application of a variety of policy-analytical practices, such as RIA and policy-oriented futures studies. They have also resulted in the institutionalisation of these types of practice in the organisational structures of Belgian administrations. This section illustrates the creation of divisions or units across levels of government in Belgium that are assigned specific tasks of policy formulation, futures studies, monitoring and/ or evaluation. The discussion highlights how some of these units are explicitly responsible for the development and use of certain *ex ante* techniques, such as regulatory impact assessment, while others fulfil a much broader task, such as that of an expertise centre or evaluation division, or are in charge of building monitoring capacity and carrying out policy-oriented futures studies.

As for the horizontal institutionalisation of policy-analytical practices and organisations at the federal level, the Agency of Administrative Simplification plays an important role. This agency within the office of the prime minister has since 2013 been tasked with the coordination of the introduction and application of RIA across the federal policy departments (DAV, 2014; OECD, 2015b). At the regional level, there are two main actors, that is, the Study Centre of the Flemish Government and the Walloon Institute of Evaluation, Foresight and Statistics (IWEPS), discussed in more detail shortly.

In Flanders, the Study Centre of the Flemish Government was for many years an autonomous agency within the department for General Government Policy, taking up a role in developing and sustaining evidence-informed policies and *ex ante* analysis. More precisely, it conducts science-based studies on demographic, societal and macro-economic developments, starting from a specific and policy-relevant information need. The centre also conducts context analysis, monitoring and futures studies itself. At the same time, it supports sectoral units carrying out monitoring, evaluation, futures studies and survey work. It predominantly works for the minister-president and the other members of the Flemish government but also delivers information to parliament and to local governments. Since 2016, it has ceased being an agency and has been integrated into the central administration for Chancellery and Governance. Its core tasks remain the same.[3]

In Wallonia policy-analytical practices were originally spread out among various administrative entities, such as the department of Environment and the studies and statistics unit of the Civil Service department. In 2004, a public agency in charge of evaluation, foresight and statistical analysis, the IWEPS, was established. The creation of IWEPS further institutionalised policy-analytical practices. It was charged with the task of centralising studies commissioned by the Walloon government and acting as a support agency for other administrations regarding methods of analysis and policy decision. The agency, however, did not fully succeed in its role of centralising statistical analysis and evaluation practices, and other public organisations started to collect their own data and to conduct or commission their own evaluations.

IWEPS currently evaluates the main regional strategic plans, through which it remains a significant actor, although all of its actions need to be based on a formal request from the government itself (IWEPS, 2012). Since its establishment, IWEPS has also increasingly positioned itself as a significant actor in the Walloon futures studies landscape. It has done so by hiring additional staff members and conducting more studies in-house (for example, on demographic transitions and the Walloon civil service), by monitoring projects launched by the Walloon government (notably in the energy, environment, economy and spatial planning sectors), and by outsourcing some of its own futures studies (for example, on energy transition, the management of an ageing population in Wallonia and poverty). IWEPS also takes up a coordinating role in the Walloon foresight landscape, exemplified by its involvement in futures studies carried out by sectoral policy units. The Autonomous Advisory Cell for Sustainable Development (CAAD) has been assigned an important role in terms of implementing the newly introduced 'examination of durability'. CAAD was created in 2013 and is linked to the department of Sustainable Development of the Walloon public services. Using the aforementioned *ex ante* examination, CAAD formulates advice to its main clients, that is, other policy departments and the Walloon government (SPW, 2014b).

Although the institutionalisation of policy-analytical practices has gained ground in Belgium, notable differences persist between policy sectors. Some policy departments conduct futures studies or policy assessments in-house (such as the Environment in Flanders, or the Sustainable Development and Research departments in Wallonia), while other departments rely more on the input of IWEPS (in Wallonia) or the Study Centre of the Flemish Government.

Moreover, some policy departments turn to external organisations such as academic research institutes or consultancies and outsource certain policy-analytical tasks. Sectoral policy-analytical capacity is indeed quite fragmented. In Flanders, for example, analytical tasks remain split between departments and agencies in certain policy sectors despite the aspirations for consolidation in the Better Administrative Policy reform (2006). It is worth noting that currently a high number of units in Flanders seem to identify policy-analytical practices (such as evaluations or futures studies) more clearly as (part of) their core task(s) (De Peuter and Brans, 2012). Also in Wallonia there are units conducting evaluation and futures studies in almost all policy sectors, situated either within the centralised departments or within the public agencies that operate at arm's length from these departments.

Professional networks for policy analysis and evaluation

The trends toward evidence-based policies, Europeanisation and professionalization have also affected the development of professional networks for policy analysis. This is especially the case for networks focusing on evaluation practices, which have been established at the regional level, both in Flanders as in Wallonia. In Flanders, the Flemish Evaluation Platform (VEP) was founded in 2007. Its aim was to develop, strengthen and diffuse an evaluation culture, to strengthen the evaluation capacity of the different actors, to raise the quality of evaluations and to stimulate the influence and use of evaluation. In Wallonia, the Walloon Society for Evaluation and Foresight (*Société wallonne de l'évaluation et de la prospective*, or SWEP) was set up earlier, in 2000. This non-profit organisation aims to promote evaluation and foresight in Wallonia to improve decision and policymaking. It does so through conferences, seminars and trainings. Both networks are targeted at (respectively French-speaking and Dutch-speaking) civil servants from all governmental levels, as well as academics and actors from the private and non-profit sector. They certainly have contributed to network and capacity building of civil servants involved in evaluation. Within the civil service, too, initiatives for training in evaluation have gained ground, in addition to those provided by academic institutions.

Another policy network active in Wallonia focuses particularly on the development of studies on spatial planning, urban planning, and territorial development. The Permanent Conference for Territorial Development (*Conférence permanente du développement territorial*, or CPDT) was created in 1998 as a platform across several universities that provides advice and policy-oriented futures studies to the Walloon government on matters of regional spatial policies (Van Cutsem and Demulder, 2011; CPDT, s.d.).

Tools at work: taking stock of policy-analytical practice

This section treats in more detail the degree to which individual civil servants in Belgium make use of a range of policy-analytical techniques, such as brainstorming, cost-benefit analysis, stakeholder analysis and decision trees. The analysis builds on the results of a series of government-wide surveys implemented at the federal level, as well as in Flanders, Wallonia, and Federation Wallonia-Brussels. After discussing the overall use of analytical techniques by civil servants across all policy levels in Belgium, the difference between these policy levels is investigated and the variation in techniques used across policy sectors is explored.[4]

Use of policy-analytical techniques in Belgium

Civil servants in Belgium make use of a variety of policy analytical techniques. A general overview of these tools is provided in Table 2.1. The table shows the relative frequency of respondents at all levels of policy in Belgium indicating that they use policy-analytical techniques 'on a regular basis'. This includes those using the different techniques either 'a few times per year', 'monthly' or 'weekly' and excludes those who have 'not' or only used these techniques 'once per year or less' during the previous two years of the legislature.

Table 2.1: Use of policy-analytical techniques in Belgium (all policy levels)

Type of tool	Average number of respondents applying policy-analytical tools on a regular basis (N=1,601)
>50%	
Brainstorming	65%
Focus group/interviews	53%
20-30%	
Cost-benefit analysis	30%
Stakeholder analysis	30%
SWOT analysis	28%
Benchmarking	24%
Multi-criteria analysis	23%
Survey analysis	20%
<15%	
Decision trees	12%
Delphi analysis	10%
Logic model	8%
Gaming	5%
Total average	24%

In Belgium, on average 24% of respondents apply analytical techniques on a regular basis in their work. These findings are similar to the results from survey research on policy-analytical techniques in Canada (Howlett et al, 2014), the Czech Republic (Nekola, 2014) and Poland (Olejniczak et al, 2015), and show that policy analysts apply not just one, but a variety of techniques.

Some analytical techniques are applied more frequently than others. Three groups of techniques can be distinguished: those that are deployed by a large share of respondents (>50%), those that are used by a substantial number (20-30%), and those for which the use seems restricted to a rather select group of civil servants (<15%). In particular, two techniques are used most frequently by respondents. Brainstorming as well as focus groups and interviews are applied regularly by more than half of them. Brainstorming is essentially a group activity. The high number of civil servants deploying this technique for analysis may be explained by this simple fact: more people are logically involved in applying this technique.

A second set of analytical techniques are used regularly by a smaller, but still substantial, number of respondents across the Belgian governments (between 20% and 30%). These techniques are traditionally considered as central to policy analysis and therefore also part of academic teaching programmes and training for policy practitioners. More precisely, around a third of respondents uses cost-benefit analysis, stakeholder analysis and SWOT analysis on a regular basis, while about a quarter regularly deploys multi-criteria analysis and carries out benchmarks or survey analysis.

A third group of five other tools is put to use regularly by a more select group, accounting for up to 15% of respondents in the survey. Whereas decision-tree and Delphi analysis are still used regularly by about 10% of respondents, the use of logic models and game theory in Belgian policy analytical practice is below 10%.

In sum, it appears that civil servants are familiar with a variety of policy-analytical techniques and that these are applied within the Belgian public administrations on a relatively frequent basis. Those applied very frequently are not the most formal techniques of analysis available, although a significant number of civil servants use the latter regularly. Of course, in terms of the deployment of different types of technique, some differences may exist between different levels of government. The next section examines these differences in more detail.

Use of policy-analytical tools across different levels of government

This section compares the application of policy-analytical techniques between the different administrative levels in Belgium: the federal level, Flanders, Wallonia and Federation Wallonia-Brussels. It pertains to the responses of civil servants indicating that they used the different techniques either 'a few times per year', 'monthly' or 'weekly', and excludes the responses of those who had 'not' or only used these tools 'once per year or less' during the previous two years of the legislature. The average number of respondents using policy-analytical techniques is quite similar across these administrations. On average, 25% to 28% of civil servants regularly deploy policy-analytical techniques. Table 2.2 provides an overview of the five *most* frequently and three *least* frequently used techniques.

Similarities across the different levels of government in Belgium include the overall importance of brainstorming, focus groups, interviews and cost-benefit analysis. The results also show the relatively limited use of logic models, Delphi analysis, and gaming in Belgium as a whole. Moreover, they are an indication of the importance of stakeholder analysis at the subnational level, which may be explained by a historically strong tradition of consultation of stakeholders by Belgian governments (see also Chapter Ten).

Use of policy-analytical tools across different policy sectors

Similar to the findings of other country case studies (Howlett et al, 2014; Nekola, 2014), the use of techniques varies between policy sectors within the same government. The sectoral variations within each of the four administrations that are found to be statistically significant are treated in more detail here.[5] Table 2.3 presents the two policy sectors whose tool use stands out as statistically significant compared with other sectors at the same level of government. Civil servants in these sectors deploy analytical techniques either significantly less or significantly more than those in other sectors. The table indicates the direction of use and the particular types of technique that are used less or more in each sector. It is notable that the results pertain to a within–government comparison, and that there is no comparison between different government levels.

Table 2.2: Most and least frequently applied techniques across policy levels in Belgium

	Federal (N=380)	Flanders (N=451)	Wallonia (N=332)	French Community (N=449)
Most frequently used tools				
1.	Brainstorming	Brainstorming	Focus group/interview	Focus group/interview
2.	Focus group/interview	Focus group/interview	Brainstorming	Brainstorming
3.	SWOT	Stakeholder analysis	MCA	Stakeholder analysis
4.	CBA	SWOT	CBA	MCA
5.	Benchmarking	CBA	Stakeholder analysis	CBA
Least frequently used tools				
10.	Logic model	Delphi	Logic model	Delphi
11.	Delphi	Logic model	Delphi	Decision tree
12.	Gaming	Gaming	Gaming	Gaming

Table 2.3: Sectoral differences in the use of analytical techniques

Policy level	Policy sector	Direction of use*	Tool
Federal	Defence	+	Focus group/interview SWOT, CBA, MCA Decision tree, logic model, gaming
	Finance	–	SWOT, stakeholder analysis
Flanders	Administrative Affairs	+	Focus group/interview, brainstorming Benchmarking, SWOT, CBA
	Work	+	Brainstorming SWOT, CBA
Wallonia	Agriculture and Environment	–	Brainstorming Benchmarking, SWOT, CBA, MCA, survey
	Finance and Budget	–	Brainstorming Benchmarking, SWOT, survey
French Community	Cultural Heritage and Infrastructures	–	Brainstorming Benchmarking, SWOT, stakeholder analysis
	Education and Youth	–	Benchmarking, stakeholder analysis

Note: * More or less use in comparison with other policy sectors indicated by + or – (within the same government, not between governments).

At the federal level, attention is drawn to one policy sector in particular. The department for Defence makes significantly more use of a range of policy-analytical techniques than any other department at this level of government. Given the historical position of Defence departments as strongholds of analytical methods, this finding does not surprise. The Defence department applies a whole range of techniques significantly more often, including techniques that are overall used very infrequently in Belgium, such as decision-tree analysis, logic models and gaming. Additionally, the results of our analysis show that the federal Finance department makes less use of SWOT and stakeholder analysis.

In Flanders, then, the departments for Administrative Affairs and for Work apply analytical techniques quite differently from the other departments. The department for Administrative Affairs makes significantly more use of five techniques than the average, while respondents at the department for Work apply three techniques significantly more often.

In Federation Wallonia-Brussels, no department makes significantly more use of analytical techniques than others. The department for Cultural Heritage and Infrastructures makes less use of brainstorming, SWOT, benchmarks and stakeholder analysis than the average department in this government. These differences are statistically significant. The department of Education and Youth also tends to use less benchmarks and stakeholder analysis than the others.

As to the policy sectors in Wallonia, the findings show that respondents in the department for Agriculture and Environment make significantly less use of six techniques than the other departments in this government (that is surveys, brainstorming, benchmarks, SWOT analysis, cost-benefit analysis [CBA] and multi-criteria analysis [MCA]). The first four analytical techniques are also deployed significantly less in the department of Finance and Budget. The lower use of CBA in these sectors is rather surprising. Given the quantitative nature of the matters dealt with in the Finance and Budget department, one would expect civil servants in this sector to make more use of this technique. Equally, it may be assumed that the department for Environment and Agriculture would apply CBA more often, given the influence of the EU in this sector.

In sum, the observed differences in use of policy-analytical techniques between the different levels of government in Belgium hide important sectoral variations. Accounting for these differences, three organisational characteristics may be potential explanations: the role of policy sectors' budget size, the sectoral dependence on EU funds, and the relative number of social scientists within a policy domain (Fobé et al, forthcoming). The findings of this recent study suggest that these factors affect the deployment of four analytical techniques, namely brainstorming, SWOT analysis, CBA and logic models. In more detail, the use of these techniques is affected by closer public scrutiny in sectors that have high levels of spending, but also by the requirements related to receiving EU funding and the focus on analytical and evaluation techniques in academic (post)graduate training programmes.

Other possible explanations for sectoral differences in the use of techniques include the conditions at the individual level of analysis, such as the professional and educational background of policy workers, or their age and prior work experience. One could also assume that the degree to which civil servants participate in training programmes (including attending general courses on policy analysis or specific courses on the deployment of certain analytical tools), affects the use of policy-analytical techniques (Fobé et al, forthcoming). These explanatory factors merit a deeper investigation from researchers both within and outside of Belgium.

Conclusion

This chapter has investigated different aspects of policy-analytical practices in Belgium, aimed at helping governments make intelligent choices for solving societal problems (Lasswell, 1971; Colebatch, 2006). It shows that several trends affect policy analysis and that their influence on the implementation of analytical practice in Belgium is quite notable. In particular, an emphasis on evidence-based policies, increased integration at EU level and the professionalisation of policy-analytical work have led to the institutionalisation of analytical practices such as RIA and futures studies, as well as to the establishment of units and professional networks for policy analysis and evaluation. Aside from developments at the organisational level, this chapter has also presented the results of a series of surveys on policy analysis in Belgium showing the extent to which civil servants use a variety of analytical techniques. The analysis considers the types of techniques used in policy analysis, and investigates differences in use between different levels of government and across policy sectors.

By reflecting on the developments and practices of policy analysis in Belgian governments, it has been shown that, overall, a significant number of civil servants engages in policy analysis, and that this is the case not only across levels of government in Belgium but also within different policy sectors. In this regard, policy analysis sustains a core function of a modern bureaucracy such as it exists in Belgium (Lasswell, 1971; Meltsner, 1976). The chapter has also demonstrated that European pressures have played an important part in fostering the adoption and institutionalisation of analytical practices in Belgium. Regulatory impact analysis and policy-oriented futures studies are two cases in point. The role of the EU and specifically the requirements related to receiving EU funding were also found to affect the use of certain analytical techniques such as or SWOT analysis at the sectoral level. Following these findings, it appears that policy analytical practice in Belgium is faced with three important challenges: strengthening the quality and role of policy analysis, reaffirming the commitment of political decision makers and establishing a common framework and language.

Despite significant developments in recent times, Belgium is not a forerunner in policy analysis. This is particularly the case when the quality and integration of the results of policy analysis in policy decisions are taken into account. While it is meant as a decision support tool, RIA often serves as a justification for decisions that have already been made and therefore has limited direct influence on policy decisions. A similar conclusion can be made for futures studies, which seem to suffer mostly from a lack of diffusion beyond the immediate actors involved, as well as from the long-term orientation that isolates it from day-to-day policy issues. In order to overcome the challenge of strengthening the quality and role of policy-analytical practices, the policy process needs to be mapped out and timed well. This would facilitate the conduct of policy analysis when needed, that is at the moment that it is deemed useful and not just when it is required. Innovative formats of displaying and communicating evidence to policymakers may improve diffusion as well, involving, for example, specific tools of visualisation of the results of policy analysis.

The influence of policy-analytical practices is curbed by the often limited extent to which policymakers are committed to using results in support of policy decisions. Policy decisions in Belgium are primarily the result of political bargaining, and are not (predominantly) supported by objective evidence and analysis. Ministerial cabinets, which take up a leading role in policy formulation in Belgium, rarely give high priority to policy-analytical practices, such as the appraisal of different policy alternatives. This brings us to a second important point, namely that the consensual nature of political decision making in Belgium is a significant obstacle to the development of policy-analytical practices within the civil service.

As this chapter has illustrated, the process of integration of policy-analytical practices within Belgium's administrations is under way. Aside from evaluation and RIA, however, there are no common standards or guidelines for carrying out policy-analytical practices. To overcome this challenge, the opportunities for formation of and training in policy-analytical practices should be expanded. By generating more insight into the variety of techniques that can be deployed in policy formulation and by learning about their strengths and weaknesses, a common framework for policy-analytical practices could be established within the civil service.

Considering that policy analysis is only an emerging profession in Belgium, a more detailed examination of policy-analytical practices is required across the different levels of government. The establishment of government-wide surveys on policy analysis in Belgium, of which some of the results were reported in this chapter, only constitutes a first step in reaching this goal. The available fragmented evidence on evaluation and foresight activities could therefore be complemented with research on SWOT analysis, stakeholder analysis or brainstorming, for example. More international research is also required, as insight into how civil servants engage in policy analysis and to what extent they apply policy-analytical techniques within particular policy settings remains relatively limited overall (Page and Jenkins, 2005; Colebatch and Radin, 2006; Howlett, 2009). Indeed, despite recent efforts to gather evidence on a large scale basis, comparative analysis across state boundaries is still wanting. Moreover, future research needs to look in more detail at the factors influencing policy-analytical practices, the conditions in which civil servants actually resort to certain analytical techniques, the hindrances to use and the ways to overcome them, and factors at the individual level of analysis including the professional and educational background of civil servants, to name but a few examples. This would move the discipline beyond merely describing what policy analysts do, and provide direction for the improvement of policy-analytical practices.

Notes

[1] OECD has also contributed to the diffusion of RIA through its Better Regulation project, covering Belgium along with 14 other EU member states (De Vos et al, 2014).

[2] These issues have been identified by Petit Jean in a series of interviews carried out in 2014.

[3] See www4dar.vlaanderen.be/sites/svr.

[4] It should be noted that this data is self-reported and all respondents may not have the same interpretation of a particular technique. The implementation of cost-benefit analysis, for instance, can range from 'very light' to 'very advanced', depending on the extent of monetisation of all variables, or depending on the extent of discounting future costs and benefits. The reader should take this into account when interpreting the data.

[5] Kruskal-Wallis test for different policy-analytical techniques by policy sector. All policy sectors in the test include a sample size of $N>10$ observations. Differences across sectors are significant if p-value for chi-square with ties <0.05.

References

Banks, G. (2009) *Challenges of evidence-based policy making*, Canberra: APSC.

Bardach, E. (1996) *The eight-step path of policy analysis (a handbook for practice)*, Berkeley, CA: Berkeley Academic Press.

Bouckaert, G. (1995) 'Improving performance measurement', in A. Halachmi and G. Bouckaert (eds) *The enduring challenges in public management: surviving and excelling in a changing world*, San Francisco, CA: Jossey-Bass, 379-412.

Bouckaert, G. and Auwers, T. (1999) *Prestaties meten in de overheid*, Bruges: Die Keure.

Brans, M. and Vancoppenolle, D. (2005) 'Policy-making reforms and civil service systems: an exploration of agendas and consequences', in M. Painter and J. Pierre (eds) *Challenges to state policy capacity. Global trends and comparative perspectives*, Basingstoke: Palgrave Macmillan, 164-84.

Brans, M., De Peuter, B. and Ferraro, G. (2012) 'Policy work old and new: challenges to bureaucratic policy work as a craft', paper presented at the Organization Studies Summer Workshop, Rhodes, 24-26 May.

Bryson, J. (2004) 'What to do when stakeholders matter', *Public Management Review*, 6(1): 21-3.

Carley, M. (1983) *Rational techniques in policy analysis*, London: Policy Studies Institute.

Carson, D. and Wellstead, A. (2015) 'Government with a cast of dozens: policy capacity risks and policy work in the Northern Territory', *Australian Journal of Public Administration*, 74(2): 162-75.

Cini, M. and Perez-Solorzano Borragan, N. (eds) (2013) *European Union politics*, Oxford: Oxford University Press.

Colebatch, H. (2006). 'What work makes policy?', *Policy Sciences*, 39(4): 309-21.

Colebatch, H.K. and Radin, B.A. (2006) 'Mapping the work of policy', in H.K. Colebatch (ed) *The work of policy*, New York, NY: Rowman and Littlefield, 217-26.

CPDT (n.d.) *Qu'est-ce que la CPDT?*, available at http://cpdt.wallonie.be/visiteurs/quest-ce-que-la-cpdt (accessed 30 December 2013).

DAV (Dienst Administratieve Vereenvoudiging) (2014) *Regelgevingsimpactanalyse. Inleiding tot praktische oefeningen*, Brussels: DAV.

Destatte, P. (2006) 'De l'histoire à la prospective', paper presented at the Conférence à l' Université du Temps Disponible, Huy, 21 September.

De Peuter, B. and Brans, M. (2012) 'Policy work: a risky profession. An analysis of policy work in the Flemish government administration from a risk management perspective', paper presented at the IPSA World Congress of Political Science, Madrid, 8-12 July.

De Vos D., Van de Walle C., Bailly N., Decoster S., Panneels C. and Quertinmont, J.C. (2014) *Regelgevingsimpactanalyse*, unpublished work.

Dobuzinskis, L., Howlett, M. and Laycock, D. (eds) (2007) *Policy analysis in Canada: the state of the art*, Toronto: University of Toronto Press.

Dunn, W. (2004) *Public policy analysis: an introduction*, Upper Saddle River, NJ: Pearson/Prentice Hall.

EFMN (European Foresight Monitoring Network) (2009) *Mapping Foresight. Revealing how Europe and other world regions navigate into the future*, Brussels: European Commission.

European Commission (2008) *Guide to cost-benefit analysis of investment projects*, Brussels: European Commission.

Fobé, E. and Brans, M. (2010) 'Toekomstverkennen in Frankrijk: van theorie tot praktijk', paper presented at the Politicologenetmaal, Leuven, 27-28 May.

Fobé, E. and Brans, M. (2012) *Toekomstverkennen bij de Vlaamse Overheid: Analyse van Praktijken en Doorwerking*, Leuven: Steunpunt Bestuurlijke Organisatie Vlaanderen.

Fobé E., and Brans, M. (2013) 'Policy-oriented foresight as evidence for policy-making: conditions of (mis)match', *Evidence & Policy*, 9(4): 473-92.

Fobé, E., Pattyn, V. and Brans, M. (forthcoming) 'Policy analytical practice investigated: exploring patterns in use of policy analytical techniques', in W. Xun, M. Howlett and M. Ramesh (eds) *Policy capacity: state and societal perspectives*, Basingstoke: Palgrave Macmillan.

Head, B.W. (2010) 'Evidence-based policy: principles and requirements', in Productivity Commission (ed) *Strengthening evidence-based policy in the Australian Federation, volume 1*, Canberra: Productivity Commission, 13-26.

Hood, C. (1991) 'A public management for all seasons?', *Public Administration*, 69(1): 3-19.

Howlett, M. (2009) 'Policy analytical capacity and evidence-based policy-making: lessons from Canada', *Canadian Public Administration*, 52(2): 153-75.

Howlett, M. and Newman, J. (2010) 'Policy analysis and policy work in federal systems: policy advice and its contribution to evidence-based policy-making in multi-level governance systems', *Policy and Society*, 29(1): 123-36.

Howlett, M., Tan, S., Migone, A. and Evans, B. (2014) 'The distribution of analytical techniques in policy advisory systems: policy formulation and the tools of policy appraisal', *Public Policy and Administration*, 29(4): 271-91.

Hugé, J. and Waas, T. (2011) 'Converging impact assessment discourses for sustainable development: the case of Flanders, Belgium', *Environment Development and Sustainability*, 13(3): 607-26.

IWEPS (Walloon Institute of Evaluation, Foresight and Statistics) (2012) *Rapport d'activité 2011*, Namur: IWEPS.

Jacqmotte, J.P. (1970) 'Tentative comparative study of RCB in France and PPBS in Belgium', *International Review of Administrative Sciences*, 36(1): 47-55.

Jenkins-Smith, H. (1990) *Democratic politics and policy analysis*, Pacific Grove, CA: Brooks/Cole.

Jordan, A., Turnpenny, J. and Rayner, T. (2015) 'The tools of policy formulation: new perspectives and new challenges', in A. Jordan and J. Turnpenny (eds) *The tools of policy formulation. Actors, capacities, venues and effects*, Cheltenham: Edgar Elgar, 267-93.

Lasswell, H. (1971) 'The policy orientation', in D. Lerners and H. Lasswell (eds) *The policy sciences*, Stanford, CA: Stanford University Press.

Linstone, H.A. and Turoff, M. (eds) (2002) *The Delphi method: techniques and applications*, Newark, NJ: New Jersey Institute of Technology.

Meltsner, A. (1976) *Policy analysts in the bureaucracy*, Berkeley, CA: University of California Press.

Nagel, S. (ed) (1999) *Policy analysis methods*, Commack, NY: Nova Science Publishers.

Nekola, M. (2014) 'The individual and organizational dimensions of the policy analytical capacity of Czech ministries', paper presented at the 23rd World Congress of Political Science, Montreal, 19-24 July.

Nilsson, M., Jordan, A., Turnpenny, J., Hertin, J., Nykvist, B. and Duncan, R. (2008) 'The use and non-use of policy appraisal tools in public policy making: an analysis of three European countries and the European Union', *Policy Sciences*, 41(4): 335-55.

OECD (Organisation for Economic Co-operation and Development) (2015a) *Impact assessment in Belgium, federal government*, Paris: OECD.

OECD (2015b) *OECD regulatory policy outlook 2015, Belgium*, Paris: OECD.

OECD (s.d.) *Better regulation in Europe: an OECD assessment of regulatory capacity in the 15 original member states of the EU. Project baseline and scope*, Paris: OECD.

Olejniczak, K., Śliwowski, P. and Trzcinski, R. (2015) 'The role of analysts in public agencies: toward an empirically grounded typology', paper presented at the 2nd International Conference on Public Policy, Milan, 1-4 July.

Page, E. and Jenkins, B. (2005) *Policy bureaucracy. Government with a cast of thousands*, Oxford: Oxford University Press.

Pattyn, V. (2014) 'Policy evaluation (in)activity unraveled. A configurational analysis of the incidence, number, locus and quality of policy evaluations in the Flemish public sector', unpublished PhD dissertation, KU Leuven.

Pattyn, V. (2015) 'Explaining variance in policy evaluation regularity. The case of the Flemish public sector', *Public Management Review*, 17(10): 1475-95.

Pattyn, V. and Brans, M. (2014) 'Explaining organisational variety in evaluation quality assurance. Which conditions matter?', *International Journal of Public Administration*, 37(6): 363-75.

Popper, R. (2008) 'How are foresight methods selected?' *Foresight*, 10: 62-89.

Radaelli, C. (2004) 'The diffusion of regulatory impact analysis – best practice or lesson-drawing?', *European Journal of Political Research*, 43(5): 723-47.

Radaelli, C. (2005) 'Diffusion without convergence: how political context shapes the adoption of regulatory impact assessment', *Journal of European Public Policy*, 12(5): 924-43.

Radaelli C. and De Francesco, F. (2007) 'Regulatory impact assessment, political control and the regulatory state', paper presented at the 4th General Conference of the European Consortium for Political Research, Pisa, 6-8 September.

Radin, B. (2013) 'Policy analysis reaches midlife', *Central European Journal of Public Policy*, 7(1): 8-27.

Rayens, M. and Hahn, E. (2000) 'Building consensus using the policy Delphi method', *Policy, Politics and Nursing Practice*, 1(4): 308-15.

SPW (Public Service of Wallonia) (2014a) 'Quelle vision du développement durable dans les analyses d'impact de la réglementation? Le cas de la Cellule autonome d'avis en Développement durable', presentation for the workshop Echange croisé: les analyses d'impact de la réglementation (Associations21), Brussels, 23 September.

SPW (2014b) *Rapport d'activités 2014 Cellule autonome d'avis en Développement durable*, Namur: Secrétariat général.

SVR (Study Centre of the Flemish Government) (s.d.) 'Methoden en Technieken', available at www4.vlaanderen.be/sites/svr/Methoden.

Thijs, N. and Van de Walle, S. (2005) 'Administrative reforms movements and commissions in Belgium. 1848-2004', *Public Policy and Administration*, 20(4): 38-54.

Turnpenny, J., Jordan, A., Benson, D. and Rayner, T. (2015) 'The tools of policy formulation: an introduction', in A. Jordan and J. Turnpenny (eds) *The tools of policy formulation. Actors, capacities, venues and effects*, Cheltenham: Edgar Elgar, 3-32.

Van Cutsem, M. and Demulder, C. (2011) *Territoires wallons: horizons 2040*, Namur: Institut Jules-Destrée.

Vandoninck, J., Brans, M., Wayenberg, E. and Fobé, E. (2016) *Ex ante beleidsevaluatie voor beleidsinstrumentenkeuze. Conclusies en pistes voor optimalisatie*, Leuven: Steunpunt Bestuurlijke Organisatie Vlaanderen.

Van Humbeeck, P. (2009) *Regulatory impact analysis in Flanders and Belgium: an update on the experience and challenges*, Antwerp: ICW.

Van't Klooster, S. (2007) *Toekomstverkenning: ambities en de praktijk. Een etnografische studie naar de productie van toekomstkennis bij het Ruimtelijk Planbureau (RPB)*, Delft: Uitgeverij Eburon.

Varone, F., Jacob, S. and Dewinter, L. (2005) 'Polity, politics and policy evaluation in Belgium', *Evaluation*, 11(3): 253-73.

Verlet, D. and De Smedt, P. (2010) 'De vooruitzichten voor Vlaanderen. Toekomstverkenningen als beleidsinstrument binnen de Vlaamse overheid', paper presented at the Politicologenetemaal, Leuven, 27-28 May.

Vésely, A. (2013) 'Conducting large-N surveys on policy work in bureaucracies: some methodological challenges and implications from the Czech Republic', *Central European Journal of Public Policy*, 7(2): 88-113.

Weimer, D. and Vining, A. (1991) *Public policy analysis: concepts and practice*, Englewood Cliffs, NJ: Pearson Prentice Hall.

Wildavsky, A. (1979) *Speaking truth to power: the art and craft of policy analysis*, Boston, MA: Little Brown.

Worthen, B.R., Sanders, J.R. and Fitzpatrick, J.L. (2003) *Program evaluation: alternative approaches and practical guidelines*, Reading: Addison-Wesley.

THREE

Political control and bureaucratic expertise: policy analysis by ministerial cabinet members

Marleen Brans, Christian de Visscher, Athanassios Gouglas and Sylke Jaspers

Belgium has a long tradition of engaging ministerial cabinets in policymaking. As a matter of fact, its ministerial cabinet system is one of the oldest in the world, and one of the closest to the ideal, the other exemplar being the French system. Ministerial cabinets (MCs) are not to be confused with cabinets of ministers. The latter refer to the core executive, in particular members of government, while the former are an extension of the core executive, located at the structural interface between politics and administration. Walgrave and colleagues (2004, p 21) define ministerial cabinets as 'a staff of personal advisers who are hired when a minister takes office and are not part of the administrative hierarchy'. These personal staff members act as the 'minister's private council' (Walgrave et al, 2004, p 7). They 'assist the minister in identifying and formulating problems, in outlining policy, and in everyday decision-making' (Walgrave et al, 2004, p 21).

Such ministerial offices and staff exist in other countries too. However, ministerial cabinets differ significantly from ministerial offices in non-ministerial cabinet systems. First, they are relatively large, comprising a mixture of civil servants and external appointees who work as advisers. The latter, at least, are expected to be sympathetic to the minister's views. Second, the minister has discretionary authority to organise and recruit the cabinet staff, including civil servants whose political allegiances are often evident. Third, members of cabinet not only advise the minister, but also provide political direction and management to the entire ministry. They issue instructions to the ministry in the minister's name, while its leading members, who usually have the right to sign documents on the minister's behalf, often represent the minister at external events and are regarded as speaking in the minister's name both within and outside the ministry (James, 2007). Moreover, members of cabinet acting as 'an extension of their minister' (instead of trustee) are in a superior position in relation to senior civil servants. They constantly put pressure on administrators in order to ensure political responsiveness, at times even meddling with civil service appointments. Finally, civil servants in ministerial cabinets have the ability to pursue careers as advisers without this hindering their progression when they return to their department.

In the golden days of Belgian partitocracy, between 1970 and 1999, the MCs functioned in full glory and were considered crucial policymakers, leading many scholars to argue that Belgian civil servants at the top of the federal administration were underperforming because their role was being usurped by advisers (Walgrave et al, 2004, p 21). The common understanding has been that MCs played a crucial role in the grip of political parties on governmental policy and that senior civil servants were marginalised in the policymaking process by ministerial advisers, who were endowed with crucial policymaking roles and colonised all stages of the policy process.

At the turn of the millennium, though, managerialist pressures at the top of the administration, as well as recurrent criticisms of the dysfunctions of ministerial cabinets, led to a tendency towards 'decabinetisation'. This is the exact opposite trend of 'cabinetisation', observed in many non-ministerial cabinet systems, both of the Westminster and continental traditions, over the past 30 years (Gouglas et al, 2015). Decabinetisation would reduce and revise ministerial cabinets in favour of strengthening the administration's role in policymaking. Indeed, public administration reforms in Belgium strengthened the policy-analytical capacity of the civil service, while relations between the administration and ministerial cabinets improved, mainly in the direction of greater complementarity of roles. However, both MC policy-related functions, as well as their size, are still issues of public debate today, with many authors claiming that ministerial cabinets have essentially been reinvented (Brans et al, 2002; Brans and Steen, 2007; Göransson and Eraly, 2015).

In this chapter, we investigate the Belgian ministerial cabinet system at the federal level and the main actors within it – ministerial advisers. Our focus is on the evolution, functions and dysfunctions of ministerial cabinets, the policymaking roles of political advisers, and their relationship with the senior civil service. Our approach is descriptive, relying on secondary source material. In the first section, we present the institutional habitat of political advisers, namely the ministerial cabinet. We describe the historical evolution of ministerial cabinets, as well as their current composition, organisation, size, functions and perceived dysfunctions. In the second section, we take a look at the agents within ministerial cabinets. For this we use past research to classify advisers' policymaking roles, both in terms of substance (what they do) and in terms of dimension (how horizontal or vertical their work is). In the third section, we address politico-administrative relations between advisers and senior civil servants.

The Belgian ministerial cabinet

This section examines the Belgian ministerial cabinet system at the federal level. It focuses on the historical evolution of the system, its contemporary structural configuration, and the functions and dysfunctions of ministerial cabinets.

History and development of ministerial cabinets in Belgium

Belgium, like France, has one of the two oldest and most representative ministerial cabinet systems. Molitor (1973) and Van Hassel (1988) point to 1840 as the year when MCs progressively started to gain momentum. According to Luyckx and Platel (1985, p 63), the development and first modest expansion of MCs occurred to satisfy the need of ministers to emancipate themselves from monarchical influence, especially in the areas of policy and personnel allocation. It almost took a century for MCs to become regulated by royal decree in November 1912 (Göransson, 2008, p 1).

However, it was only in the aftermath of the Second World War that the institution started to expand significantly in both numbers and scope (Brans and Steen, 2007, p 66). Before the Great War, a typical cabinet would comprise on average four advisers, of which 90% would be civil servants. The end of the First World War witnessed a great increase in the size of ministerial cabinets, among others reasons, in order to accommodate the need for reconstructing the country. In 1937, the Camu administrative reform attempted (and failed) for the first time to limit politicisation by offering 'protection against the arbitrary intervention of political power in the recruitment and promotion of civil servants' (de Visscher et al, 2011, p 169). The Camu Statute formed the basis of the so called 'old public service bargain' between politicians and administrators, seen as a mix between a 'trustee' (consociational) and an 'agency' (serial loyalist) bargain (de Visscher and Salomonsen, 2013). Ever since, as the numbers of ministerial advisers continued to soar, politicians expanded the avenues of political control over the civil service. Consequently, the need for a delimitation of political roles, including adviser numbers, has been a recurrent theme of the public debate. Wilwerth (2001, pp 17-18) documents an attempt by the Ministry of Finance to suppress MCs in 1962, which did not find unanimity within the Belgian government.

The period 1970-99 was coined as the heyday of Belgian partitocracy, with Deschouwer (1996, p 296) even claiming that Belgium is a consociational partitocracy. Partitocracy and MCs are associated, with MCs playing a crucial role in the partitocratic grip of political parties on governmental policy and on the selection of public sector personnel. In the glory days of partitocracy, this was reflected both in advisers' career patterns, but also cabinet size. Walgrave et al (2004, pp 10-11) specify that the total number of advisers in government increased from about 300 to 900 in the 1980s due to the process of federalisation and devolution that overloaded the political agenda in that period. By the year 2000, there were 25 MCs for 17 cabinet ministers. A minister combining different portfolios could have a 'small army' of up to 150 personal aids. In a standard MC, a minister was estimated to have at his/her disposal 40 technical and administrative collaborators and a core of 10 policy collaborators.

It was only in the late 1990s that pressure for politico-administrative reform 'became alarmingly apparent' due to 'the lack of legitimacy of the politico-administrative system' caused by a series of political scandals and cases of maladministration (Brans and Steen, 2007, p 68). The result of this pressure was an ambitious reform at the end of the millennium, which the press labelled Copernicus, after the astronomer who caused a revolution by no longer conceiving the earth as the centre of the universe (Brans and Steen, 2007, p 74). The

Copernicus reform aimed at the 'responsibilisation' of the senior civil service, through the strengthening of its policy role, the rebalancing of the relationship between politics and administration, and, finally, its 'depoliticisation'. Within ministries, direction committees were created, staffed with senior civil servants. Strategy boards in turn were installed to create an interface between the direction committees and the reformed ministerial cabinets. This meant that politics and administration were institutionally obliged to work together as well as share information. Moreover, the increase of senior civil servants' financial autonomy and a new system of less politicised appointments at the top all pointed in the direction of a new-found balance between politics and administration. Moreover, while it is debated whether complete abolition was intended in the first place, the Copernicus reform did actually make an attempt at decabinetisation. The intention was to substitute MCs, introducing in their place smaller strategic cells, general policy cells and a small administrative secretariat of the minister. By 2003, however, subsequent government reforms, among others the abolition of the strategy boards and the reinstatement of political discretion over appointments, led to the reinvention of ministerial cabinets, albeit not in name (Brans and Steen, 2007, p 77).

Contemporary ministerial cabinet composition, organisation and size

Ministerial cabinets at the federal government level in Belgium have traditionally been regulated by a series of royal decrees.[1] The royal decrees of 2000 and 2001 contain regulations that attempt to suppress in both name and functions the old Belgian ministerial cabinet system, while at the same time strengthen the policy role of the administration. They are in this respect in line with the spirit of the Copernicus reform. Ministerial cabinets are broken up into strategic cells, general policy cells and a secretariat of the minister. The position of the senior civil service, in turn, is strengthened by the creation of a direction committee staffed by civil servants, and by the installation of a strategy board to coordinate all organs. More recent royal decree modifications, however, suppressed the role of the strategy board, without at the same time institutionally assuring the involvement of the senior civil service in the decision-making process.

According to the provisions in force on March 2014, every member of the government forms a strategic cell, a political cell and a secretariat in order to assist with government work. The strategic cell is headed by a director, appointed by the minister. It comprises smaller nuclei, reflecting various policy portfolios, which in turn have appointed heads. According to the provisions in force, the strategic cell is also staffed by members of cabinet, following specific policy portfolios or facilitating the execution of policy. The prime minister and vice-prime ministers also have at their disposal a general policy cell alongside the strategic cell.[2] In the case of the prime minister's office, this is called the cell of general policy coordination. It is responsible for assisting with preparing and evaluating general government policy. General policy cells are envisaged as organs for general government political and policy coordination and are headed by a director, without further provisions relating to their internal organisation. Finally, the secretariat, again headed by a director, is there to assist ministers on administrative issues. These organs constitute the Belgian federal government ministerial cabinet, although the term ministerial cabinet *per se* is nowhere to be found in statutory provisions.

There are no strict legally binding limitations regarding the size of ministerial cabinets, the hiring of personnel or staff job descriptions. Cabinet size is limited to budget availability and is fixed at the beginning of the legislative period. MCs contain a mixture of seconded civil servants and externally appointed staff. The appointment/secondment of ministerial cabinet staff and the assignment of roles is a competency of the minister. In relation to job descriptions, as the Organisation for Economic Co-operation and Development (OECD, 2011, p 29) pointed out, 'Belgium once used them, before dispensing with them in its 2005 *vademecum* for each type of ministerial staff'. Ministerial staff are appointed or seconded at the sole discretion of the minister for the duration of the ministerial mandate. Nevertheless, ministerial staff must respect some basic requirements. For the strategic cells, this translates into being holder of a level A or B on the civil service scale.[3] In case they are externally appointed, they need to have a degree or specific certificate, which under normal circumstances would make them eligible to participate in a selection process at this level. For the secretariat, the level is set at D. The general policy cells are exempt from this rule. The terms of employment depend on each person's legal status before being appointed. The general employment framework governing the statutory personnel applies to seconded civil servants, while labour law applies to externally appointed staff. Finally, the royal decrees also regulate payment issues. Seconded civil servants are paid by their department of origin. All ministerial cabinet staff benefit from a wage relevant to their grade scale plus a series of extra allowances.

In March 2014, 18 cabinets served the government: the cabinet of the prime minister, six vice-prime ministerial cabinets, six ministerial cabinets and five state secretary cabinets. A total of 564 staff worked in the Belgian federal MCs, of which 440 performed advisory tasks (see Table 3.1). The average number of employees in each MC was around 30, 25 of whom performed various advisory duties. If considering only official job titles, the number of 'advisers' evidently drops. However, an analysis of work-related data published online reveals that many staff perform advisory duties by being responsible for policy portfolios without carrying the official title of 'adviser'. Overall, the March 2014 ministerial cabinet staff snapshot reveals that the Copernicus reform appears not to have significantly reduced cabinet size. This in turn confirms past findings in a study conducted by Pelgrims and Dereu (2006) and published in an official report commissioned by the Belgian Senate (2008, p 5). According to that report, the average number of advisers in MCs in the period 1999-2003 increased from 16.2 to 28 per minister, equivalent to an increase of 73%. Another source confirms this steady increase of ministerial advisers in individual ministries in Belgium, from 275 in 2000 to 326 in 2010 (OECD, 2011, p 51).

Cabinet functions and dysfunctions

The very *raison d'être* of MCs in Belgium is associated with the functions they perform (Göransson and Eraly, 2015). As Walgrave et al (2004) have argued, these functions can be divided into partitocratic and non-partitocratic ones. In a rather similar vein, Brans and Steen (2007, p 66) distinguish between political and policy functions.

On the more partitocratic and political front, MCs allow for a firm hold of partisan politics on the administration (Walgrave et al, 2004, p 8; Göransson and Eraly, 2015). They are tools for party control over ministers and for supporting party organisations, with political parties imposing senior personnel and at times even forcing less well qualified personnel on the minister (De Winter, 1981; Dewachter, 1981; Göransson and Eraly, 2015; Walgrave et al, 2004). Moreover, MCs appear to form career pools and recruitment mechanisms for professional politicians (Brans and Steen, 2007, p 66). Finally, MCs sharpen the grasp of political parties on the civil service and the wider public sector as a whole, especially through facilitating the appointment and promotion of befriended civil servants (Walgrave et al, 2004, p 8; Göransson and Eraly, 2015). MCs do this by negotiating the allocation of personnel, taking human resource management out of the hands of the civil service, and rewarding MC members with top civil service positions.

In relation to the latter, a series of studies conducted since the 1970s revealed that the appointment of a civil servant in an MC positively affects his/her future career (Depré, 1973; Hondeghem, 1990; Walgrave et al, 2004). Comparing the MC member database with the top 10 civil servants in 2000, Walgrave et al (2004, p 8) found that all of these actors served in an MC at least for a little while. This is comparable to France where 'several spells as a ministerial adviser or a cabinet member is a more or less essential stage in the upward progress of a politician or senior civil servant' (James, 2007, p 11). Past findings are corroborated by more recent work by Göransson and Eraly (2015) who argue that cabinets not only look to control recruitments, promotions and nominations, but also actively place their members in the administration in order to thank them for past services and to facilitate their further careers.

Ministerial cabinets' functions go beyond partitocracy. Göransson and Eraly (2015) have recently pointed to a series of such functions: secretarial and administrative support, provision of political and policy advice, political negotiation, coordination with the administration, public relations and relations with the minister's party, relations with parliament, coordination with stakeholders and constituency relations. Overall, MC functions can be categorised into four tasks and functions: communication, expertise, flexibility and loyalty (Walgrave et al, 2004, p 9). Communication refers primarily to coordination of the

Table 3.1: Belgian federal ministerial cabinets: numbers and staff (2011-14)

Belgian federal MCs (legislature 2011-14), March 2014	Staff	Staff performing advisory tasks	Number of advisers: strict definition (based on title)		
			Total	Male	Female
Prime Minister	31	23	14	11	3
Vice-Prime Minister and Minister of Defence	36	33 GPC: 13 SC: 20	22 GPC: 11 SC: 11	18 GPC: 10 SC: 8	4 GPC: 1 SC: 3
Vice-Prime Minister and Minister of Foreign Affairs, External Trade and European Affairs	48	40 GPC: 13 SC: 27	26 GPC: 9 SC: 17	18 GPC: 7 SC: 11	8 GPC: 2 SC: 6
Vice-Prime Minister and Minister of Economy, Consumers and the North Sea	33	27 GPC: n.d. SC: n.d.	19 GPC: n.d. SC: n.d.	15 GPC: n.d. SC: n.d.	4 GPC: n.d. SC: n.d.
Vice-Prime Minister and Minister of Pensions	32	25 GPC: 18 SC: 7	21 GPC: 15 SC: 6	13 GPC: 10 SC: 3	8 GPC: 5 SC: 3
Vice-Prime Minister and Minister of Interior and the Equality of Chances	51	40 GPC: 16 SC: 24	26 GPC: 8 SC: 18	11 GPC: 5 SC: 6	15 GPC: 3 SC: 12
Vice-Prime Minister and Minister of Social Affairs, Public Health, with responsibility for Beliris and the federal cultural institutions	44	40 GPC: 11 SC: 24	32 GPC: 10 SC: 22	23 GPC: 9 SC: 14	9 GPC: 1 SC: 8
Minister of Justice	30	25	20	16	4
Minister for the Middle Class, the SMEs and the Self-employed and Minister of Agriculture	26	18	11	9	3
Minister of the Budget and Administrative Simplification	24	22	14	10	4
Minister of Employment	22	16	10	8	2
Minister of Public Enterprises and Cooperation of Development, with responsibility for the big cities	15	7	1	0	1
Minister of Finance, with responsibility for the public service	29	24	16	6	10
Secretary of State for the Environment, Energy and Mobility and Secretary of State of Institutional Reforms	27	19	12	10	2
Secretary of State of Social Affairs, Families and Persons with a Handicap, with responsibility for professional risks	27	16	10	5	5

Belgian federal MCs (legislature 2011-14), March 2014	Staff	Staff performing advisory tasks	Number of advisers: strict definition (based on title)		
			Total	Male	Female
Secretary of State of Institutional Reforms and Secretary of State for the Organisation of Building, with responsibility for the public service	22	14	9	6	3
Secretary of State of Asylum and Migration, Social Integration and the Fight against Poverty	30	23	16	8	8
Secretary of State of Public Service and the Modernisation of Public Services, with responsibility for the public service	19	11	8	4	4
Secretary of State of the Battle against Social and Fiscal Fraud	19	13	7	6	1
Total	**534**	**413**	**280**	186	94
Total Flemish Christian Democrats	106	82	55	34	21
Total Francophone Socialists	86	63	43	28	15
Total Francophone Liberals	98	80	51	37	14
Total Flemish Socialists	74	56	36	29	7
Total Flemish Liberals	92	72	57	37	20
Total Francophone Christian Democrats	78	59	38	21	17

Notes: GPC: general policy cell; SC: strategic cell; n.d.: Not defined.

coalition government. Brans and Steen (2007, p 66) refer to MCs as centres of communication and coordination that facilitate the continuity of coalition government. Beyond this, MCs are also projected as 'brain trusts' that pool expertise (De Winter, 1981, p 66). However, the production of policy advice occurs in ways that combine technical expertise with political feasibility (Brans and Steen, 2007, p 67). In addition to communication and expertise, MCs allow for organisational flexibility. This refers to the customised nature of the organisation of a cabinet, so as to fit the needs of the political executive. MCs comprise ad hoc task forces that work more smoothly than rigid bureaucracies (Walgrave et al, 2004, p 9). Ultimately, MCs have a fourth non-partitocratic function, which is the safeguarding of loyalty to the person of the minister.

Despite these functions, ministerial cabinets in Belgium, as everywhere, have been associated with serious dysfunctions: incompetence stemming from a lack of qualifications; bad wages and difficult working times; deficient organisation of work; substitution of the administration; elitism; partisan affiliations and a culture of mistrust even among ministerial cabinets; enclosure in an ivory tower; and information bias (Eraly, 2001, p 77).

As previously discussed, the Copernicus reform failed and the ministerial cabinets were reinvented. So it can be assumed that these dysfunctions are still present today. A more recent evaluation of MCs' dysfunctions concludes that the current policy cells still show many similarities with the former ministerial cabinets. According to De Jaegere (2010), the policy cells still perform the same functions as did the ministerial cabinets, and the latter's old dysfunctions still keep the government from operating in an optimal way. They still monopolise policymaking. The politicisation of both MC members and top civil servants still engenders distrust between the administration and MC members. Furthermore, policies are discontinued, with each new legislature installing new policy cells (De Jaegere, 2010, pp 606–7).

Göransson and Eraly (2015) confirm these findings in qualitative research comparing the (dys)functions of ministerial cabinets before and after the Copernicus reform. Five major dysfunctions are highlighted: the exclusion of civil servants from policymaking in what is described as deresponsibilisation; the meddling of the ministerial cabinet in administrative affairs; the short-circuiting of the senior civil service by members of cabinet, who give direct instructions to lower-ranking civil servants; the destabilisation of departments through secondments; and the politicisation of the administration. According to the same authors, these dysfunctions persist because of the characteristics of the Belgian political system: the coalition regime, the federal regime and partitocracy.

Inside the cabinet: political advisers and policymaking

Scholarly focus on the agents working inside the Belgian ministerial cabinets has been rather limited. In this section, we take a look at ministerial cabinet advisers on the basis of what we know from a limited number of recent studies on the topic. We start with a short description of advisers' socio-demographic profile and proceed with a discussion of the substantive and dimensional aspects of their work.

Who are advisers and what is their background?

The Belgian adviser is predominantly male. In March 2014, 186 of the advisers employed in federal government ministerial cabinets were male (66%) and 94 female (34%) (Table 3.1). This gender (im)balance constitutes a slight improvement compared with the 1995–99 legislature (70% male to 30% female) (Walgrave et al, 2004, p 15). However, it is a change in degree not in kind. As far as age is concerned, the majority of advisers fall within the 35–50 age cohort (Suetens and Walgrave, 1999, pp 506–7; Gouglas et al, 2015; Jaspers, 2015).

As for educational background, advisers are highly educated. A recent study of 35 federal government advisers employed in 2014 revealed that 94% hold a university degree, of which 3% hold a doctorate. This confirms past research findings according to which 81% of Belgian members of cabinets were found to hold a university degree, 33% more than one degree, and 7% a PhD (Walgrave et al, 2004, p 12).

As far as policy expertise is concerned, the literature reveals that Belgian advisers are not only highly educated, but also share important previous public sector experience. Nevertheless, they appear to be generalists, since they are usually assigned portfolios that do not necessarily match their individual expertise (Gouglas et al, 2015; Jaspers, 2015). Walgrave et al (2004, p 13) highlight that advisers shift competencies by taking up positions in MC policy fields outside their field of expertise. Altering their positions frequently, Belgian advisers project a high degree of heterogeneity in the ministerial portfolios they serve. For the period 1970-99, the average MC career was 37.9 months for every 1.73 policy domain. This means that every two years an adviser changes over to another policy domain (Walgrave et al, 2004, p 13). Today the average career of the Belgian adviser is estimated at around 48 months (OECD, 2011, p 38).

What do advisers do? Adviser types

Connaughton (2010a, 2010b, 2015) suggests that ministerial advisers can be categorised into four types:

- Type I is the expert, a 'highly qualified political outsider' who works as a specialist on a specific departmental policy portfolio (Connaughton, 2015, p 38). The currency of the expert is knowledge and the added value of her/his work the expertise she/he brings into a specific field.
- Type II is the exact opposite. She/he is partisan, 'predominantly appointed thanks to political affiliation'. She/he acts as a highly political agent, attentive to the minister's mission and primarily aims to achieve electoral gains and political dominance.
- Type III is the coordinator. Coordinators are generalists; they understand and respond to the strategic and political context, yet their main job is to provide oversight to the government programme, and to fix, mend, liaise and monitor policy. Their added value is political and policy steering, their impact being political and process management.
- Type IV is the minder. Unlike the partisan who is a 'party apparatchik', the minder is the minister's bodyguard, always looking 'for issues potentially harmful' to the political executive (Connaughton, 2010a, p 63; 2010b, pp 351-2). The relationship between the minder and the minister is characterised by trust, affinity and mutuality.

Past research reveals that ministerial advisers in Belgium fulfil foremost 'partisan and promotional functions', being 'party soldiers' and 'faithful executors of their minister's partisan will' (Walgrave et al, 2004, pp 20-1). A recent classification of Belgian advisers along the four types suggested by Connaughton (2010a, 2010b) challenges the partisan thesis (Gouglas et al, 2015; Jaspers, 2015). The majority of Belgian advisers, about 40%, appear to fit the pure coordinator type. The rest are classified as hybrids, revolving around the coordinator and minder types (Table 3.2).

However, the dominant type of adviser differs according to whether advisers work in general policy or in strategic cells (Gouglas et al, 2015; Jaspers, 2015). Advisers in strategic cells are primarily fixers who manage and coordinate policy. On the one hand, they get their hands 'dirty' with policy at the technical level.

Table 3.2: Individual types of Belgian adviser

Adviser type (N=34)	Frequency	Percentage
Expert	2	5.9
Partisan	I	2.9
Coordinator	13	38.2
Minder	3	8.8
Coordinator and minder	4	11.8
Expert and minder	2	5.9
Minder and partisan	I	2.9
Coordinator and expert	3	8.8
Coordinator and partisan	I	2.9
Minder, coordinator and partisan	I	2.9
Expert, coordinator and partisan	I	2.9
Minder, partisan and expert	I	2.9
Total	34	100.0

On the other hand, they indulge in political and policy steering. Such steering involves agenda and time management, mobilisation and direction of the civil service, final text processing and coordination with stakeholders. In relation to politics, the average strategic cell adviser is seen as a political bodyguard of the minister, protecting him from potential harm.

On the contrary, advisers in general policy cells are tasked with maintaining a political line in inter-cabinet negotiations on different policy areas (Jaspers, 2015). Despite having a coordinating and managerial role too, this role is of less importance for general policy cell advisers than for the strategic cell advisers. Advisers in general policy cells are 'political animals' whose main impact in the cabinet and outside is political dominance.

Dimension of advisers' work

Maley (2015, p 47) argues that it 'is useful to understand the policy work of partisan staff as occurring in three different arenas: working with the department;

working with other ministers (within the political executive) and working with stakeholders'. A crucial question here is whether the work of advisers across the three arenas is an institutional responsibility or an ad hoc opportunity advisers grasp at will. The Belgian consociational democracy in conjunction with its moderately strong corporatist system of interest intermediation demands that Belgian ministerial advisers are active in all three arenas. However, individual adviser idiosyncrasies and skills, ministerial preferences and the policy portfolio, as well as whether an adviser works in a general or strategic policy cell, can result in significant departures from this general picture.

According to recent research (Gouglas et al, 2015; Jaspers, 2015), the majority of Belgian ministerial advisers are highly active across all three arenas (Table 3.3). Looking at advisers in strategic cells and advisers in general policy cells, the two studies find that strategic cell advisers consider working with the department, across the executive (with other advisers) and with stakeholders as a core job responsibility. On the contrary, general policy cell advisers are less involved in departmental work. Their core work responsibility lies in political coordination across the coalition government, the legislature and the relevant stakeholders.

Working with the department and coordinating across the executive branch is a core work responsibility for strategic cell advisers. It is within the first arena that coordinators and minders 'supervise', 'orientate' and 'mobilise' the department (Maley, 2015, p 48). The second arena is where 'decision making is facilitated', 'policy conflicts are resolved' and 'policy coordinated' (Maley, 2015, pp 51-2). Belgian coalition government politics requires intensive coordination and heavy political and policy work not only within the department, but also across the coalition government parties. This is a stage dominated by advisers of the partisan type. As Göransson and Eraly (2015) point out, important policy portfolios are presented, discussed and pre-negotiated within teams of advisers from various ministries. Depending on the case, they then enter the agenda of chiefs of cabinets and later that of the chiefs of vice-prime ministers. During this whole process, each member of cabinet is in a position to control and contest policy proposals on both political and policy grounds, always keeping in mind the coalition agreement. This in turn means that advisers spent an essential part of the time examining the policy portfolios of other ministers.

Finally, in the third arena, ideas and interests are linked, and bargaining and negotiation with stakeholders take place (Maley, 2015). The moderately strong corporatist nature of interest intermediation in Belgium means that there is a coordinated, cooperative institutionalised system of policymaking in place. Advisers at the federal level liaise with stakeholders as part of their core work. It is for them a responsibility rather than an opportunity they grab at will.

Relations with the administration

A comparative international study conducted by the OECD (2011) on ministerial advisers in 27 countries revealed that tension, blurred politico-administrative boundaries, and a risk of politicisation of the civil service are characteristics of most systems when it comes to adviser–civil servant relations. However, these dangers are much more pronounced in ministerial cabinet systems where ministerial cabinet advisers command and steer civil servants, increase pressure for politicisation and facilitate the development of shadow administrations, which encroach on the administration and shield it from information (James, 2007). This section looks at the politico-administrative relations in Belgium with a twofold approach. First, using material from past studies, Belgian politico-administrative relations are classified on the basis of some of the most state-of-the-art typologies found in the literature. Second, the Belgian 'public service bargain' (de Visscher and Salomonsen, 2013) is presented as a 'ministerial *ménage à trois*'.

Table 3.3: Number of highly active adviser types per arena (N=33)

Arena	Frequency	Frequency of adviser type
(1) Working with the department	1	Expert (1)
(2) Working with other ministers	4	Minder (1) Expert, coordinator and minder (1) Expert (1) Minder, partisan and expert (1)
(1 + 2 + 3) All 3 arenas	19	Coordinator (11) Partisan (1) Minder (1) Coordinator and partisan (1) Coordinator and expert (2) Coordinator and minder (1) Minder, coordinator and partisan (1) Expert, coordinator and partisan (1)
(1 + 2) Working with the department and with other ministers	6	Coordinator and minder (2) Expert and minder (1) Minder and partisan (1) Coordinator (1) Coordinator and expert (1)
(1 + 3) Working with the department and with stakeholders	1	Coordinator (1)
Intra-executive coordination and horizontal coordination	2	Minder (1) Expert and minder (1)
Total	33	33

Source: Gouglas et al, (2015); Jaspers, (2015)

Politico-administrative relations: typologies and the dichotomy ideal

Belgian politico-administrative relations can be examined through the lens of a typical Weberian dichotomy (Brans et al, 2005, 2006). De Visscher and Salomonsen (2013, p 81) appear to have agreed with this approach. Belgium is a Weberian bureaucracy, originally influenced by the Napoleonic tradition. Political power is concentrated at the top and there is a strong division of labour between politicians and civil servants. In view of this, it may be argued that Belgian politico-administrative relations best fit Peters' (1987) formal/legal model, which is equivalent to this Weberian–Wilsonian dichotomy ideal.

Not disregarding the reality of the Napoleonic tradition, engrained into Belgian administrative law and culture, Schreurs and colleagues (2010, pp 21-2) more recently challenged the politics–administration dichotomy in Belgium. Given that MCs have developed a relatively large share even of executive tasks and that the policymaking process is characterised by politicisation, Belgian politico-administrative relations arguably best fit Svara's (1999) political dominance type, where 'administrative independency is low, because of the close watch of the political executive on the administration and the strict instructions they offer, while obviously political control is high' (Schreurs et al, 2010, p 18).

An interesting question arises here as to the extent of political dominance of politicians and advisers. Is it absolute or is it significantly smoothened? As discussed earlier, the Copernicus reform at the end of the millennium was designed to rebalance politico-administrative relations, by 'responsibilising' and depoliticising the civil service, while also suppressing the size and policy scope of ministerial cabinets (Brans and Steen, 2007). Despite the reinvention of MCs, including the reinvention of mechanisms of political control over the administration, it is argued that the Copernicus reform did at least lead to a new politico-administrative balance, through a 'confined involvement of the senior civil servants in the [policy] process' (Schreurs et al, 2010, p 22).

Public service bargains: a ménage à trois à la Belge

An alternative way to look into the relations between politics and administration in Belgium is to investigate the public service bargain. Public service bargains denote an agreement – be it explicit or implicit – between public servants and elected politicians or society at large. Hood (2000, p 8) defines a public service bargain as 'any explicit or implicit understanding between (senior) public servants and other actors in a political system over their duties and entitlements relating to responsibility, autonomy and political identity, and expressed in conventions or formal law or a mixture of both'. Public service bargains conceptualise a reciprocal exchange relationship between civil servants and other actors in their social or political environment.

Hood and Lodge developed eight types of bargain based on the distinction between trustee and agency bargains. In trustee bargains, civil servants act as trustees loyal to a constitutional order and 'above politics'. In this relationship, civil servants are 'expected to act as independent judges of the public good (that is interests of their beneficiaries) to some significant extent, and not merely to take their orders from some political masters' (Hood and Lodge, 2006, p 26). In agency bargains, the civil service is loyal to either successive ministers (serial loyalty), the Schafferian type, or to a specific minister (personal loyalty), the hybrid type (Hood and Lodge, 2006, p 21).

The Belgian model borrows several elements from the consociational, trustee type of bargain. First, the parity rule between high-ranking French- and Dutch-speaking civil servants can be seen as a means of ensuring a balance of power in order to preserve the Belgian state. Second, until recently, senior officials have enjoyed permanent tenure, and were thus not wholly dependent on the government of the day. Third, even if there are few limitations to the political activities of civil servants (Hondeghem, 2011), they (and the social groups they represent) are expected to be loyal to the state in exchange for their 'fair share' in the bureaucracy (de Visscher et al, 2011).

The Belgian public service bargain also contains elements of the agency type. Top civil servants are considered as agents of their political masters. They take their orders from their successive ministers and their career is set by the government by means of royal decree (de Visscher et al, 2011, p 169). This agency type of bargain includes a third player, namely the MC advisers. In other words, the Belgian model may be characterised as a *ménage à trois* in which the minister is served by two groups of servants, the top civil servants, who may be portrayed as 'serial loyalists', and MC advisers, whose loyalty is linked to a specific minister or to the party she/he belongs to. In contrast to the top civil servants, these 'personal loyalists' (de Visscher and Salomonsen, 2013, p 75) are to be responsive to the minister's political needs, providing not only technical advice but also advice related to party politics, the minister's constituency and links to media. But how loyal is every actor in this trilateral relationship?

From a public service bargain perspective, 'bargaining relationships involve parties that either deliver or cheat' (de Visscher and Salomonsen, 2013, p 75). According to Hood (2000), when both parties deliver, there is a balanced bargain characterised by mutual trust, cooperation and mutual respect. In the opposite situation, however, where at least one party cheats, the bargain is characterised by distrust and even degenerates into conflict. Ministers may cheat by undermining the representativeness of the civil service, while the senior civil servant may cheat by being disloyal to the minister, allowing for the capturing of politics by organisational and administrative interests, policy sabotage or leaking of information (de Visscher and Salomonsen, 2013, p 75). Leaking of information may also be an indication of advisers' cheating on their minister, as is changing minister frequently. The minister may also cheat advisers by not offering protection or blaming them for political executive failures (de Visscher and Salomonsen, 2013, p 75). However, advisers can also cheat civil servants. The personal loyalists can influence the advice provided to the minister by the serial loyalists, resulting in what Eichbaum and Shaw (2008, p 343) termed 'administrative politicisation' (de Visscher and Salomonsen, 2013, p 75). In this situation, the advice provided by the civil service becomes subordinate to that provided by the adviser. This happens both when advisers procedurally block the flow of advice to the minister and substantively when advisers question the competencies of the civil service (de Visscher and Salomonsen, 2013, p 75).

In the case of Belgium, cheating behaviour from the permanent civil service is considered rare, but not uncommon on the side of ministers and advisers. Ministers appear to be cheating by promoting political appointments of senior civil servants. Despite the Copernicus reform, the system of mandates and the comparative selection procedure under the auspices of the public recruitment agency, SELOR, political–party criteria still carry significant weight when picking candidates at the final stage (de Visscher and Salomonsen, 2013, p 82). Additionally, ministers may also be tempted to shift blame to senior civil servants. Advisers in turn may seize opportunities to cheat as ministerial cabinets' size and scope expand to include technical expertise, as well as advice on party-political matters. Moreover, as indicated earlier, they intervene in all stages of the policy cycle, thus resulting in a 'functional colonisation' of the prerogatives of the civil service (Pelgrims, 2008; de Visscher et al, 2004). Finally, in the case of Belgium, as is usually the case in other ministerial cabinet systems, advisers also cheat by steering civil servants.

Whether changing ministers frequently may also be considered a form of cheating on the part of an adviser depends on where ministerial cabinet advisers' loyalty lies. It has been argued that MCs comprise three types of adviser in terms of loyalty: *chiens, chats et singes* (dogs, cats and monkeys) (Thuillier, 1999; quoted in Wilwerth, 2001, p 19). The *chiens* refer to advisers who, like dogs, are always loyal to their boss, the minister, moving wherever she/he moves. The *chats*, like cats, are loyal to the house, in this case the ministry and its cabinet. Finally, the *singes* are not loyal to either the minister or the house. They move around from cabinet to cabinet and from ministry to ministry, like monkeys jumping from one branch to the next, according to need, opportunity and chance. Based on Walgrave and colleagues' data (2004, pp 12, 14-18), the Belgian adviser appears to fit the *singes* type. Despite evidence of personal loyalty, the data points to rather high levels of ministerial mobility among advisers, showing that a typical adviser works for 1.56 different ministers during his short average career. This in turn shows the limits of advisers as ministers' personal loyalists. Loyalty first and foremost means loyalty to the party of the minister. Advisers may frequently move to another minister of the same party, but very rarely will advisers move to a minister from a different party.

Conclusion

Since their inception in the 1840s, Belgian ministerial cabinets have come a long way. Conceived initially as institutions to counterbalance monarchical influence, especially in the areas of policy and personnel allocation, ministerial cabinets progressively evolved as the central locus of politics and policy in the Belgian national and later federal policy advisory system. Ministerial cabinets perform important political and policy functions (Walgrave et al, 2004; Brans and Steen, 2007). On the political front, they are thought of as mainly performing 'partitocratic' functions. They are tools for political control, both party-political and executive, over the administration. Ministerial cabinets' functions go beyond partitocracy though. They facilitate policy coordination, thus enabling the continuation of fragile coalition government. They are also 'brain trusts' that pool expertise together in order to produce policy advice in ways that technical expertise is combined with political feasibility (De Winter, 1981; Brans and Steen, 2007). They also allow for organisational flexibility, so as to fit the needs of the political executive, while safeguarding staff loyalty to the minister.

Some examples of serious cabinet dysfunctions, associated first and foremost with the negative side of Belgian partitocracy (Eraly, 2001), have caused concern. Political control has traditionally been thought to suppress bureaucratic expertise and the policy role of the civil service. Moreover, MCs are broadly seen as mechanisms through which government policymaking is politicised. They also raise the levels of distrust between the political and administrative levels by, among other reasons, excluding civil servants from policy work. This in turn results in demotivation on the part of civil servants, duplication and inefficient organisation of work, and incompetence.

The close association of ministerial cabinets with partitocracy and its dysfunctions was a prominent feature of the Belgian policy advisory system in the period 1970-99 (Walgrave et al, 2004). This led scholars to describe the Belgian politico-administrative setting as best fitting Svara's (1999) political dominance type (Schreurs et al, 2010). This entails a politico-administrative arrangement where low levels of administrative independence coexist with high levels of political control. The Copernicus administrative reform attempted to do away with ministerial cabinets and address partitocratic dysfunctions. To a certain extent, it moved things forward. The political executive is nowadays assisted by a strategic cell, a general policy cell and a secretariat. There have been important steps towards rebalancing the relationship between politics and administration. Although formal institutionalisation of politico-administrative cooperation was soon dismantled through the suppression of strategy boards, nowadays the civil service is involved in the policy process to some extent. Civil service independence increased while political dominance was smoothened. Yet, despite significant changes, ministerial cabinets still have an enduring functionality in a polity characterised by fragile coalition government and strong pressure for political control. Since 2003, cabinets have arguably been 'reinvented' (Brans and Steen, 2007). This is evident in the *ménage à trois à la Belge* (De Visscher and Salomonsen, 2013). The trilateral relationship between ministers, advisers and civil servants is a combination of consociational and trustee bargains, with advisers expected to be personal loyalists and top administrators serial loyalists to the political executive. However, the deal is frequently broken on both sides when they are caught systematically cheating on one another.

Finally, recent research on the political and policymaking roles of ministerial cabinet advisers reveals a difference between the golden days of Belgian partitocracy (1970-99) and today (Gouglas et al, 2015; Jaspers, 2015). Traditionally seen as partisans, 'party soldiers' and 'faithful executors of their minister's partisan will' (Walgrave et al, 2004), nowadays ministerial advisers appear rather to be coordinators and minders (Gouglas et al, 2015; Jaspers, 2015). As coordinators, Belgian advisers are fixers who steer and mend policy. As minders, they primarily work as the minister's 'bodyguards', offering protection from potentially harmful issues. Advisers working in strategic cells are closer to this ideal role than their colleagues working in general policy cells. The latter still best fit the partisan adviser type. These actors are primarily concerned with following up and maintaining the party line, as well as monitoring and coordinating the implementation of the coalition government programme (Gouglas et al, 2015; Jaspers, 2015).

Where does this all leave us then? In terms of future research, there is a need for more empirical studies on advisers' policymaking roles. Given that the literature is rife with analyses of ministerial cabinets as the institutional habitat of advisers, a focus on agents is set to significantly improve our understanding of the relationship between bureaucratic expertise and political control, as well as of the trilateral relationship among advisers, politicians and civil servants in this *ménage à trois à la Belge*.

Notes

[1] On March 2014, at the end of the 2010-14 legislature, there were two royal decrees in force: the royal decree of 7 November 2000, modified on 27 April and 8 May 2008; and the royal decree of 19 July 2001, modified on 21 December and 30 December 2013.

[2] A vice-prime minister can take the position of acting prime minister when the prime minister is temporarily absent due to travel abroad, illness or absence. All the political parties comprising the coalition government have a vice-prime minister, and together they form the core cabinet, charged with preparing the meetings of the full cabinet.

[3] There are four levels of civil servant position in Belgium, depending on levels of education. Level A requires a university degree, B higher education other than a university degree, and C a secondary education degree. For level D, no qualifications are required.

References

Belgian Senate (2008) 'Proposition de résolution visant à supprimer progressivement les "cabinets ministériels"', 4-1106/1, 2008-09 session, 9 January 2009.

Brans, M. and Steen, T. (2007) 'From incremental to Copernican reform? Changes to the position and role of senior civil servants in the Belgian federal administration', in E. Page and C. Wright (eds) *From the active to the enabling state*, New York, NY: Palgrave Macmillan, 63-80.

Brans, M., Hoet, D. and Pelgrims, C. (2002) 'Abolishing ministerial cabinets for re-inventing them? Comparative observations on professional policy advice and political control', paper presented at the 63rd annual Conference of the American Society for Public Administration, Phoenix, 23-26 March.

Brans, M., Hoet, D. and Pelgrims, C. (2005) 'Politico-administrative relations under coalition governments: the case of Belgium', in B. Peters, T. Verheijen and L. Vass (eds) *Coalitions of the unwilling? Politicians and civil servants in coalition governments*, Bratislave: Nispacee, 207-35.

Brans, M., Hoet, D. and Pelgrims, C. (2006) 'Comparative observations on tensions between professional policy advice and political control in the Low Countries', *International Review of Administrative Sciences*, 72(1): 57-71.

Connaughton, B. (2010a) '"Minding" the minister: conceptualising the role of the special adviser in Ireland', *Administration*, 58(1): 55-75.

Connaughton, B. (2010b) '"Gloriefied gofers, policy experts or good generalists": a classification of the roles of the Irish ministerial adviser', *Irish Political Studies*, 25(3): 347-69.

Connaughton, B. (2015) 'Navigating the borderlines of politics and administration: reflections on the role of ministerial advisers', *International Journal of Public Administration*, 38(1): 37-45.

De Jaegere, J. (2010) 'Beleidscellen op federaal niveau: evaluatie van de Copernicushervorming', *Jura Falconis*, 46(4): 575-608.

Depré, R. (1973) 'De topambtenaren van de ministeries in Belgie: een bestuurssociologisch explorerend onderzoek', Leuven: KU Leuven.

Deschouwer, K. (1996) 'Of the Belgian parties and the party system', *Res Publica*, 38(2), 295-306.

De Visscher, C. and Salomonsen, H.H. (2013) 'Explaining differences in ministerial "ménages à trois": multiple bargains in Belgium and Denmark', *International Review of Administrative Sciences*, 79(1): 71-90.

De Visscher, C., Le Bussy, G. and Eymeri, J.M. (2004) *La relation entre l'autorité politique et la haute administration*, Ghent: Academia Press.

De Visscher, C., Hondeghem, A., Montuelle, C. and Van Dorpe, K. (2011) 'The changing public service bargain in the federal administration in Belgium', *Public Policy and Administration*, 26(2): 167-88.

Dewachter, W. (1981) 'Noodzaak en overzicht van de politieke partij in de polyarchie', *Res Publica*, 23(1): 125-51.

De Winter, L. (1981) 'De partijenstaat in de westeuropese polyarchie: een proeve tot meting', *Res Publica*, 23(1): 53-107.

Eichbaum, C. and Shaw, R. (2008) 'Revisiting politicization: political advisers and public servants in Westminster systems', *Governance*, 21(3): 337-63.

Eraly, A. (2001) 'Les cabinets ministériels et la décision politique', in H. De Croo (ed) *Les cabinets ministériels et autres. Statuts, rôles et pouvoirs*, Brussels: Bruylant, 65-88.

Göransson, M. (2008) *Les cabinets ministériels: analyse et comparaison de leur nécessité au sein du système politico-administratif*, Working Paper CEB No. 08/038, Brussels: Centre Emile Bernheim.

Göransson, M. and Eraly, A. (2015) 'Les cabinets ministériels en Belgique: entre coalition et particratrie', in J.M. Eymeri-Douzans, X. Bioy and S. Mouton (eds) *Le règne des entourages. Cabinets et conseillers de l'exécutif*, Paris: Presses Science Po, 703-19.

Gouglas, A., Brans, M. and Jaspers, S. (2015) 'Political advisers and policymaking in ministerial cabinet systems: the case of Belgium, Greece and the European Commission', paper presented at the International Conference on Public Policy, Milan, 1-4 July.

Hondeghem, A. (2011) 'The national civil service in Belgium', in F. Van der Meer (ed) *Civil service systems in Western Europe*, Cheltenham: Edward Elgar, 115-49.

Hood, C. (2000) 'Paradoxes of public–sector managerialism, old public management and public service bargains', *International Public Management Journal*, 3(1): 122.

Hood, C. and Lodge M. (2006) *The politics of public service bargains. Reward, competency, loyalty – and blame*, Oxford: Oxford University Press.

Hondeghem, A. (1990) *De loopbaan van de ambtenaar. Tussen droom en werkelijkheid*, Leuven: Symons.

James, S. (2007) *Political advisors and civil servants in European countries*, SIGMA Paper No. 38, Paris: OECD.

Jaspers, S. (2015) *Political advisors in Belgian federal ministerial cabinets and their policymaking role*, Leuven: KU Leuven.

Luyckx, T. and Platel, M. (1985) *Politieke geschiedenis van Belgie. Deel 1*, Antwerp: Kluwer.

Maley, M. (2015) 'The policy work of Australian political staff', *International Journal of Public Administration*, 38(1): 46-55.

Molitor, A. (1973) *Les superstructures des administrations centrales*, Paris: Cujas.

OECD (Organisation for Economic Co-operation and Development) (2011) *Ministerial advisors: Role, influence and management*, Paris: OECD.

Pelgrims, C. (2008) *Bestuurlijke hervormingen vanuit een politiek perspectief. Politieke actoren als stakeholders in Beter Bestuurlijk Beleid en de Copernicushervorming*, Bruges: Van den Broele.

Pelgrims, C. and Dereu, S. (2006) 'Ministeriële kabinetten in de Copernicushervorming. De terugkeer van iets dat nooit weg was', *Burger, Bestuur en Beleid*, 3(1): 25-33.

Peters, B.G. (1987) 'Politicians and bureaucrats in the politics of policy-making', in J.E. Lane (ed) *Bureaucracy and public choice*, Bristol: Sage Publications, 256-82.

Schreurs, F., Vandenabeele, W., Steen, T. and Brans, M. (2010) *Politico-administrative relations in top civil service*, Report commissioned for the Belgian presidency of the EU, Brussels: EGPA/IIAS.

Suetens, M. and Walgrave, S. (1999) 'Leven en werk van de kabinetsleden. Wie zijn de mannen achter de minister en wat doen ze?', *Res Publica*, 41(4): 499-528.

Svara, J.H. (1999) 'Complementarity of politics and administration as a legitimate alternative to the dichotomy model', *Administration and Society*, 30(6): 676-705.

Thuillier, G. (1999) *Pour une histoire de la bureaucratie en France*, Paris: IGPDE.

Van Hassel, H. (1988) 'Le syndrome du cabinet dans une perspective historique', *Bulletin trimestriel du Crédit communal de Belgique*, 166: 11-35.

Walgrave, S., Caals, T., Suetens, M. and De Swert, K. (2004) 'Ministerial cabinets and partitocracy. A career pattern study of ministerial cabinet members in Belgium', PSW Paper 2004/7, Antwerp: University of Antwerp, Faculty of political and social sciences.

Wilwerth, C. (2001) 'Introduction générale', in H. De Croo (ed) *Les cabinet ministériels et autres: statuts, rôles et pouvoirs*, Brussels: Bruylant, 11-21.

Part Two
Policy analysis in the government and legislature

FOUR

Policy analysis in the central and regional governments

David Aubin, Marleen Brans and Ellen Fobé

Policy analysis is the application of intellect to the definition of and solution to policy problems. Thus understood, policy analysis is a craft (Weimer, 1998), drawing on both specialist and generalist knowledge and skills (Colebatch and Radin, 2006). It draws on the application of more or less formalised policy-analytical skills, but also on the ability to engage in interactions with stakeholders, and to communicate effectively with political executives. In this sense, policy analysis is only loosely defined and encompasses policy-analytical activities that garner and analyse information as well as the activities of policy workers aimed at integrating policy-relevant political judgement, experience and the value positions of stakeholders.

This chapter analyses the locus and modus of in-house policy analysis in the Belgian central and regional governments. It describes the way in which policy-analytical roles within the departments and agencies are organised, and what kind of resources civil servants have for conducting policy analysis. The analysis draws on a survey conducted in 2013-15, specifically designed with this book in mind.

In-house policy analysis has long been recognised as a core function of modern bureaucracies (Lasswell, 1971; Meltsner, 1976; Peters, 1989). Even when acknowledging that civil servants are not the only actors engaged in policy analysis, and many external policy-analytical activities contribute to policy framing, agenda setting and other stages in the policy process, in-house policy analysis remains a relevant object of study because the very production of public policy is still located within the authoritative sphere of government. The translation of ideas, representations of problems and their solutions, and causal models into legal texts, policy instruments and the provision of public goods and services still remains a government activity. Because of their proximity to the political executives who ultimately carry the responsibility for policy decisions, the people serving these executives are a special kind of stakeholder in the policy process, and deserve special scrutiny as they act as gatekeepers, arbitrators and writers committed to legal drafting.

In Belgium, the people who serve the government are both civil servants and ministerial advisers. While Chapter Three delves into the policy-analytical roles and tasks of ministerial advisers, this chapter focuses on the location of in-house policy analysts, their analytical and information-processing activities, and their advice-seeking behaviour.

The survey was designed to give an account of the actual contribution of civil servants to the policy process, not only of the statutory policy analysts but of all university-graduated civil servants within the central and regional governments (see Chapter One). It investigates three aspects of policy analysis. First, the analysis of the survey results serves to contextualise policy-analytical work. The survey inquired about the number of units specialising in policy analysis as well as the time devoted to a range of basic policy-analytical activities, and requested a self-assessment of each organisation's policy-analytical capacity. Second, it asked questions relating to the kind of policy-analytical tasks conducted by civil servants. This was particularly useful for situations where several civil servants are supposed to be involved in policy work, but policy work may not be their primary activity. Civil servants were questioned about their role in the preparation of a series of documents, their participation in analytical or procedural activities, and their involvement in political debate. Third, civil servants were asked about the kind of information they use in their policy-analytical work. How do they get access to information on a day-to-day basis? How do they proceed when required to find information quickly and how frequently do they seek or receive advice from colleagues or stakeholders?

Based on the survey results, the following sections consecutively present a picture of in-house policy-analytical work in the federal and Flemish governments and in Francophone Belgium.

Policy analysis in the Belgian federal government

Policy analysis at the Belgian federal level is situated predominantly within the centralised services known as the 'federal public service'. This section discusses the results of the federal survey and is based on fully or partially completed questionnaires by federal university-graduated civil servants (N=904).

Location of policy analysis

Survey participants in the federal public service were invited to indicate the type of functional unit they work in. Unsurprisingly, half of them are linked to a unit that predominantly carries out tasks related to policy implementation (43%) or inspections (7%). Only 18% actually work in a unit that focuses on policy formulation. Another third of respondents reported their unit's main function as being either policy coordination (14%), policy evaluation (3%) or research (14%).

Civil servants working on policy-related matters spend their time carrying out various activities, such as reading or writing texts or going to meetings (see Figure 4.1). About 30% of respondents in the federal government spend more than 15% of their time writing policy-related texts, and less than a half reading reports and notes. About half of respondents report that meetings with colleagues, members of ministerial cabinets, or stakeholders and researchers also take up a significant amount of time. A more select group participates in or follows up on research studies. In all, less than 20% of respondents spend more than 15% of their time on policy-related activities. These results indicate that such tasks are carried out by a wide range of civil servants, even if only a fraction is more involved in policy formulation.

Figure 4.1: Time spent on tasks by federal civil servants (N=303-387)

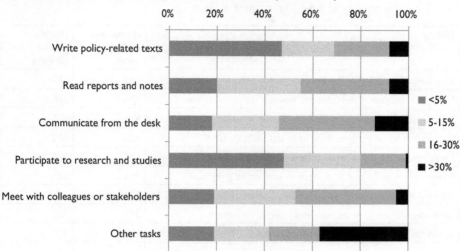

When questioned about their perceptions of the general policy capacity of their organisations, the respondents take up a fairly positive stance as regards their access to informational resources to conduct their work, and ways to coordinate on cross-sectoral issues (see Table 4.1). They also recognise that their hierarchy is supportive of the policy work that they carry out and have a favourable perception of the impact of their work on the decision-making process. However, respondents are less satisfied about their organisation's general personnel policies. Specifically, they report a lack of opportunities for development and training, too little time to follow up on recent scientific research results and too few personnel. These results may have been affected by recently announced cutbacks that would have had a negative impact on the respondents' perceptions of the overall policy capacity of their organisations.

Tasks

Civil servants generally perform a number of policy-related tasks. This section elaborates on the degree to which the federal respondents are involved in the preparation of policy documents and the extent to which they carry out a range of policy-related activities.

As far as the preparation of specific policy documents is concerned, a large group of federal civil servants regularly work in close cooperation with their political principal and his/her personal advisers (see Table 4.2). Half of the respondents answer questions from their minister regularly, while about 40% also answer parliamentary questions or contribute to briefings, presentations or reports for their political principal. A much smaller group is involved in the preparation of strategic policy documents.

Table 4.1: Policy capacity of federal government organisations

N=370	(Somewhat or fully) agree	(Rather or fully) disagree
There is too little concern for long-term issues in policy work	71%	10%
I can quickly make use of information and knowledge relevant to my work	62%	16%
The ministerial cabinet plays a dominant role in policy formulation	57%	13%
The work I do has an impact on the decisions that are finally taken	47%	21%
I receive strong support from my superiors to carry out policy work	47%	24%
I know where to go if I need to coordinate on cross-sectoral policy issues	45%	24%
The ministerial cabinet's role in policy formulation is too dominant	31%	23%
The training offer related to the policy work I carry out is sufficient	28%	45%
My unit has enough personnel to carry out policy work	22%	62%
I have enough time to follow up on scientific work related to my policy work	12%	69%

Notes: The answers to these questions ranged on a scale from 1 to 5, where a score of 1 and 2 indicates that respondents 'rather' or 'fully' disagreed', and a score of 4 and 5 indicates that they 'somewhat' or 'fully' agreed with the statement. A 'middle of the road' option, with a score of 3, was also included (contrary to the survey in the Flemish administration) and respondents could indicate that they did not know the answer to the question.

The results also indicate that the federal administration, or at least the group of graduate civil servants in the survey, is not often directly involved in the preparation of government coalition agreements. This task, which is moreover restricted to times of government turnover, remains the concern of ministerial cabinets and political parties' study centres (see also Chapter Eight). Some respondents report involvement in the preparation of evaluations and green or white papers. While it is fair to assume that these activities are concentrated within a small subset of the federal government's administration, they are indicative of evaluation and green papers as emergent practices.

Respondents were presented with a list of specific policy-related activities pertaining to the formulation of policies, or to aspects of implementation and evaluation (see Table 4.3). Almost half of respondents perform implementation tasks regularly, and around 30% assess the legal acceptability of policies. This important aspect of policy development may be explained by the fact that a large group of civil servants at the federal level holds a law degree (see Chapter One), and by the types of policy sector that are embedded in the federal administration (including Justice and Interior).

Table 4.2: Federal civil servants' involvement in the preparation of policy documents

N=408	Often or always	Rarely (or never)
Questions from ministerial cabinets	49%	22%
Parliamentary questions	42%	24%
Briefings, presentations or reports to the minister	39%	35%
Internal strategic notes to the administration	34%	33%
New regulation	34%	40%
Strategic policy notes to the minister	26%	48%
Research reports	13%	59%
Budgetary documents	13%	69%
(Cross-sector) policy plans	10%	62%
Government coalition agreement	10%	75%
Foresight	9%	68%
Regulatory impact assessment	9%	74%
Programme evaluations	6%	78%
Green or white papers	5%	80%

Note: The score for 'occasionally' is not presented, but can be easily deduced from the sum of the two others.

Table 4.3: Involvement of federal civil servants in policy-related tasks

N=406	Often (or always)	Rarely (or never)
Implementing policies	49%	33%
Assessing legal acceptability	29%	52%
Testing timing and feasibility of policy options	16%	58%
Determining budgetary impacts	16%	65%
Assessing (cross-sector) effects	15%	62%
Investigating political risks for the minister	15%	67%
Assisting the cabinet in inter-cabinet meetings	13%	65%
Deciding on policy options	10%	66%
Testing societal support for policies	10%	71%
Following up on commissioned research or evaluation	9%	70%
Assisting the minister in parliament	6%	84%

Note: The score for 'occasionally' is not presented, but can be easily deduced from the sum of the two others.

Other types of policy assessments are limited to a small, but still significant group of respondents (about 15%) who regularly carry out analyses of the cross-sectoral or financial effects of policies. They also report being involved in the assessment of political risks to the minister and societal support for policies, which were expected to be the domains of the personal advisers to the minister rather than the civil servants. Ministers seem to rely on the administration for some policy work.

In terms of the salience of issues addressed, firefighting is a recurrent theme for almost 40% of respondents, who spend more than 30% of their time on such matters (see Figure 4.2). This is a remarkable result, even if civil servants are on average predominantly involved in issues that receive relatively little media attention, such as long-term dossiers or smaller cases that are politically less important.

Figure 4.2: Salience of issues addressed within the federal government (N=376)

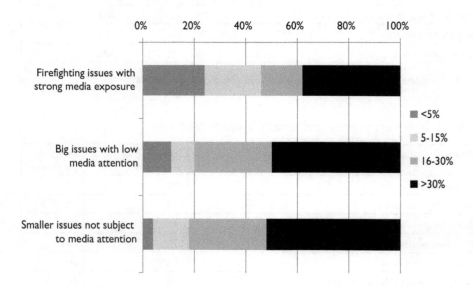

Information sources

The sources of information and knowledge that civil servants rely on are quite varied. Knowledge is indeed produced by different types of actor, such as governmental actors, scientists, and societal actors.

Two thirds of federal civil servants rely predominantly on regulatory documents (see Table 4.4). Moreover, the use of press articles and documents from the political principal is widespread. Considering that External Affairs, Defence and Sustainable Development are federal competencies, documents produced by international organisations (such as the Organisation for Economic Co-operation and Development and the European Commission) are important for a third of respondents. A quarter also regularly consult scientific articles and parliamentary documents. Somewhat surprising is the limited use of studies produced by scientific research institutes that are closely linked to the government, and of evaluation studies carried out in-house or by external actors. These kinds of report seem to inform policy-analytical work at the federal level only to a limited degree.

Table 4.4: Information sources used in policy work by federal civil servants

N=380	Often (or always)	Rarely (or never)
Current regulations and programmes	65%	12%
Documents from the minister or his/her cabinet	40%	27%
Press articles	39%	28%
Reports from international or European organisations	33%	41%
Parliamentary documents	28%	45%
Scientific articles	26%	47%
Reports from NGOs or civil society	21%	51%
Reports from the Court of Audit, Planning Bureau or National Bank	13%	63%
Think-tank reports and studies	11%	70%
Reports from not-for-profit research and policy foundations	8%	72%
Reports from governmental research centres	8%	77%
Evaluation reports	7%	76%

Note: The score for 'occasionally' is not presented, but can be easily deduced from the sum of the two others.

When relevant information must be gathered quickly, civil servants do not seek external documents but rely heavily on colleagues inside their own unit or organisation (84%), or on other actors within government (76%) (see Table 4.5). Thus, it seems that in-house policy workers in federal Belgium are still very much inward-looking when carrying out their work. Their second recourse is, of course, to 'Google' the information they need or to browse scientific websites. They are much less likely to call on personal contacts outside government.

This reliance on internal sources of knowledge is further supported by the findings on which actors' advice they actively solicit or passively receive (see Table 4.6). Internal sources of advice are consulted more regularly than external sources. Similar to the findings on sources of information, the results point to a relatively substantial number of respondents asking advice from actors situated in different levels of government in Belgium (25%) and abroad (20%). They also receive advice from these actors quite regularly. These results confirm Halligan's (1995) location-based model of advice.

Table 4.5: Sources used by federal civil servants to gather relevant information quickly

N=371	To a large extent or (very) frequently	Very little or rather little
I use the information available within my unit or department	84%	5%
I call on personal contacts within the administration or cabinet	76%	10%
I 'Google' the information required	59%	20%
I browse scientific articles	30%	49%
I browse the websites of known companies or civil society organisations	28%	46%
I browse the websites of renowned scientific institutions	28%	47%
I search in reports and press archives	24%	50%
I call on personal contacts in companies or civil society	20%	57%
I call on personal contacts within the scientific community	14%	62%
I browse social networks	5%	85%

Note: The scores range on a scale from 1 to 5, where 1 and 2 indicate that the source of information is turned to 'very little or rather little', and 4 or 5 indicate that it is counted on 'to a large extent or (very) frequently'. A 'middle of the road' option was also included by score 3 (contrary to the questionnaire in Flanders).

In addition, and somewhat puzzling, is the finding that 5% of respondents regularly receive advice from individual citizens, which is more than those who report receiving advice from private companies, consultants or scientific actors. Federal research institutes seem to be the exception here: 16% of respondents receive advice from such actors, whereas only 5% actively solicit advice from them. This may be explained by the fact that these federal research institutes actively disseminate their results across the federal government's administrations (for example, the Belgian Health Care Knowledge Centre, the Royal Belgian Institute of Natural Sciences and the Institutes for Tropical Medicine and for Middle Africa, to name but a few).

In sum, this section has shown that policy analysis is regularly conducted by the federal civil servants who participated in the survey. These civil servants spend a considerable proportion of their time writing policy-related documents and contributing to various related policy-analytical tasks, including assessing the legal acceptability or budgetary feasibility of policy proposals. In addition, they make use of a wide variety of sources of information and advice, although they are, as Meltsner (1976) attested, still mainly reliant on internal contacts for this. The survey underlines the need for maintaining and managing this policy-analytical capacity.

Table 4.6: Advice requested or received by federal officials in their search for information

N=342-365	Advice requested at least monthly	Advice received at least monthly
Officials in the same sector	70%	57%
Officials from other sectors	32%	27%
Other public organisations at a different policy level	25%	19%
International or European organisations	20%	23%
Advisory bodies	10%	9%
Sectoral federations	9%	8%
NGOs and other civil society organisations	7%	8%
Trade unions or employers' organisations	6%	7%
Federal research institutes	5%	16%
Individual citizens	2%	5%
Think tanks	2%	4%
Individual private companies	2%	3%
Private consultants	2%	2%
Individual scientists	2%	2%
Scientific research groups	2%	1%
Political parties' study centres	1%	2%
Citizen movements	1%	1%

Policy analysis in the Flemish government

Although in the Flemish government ministerial cabinets play an important role in support of policymaking, policy analysis also takes place within the Flemish government's centralised policy departments and agencies. This section examines in-house policy analysis based on the results of the survey for Flanders (N=499). As explained in Chapter One, the sampling of Flemish university-graduated civil servants was more narrowly focused on their assumed engagement in policy-analytical activities.

Location of policy analysis

Given this narrow focus on policy analysts and policy advisers, 55% of respondents understandably indicate that their unit is predominantly involved in policy formulation (43.5%), coordination (11%) and evaluation (1%). Aside from this, another 7% assign the task of studying and researching to their unit, whereas 28% consider that implementation is their unit's main function and 3% of identify their unit as mainly carrying out inspections.

When consulted about the extent to which they devote their time to various sorts of activity, 40% of respondent Flemish civil servants indicate that they spend more than 15% of their time writing policy-related texts, while a third spend a similar amount of time reading reports and notes (see Figure 4.3). Meeting with colleagues and stakeholders also takes a fair amount of their time. A more limited group of civil servants (20%) spends quite some time participating in or following up on research and policy relevant studies.

Figure 4.3: Time spent on tasks by Flemish civil servants (N=407-475)

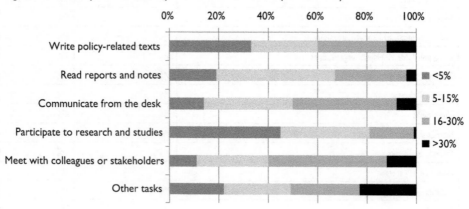

Concerning assessment of their organisation's policy capacity, almost all the respondents have sufficient access to relevant information and contact persons when required (see Table 4.7). Overall they seem quite positive about the impact that they have on the decision-making process (73%). Thus, their judgement of their organisation's capacity is fairly positive, and is certainly a consequence of the huge efforts made by the Flemish government to reform its administration over the past 20 years.

However, Flemish civil servants still consider that their organisations lack time, staff and strategic vision. For example, they would appreciate the opportunity to follow up on relevant scientific research. They also overwhelmingly agree that long-term issues in public policy should receive more attention (77%). This is rather worrisome, since the civil service seems the most appropriate body within government to develop such a long-term, strategic vision, away from political and media attention. Firefighting takes up a significant part of the civil servants' time and helping ministers answer parliamentary questions may crowd out other core policy-analytical activities (see the following section).

Table 4.7: Policy capacity of Flemish government organisations

N=397	(Somewhat or fully) agree	(Rather or fully) disagree
I can quickly make use of information and knowledge relevant to my work	83%	15%
There is too little concern for long-term issues in policy work	77%	19%
The work I do has an impact on the decisions that are finally taken	73%	18%
I receive strong support from my superiors to carry out policy work	69%	28%
I know where to go if I need to coordinate on cross-sectoral policy issues	69%	26%
The training offer related to the policy work I carry out is sufficient	58%	35%
The ministerial cabinet's role in policy formulation is too dominant	49%	39%
My unit has enough personnel to carry out policy work	46%	51%
I have enough time to follow up on scientific work related to my policy work	28%	69%

Notes: The answers ranged on a scale from 1 to 4, where a score of 1 and 2 indicates that respondents 'rather' or 'fully' disagreed', and a score of 3 and 4 indicates that they 'somewhat' or 'fully' agreed with the statement. A 'middle of the road' option was not included in the answer range for Flemish civil servants (contrary to the surveys at the federal level and in French Belgium), which renders the information presented in the table more dichotomous. Respondents could, however, indicate that they did not know the answer to the question.

Tasks

Civil servants within the Flemish government perform many policy-analytical tasks. A large proportion of the surveyed population in Flanders is involved in the preparation of policy documents, at least occasionally (see Table 4.8), and a majority provide frequent support to ministers. This includes answering questions coming directly from ministerial cabinets, as well as parliamentary questions addressed to the ministers, and contributing to strategic notes, policy notes and policy briefs. This finding confirms that policy work is an activity shared between the Flemish administration and ministerial cabinets (Vancoppenolle and Brans, 2010).

Likewise, a relatively large group of respondents is regularly involved in the preparation of new regulations, internal strategic notes and cross-sectoral policy plans. A more limited subset of Flemish civil servants, probably generalists, is involved in the production of specific types of analytical document, such as evaluations and foresight reports. Additionally, a third of respondents indicate that they (often) contribute to the government coalition agreement at the beginning of the legislature. The involvement of the civil service in these wide-ranging political negotiations is more institutionalised in Flanders than in any other Belgian government (Brans et al, 2012).

Table 4.8: Flemish civil servants' involvement in the preparation of policy documents

N=492	Often or always	Rarely (or never)
Questions from ministerial cabinets	56%	14%
Parliamentary questions	55%	13%
Strategic policy notes to the minister	51%	25%
Briefings, presentations or reports to the minister	45%	26%
New regulation	43%	33%
Internal strategic notes to the administration	41%	27%
Government coalition agreement	38%	39%
Cross-sector policy plans	32%	37%
Research reports	22%	44%
Programme evaluation	16%	58%
Foresight	15%	60%
Budgetary documents	15%	68%
Regulatory impact assessment	11%	71%
Green or white papers	10%	71%

Note: The score for 'occasionally' is not presented, but can be easily deduced from the sum of the two others.

The second question about tasks relates more to specific activities than to the kinds of document civil servants produce. Even if the population is narrowed down to policy analysts, policy implementation remains an important task for half of the respondents (see Table 4.9). Policy formulation is a regular activity for only a quarter of respondents. In terms of tasks, this relates to assessing policy options regarding societal support, timing and feasibility, legal acceptability, as well as considering the financial impact of proposals and political risks to the minister. Providing direct assistance to the minister is confined to a much smaller group of public servants. As a task gets closer to supporting a particular policy option, civil servants clearly become somewhat less active and the ministerial advisers take their place.

So precisely what type of issue do civil servants within the Flemish government deal with? Respondents are predominantly involved in issues that receive relatively little media attention (see Figure 4.4). About 60% of the respondents assign more than 30% of their time to important cases that do not receive much media attention but that are of concern to the minister, and another half to less high-profile issues and dossiers produced inside the civil service. Nevertheless, firefighting, that is the management of short-term events and crises, affects (at least to a certain extent) the policy work of a significant number of Flemish civil servants.

Table 4.9: Involvement of Flemish civil servants in policy-related tasks

N=491	Often (or always)	Rarely (or never)
Implementing policies	50%	30%
Following up on commissioned research or evaluation	30%	42%
Testing societal support for policies	28%	40%
Testing timing and feasibility of policy options	26%	42%
Assessing (cross-sector) effects	26%	44%
Assessing legal acceptability	26%	55%
Determining budgetary impacts	19%	54%
Investigating political risks for the minister	18%	61%
Deciding on policy options	16%	60%
Assisting the cabinet in inter-cabinet meetings	12%	65%
Assisting the minister in parliament	4%	81%

Note: The score for 'occasionally' is not presented, but can be easily deduced from the sum of the two others.

Figure 4.4: Salience of issues addressed within the Flemish government (N=462)

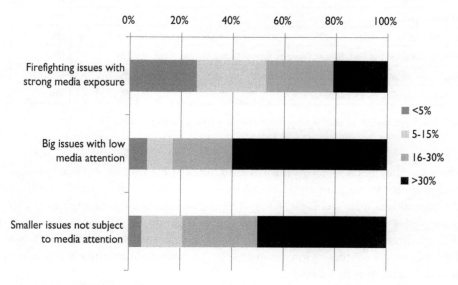

Information sources

Specific policy documents and documents from the political principal serve as the main sources of information to a majority of respondents (see Table 4.10). In addition, more than 40% make regular use of press articles, and about 30% make use of scientific information produced in journals or by governmental research centres. Parliamentary documents and reports produced by civil society organisations are also consulted frequently by a significant proportion of Flemish civil servants. Respondents assigned only relative importance to evaluation reports in policy work: 5% consult regulatory impact assessments regularly, and 20% make more than regular use of information stemming from other evaluations. Less widely used sources of information are economic reports and audits produced, for instance, by the National Bank, as well as information made available through think tanks and policy foundations. The role of such actors as sources of information for policy work seems fairly limited within the Flemish government.

Table 4.10: Information sources used in policy work by Flemish civil servants

N=450	Often (or always)	Rarely (or never)
Current regulations and programmes	82%	6%
Documents from the minister or his/her cabinet	57%	12%
Press articles	41%	22%
Scientific articles	32%	32%
Reports from governmental research centres	28%	35%
Parliamentary documents	25%	35%
Reports from NGOs or civil society	24%	34%
Evaluation reports	19%	47%
Think-tank reports and studies	10%	63%
Reports from the Court of Audit, Planning Bureau or National Bank	9%	68%
Reports from not-for-profit research and policy foundations	7%	63%
Results from regulatory impact assessments	5%	80%

Note: The score for 'occasionally' is not presented, but can be easily deduced from the sum of the two others.

Whenever they need to access information quickly, Flemish civil servants assign much importance to their contacts inside the government apparatus (more than 90% of respondents) (see Table 4.11). The use of internet search engines is also considered a relevant means. Surprisingly, a large group of respondents still relies on direct or indirect access to scientific and societal sources. Other types of (social) media sources of information seem to matter comparatively less when immediate action is required.

Table 4.11: Sources used by Flemish civil servants to gather relevant information quickly

N=395	To a large extent or (very) frequently	Very little or rather little
I use the information available within my unit or department	97%	3%
I call on personal contacts within the administration or cabinet	96%	4%
I 'Google' the information required	89%	11%
I browse scientific articles	60%	40%
I browse the websites of known companies or civil society organisations	59%	41%
I call on personal contacts in companies or civil society	56%	44%
I call on personal contacts within the scientific community	51%	49%
I browse the websites of renowned scientific institutions	49%	51%
I search in reports and press archives	37%	63%
I browse social networks	12%	88%

Notes: The scores range on a scale from 1 to 6. A score of 1 to 3 indicates that the source of information is considered to a 'very little or rather little' extent, and a score 4 to 6 indicates that it is turned to 'to a large extent or (very) frequently'. Contrary to the federal level and the questionnaire in French Belgium, there was no 'middle of the road' option in the Flemish survey. The results presented here are therefore more dichotomous in comparison with the two other governmental levels.

Aside from looking up documents and reports relevant to their policy work, public servants in Flanders obtain access to relevant information by soliciting or receiving advice from other actors. On average, they tend to solicit advice more frequently than they would receive advice without having requested it, and this advice is mainly formulated by colleagues inside the Flemish government (see Table 4.12). It appears that civil servants are still largely oriented inwards, thus again confirming Halligan's location-based model of advice (1995). Advisory actors that are located relatively close to the government (such as local or federal public organisations, institutionalised advisory bodies, and policy research centres set up by the Flemish government) are consulted at least on a monthly basis by 10–20% of policy-engaged civil servants. External or societal actors are regularly consulted by a much smaller subset of respondents.

This section has shown that civil servants are regularly involved in policy analysis in Flanders. They are active in the production of policy-related documents and contribute to a range of policy-analytical tasks, such as testing societal support, budgetary feasibility and cross-sectoral effects of policy proposals. They also make use of a wide variety of sources of information, and they turn for advice to various actors, although most of these are confined to the governmental arena.

Table 4.12: Advice requested or received by Flemish civil servants in their search for information

N=393-412	Advice requested at least monthly	Advice received at least monthly
Officials in the same sector	77%	48%
Officials from other sectors	37%	20%
Other public organisations at a different policy level	17%	11%
Advisory bodies	13%	10%
Experts from Flemish policy research centres	10%	7%
International or European organisations	9%	10%
Scientific research groups	7%	6%
NGOs and other civil society organisations	6%	7%
Sectoral federations	6%	6%
Trade unions or employers' organisations	5%	5%
Private consultants	3%	3%
Individual private companies	3%	3%
Citizen movements or individual citizens	3%	3%
Think tanks	1%	1%
Political parties' study centres	0%	0%

Policy analysis in Francophone Belgium

In Francophone Belgium, policy analysis is in theory mainly located in ministerial cabinets. However, the central administration and agencies are involved too. The survey addressed all the graduate civil servants of Wallonia and Federation Wallonia–Brussels, two autonomous Belgian federated entities (N=1,314). These civil servants feed back to the cabinets, help the minister design public policies, and advise on the feasibility of proposals.

Location of policy analysis

Policy units are rather scarce in Francophone Belgium. The regional administrations are mainly concerned with policy implementation, including inspection and control (64%). Only 4% of the respondents consider that policy formulation is their unit's main function. However, grouping together policy formulation, coordination, evaluation and studies, the answers relating to policy analysis reach 20%. Some differences appear between Wallonia and Federation Wallonia–Brussels, the latter reporting fewer units specialising in policy-related activities (14%).

Individually, civil servants in Francophone Belgium estimate that their work is devoted to a series of policy-related activities. A majority is involved in writing policy-related texts, with most civil servants devoting 5–15% of their time to this activity and 14% spending 16-30% of their time on the task (see Figure 4.5). Hence, policy analysis is not a specialised function, but an activity widely shared within the public service.

Figure 4.5: Time devoted to policy work by Francophone Belgian civil servants (N=683-844)

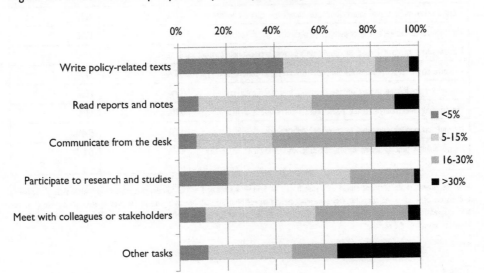

The civil servants of the Francophone Belgian administrations are divided over the policy-analytical capacity of their organisation (see Table 4.13). A small majority agrees that their knowledge base and resources are sufficient to conduct their work (46%) and coordinate on cross-sectoral issues (41%). They also recognise that their hierarchy is supportive of their policy-related work (38%). However, a significant proportion expresses a neutral position (neither agreeing nor disagreeing) or does not take a position, which may express a mixed view of their organisation's capacity.

In terms of weaknesses, civil servants agree that the ministerial cabinets dominate the policy process (70%), and that this dominance is too strong (44%). They regret the lack of concern for long-term issues (68%), and also identify a lack of public policy training opportunities (44%), staff shortages (54%) and lack of time to follow up on scientific work (61%). Thus, the policy capacity in Francophone Belgian administrations is sufficient for day-to-day functioning, but the margins for improvement are significant.

About 20% of respondents in Wallonia and 14% in Federation Wallonia-Brussels are attached to units that primarily conduct policy-analytical work, even when policy formulation units are almost inexistent in both governments. In addition, a majority of respondents are involved in writing policy-related texts, even when this activity represents only a portion of their workload. This task appears to garner sufficient resources even if margins of improvement remain considerable.

Table 4.13: Francophone civil servants' perception of the organisation's policy capacity

N=589	(Somewhat or fully) agree	(Rather or fully) disagree
The ministerial cabinet plays a dominant role in policy formulation	70%	6%
Concerns for long-term issues are too limited in policy work	68%	8%
I can quickly make use of information and knowledge relevant to my work	46%	22%
The ministerial cabinet's role in policy formulation is too dominant	44%	15%
I know where to go if I need to coordinate on cross-sectoral policy issues	41%	23%
I receive strong support from my superiors to carry out policy work	38%	22%
The work I do has an impact on the decisions that are finally taken	32%	25%
The training offer related to the policy work I carry out is sufficient	23%	44%
My unit has enough personnel to carry out policy work	17%	**54%**
I have enough time to follow up on scientific work related to my policy work	15%	**61%**

Note: The answers to the questions ranged on a scale from 1 to 5, where a score of 1 and 2 indicates that respondents 'rather' or 'fully' disagreed', and a score of 4 and 5 indicates that they 'somewhat' or 'fully' agreed with the statement. A 'middle of the road' option, with a score of 3, was also included (contrary to the survey in Flanders, but similar to the one at the federal level) and respondents could indicate that they did not know the answer to the question.

Tasks

Many civil servants in Francophone Belgium are involved in the preparation of policy documents. About a quarter are at least often involved in the writing of policy documents, but for most this involvement is only occasional or limited to incidental activities (for example, if 42% are rarely or never involved in writing strategic policy notes to the ministers, it means that 58% are at least occasionally involved in such activity, and 25% rather frequently) (see Table 4.14).

The most frequently cited activity is answering questions from ministerial cabinets (35%). This denotes that Francophone civil servants have a function of supporting ministers and their cabinets, who are the true policy designers and decision makers. This activity should not devalue the importance of other policy-formulation activities that civil servants conduct. Around 25% report a repeated involvement in the preparation of strategic notes, either to the minister, or internal to the administration. A smaller group is involved in writing new regulations, policy notes or reports to the minister, or preparing budgetary documents (about 15-20%). Naturally, most of these activities are conducted in close collaboration with the minister, but nevertheless demonstrate that civil servants are part of policy work. The division of tasks between formulation and implementation is not as clear-cut as one might assume. Ministers need the support of the administration, which is involved in policy-analytical tasks to a greater degree than expected.

Table 4.14: Francophone civil servants' involvement in the preparation of policy documents

N=933-937	Often or always	Rarely (or never)
Questions from ministerial cabinets	35%	31%
Internal strategic notes to the administration	26%	41%
Strategic policy notes to the minister	25%	42%
Parliamentary questions	24%	45%
Budgetary documents	22%	57%
New regulations	21%	47%
Briefings, presentations or reports to the minister	16%	56%
Foresight	10%	70%
Research reports	7%	74%
Programme evaluation	6%	81%
Government coalition agreement	5%	81%

Note: The score for 'occasionally' is not presented, but can be easily deduced from the sum of the two others.

Only a few respondents report frequent involvement in study activities; less than 10% are often involved in research, policy evaluation and foresight. It also appears that the preparation of government coalition agreements remains a purely political activity that does not require knowledge or input from the administration. This is quite surprising given the degree of detail in these agreements, which set most of the policy agenda for the whole legislature.

The involvement of civil servants in the preparation of policy tasks can be manifold (see Table 4.15). It consists mainly of implementing policy decisions, or assisting the minister and his or her cabinet in the formulation phase. Forty-one percent of respondents are frequently involved in implementing public policies. It is more surprising to see that the same proportion considers that they are not really involved in policy implementation. This may reflect the way in which the question has been interpreted, with respondents assuming that activities of follow-up, inspection or control are not part of policy implementation. It may also reflect the extent to which civil servants are involved in support functions such as IT, human resource management, or infrastructure maintenance.

The role of civil servants as auxiliaries to ministers and their (ministerial) cabinets is evident from the survey but only concerns a minority. About 13% of graduate civil servants declare being often involved in following up research or evaluation that has often been commissioned by the ministers. They also assess the legal acceptability and budgetary impacts of policy proposals. The five areas most closely associated with policy formulation or policy advice are reported as being the concern of a mere 5% of respondents (from testing the feasibility of policy options to making policy decisions). This confirms the finding that civil servants are mainly indirectly involved in the formulation of policies. They participate, but usually on the side lines; only a few are more directly involved.

Table 4.15: Involvement of Francophone civil servants in policy-related tasks

N=916-923	Often (or always)	Rarely (or never)
Implementing policies	41%	41%
Following up on commissioned research or evaluation	13%	69%
Assessing legal acceptability	13%	72%
Determining budgetary impacts	12%	70%
Testing timing and feasibility of policy options	7%	79%
Assessing (cross-sector) effects	6%	80%
Investigating political risks for the minister	5%	87%
Testing societal support for policies	4%	91%
Deciding on policy options	3%	89%

Note: The score for 'occasionally' is not presented, but can be easily deduced from the sum of the two others.

This contribution to policy from behind the scenes is confirmed by answers to the question about the salience of the issues dealt with by the Francophone civil servants. On average, civil servants tend to manage issues of little interest to the media (see Figure 4.6); 56% of respondents spend more than 30% of their time on issues of limited scope, and another 45% on issues that are more wide-ranging but have little salience. These issues tend to concern the policy priorities of the governments (for example, the Marshall Plan in Wallonia or the introduction of an internal audit system in Federation Wallonia-Brussels), but do not attract much interest from the media. They are developed internally and have a long term orientation.

Figure 4.6: Salience of issues addressed within the Francophone Belgian government (N=751-778)

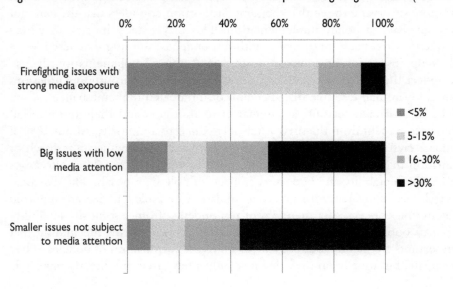

On average, civil servants are not subject to strong media scrutiny and are not directly involved in firefighting. This is usually the preserve of ministerial advisers, although a small proportion of respondents spend a fair amount of their time in this way. Around 25% declare that they spend more than 16% of their time firefighting, with a larger proportion being involved from time to time. This indicates once again that civil servants are strong supporters of ministers and their cabinets when it comes to dealing with highly salient issues, even if they remain behind the scenes. Part of their work is devoted to policy formulation and subsequent political reaction.

Information sources

The most frequently used documents in policy work are current regulations or strategic plans. Sixty-two percent of respondents declare using them often or always, and only 15% rarely or never (see Table 4.16). Political documents from the minister are also widely used, with 36% using them often and 29% occasionally. Many civil servants obtain relevant information from newspapers, but, surprisingly, scientific articles come fourth in the list of most frequently consulted sources, with 29% of respondents using them often and 57% at least occasionally. It is possible that, as specialists, civil servants are university graduates and are familiar with scientific writings. Below scientific articles, the next most frequently used documents are reports and studies from internal research units or European and international organisations. Other external sources of information are more scarcely used, except by the top 10% of civil servants who seem to be most closely connected to policy advice.

Table 4.16: Information sources used in policy work by Francophone civil servants

N=759-763	Often (or always)	Rarely (or never)
Current regulations and programmes	62%	15%
Press articles	41%	27%
Documents from the minister or his/her cabinet	36%	35%
Scientific articles	29%	43%
Reports from governmental research units	23%	52%
Reports from European and international organisations	19%	56%
Parliamentary documents	16%	57%
Reports from the Court of Auditors, Planning Bureau or National Bank	13%	63%
Reports from NGOs or civil society	12%	67%
Evaluation reports	11%	72%
Reports from not-for-profit research and policy foundations	8%	75%
Results from regulatory impact assessments	6%	81%
Think-tank reports and studies	4%	87%

Note: The score for 'occasionally' is not presented, but can be easily deduced from the sum of the two others.

When in a rush, civil servants rely on their immediate colleagues and internal information sources (see Table 4.17): 78% use to a large extent the information available in their own unit or department, and 68% their personal contacts within the administration or cabinet. At the same time, fewer respondents search external information sources. It appears that the capacity to manage information internally is still critical to the way in which public administrations operate, despite the current trends toward outsourcing and co-production.

Table 4.17: Sources used by Francophone civil servants to gather relevant information quickly

N=743-751	To a large extent or (very) frequently	Very little or rather little
I use the information available within my unit or department	78%	11%
I call on personal contacts within the administration or cabinet	68%	15%
I 'Google' the information required'	59%	19%
I browse the websites of renowned scientific institutions	37%	35%
I browse the websites of known companies or civil society organisations	32%	43%
I browse scientific articles	29%	50%
I search in reports and press archives	26%	47%
I call on personal contacts within the scientific community	22%	57%
I call on personal contacts in companies or civil society	19%	63%
I browse social networks	3%	92%

Notes: The scores in the survey ranged on a scale from 1 to 5, where 1 and 2 indicate that the source of information is turned to 'very little or rather little', and 4 or 5 indicate that it is counted on 'to a large extent or (very) frequently'. An 'occasionally' option was also included, with a score of 3 (contrary to the surveys in Flanders but similar to the one at federal level). It is not presented, but can be easily deduced.

In their analytical tasks, civil servants not only consult documents, but also request advice from colleagues or external experts. In Francophone Belgium, as elsewhere, the most important requests are directed to civil servants in the same sector (see Table 4.18). Sixty-one percent of respondents consult their immediate colleagues at least once a month; 52% also receive advice from colleagues without requesting it. Respondents also ask advice of civil servants from other sectors (26%), other national public organisations (19%) and, less often, experts from in-house research institutes (10%). In-house communication remains critical.

Consultation of stakeholders is less frequent, with the exception of advisory bodies, which are regular suppliers of advice for 16% of respondents. This is not surprising in light of the decision-making process in Francophone Belgium where bills must be sent to advisory bodies before being sent to parliament for approval. In return, some officials (10%) use advisory bodies as a means of seeking information from stakeholders. Otherwise, advice from private actors, including social interlocutors, is limited. In a multi-level polity, it is remarkable that requests for advice from international and European organisations are also limited, although the survey covers all policy sectors under the remit of the Belgian regions and communities, many of which are not directly influenced by supranational organisations (for example, culture, education and road maintenance).

Table 4.18: Advice requested or received by Francophone civil servants in their search for information

N=515-669	Advice requested at least monthly	Advice received at least monthly
Officials in the same sector	61%	52%
Officials from other sectors	26%	22%
Other public organisations	19%	9%
Advisory bodies	10%	16%
Experts from in-house research units	10%	8%
International or European organisations	8%	8%
Trade unions or employers' organisations	7%	5%
Individual private companies	6%	1%
Sectoral federations	6%	3%
NGOs and other civil society organisations	4%	1%
Private consultants	2%	2%
Scientific research groups	2%	6%
Think tanks	0%	9%

Policy analysis does take place in the central administrations and agencies of Wallonia and Federation Wallonia-Brussels, but activity is quite dispersed. Only a small group of civil servants (around 5-10%) is involved to any great extent in policy-analytical work (that is, policy formulation, coordination, research and evaluation) or is committed to writing policy documents and performing other policy-related tasks.

Conclusion

In-house policy analysis is an important object of study. Even if civil servants are not the only actors engaged in policy analysis and external policy analytical activities have a bearing on agenda setting, policy formulation and other stages of the policy cycle, the ultimate practice of public policy remains located within the authoritative sphere of government. This chapter has presented the locus and modus of in-house policy analysis in the Belgian central and regional governments. It has described and analysed the way in which policy-analytical roles within departments and agencies are organised, which tasks civil servants perform when engaged in policy work, what resources they use for conducting policy analysis, and how they rate the policy-analytical capacity of their organisations.

The Belgian administrations do not have a long-standing tradition in locating policy analysis in distinct organisational units. Only the Flemish administration has in its move to agencification in the mid-2000s formally articulated policy formulation and policy evaluation as tasks to be performed by departments. The results of the survey confirm that in the Flemish administrations a substantive number of civil servants engaged in policy work attribute policy formulation, coordination and evaluation functions to their units. At the same time, as in the other administrations, policy-analytical tasks are dispersed over a relatively large number of civil servants whose policy-analytical tasks complement other duties.

When reviewing the results of the surveys in the different administrations, it is clear that a number of characteristics of policy-analytical work are widely shared in Belgium. A lot of policy work is devoted to writing policy-related documents of all kinds, ranging from strategy notes, to policy briefs, or notes to the ministerial cabinets. Civil servants also contribute to policy-analytical tasks such as providing legal and financial feasibility checks on policy proposals. In performing their policy-analytical tasks, civil servants in the different administrations make use of a variety of sources of information, and the use of search engines for garnering information is an indicator of the widespread use of this new kind of policy analytical heuristics. As to the search for and receipt of advice, all administrations predominantly look inwards instead of outwards. They predominantly consult their colleagues from their own units, other units within the same government, or across levels of government. The rather limited consultation of scientific actors is striking, and so is the relatively scarce use of evaluation reports.

In all administrations, there is some concern about the maintenance and strengthening of policy-analytical capacity. While there is an appreciation of the hierarchy's support for policy-analytical work, large numbers of civil servants across the different organisations agree that ministerial cabinets dominate the policy process and that this dominance is too strong. The reported insufficient interest in long-term issues is another sore point, given that large numbers of policy-engaged civil servants spend quite some time on firefighting and regret not having enough time to follow up scientific work. In the Flemish administration, it is moreover notable that answering parliamentary questions risks crowding out more essential policy-analytical work.

From the analysis it appears that there is still room for improving the scope and the depth of policy-analytical work. In addressing the dimensions of professional policy work that have occupied the international agenda for professional policymaking (Brans and Vancoppenolle, 2005), Belgian administrations are challenged to move ahead with outward- and forward-looking evaluation and evidence-based policy analysis. The surveys in the different administrations have indeed shown that in-house policy analysis is still very much inward-looking, that the long term aspects of policy work are frequently challenged, and that the relatively scarce deployment of evaluation and scientific research threatens to constrain the evidence base of policymaking.

References

Brans, M., De Peuter, B. and Ferraro, G. (2012) 'Policy work old and new: challenges to bureaucratic policy work as a craft', paper presented at the Organization Studies Summer Workshop, Rhodes, 24-26 May.

Brans, M. and Vancoppenolle, D. (2005) 'Policy-making reforms and civil service: an exploration of agendas and consequences', in M. Painter and J. Pierre (eds) *Challenges to state policy capacity: global trends and comparative perspectives*, Basingstoke: Palgrave Macmillan, 164-84.

Colebatch, H.K. and Radin, B.A. (2006) 'Mapping the work of policy', in H.K. Colebatch (ed) *The work of policy: an international survey*, Lanham, MD: Lexington Books, 217-26.

Halligan, J. (1995) 'Policy advice and the public sector', in B.G. Peters and D.T. Savoie (eds) *Governance in a changing environment*, Montreal: McGill-Queen's University Press, 138-72.

Lasswell, H.D. (1971) *A preview of policy sciences*, New York, NY: American Elsevier.

Meltsner, A.J. (1976) *Policy analysts in the bureaucracy*, Berkeley, CA: University of California Press.

Peters, B.G. (1989) *The politics of bureaucracy*, New York, NY: Longman.

Vancoppenolle, D. and Brans M. (2010) 'Een vergelijkende analyse van de beleidsinteracties van kabinetsmedewerkers en ambtenaren in de Vlaamse beleidsvorming', *Res Publica*, 52(4): 483-510.

Weimer, D.L. (1998) 'Policy analysis and evidence: a craft perspective', *Policy Studies Journal*, 26(1): 131-46.

FIVE

Local planning in Belgium: A myriad of policy styles?

Ellen Wayenberg, Min Reuchamps, Marine Kravagna and Catherine Fallon

What policy style(s) does local government display in Belgium? This seemingly straightforward question does not have an easy answer. After all, the country is renowned for its institutional complexity and thickness, two features that have a significant impact on local government's way of working. In the wake of state reforms, the federal government granted the three Belgian regions (Walloon, Flemish and Brussels) key competencies over the cities and municipalities standing on their territory (Deschouwer and Reuchamps, 2013; Reuchamps, 2013). In 2001, regions were even given powers over and above those granted in the basic local government legislation, regulating to a large extent local political and administrative institutions and practices. A new and influential layer of central government has thus been created: all regions have grasped their new powers to introduce policy tools and instruments on the local level, according to their own needs and policy orientation (Wayenberg et al, 2011). This federalisation process added diversity between cities and municipalities that were already very heterogonous in size, financial status and political dynamics, to name but a few of their basic characteristics (De Rynck and Wayenberg, 2013). As a result, local government in the three Belgian regions now operates under different regulatory frames.

This chapter explores whether local government in Belgium displays a specific style of policy analysis. To this end, we use a two-level comparative analysis that allows us to shed light on local policy analysis in the context of the specificity of the Belgium's regions. The first level is a comparison of the Flemish and the Walloon regions. The focus on them is not only a matter of size, as Flanders and Wallonia respectively count for 308 (52%) and 262 (45%) of the 589 Belgian municipalities, but also a matter of policy analysis. Indeed, they represent the country's two main administrative traditions, being located in the Dutch-speaking north and the French-speaking south. Both have also made use of their competency to legislate on local government's political and administrative institutions and practices, and have promulgated local government legislation to this end. That is not the case with the Brussels-Capital Region, which accounts for 19 municipalities (3%) still functioning according to the Belgian legislation of 1988 (De Rynck and Wayenberg, 2013). The case of Brussels will therefore not be covered by this chapter nor will the peculiar case of the nine German-speaking municipalities that are attached both to the Walloon Region and the German-speaking community (Bouhon et al, 2015).

As such, we aim at finding out which policymaking tools and instruments are currently in use at the local level and which are emerging, via a thorough document analysis of local government legislation in both regions. The second comparative level is a case study of two local governments with the aim of verifying the implementation of the new regional tools and instruments. Are these reforms actually embedded in local government practice, thus shaping local policy style? To this end, we consider one Flemish and one Walloon local government, Deinze and Gembloux respectively. These cities are quite similar in terms of their main institutional features: both are medium-sized, financially healthy and have been governed since 2006 by the same parties. They are neither well-known 'success stories' nor criticised as 'worst cases' as far as planning practice is concerned. Rather, they are supposed to be 'business as usual' stories that could provide meaningful insights regarding local policy analysis in Belgium. These two case studies are thus suitable to gather context-rich insights into local government's style(s) of policy analysis and the interrelations between local actors and the processes of governance. This data highlights any gaps between local practices and regional injunctions, as well as the differences between the two regions. Before turning to the two-level comparative analysis, we start by clarifying the policy-style concept that is central to our analysis.

Policy style and local government

Up until now, the concept of policy style has rarely been used as a heuristic tool to understand policy analysis in local government. Rather, it is commonly applied to the national level for comparing policy communities within as well as between political systems in terms of commonalities in their policymaking patterns (Richardson et al, 1982; Parsons, 1995; Knill and Tosun, 2008). The concept provides a simple and effective framework for comparison. An overview of the literature suggests that simplicity springs from the limited variance on standard operating procedure taken into account to grasp a government's policy style. The work of Richardson and colleagues seems to have set the tone in this regard (1982), promoting the style concept and serving as a starting-point for various typologies ever since. According to Richardson et al (1982), only two dimensions are needed to satisfy the concept's applicability. The first one covers how policymakers acknowledge societal issues and their approach to problem analysis. The second concerns their relative autonomy vis-à-vis other actors involved in policymaking and implementation. Do policymakers seek consensus among these parties or simply impose their decisions on them? Together, both dimensions give rise to a framework that has been used repeatedly to compare national governments according to their pattern of policymaking (Freeman, 1985; Bovens et al, 2001).

The effectiveness of the framework can be ascribed to its ability to identify a government's operating procedure from a policy-analytical point of view. According to the literature, there are several ways of performing policy work and each way can be associated with one or more specific clusters of activity that policy analysts perform. Clarifying as well as developing values and arguments is one of these widely recognised clusters. Typically, these activities are performed by policymakers who are primarily concerned with the social construction of policy problems, policy discourses and the politics of the policy process. In 2000, Radin labelled those policymakers as post-modern in their performance, a label that falls under the anticipatory style (2000). A second activity cluster is characterised by a reactive way of working, typical for policymakers who spend their time mainly on researching and analysing facts, causes and effects. At least to a large extent, they assume the world to be empirically knowable and measurable and that policy knowledge should and could be provided as complete and unbiased as possible, capable of withstanding scientific scrutiny. According to Thissen and Walker, these activities and assumptions typify traditional policy analysis (2013).

In addition these two activity clusters, that is to clarify/develop values and arguments and to research and analyse, four others are defined by Mayer and colleagues (2004). All of them can be associated with the operating procedures of Richardson's second dimension as they refer to interactions and power relations between government and other actors involved in policymaking. As mentioned earlier, a government can impose policy solutions in a top-to-down hierarchical style. Policymakers will then (have to) act strategically as well as design clear policy processes as main clusters of activity. Alternatively, a government can opt for a bottom-up inclusive and participatory style and seek consensus with other key parties involved. Policymakers' main cluster of activity will then (have to) consist of democratising policies and/or mediating between parties. As visualised in Table 5.1, each cluster can be related to a specific policy style. In association, they provide an understanding and comparison of the main governmental policy pattern(s).

Table 5.1: Policy styles and main clusters of policy-analytical activity

	Anticipatory To clarify/develop (new) values and arguments	Reactive To research, analyse and develop knowledge of problems and solutions
Consensus seeking To democratise policies and/or to mediate between parties involved in policymaking to unveil groups' standpoints and worldviews and to support mutual understanding	Post-modern	Communicative
Coercive To act strategically to integrate the interests of actors involved and/or to design clear policy processes	Strategic	Traditional

Source: Richardson et al (1982); Mayer et al (2004)

Applying this framework at the local level helps to reveal the diverse configurations of local actors and their impact on policy style. However, it cannot be applied without analysing the contextual conditions – quite important in policy analysis, particularly when the issue at stake is 'ambiguous' with no clear-cut, defined solution (Matland, 1995). The variety of local conditions in Belgium should therefore not be underestimated: the power and diversity of local (un)elected actors depend on long-term historical and institutional trends as well as on the recent remodelling of political forces, due to socioeconomic and demographic transformations. This variety is examined in more detail in the next section.

Local government in the federal state of Belgium

According to the Belgian constitution, local government can take whatever initiative it wants as long as it is beneficial to local interests and no other government has legal responsibility for the field of action concerned. As such, each local government can operate autonomously on its own territory, a principle that is institutionally reflected in the direct election of its legislative council. However, the Belgian reality of local policymaking is far from one of (full) local government autonomy and power. After all, throughout successive rounds of state reform, Belgium has evolved into a state of complexity with an additional governmental layer created and active ever since (Wayenberg et al, 2010). In particular, two types of sub-central non-local government have thus been installed: three regions on the one hand – the Brussels, Flemish and Walloon regions – as socioeconomic entities with competency over hard policy domains such as housing, transport and spatial planning, and three communities on the other – the Flemish-, French- and German-speaking communities – as language-based entities dealing more with soft policy fields such as education, culture and youth policy. Their respective territory does not fully coincide.[1] On top of this, there is no clear hierarchy of legal norms in the trade-off between federal government and regions/communities. Put differently, the latter cannot be overruled by their federal counterpart within their fields of competencies. In those fields, they act as the only national government while in other fields – including social and economic matters – policymaking is the result of their bargaining with federal government. From local government's point of view, the overall impact of Belgium's federalisation process is straightforward: a new layer of central government has thus been created as regions and communities have been steering their local counterparts in the respective territory- and person-related policy fields for which they hold competency. Apart from the resulting centralisation of the local sphere of action, the regions have also gradually been granted specific key competencies with regard to the local government system on their territory. These competencies include central supervision over local government (1980), the municipal fund (1988), inter-municipal cooperation (1993) and, most importantly, local government's basic legislation (2001), thus turning regions into Belgium's main central governments from the local point of view (De Rynck and Wayenberg, 2009).

In this chapter, the two cities selected as 'case studies', Deinze and Gembloux, are positioned in the framework presented above. To this end, each case study starts with the discussion of the major reforms that the regional government has introduced over the last years (first level) and that affect local policymaking. They include financial repercussions concerning the expenditure and revenue dimensions of local government operations, and structural ones dealing with the number, type and size of municipalities, quasi-municipalities and local special-purpose bodies. However, first and foremost, the chapter considers the reforms that have stimulated local elected councils and/or administrative units to adopt new or renewed ways of policymaking. These reforms are discussed through interviews with a selection of political and administrative policymakers of the two cities under study (second level). This allows an appreciation of the social embeddedness of these reforms as genuine instruments of local policy practice/style as well as the specific local issues these new tools may (or may not) address. The Flemish and Walloon cases are subsequently presented, followed by a thorough comparison to find out whether there is ground to assume a specific local style of policy analysis in Belgium.

Local policy analysis in Flanders

Regional setting

In Flanders, recent modernisation of local government is mainly the result of injunctions from the Flemish regional authority. As explained earlier, the latter gained key competencies vis-à-vis the local level during various rounds of Belgian state reform. And it has used these powers consistently to steer its local counterpart towards performing more efficiently and effectively, and with greater customer focus, within a (re-)new(-ed) public management (NPM). Over the years, strategic planning has been one of the Flemish government's main instruments to this end. Initially, in the early 1990s, planning was introduced as a prerequisite for Flemish subsidisation of local government in a select number of policy fields, including social, mobility and environmental policy. By the turn of the century, it had evolved into standard practice in practically every field of local policymaking, amounting to more than 30 different sectoral policy plans being drafted at the local level (Vlaamse Regering, 2006).

Repeatedly, Flemish local governments have complained about this practice resulting in too much 'planning burden'. In essence, their complaints are threefold (VVSG, 2006). First, they have criticised the high number of regional planning and reporting requirements imposed in a range of policy fields. In 2007, each local government was drafting up to 27 different policy plans, often forcing them also to adopt the Flemish intra-organisational structure (Dienst Wetsmatiging, 2007). Second, these requirements have often been criticised for being too detailed. In various fields, they leave little or no policy leeway for local government. The latter is thus forced to act as a regional agent in order not to be deprived of financial means that are locally deemed essential for any policymaking at all. Third and finally, the divergence among planning requirements causes local distress. These requirements differ substantially from one policy field to another with regard to – among other things – policy duration, result orientation and monitoring. And these sectoral differences hinder every local government in efforts to join up its plans.

Since the mid-1990s, subsequent Flemish governments acknowledged the local planning problems and each in turn took steps towards their remediation. On 20 June 1995, the first directly elected Flemish government took office. In its coalition agreement, this government expressed its intention to work with local government to achieve optimal intergovernmental relations (Vlaamse Regering, 1995). On 8 March 1999, it finally signed a pact with the local representative organisation to this effect. The pact contained 63 action points, including one to harmonise Flemish sectoral subsidisation vis-à-vis the local level. However, little implementation took place as the Flemish legislature ended a few months later. The divergent subsidisation requirements as well as their overall number were also at stake during the so-called core task debate for Flanders. This debate was launched by the newly installed Flemish government in 1999 (Vlaamse Regering, 1999). From the beginning, two questions were at the fore, that is, what tasks does the Flemish government have vis-à-vis the private sector and how should the governmental tasks be divided among the Flemish, provincial and local administrations as the three democratically elected layers of government? To deal with this second question, numerous intergovernmental debate groups were set up across all sectoral policy fields. Their activities resulted in the signing of the so-called 'core task agreement' on 25 April 2003 between the Flemish government and the provincial and local representative organisations. Among other actions, these parties thus agreed to make an inventory of all Flemish intergovernmental subsidies with a view to harmonising their requirements concerning sub-central planning and reporting as well as reducing their overall number. But again, this agreement ended in the second half of the Flemish legislative term and few concrete actions to lift the local planning burden were taken at that time.

The situation somewhat improved after the 2004 elections. A new Flemish government took office on 20 July 2004. In its coalition agreement, this government immediately announced an audit of its sectoral planning and reporting requirements vis-à-vis the local level with the purpose of simplifying and reducing them (Vlaamse Regering, 2004). To this end, two research reports were ordered and written, by academics and civil servants respectively. Both of them contained concrete recommendations to harmonise planning and reporting requirements across sectors or even abolish them altogether. Next to this, there was the critical report of the advisory Committee on Efficient and Effective Government that the Flemish government had installed in its endeavour to evolve into one of Europe's five top regions by 2020. The committee report made a clear plea for a drastic reduction in the number of sectoral planning and reporting requirements to an absolute minimum as well as for their mutual integration into an all-embracing legislative framework (Commissie Efficiënte en Effectieve Overheid, 2009). And precisely these ideas were central to the way in which the next Flemish government tackled the local planning burden.

This government took office on the 13 July 2009. In its coalition agreement, it clearly committed itself to unburdening its local counterparts from unnecessary planning and reporting (Vlaamse Regering, 2009). Central to this was the Flemish idea of a Policy and Management Cycle (PMC) in local government aligned to the six-year term of the latter. After all, that six-year cycle of planning, budgeting and reporting would encompass all local policy fields and objectives, thus reducing the necessity for and number of separate sectoral plans at the local level. Moreover, the Flemish government would restrain from excessive top-down interference in local government PMC and would confine its involvement to controlling outcomes. Finally, the accompanying planning and reporting requirements would apply to all policy fields, thus preventing their mutual divergence. In sum, the PMC planning reform holds the key to a lower local planning burden, at least from the Flemish point of view.

The PMC was legally enforced on 25 June 2010 (Vlaamse Regering, 2010). The Flemish government then altered the basic local government decree to require every municipality to adopt a six-year planning, budgeting and reporting cycle. However, this legislative step alone was deemed insufficient for any meaningful reform of local planning in Flanders. This was the view taken, among others, by the then Committee for Efficiency Gains in Local Government (CEGLG), a Flemish advisory committee including local representatives. In its view, the success of the PMC also relied on a drastic turnaround in Flemish subsidy practices. After all, the planning burden on local governments intrinsically springs from the numerous, detailed and divergent requirements of Flemish departments and agencies operating in accordance with central directives in various areas. There was a danger that the PMC reform might even increase the local burden by introducing yet another cycle of policy planning on top of all the rest, hence the CEGLG's urge to add a sectoral slant (Commissie Efficiëntiewinst voor de Lokale Besturen, 2010). Sensitive to this concern, the Flemish government drafted an Act on the local planning burden aimed at stipulating clear principles for future sectoral subsidisation. It took more than a year – until 15 July 2011 – before that second legislative step was taken (Vlaamse Regering, 2011). Notwithstanding various alterations to its principles, the Act was approved in parliament and the number of Flemish regulations within its scope were drastically reduced. Initially, the Flemish government intended to streamline 14 sets of sector-specific directives concerning local planning. Finally, only ten remained and were redrafted between November 2011 and September 2012. These Flemish regulations were thus integrated with the planning burden requirements before the local elections of October 2012 that signalled the start of the first six-year term of PMC implementation. In no particular order of importance, the areas of policy areas affected are sports, integration, urban affairs, developing aid, youth, welfare, culture, heritage, education and service economy.

What are the specific principles now guiding local planning reform in these fields (Dienst Wetsmatiging, 2010)? As noted earlier, the PMC places new planning, budgeting and reporting requirements on local government. These include drafting a six-year strategic policy plan and annual evaluation reports. All documents resulting from the PMC should serve local needs as well as local government applications for sector-specific subsidy. Separate local documents would undermine Flemish administrations' 'use of PMC' as the first principle embedded in the Act on the local planning burden. The second principle aims at 'more local autonomy'. Seemingly contradictory at first sight, the Act subscribes to the Flemish use of top-down subsidies for the purpose of achieving policy objectives. But in doing so, each Flemish objective should aim to grant local government enough leeway to align its intentions with specific local needs and objectives. After all, policy made at the local level ought to be local. Accordingly, the third principle of the Act requires the Flemish government to 'shift from input- to output- and outcome-oriented influence and control' at the local level. Consequently, a subsidising administration may regulate its local counterpart primarily in terms of local output and outcomes, but may no longer tie subsidies to specific local input actions, such as the appointment of an official with particular qualifications or the design of the local organisational structure. Local government has now been granted the full prerogative in such cases. However, the same cannot be said when it comes to the involvement of local stakeholders. While the fourth planning burden principle underlines 'the importance of local participation', it clearly preserves the Flemish prerequisite of requiring local government to account for the involvement of specific local stakeholders throughout the PMC. The fifth and final principle concerns 'co-financing'. The Flemish Government no longer has an obligation to cover all costs arising from the implementation of its policy objectives at the local level. Local government is now expected to invest up to the amount of any subsidy granted.

Box 5.1 lists the five principles of the Flemish Act on the local planning burden. All of them are instrumental in the quest towards greater policy integration and coordination at the local level. These targets are typical within the so-called post-NPM period, the ongoing era of administrative reform since the early 2000s.

The next section examines how local policymaking works in practice, using Deinze as an example of a city operating under the Flemish regulatory framework of local planning reform.

Box 5.1: Principles of Flemish subsidisation according to the 2011 local planning burden Act

Use of the PMC

More local autonomy

A shift from input-oriented to output- and outcome-oriented influence and control

The importance of local participation

Co-financing

The case of Deinze

Deinze is a medium-sized city of approximately 30,000 inhabitants, located in the province of East Flanders near the provincial capital of Ghent. The city has no specific problems or exceptional assets and does not deserve specific attention by the regional authorities, which is why we have chosen it as a case study. The local politico–administrative structure is large enough to require efficient forms of organisation. Deinze is governed by a coalition of Christian Democrats (CD&V) and Liberals (Open-VLD+) that was re-elected in October 2012 for a second term. Shortly after the elections, the PMC was introduced locally as required by the Flemish local government decree. With a view to thoroughly canvassing the local area as part of the PMC, the city and the public centre for social welfare jointly organised a survey of 5,000 inhabitants.[2] To complement this exercise, several citizen focus groups took part in the project *Als je 't mij vraagt* ('If you ask me'). The city appointed an extra staff member to carry out these initiatives. It also refrained from hiring consultants for other stages of the PMC, motivated by a willingness to get to know and work with the planning tools that the Flemish government had introduced locally. As such, an intense but very informative consultation period took place lasting over a year and ending successfully on 19 December 2013 when the city council approved the resulting multi-annual policy plan and a balanced budget for 2014-19 (Stad Deinze, 2014a, 2014b). The plan contains 13 policy goals. All are embedded in various programmes and action plans grounded in information that was gathered via the canvassing exercise. They all reflect Flemish policy priorities and were approved by the city administration, which added more detail into the PMC documents than was legally required. After all, these plans and reports form the basis of Deinze's future and deserve to be fully evidence-based.

What policy style(-s) did Deinze demonstrate during the process of drafting its policy plan and budget? By approaching its citizens through a survey and focus groups, the city initially aimed to expand its knowledge of its inhabitants' needs and desires. Launching (new) policy ideas was not a primary objective. First and foremost, the city took a reactive stance and looked backwards in order to better understand what was already 'alive and kicking' in its own community. In retrospect, the survey and focus group results were not really surprising. As the mayor put it:

> "The answers affirmed that we – as policymakers of Deinze – basically want to move in the same direction as our citizens. For example, we have wanted a cultural centre on our territory for a long time now and clearly, that same desire lives among our citizens. Mobility is another issue that really concerns people but of course, we already knew that as well."

Nevertheless, both of these exercises were locally regarded as very valuable, not least because of their ability to temporarily bridge the gap between policymakers and citizens. The focus groups turned out to be particularly instrumental in this regard. Eleven focus groups were organised between February and May 2013. Each focus group gathered six to 10 residents to jointly discuss and propose innovative solutions to improve the city's way of working. One area singled out for improvement was the city's e-services. Although it was well known that the service was little used, the reasons for this were not fully understood. By getting several groups to focus on this issue, the city actually gained in more ways than one. As well as gathering ideas about how to make its e-services more citizen-friendly and accessible, it could use the focus groups as a test-bed for the workability of the proposed solutions, which passed the first – and critical – customer test. Of course, not all policy ideas launched via the survey and focus groups were adopted by the city. In the words of the city manager:

> "Some ideas – such as digging a tunnel under the town centre to solve the mobility problem – might be interesting but they are just too expensive and not feasible to realise. And finally, it is our job to make ends meet."

By explicitly opting for dialogue with its citizens, the city had more time to explain its policy standpoints, which in turn meant that citizens could gain greater understanding of (the limitations of) its policy work. Overall, the city clearly adopted a communicative stance during the first stage of drafting an all-round and financially feasible policy plan for the upcoming legislature. It actively researched and analysed its citizens' needs and desires, and combined this with a consensual way of working by opting for negotiation and dialogue instead of just unilaterally translating the knowledge gained into a series of goals and actions.

However, throughout the policy implementation period, the city also showed signs of operating according to another style. The mayor's attitude towards the so-called 'blue-bike' project is indicative of this. Deinze had an initiative of renting bicycles daily at a very low rate in order to reduce the number of cars passing through the city. A great supporter of the project, the mayor admitted:

> "One day, I counted the number of people that I still would have to convince to start cycling in our city, given the fact that I only have five more years to go. More than 150 a day. Of course, that is not possible. But that does not stop me from promoting this idea another 200 or even 300 times, at every possible occasion. Because that is what you have to do: you have to believe and defend your beliefs wherever and whenever you can."

Here the mayor explicitly takes on an anticipatory approach in addition to a merely reactive one. According to the city manager, this stance is typical:

> "Local politicians are much more citizen-focused. And that is common practice. After all, politicians are judged by the citizen whilst we are not. And so, they are the ones having to explain the choices that are locally made".

But for their part, local administrators do not just stand aside but often play a crucial part in preparing political speeches and making sure that policy ideas are highlighted at the right time and place. In short, they turn out to be indispensable to the implementation process once ideas have been adopted. And in Deinze, this strategic style increasingly complemented a primarily communicative way of working once the planning process began to evolve from the kick-off phase into its current executive stage.

Local policy analysis in Wallonia

Regional setting

In 2004, the Walloon government defined the conditions of local governance in a unique document, the Code of Local Democracy and Decentralisation (*Code de la démocratie locale et de la décentralisation*, or CDLD), which applies to the organisation of municipalities and of provinces, the designation of governing bodies and the management of local policies. Matagne et al (2011) observe a twofold change stemming from the introduction of the code. On the one hand, it increases local authorities' powers of intervention. On the other hand, it opens up the local governance to the citizens and civil society. Thus, the candidate with the highest number of votes in the list with the highest number of votes among the lists of the governing coalition is directly elected as mayor (CDLD, art. 1123-4, par. 1, al. 1er). A new principle also appears, that of 'constructive mistrust', which reinforces the democratic accountability of the executive: one (or more) member of the executive body can change during the legislature on at the local council's request. Finally, the president of the public social welfare centre (CPAS) acts as a member of the local executive, which supports an increase in transversal policies. Matagne et al (2011) present these transformations as a tendency towards a stronger democracy of and for the public, with a decrease in political parties' power.

In recent decades, the Walloon government has supported the implementation of several new policy tools at the local level, each of them imposing a strategic and participatory implementation pattern. Among them we analyse the Communal Plan for Rural Development (*Plan communal de développement durable*, or PCDR) and the Transversal Strategic Plan (*Plan stratégique transversal*, or PST), which contribute to a new framework for local policy analysis in Wallonia. These new instruments (none of them are compulsory) refer to different sectors that usually vary a lot as far as their level of influence over local government is concerned. Nevertheless, they share three important characteristics: they are bottom–up and based on a strategic diagnosis and analysis of the current situation. They are innovative in the sense that they emphasise communal strategic autonomy and support local strategic competencies in policymaking. But the local autonomy is very narrowly framed by the regional government, which defines precisely the local procedural approaches for accessing financial resources, while leaving room for manoeuvre for the municipality to allocate resources to specific, locally defined projects. We propose to use these new tools to highlight the governmental style in Wallonia and to analyse our local case study, the city of Gembloux. This leads to the following twofold question: do these tools influence the local policy style and how do local policymakers and administrations appreciate these new tools with regard to the main characteristics mentioned above?

In 1991, Wallonia adopted egislation intended to support local development policies in a participatory approach that established the *Plan communal de développement durable* (Godart and Deconinck, 2003). The PCDR comprises a set of coordinated development and planning actions undertaken in rural areas, whose operations are financially supported by the region (up to 80%).[3] The strategic planning (with a vision of up to 10 years) derives from a third-party diagnosis report and thorough public consultation, and establishes a local development coordinated strategy based on a deep analytical, prospective and shared diagnosis of the territory. The main driver behind the definition of the projects to be launched – with large regional subsidies – is the local commission for rural development *(Commission locale de développement rural*, or CLDR). This group comprises 10 to 30 inhabitants representing different political, economic, socio-professional and cultural sectors and backgrounds. Its mission is to prepare the diagnosis, produce the plan and implement the different projects, with the support of a technical designer. The PCDR dynamics rely strongly on an ascending participatory process of co-construction with the stakeholders and inhabitants, as well as the involvement of technical experts. Management of the CLDR must be outsourced to a regional company specialising in social intervention. This instrument has only marginally been modified since 1991 and is still very important for local policy analysis.

In 1999, the regional government presented a new strategic plan, entitled Contract for the Future of Wallonia (*Contrat d'avenir pour la Wallonie*), developing a strategic vision for the economic redeployment of the region (Decoster et al, 2003). As a consequence, in 2003, local authorities were required to define their own local Contract for the Future (Van Cauwenberghe, 2003): each entity is asked to develop a strategic vision with reference to the regional priorities. This proposition was met with little support. What the local authorities were waiting for was a new local strategic management system, which would not involve the heavy or complex planning required by the Contract for the Future.

In 2009, the Walloon government launched a new tool for local authority management: the Transversal Strategic Plan (*Plan stratégique transversal*, PST). This contains the global policy strategy of the commune (that is the municipality) and aims to create a better culture of planning and evaluation (Union des villes et des communes de Wallonie, 2011; Boverie et al, 2013a).[4] The regional minister in charge of the local bodies proposed developing a pilot action with voluntary local authorities, which were invited to initiate a local planning strategy based on production of a local diagnostic and the definition of transversal local priorities of action. The project aims to establish such an approach for the next local term (2018-24). Half of the communes (132) showed an interest, and 24 were selected to receive specific support during the pilot phase and to test the system. They were asked to finalise their PST and to make the document public, as well as to take part in the development of common tools and management systems to support the new dynamics of policy analysis, implementation, follow-up and evaluation. The diagnostic was mostly written by the local administration with the use of data from a new website designed by the Walloon Institute of Evaluation, Foresight and Statistics.

This strategic tool, close to the Flemish local planning and reporting cycle, is prepared by the local authorities and the local administration in the year after the local elections, with very limited public participation. It combines in the same document internal components and resources (local administration) and the strategies for local policies for the next six years, presenting a comprehensive overview of all local actions and policies, and other strategic or sectoral local plans. At the core of any PST is the political project of the political authorities, which is supposed to be in line with the local diagnostic. These priorities are translated into operational targets and relevant resources.

The writing of the plan itself is based on the involvement of the local executive body (the College) and of the local administration. The political authorities are responsible for drafting the main strategic goals (with reference to questions such as 'What do we want to achieve in the next six years?') and to translate them in relation to available resources – not only local resources and competencies within the administration itself, but also external subsidies and support from local partnerships with public or privates bodies. The plan must translate the political vision into operational priorities and concrete actions, taking into consideration the limited resources available (reality principles) and the possible partnerships to be established.

What is new is the internal side of the plan: besides the political projects, the administration itself can design its own strategic vision, in order to manage the requirements imposed by the political authorities as well as to develop modern modes of management. This part of the PST is often presented as a possible 'contract' between the administration and the political authorities: even if it still remains an informal contract, it reconfigures the action of the administration, its forms of cooperation and the modalities of accountability with regular reporting of the achievement of the PST.

In 2013, two new regional laws reformed the status and modes of action of heads of the local administration.[5] They reinforced the role of the head of administration as general manager (director-general, DG) and head of local staff: their higher status was confirmed by a major salary increase (Durviaux and Fisse, 2015, p 71). These laws launched a compulsory reform of local administration's top management by changing the status of high local civil servants and by redefining the relationship between the local authority and its administration thanks to the setting up of new management tools (Boverie et al, 2013b).

The objective of this reform is often presented as the 'modernisation of the management of local administrations' (Walloon parliament, 2012-2013, p 2), translated into concrete tools for a more transversal and project-based governance. The DG is required to produce a written document for the legislature – the statement of mission (*lettre de mission*) – outlining how the political objectives will translate into strategic guidelines, operational aims and projects. This document combines an account of strategic policy and an annual evaluation of the DG's objectives with a description of the main political priorities of the College and its own resources and mission. For his part, the DG has to produce a performance contract (*contrat d'objectifs*), which presents his vision for the operationalisation of the political mandate and details of concrete actions arising from his strategy. The aim of this 'translation process' is to enable better operationalisation by the administration of the political will. By doing so, the administration remains the executor of the political will. The goals it has to achieve are clear and feasible and the political authority can have a better view of the degree of implementation of its goals. This concept of contract is quite new for the DG and is a sign of greater cooperation between the political bodies and the administration (through the DG). In practice, very few such contracts have been completed and signed so far.

Moreover, the reform has resulted in the establishment of an executive committee (*comité de direction*) in charge of organisational and operational issues, ensuring transversal communication between services and direct contact with the local authorities. It is also charged with ensuring that new human resources (HR) management tools are developed (such as organigrams).

Last but not least, the head of the local administration should ensure that the local public authorities' actions are regularly evaluated, in order to check the quality of management and the degree of realisation of missions and objectives. Evaluations are organised by the political authorities with the support of external experts.[6] If the evaluation is negative or 'unfavourable', the local council can propose to end the contract with the DG on the basis of professional ineptitude (Durviaux and Fisse, 2015, pp 143-4).

With regard to financial resources, the financial head of administration is obliged to give legal advice on every project with a budget of more than €22,000[7] and on the budgetary aspects of the PST; advice is given at the planning stage, making the projections of the political strategic priorities more realistic. This reform gives the financial head a more active role, transforming the local politico-administrative equilibrium. It is in light of these changes that we study the local policy style in Gembloux.

The case of Gembloux

Among the 262 Walloon communes, Gembloux is a medium-sized municipality with over 25,000 inhabitants, a steadily rising population that increased by 25% from 2000 to 2010. It is a university town, in a rural area, situated between Namur and Brussels. Its increase in size and importance, coupled with the growing complexity of local matters, has left the local authorities facing new challenges such as mobility, land use and impoverishment in the inner centre. It has therefore implemented the three regionals instruments described earlier.

Gembloux adopted a PCDR in 2005 in order to identify and meet the needs of its residents through citizen involvement. The input of inhabitants and stakeholders, as well as the outcomes, were considered to be great achievements. Local stakeholders and citizens were very receptive to the implementation of the PCDR, and the process was characterised by a lack of politicisation. As one of the aldermen stated:

> 'We have at the participatory level quite some tools where citizens participate in function of their interest but also the associations, lobbies, and so on. This works pretty well because this is not at all politicised or almost not politicised.'

The local authorities had introduced participation mechanisms in many areas (such as schools management, social policies and territory planning), but none of them involved the same co-construction dynamics that occurred in the PCDR.

Local authorities seem therefore to have integrated into their policymaking the consensus-seeking style of this tool. Nevertheless, the process was not without its challenges: chiefly, this type of participation is time-consuming. The DG noted that: "This is really, really time-consuming to implement. The public consultation of all the villages took us two years. And for little impact on the population". The local authorities were also critical of the fact that the PCDR suffers from inflexibility and a lack of adaptability to an evolving context, especially when the slow pace of the procedure implies that the planned projects need several years to come to fruition. However, Gembloux intends to reiterate the process, which suggests that the potential subsidies, the technical support provided by the region and the participatory and anticipatory dynamics of the PCDR overcome its weaknesses.

Gembloux was also a candidate to be a pilot for the development of a PST (2013–18). Compared with the PCDR, the commune had more freedom to develop the PST. Gembloux used the services of an external consultant for the methods but the content was produced by the local public servants and the political actors themselves. The commune could really adapt the PST to its own vision, and it decided to match the PST to its statement of local policy *(déclaration de politique communale)*, the roadmap agreed by the coalition partners for the six-year term. The compulsory reform of the administration had the effect of formalising existing practice. Limited to organisational issues, the reform reaffirmed the relationship between political and administrative authorities, allowing some room for management by the DG while retaining the decision-making powers of the political authorities. The administration was already organised on the basis of specialised areas whose heads met regularly, forming the executive committee. The DG has to play more of a coordination and management role, but his or her vision of the way the commune should function also has a great influence on the communication between the political and administrative authorities.

The transversal dimension of the PST is recognised and supported by both the political and administrative actors, but their perception of its added value differs somewhat. From the political point of view, the PST is a transversal, complete, flexible, evolving and very useful tool that enables the commune to clearly set priorities while taking the budgetary dimension into account. For the administration, the PST did not bring much added value. While the idea behind the PST is to urge communes to adopt a transversal and strategic vision, Gembloux had already embraced this logic when it gained ISO certification from the International Organization for Standardization in the 2000s. For this reason, the administration perceived the PST as the compulsory duplication of work that did not address the real need, that is, the lack of communication between the political authorities and the administration as well as within the administration. Nevertheless, the PST introduced an evaluation component as well as a new procedure for long-term analysis in resource management and budgeting, forcing the commune to choose its goals for the coming three years.

The case of Gembloux also reveals an increase in the complexity of local responsibilities and the importance of qualified and skilled staff to address this complexity. The ability of the commune to hire professionals such as lawyers and architects for specific areas of activity while maintaining transversal contacts and insight is critical. The administration has a duty to carry out the strategic planning function using the regional tools, so the skills of its personnel are as important as the tools. Technical support and HR development are needed to help it gather the necessary competencies for planning and managing more complex projects.

The clear common goal of these – relatively new – tools is to help the communes to face the growing complexity of their jurisdiction through a strategic approach. However, the participatory planning tool (PCDR) has a patent disadvantage: the slow pace and cumbersome nature of procedures and regional control, as well as the amount of human and financial resources needed to develop and follow up such a strategic, bottom-up, diagnosis-based approach. In the light of the case study of Gembloux, the contrast between regional embedded local policies and pure local policies seems to be salient, the latter being achieved much faster but also involving smaller budgetary items and consequently less structural, as it was put at the fore for the PCDR larger projects. With the two managerial reforms (PST and the 2013 law on the status of heads of staff), the region also tends to impose new policy processes at the local level, with stricter budgetary control, a more strategic management style and a more transversal approach. Evaluation is also being introduced at the local level (with reference to the evaluation of PST and of heads of staff themselves).

Conclusion

To explore local policy planning in Belgium, this chapter has focused on the country's two largest regions – Flanders and Wallonia respectively. The Flemish and Walloon regional governments have opted to regulate local planning differently. Their central rules and regulations frame local governments' adoption and implementation of a policy plan, but they are not crucial to this end. Indeed, and put differently, local government in both regions still have considerable leeway to decide on specific ways of working when dealing with the needs and desires of its environment and citizens, and involving other local actors. The former may take an anticipatory or reactive approach while the latter may adopt a consensus-seeking or coercive stance. This leads us to distinguish four policy styles, whereby local government can plan in a post-modern (that is anticipatory and consensus-seeking), communicative (that is reactive and consensus-seeking), strategic (that is anticipatory and coercive) and traditional (that is reactive and coercive) way. These planning styles are not mutually exclusive, as both cases studies have illustrated.

Deinze and Gembloux, which are supposed to be 'business as usual' stories, provide meaningful insights regarding local policy analysis in Belgium. Their different regional frameworks show how municipalities may face regional intervention and the imposition of requirements at the same time as acquiring the ability to broaden their scope of action. Greater breadth of action and more complex policy fields call for higher levels of competence in local administration. In the current times of budget restrictions, especially in the case of small municipalities, these conditions are likely to set a trend for the pooling of relevant competencies across municipalities as well as the reinforcement of networks with surroundings communes.

Our case study of Deinze shows that the city initially chose a communicative style but consciously opted to complement it with a more strategic way of working in the later executive phases of the planning process. Clearly, this observation points to Flemish local government's capacity and flexibility when it comes to analysing policy. Deinze has shown to deal with its environment in an anticipatory as well as a reactive way and to involve citizens in a consensus-seeking as well as a more coercive fashion. This finding urges us to extend our typology of policy styles. The case of Deinze illustrates the necessity to consider at least one combination type of communicative and strategic policy style in order to empirically grasp planning practice.

In Wallonia, the government has established different tools outlining different policy styles. Two of these tools have been used in Gembloux. With the introduction of PCDR, policy content is mainly co-constructed by the non-political actors, on the basis of a thorough diagnosis of the state of affairs in the local environment and an anticipatory approach defining the long-term objectives as a ten-year vision. The PCDR reveals a consensus-seeking and anticipatory approach that is valued by the local authorities: this style, and the participatory dynamics involved, were fruitful but considered by the local authorities to be very time-consuming. The other main tool is the more recent PST, a comprehensive tool linking ambitious strategies to specific actions. In terms of policy style – designing the policy process without involving citizens – it may be regarded as coercive, and it aligns local policy analysis with a process-oriented style. Yet, it can be argued that it has more to do with rationalisation of implementation (with regard to the means of action) and with the modernisation of local public services than with actual definition of policies. The PST focuses chiefly on the implementation of policy goals by translating them into operational actions and on their assessment and adjustment in line with available means and resources. This new tool, proposed by the regional authorities to support local reforms in policy style, suggests a more coercive policy style.

The insights from the two local case studies reveal the importance of the regional frame, which provides opportunities and constraints for policy, as well as the local autonomy remaining under that frame. This study has shown that there are possibilities for a myriad of policy-analytical planning styles at Belgian's local level, worthy of further research and exploration. The case studies lead us to two new branches in the development of a policy analysis framework. First, proximity at the local level between political authorities, administrations and citizens should be considered, specifically to enrich the explanatory potential of a framework. Second, the local level lends itself in particular to the transversal policy approach, where policy analysis in different sectors and with different tools reveals a mix of styles within the same political administrative setting. This typifies local policy analysis regimes.

Finally, policy styles should give greater attention to relations with higher authorities; in Flanders and Wallonia there appears to be a trend for regional authorities to take back the reins and reduce local autonomy by imposing on local authorities new policy styles in more policy domains and areas of competency, with a view to modernising local government and controlling resources. However, even though their functioning is largely constrained by regulations common to every municipality, each commune is a unique entity in itself, with its own traditions, rules and actors, and consequently with the means to adapt regional policy tools to the local context in a style of its own choice.

Notes

1   In Flanders, region and community have been merged. The German-speaking municipalities are part of the Walloon Region for policy matters under the competency of the regions. In Brussels, the Flemish and French Communities are responsible for local issues in their own community, except for those issues that affect both language communities, in which case a Joint Community Commission has competency).

2   There is a public centre for social welfare in every Belgian municipality. It provides social support and fights poverty.

3   To date, the PCDR is not a compulsory tool for the Walloon communes; so far, 92 have adopted a PCDR out of a total of 124 rural communes. More information about the workings of PCDRs is available at www.pcdr.be/operation-de-developpement-rural-odr (accessed on 6 February 2013).

4   The first such PSTs were adopted in 2012 by 24 pilot communes for the 2012-18 legislature.

5   Regional law of 18 April 2013 (*Décret du 18 avril 2013 modifiant certaines dispositions du Code de la démocratie locale et de la décentralisation*) and a second regional law of 18 April 2013 (*Décret du 18 avril 2013 modifiant certaines dispositions de la loi du 8 juillet 1976 organique des centres publics d'action sociale*).

6   Decree of the Walloon government of 11 July 2013 (*Arrêté du Gouvernement wallon du 11 juillet 2013 fixant les règles d'évaluation des emplois de directeur général, directeur général adjoint et directeur financier communaux*), art. 4, § 6.

7   CDLD, art. L1124-40, § 1er, 3°.

References

Bouhon, F., Niessen, C. and Reuchamps, M. (2015) 'La Communauté germanophone après la sixième réforme de l'état: état des lieux, débats et perspectives', *Courrier hebdomadaire du CRISP*, no. 2266-2267.

Bovens, M., Hart, P. and Peters, B.G. (eds) (2001) *Success and failure in public governance*, Cheltenham: Edward Elgar.

Boverie, M., Maitre, A. and Van Driessche, L. (2013a) 'Gouvernance – fiche 2 – le PST: programme stratégique transversal communal', in *Focus sur la commune – 161 fiches pour une bonne gestion communale*, Namur: Union des Villes et Communes de Wallonie.

Boverie, M., Maitre, A. and Van Driessche, L. (2013b) 'Gouvernance – fiche 4 – les nouveaux principes de gouvernance locale en Wallonie – la réforme des grades légaux', in *Focus sur la commune – 161 fiches pour une bonne gestion communale*, Namur: Union des Villes et Communes de Wallonie.

Commissie Efficiënte en Effectieve Overheid (2009) *Een slagkrachtige overheid in Vlaanderen*, Brussels: Commissie Efficiënte en Effectieve Overheid.

Commissie Efficiëntiewinst voor de Lokale Besturen (2010) *Rapport met aanbevelingen*, Brussels: Commissie Efficiëntiewinst voor de Lokale Besturen.

Decoster D.P., Fontaine, P., Niarchos, C., Piraux, J., Rosinski, Z., Roufosse, C. and Vissers, F. (2003) *Vers des contrats d'avenir locaux. Elaborer et réussir sa stratégie de développement communal*, Brussels and Liège: ULG-IGEAT.

De Rynck, F. and Wayenberg, E. (2009) 'Local government in Flanders, Brussels and Wallonia. Towards more convergence or divergence in Belgian's local government systems?', in E. Page and M. Goldsmith (eds) *Central and Local Government Relations*, London: Sage Publications, 14-29.

De Rynck, F. and Wayenberg, E. (2013) 'Hoofdstuk 7. De lokale besturen', in A. Hondeghem, W. Van Dooren, F. De Rynck, B. Verschere and S. Op de Beeck (eds) *Handboek bestuurskunde*, Bruges: Vanden Broele, 191-230.

Deschouwer, K. and Reuchamps, M. (2013) 'The Belgian federation at a crossroad', *Regional & Federal Studies*, 23(3): 261-70.

Dienst Wetsmatiging (2007) *Administratieve lastenmeting planverplichtingen lokale besturen: finaal rapport*, Brussels: Vlaamse Overheid.

Dienst Wetsmatiging (2010) *Implementatietraject kaderdecreet planlasten voor lokale besturen*, Brussels: Vlaamse Overheid.

Durviaux, A.L. and Fisse, D. (2015) *Droit de la fonction publique locale. Bruxelles, Flandre, Wallonie*, Brussels: Larcier.

Dyson, K. (1982) 'West Germany: the search for a rationalist consensus', in J. Richardson (ed) *Policy styles in Western Europe*, London: Allen & Unwin, 17-46.

Freeman, G.P. (1985) 'National styles and policy sectors: explaining structured variation', *Journal of Public Policy*, 5(4): 467-96.

Godart, M.F. and Deconinck, M. (2003) 'Développement territorial en milieu rural: quelques exemples en région wallonne', *Revue d'économie régionale et urbaine*, 5: 909-24.

Knill, C. and Tosun, J. (2008) 'Policy making', in D. Caramani (ed) *Comparative politics*, Oxford: Oxford University Press, 495-519.

Matagne, G., Radoux, E. and Verjans, P. (2011) 'La composition du collège communal après la réforme du Code wallon de la démocratie locale', *Courrier hebdomadaire du CRISP*, no. 2094.

Matland, R.E. (1995) 'Synthesizing the implementation literature: the ambiguity-conflict model of policy implementation', *Journal of Public Administration Research and Theory*, 5(2): 145-74.

Mayer, I.S., Van Daalen, C.E. and Bots, P.W.G. (2004) 'Perspectives on policy analysis: a framework for understanding and design', *International Journal Technology, Policy and Management*, 4(1): 169-91.

Parsons, W. (ed) (1995) *Public policy*, Aldershot: Edward Elgar.

Radin, B.A. (ed) (2000) *Beyond Machiavelli: policy analysis comes of age*, Washington, DC: Georgetown University Press.

Reuchamps, M. (2013) 'The current challenges of Belgian federalism and the sixth reform of the state', in A. López-Basaguren and L. Escajedo San-Epifanio (eds) *The ways of federalism in Western countries and the horizons of territorial autonomy in Spain*, Heidelberg: Springer, 375-92.

Richardson, J., Gustafsson, G. and Jordan, G. (1982) 'The concept of policy style', in J. Richardson (ed) *Policy styles in Western Europe*, London: Allen & Unwin, 1-16.

Stad Deinze (2014a) *Financiële nota 2014-2019*, Deinze: Stad Deinze.

Stad Deinze (2014b) *Meerjarenplanning 2014-2019*, Deinze: Stad Deinze.

Thissen, W.A.H. and Walker, W.E. (eds) (2013) *Public policy analysis. New developments*, Delft: Springer.

Union des Villes et Communes de Wallonie (2011) 'Le programme stratégique transversal communal (PST) Une démarche stratégique pour les villes et communes', *Mouvement Communal*, 863 (hors-série).

Van Cauwenberghe, J.-C. (2003) 'Préface', in D.-P. Decoster, P. Fontaine, C. Niarchos, J. Piraux, Z. Rosinski, C. Roufosse and F. Vissers (eds) *Vers des contrats d'avenir locaux. Élaborer et réussir sa stratégie de développement communal*, Brussels and Liège: ULG-IGEAT.

Van Overmeire, K. (2013) 'La situation financière des communes wallonnes', *Mouvement communal*, 6: 21-26.

Vlaamse Regering (1995) *De Vlaamse Regering 1995-1999. Bakens voor de 21ste eeuw*, Brussels: Vlaamse Overheid.

Vlaamse Regering (1999) *De Vlaamse Regering 1999-2004. Een nieuw project voor Vlaanderen*, Brussels: Vlaamse Overheid.

Vlaamse Regering (2004) *De Vlaamse Regering 2004-2009, Vertrouwen geven, verantwoordelijkheid nemen*, Brussels: Vlaamse Overheid.

Vlaamse Regering (2006) *Inventaris Vlaamse regering planningslasten lokale besturen en provincies*, Brussels: Vlaamse Regering.

Vlaamse Regering (2009) *De Vlaamse Regering 2009-2014. Een daadkrachtig Vlaanderen in beslissende tijden. Voor een vernieuwende, duurzame en warme samenleving*, Brussels: Vlaamse Overheid.

Vlaamse Regering (2010) 'Besluit van de Vlaamse Regering van 25 juni 2010 betreffende de beleids- en beheerscyclus van de gemeenten, de provincies en de openbare centra voor maatschappelijk welzijn', *Belgisch Staatsblad*, 7 October.

Vlaamse Regering (2011) 'Decreet van de Vlaamse Regering van 15 juli 2011 houdende vaststelling van de algemene regels waaronder in de Vlaamse Gemeenschap en het Vlaamse Gewest periodieke plan- en rapporteringsverplichtingen aan lokale besturen kunnen worden opgelegd', *Belgisch Staatsblad*, 11 August.

VVSG (Association of the Flemish Municipalities) (2006) *Inventaris plannen lokale besturen*, Brussels: VVSG.

Wayenberg, E., De Rynck, F., Steyvers, K. and Pilet, J.-B. (2010) 'Belgium: a tale of regional divergence', in F. Hendriks, A. Lidstrom and J. Loughlin (eds) *The Oxford handbook of local and regional democracy in Europe*, Oxford: Oxford University Press, 71-95.

Walloon parliament (2012-2013) *Projet de décret modifiant certaines dispositions du Code de la démocratie locale et de la décentralisation*, Exposé des motifs, Parl. w., sess. ord. 2012-2013, n°744/1.

SIX

Policy analysis in the Belgian legislatures: the marginal role of a structurally weak parliament in a partitocracy with no scientific and political tradition of policy analysis

Lieven De Winter and Wouter Wolfs

This chapter analyses the use of policy advice of the federal Chamber of Representatives (*Kamer van Volksvertegenwoordigers/Chambre des représentants*) as well as two regional assemblies, the Flemish Parliament (*Vlaams Parlement*) and the Walloon Parliament (*Parlement wallon*). Their main duties are to co-legislate and scrutinise their respective executives. This chapter analyses the role of parliaments in shaping public policy as well as its tools to feed the evidence base of political debates about policy choices. The chapter begins with some methodological remarks. It sketches the role of parliamentary committees and MPs and the constraints and political factors that influence the effectiveness of MPs and parliaments as agents of public policy within the context of partitocratic governance. As to the instruments that are developed to gain relevant expertise, the chapter analyses the functioning of parliamentary committees and hearings in the garnering and use of policy expertise, as well as the in-house resources MPs have at their disposal, individually and collectively, to increase the research and evidence base of their interventions. In-house resources comprise individual collaborators of MPs, legislative research staff, the administration of parliament and para-parliamentary agencies. The chapter also touches on the external expertise provided to MPs by the study units of political parties and ministerial cabinets, but these are discussed in more detail in Chapters Three and Eight.

Conceptual and methodological remarks

The interviewees in our study were given a general definition of policy analysis relevant to parliament: all information (based on facts, research, expertise/expert opinions, stakeholder opinions, media reporting, and so on) relevant to the legislative and oversight role of Belgian parliaments, produced for/by individual MPs, parliamentary groups, and parliament as a whole.

Case selection and period

Even though there are seven legislative assemblies at the federal and regional/ community level, the study focuses on policy analysis from 1995 to 2015 in three legislative assemblies only, that is, the most important federal, Flemish and French-speaking administrations. At the federal level, it analyses the Chamber of Representatives, but not the Senate, given the fact that the latter has been deprived of considerable power and influence since 1995, and in 2014 lost all political significance. At the regional level, it considers the Flemish parliament, that is, the merged assembly of the Flemish Region and Flemish Community. On the French-speaking side, the study focuses on the Walloon rather than the Brussels parliament or the assembly of the Federation Wallonia-Brussels (French Community) because of the hybrid nature of the latter two. Neither does the study consider the assembly of the German-speaking community, given its small size and the fact that it operates on a part-time basis only.

Data collection

The authors conducted face-to-face interviews with the political secretaries of all parliamentary parties in the Chamber of Representatives and Flemish and Walloon parliaments. In addition, a number of in-house and para-parliamentary bodies involved in the provision of policy advice were interviewed in each legislature. In total, the interviews covered 10 parliamentary group secretaries and six officials in the federal chamber, all the seven parliamentary group secretaries as well as four officials of the Flemish parliament, and all the four parliamentary group secretaries and one official of the Walloon parliament. The 32 interviews were conducted inside the respective parliamentary buildings.

With regard to the second main source of information, that is, recorded parliamentary outputs, the authors examined annual parliamentary activity reports, as well as the activity reports of specific intra- and para-parliamentary bodies, focusing on the most recent complete legislative term.

Comparisons

We sometimes make comparisons over time, to avoid bias towards the most recent legislative term, and to reflect factors such as the record length of government formation (541 days). For inter-parliamentary comparisons, we use the last full relevant legislative term ending in April 2014. For longitudinal comparisons, we mainly consider averages per legislative term for the period 1995-2014 (drawn from Table 6.1, which shows activities per legislative year).

Structural features and constraints of parliamentary policy analysis within a partitocratic regime

The federal parliament has shifted from strong bicameralism to insignificant bicameralism (Lijphart, 1999). Federalisation not only disempowered the Senate, it created an entirely new chain of delegation in the regions and communities, each of which has its own directly elected legislature, a coalition cabinet headed by a minister-president, and a civil service. This regional level of government now controls more public spending than the federal government (De Winter and Van Wynsberghe, 2015).

Extreme fragmentation of the party system

The Belgian party system is one of the most fragmented in Western Europe. The 'number of effective parties' peaked at 9.1 in 1999 (8.4 in 2010, 7.8 in 2014), expressing a multitude of cleavages and policy dimensions: left–right, clerical–secular, regional–linguistic, materialist–postmaterialist and system–antisystem. There are no relevant national parties left, that is, parties with candidates in all 11 constituencies. All parties are homogeneously Flemish or Francophone, and contest only Flemish or Francophone constituencies (with the exception of the bilingual Brussels constituency).

Unstable multiparty coalitions and complex government formation and maintenance

This fragmentation means that since the 1970s cabinets have been rather unstable coalitions of between four and six parties (41 cabinets between 1946 and 2014, with an average duration of 542 days). Since the early 1970s, Belgium has undoubtedly had the most complex coalition bargaining system in Western Europe, and government formation has become its most crucial policy decision-making stage. The length of time taken to form government is on the rise (with a 'world record' of 541 days after the 2010 elections). The increasing number of coalition parties feeds uncertainty and potential for shirking responsibility, thus undermining cabinet stability. In order to reduce loss of agency and cabinet instability, parties have developed an elaborate set of *ex ante* and *ex post* delegation control mechanisms that makes governmental decision making extremely collective, and tends to reduce cabinet ministers as well as majority MPs to pure party agents (Dumont and De Winter, 1999; De Winter and Dumont, 2000).

The most central *ex ante* control mechanism is 'contract design', that is, the government agreement or coalition policy programme. This comprehensive policy package deal, whose length has grown over time (the 2011 one counting 180 pages), sometimes contains explicit statements about the behavioural rules that coalition members are expected to follow. The 1992 and 1995 agreements concluded with the statement that 'also for all matters not included in the coalition agreement the majority parties have agreed to observe the classic rule of consensus within the cabinet and in parliament'. This meant that majority MPs and ministers could only launch new policies when their initiative was explicitly approved by all coalition parliamentary parties or by the full cabinet.

The coalition composition and policy agreement become definitive after they have been submitted to the party congresses – the party's supreme decision-making body representing the local or constituency party organisation. Congress decisions bind the entire party to the coalition contract. Any party organ's criticism of the policy of their own or other ministers' parties can be condemned as a breach of party discipline, as long as the policy is part of the coalition agreement. Thus, the coalition agreement not only ties coalition parties to each other, but also enhances discipline within each coalition party and its parliamentary group, and therefore undermines the relevance of policy analysis by MPs and parliament as a collective actor.

The necessary reduction of the role of parliament

To guarantee a minimum degree of cohesion and stability, governmental parties minimise the interference of other political actors: voters, party rank-and-file, individual ministers, civil servants and even the judiciary. Hence, it comes as no surprise that the decision-making role of parliament as a whole and of individual MPs is perceived to have declined vis-à-vis the 'new principal' in the democratic chain of delegation: the coalition parties (De Winter and Dumont, 2003).

In fact, in comparison with the powerful inter- and intra-party tools that parties use to monitor government, the traditional tools for parliamentary monitoring of the executive (legislation and various oversight devices) seem quite ineffective. Parliamentary government in Belgium can only function properly if the MPs of the majority parties are able to guarantee permanent support for the government. Until the introduction of the constructive motion of censure in 1995, the cabinet had to mobilise a majority of votes from the majority parties on every single governmental initiative introduced in parliament. 'Alternative majorities' (that include the votes of some opposition parties and exclude some of the majority parties) might have existed on specific issues, but have never been used in the post-war period (at least on government-initiated proposals) because doing so would trigger the downfall of the government. Hence, members of the majority are permanently faced with the dilemma of having to approve governmental actions unconditionally, or forcing the cabinet to resign. Consequently, parliamentary groups have historically been well disciplined in voting (and still are in spite of the constructive motion of censure) (Depauw and Martin, 2009).

Formal and informal party constraints further enhance voting discipline. First, the statutes of all parties give supreme authority to the party's national congress, and between congresses, to the party executive or president.[1] Most party statutes define the role of their public office holders in agency terms: office holders are agents of the party, and they are obliged to carry out the party programme. In almost all parties, MPs must ask permission from their group (leader) to introduce a private members' bill or amendment, hold interpellations, or support a bill sponsored by another party. The parliamentary group can explicitly sanction voting rebellions in a variety of ways – from a simple warning to exclusion from committees, the parliamentary party group and/or the party. The composition of electoral lists is also determined by the party executive. The quasi-closed list system for federal and regional elections means that an MP's position on the list is decisive for his/her chance of getting re-elected, which magnifies the dependence of the MP on the party executive (De Winter, 1988; Vandeleene et al, 2016). Given this *Kadaverdiziplin* imposed by parties, MPs have little incentive to seek policy advice.

There is also the problem of increasing levels of turnover. High turnover weakens parliamentary groups' social cohesion, relationships and political trust among MPs, which undermines in particular the efficacy of committee work and MPs' capacity to specialise in specific policy fields. Nowadays, at each election, half of the incumbents are replaced (Put et al, 2015).

Policy analysis resources of Belgian parliaments

Before investigating in detail the role that parliamentary committees, and to some extent also the plenary assemblies, play in policy oversight and legislative processes, we first examine the policy advice resources allotted to the parliament as a collective body, and to committees, parliamentary party groups and individual MPs.

The Belgian parliaments are characterised by meagre collective resources in terms of collective staff. As personnel are required to be neutral, their advice is restricted to mere technical and procedural advice. The argument is that policy advice and the selection of information can never be truly neutral and should therefore take place in the political groups of the parliaments.

The modest staff allocation in parliamentary groups is in most parties transferred to the party research centres (see Chapter Eight), which adds to the MP's dependency on his party organisation. MPs often rely on information provided by their research centre in drafting bills, amendments and interpellations. For most policy sectors, a group of paid experts and volunteer specialists associated with the research centres prepare the party's proposals in collaboration with the MPs who specialise in these areas. Thus MPs are to a large extent dependent on their party's brain-trust.

Collective parliamentary staff

The Chamber of Representatives is relatively poorly staffed, currently with around 600 permanent employees, over a quarter of whom are university educated. Of the latter, over a quarter work for the legislative services and 10 for the library, providing intellectual assistance to individual MPs. The collective staffs of the Walloon and the Flemish parliaments are even smaller: 95 and 250 respectively.[2]

Legislative and judicial services

In the three legislatures, MPs are assisted by functionaries of the legislative services, but their role is limited to technical support; none of them provides genuine policy advice. In the Chamber of Representatives, each parliamentary committee is supported by two or three committee secretaries, whereas in the Flemish and Walloon parliaments there is one secretary for each committee. Most of these officials have a long service record and have built up significant expertise in their policy field. However, as a consequence of the basic principle of administrative neutrality and the primacy of the political level, their role is limited to administrative, legalistic and procedural support. The administrators support the committee chair in the day-to-day functioning of the committee, in particular by giving procedural advice based on the internal rules of procedure. They are also responsible for drafting the minutes and reports of meetings and hearings, in which they may list a number of draft findings and conclusions by summarising the information. Furthermore, they provide advice on the terminology used in private members' bills (PMBs) or amendments to improve the legal quality of the texts. In the Flemish parliament, the committee secretaries also advise the committee chair on whether MPs' oral questions are admissible, based on the usefulness and seriousness of the question.

A similar situation exists with regard to the judicial services. In the Chamber of Representatives, the administrators of the judicial service examine the legislative proposals that have been voted in by the committee and prepare a note with suggestions for improvements to the legal terminology. In the Walloon parliament, the (very small) judicial service also merely provides legalistic advice for PMBs and amendments. In the Flemish parliament, the judicial service only provides legal advice on the division of competencies between the different governmental levels in Belgium and only on direct request of the bureau of the parliament.

Library services

The three parliamentary assemblies are also equipped with library services. Although these services may provide support to MPs, such support is limited to information provision and does not include policy advice. MPs can ask library administrators to supply them with background information on a specific topic, which is limited to the collection of data, that is, 'unprocessed source material'. Library staff gather existing articles and papers on the topic, but do not produce summary notes or briefing papers, although the library services of the Chamber of Representatives may draft dossiers on certain topics for MPs. Overall, none of the parliaments uses the services of the library often.

Specialised in-house think tanks

Unlike the other two assemblies, the Flemish parliament has two specialised in-house think tanks: the Flemish Peace Institute and the Children's Rights Commissioner.[3] These think tanks are directly financed by the parliament, but enjoy a high degree of autonomy and produce policy advice through in-depth studies and recommendations.

The Flemish Peace Institute comprises five researchers and focuses on arms trafficking, foreign policy and the prevention of violence. The institute publishes regular reports that can be issued on the occasion of a specific legislative proposal or governmental action, such as the annual arms export report of the Flemish government, or on the initiative of the institute itself.

The Children's Rights Commissioner acts specifically as an ombudsman for the rights and interests of children. This body consists of 10 policy advisers who advise the Flemish Parliament on legal issues and problems with children's rights in Flemish legislation. They supply the Flemish parliament with policy papers and reports on a wide range of children's issues and evaluate all new policy initiatives on the basis of the United Nations Convention on the Rights of the Child. The think tank also publishes an annual report with specific recommendations that are discussed in the appropriate parliamentary committees.

Parliamentary ombudsmen

Belgium has two federal ombudsmen (one French-speaking, the other Dutch-speaking), who publish a yearly report that is discussed in the Committee of Petitions of the Chamber of Representatives. Within each permanent committee, an *Ombudspromotor* is appointed to follow up on the recommendations of the ombudsmen. The yearly reports of the federal ombudsmen, together with those specific to certain administrations (pensions, public transport and so on), provide useful advice about the circumstances in which policies and their implementation fail, and may lead to parliamentary questions and PMBs.[4] As usual, this information is mainly used by opposition MPs.

The Flemish and Walloon parliaments also each have an ombudsman. The Flemish ombudsman publishes an annual report, in which it may propose specific measures and recommendations to improve existing legislation for discussion in the relevant permanent committees of the Flemish parliament. The ombudsmen also provide MPs with reports on citizens' problems with governmental services and make recommendations for remedies and improvements. The annual reports are extensively debated in parliament and stimulate MPs' oral and written questions. In the Walloon parliament, the reports of the ombudsman are also examined in all committees and can be used to inspire opposition against a particular minister, although they are not considered to be an important source of parliamentary work.

The Court of Audit (Rekenhof/Cour des Comptes)

The Court of Audit is the institution responsible for the control of the budget, finances and accounts of the different executive levels in Belgium. It verifies revenues and expenses, and examines whether there is sufficient legal basis for the expenses and whether state funds are spent efficiently and effectively. The Court of Audit is not part of the governmental services, but works directly for the parliaments at the different levels. Its reports are delivered directly to the parliamentary assemblies. The Court of Audit publishes yearly reports as well as specific reports. As usual, the *ex post* information contained in the yearly reports, often referred to as the 'blunderbooks', is most used by opposition MPs. Most groups call systematically for advice on the budgetary costs of PMBs, in order to avoid delays at a later point by parties opposing the PMB.

Cooperation between the Flemish parliament and the Court of Audit has significantly increased over the years. The Court of Audit is frequently asked by one of the parliamentary committees to investigate a certain policy issue or conduct a specific audit. In the Walloon parliament, the Court of Audit is mainly used as a source of budgetary information, but may also be required to conduct specific audits or studies. Its reports are sent to all MPs and to relevant committees, which may organise special hearings inviting auditors to comment on their reports and studies.

Staff allotted to individual MPs and parliamentary party groups

The Chamber of Representatives currently grants to every recognised parliamentary group 1.05 university-educated assistants per group MP.[5] These assistants are on the official payroll of the Chamber of Representatives and are allotted to the group collectively. In addition, each MP receives the means to engage an 'administrative' collaborator paid at the 'clerk' level, where a university degree is not required. MPs who are group leaders, the vice-presidents of the Chamber of Representatives, quaestors (MPs elected to look after Members of their Parliament) and committee chairs, all receive an additional collaborator (who is rarely used for group work).

In the Flemish parliament, each political group is granted a secretariat, consisting of one group secretary, one clerk and one policy adviser. The group receives an extra policy adviser for every three MPs. Furthermore, every MP is entitled to one personal assistant. Members of the bureau are granted an additional policy adviser.

Notwithstanding its meagre collective resources, the Walloon parliament grants generous personnel resources to its parliamentary groups and individual MPs. First, each parliamentary group is allocated one political secretary (and two deputies), one *chef de cabinet*, one group secretary, two administrators, and for each MP, the group is allocated a quarter-time administrator. In addition, the group members of the parliamentary bureau (N=6) as well as the committee chairs receive an additional assistant with higher education qualifications. In addition, each MPs is allotted one university-educated assistant, and the equivalent of one-and-a-half 'administrative' collaborators.

In practice, however, in each parliament there is a wide variety between parties in terms of patterns of usage of these two types of assistant. In most parties, some of the collective group assistants are delegated to the party research centre or to the party central office. The degree of 'mutualisation' or 'pooling' of these collaborators varies significantly: in one party all university-educated and 'personal' administrative assistants are pooled in the party research centre, while other parties skim off just a few collaborators for their own needs.

For instance, in the extreme right Vlaams Belang party, until 2012, most of the university-educated and administrative personal assistants allocated to their representatives were delegated to the central party office, and then transferred to the constituency parties in order to work at enhancing local organisational and electoral expansion. MPs were thus entirely dependent on their party for policy advice (if any), as well as secretarial assistance. At the other extreme, in terms of mutualisation/personalisation of university-educated policy advisers, we find, surprisingly, the 'collectivist' Parti Socialiste, in which each MP has a 'drawing right' on a half-time university collaborator as well as an administrative collaborator. Some parties display rather unusual patterns. For instance, the Francophone Christian Democrats (cdH) and the Flemish-nationalist N-VA both merged their pool of university-educated assistants from the Chamber of Representatives and the Senate. The two ecologist parties, the French-speaking ECOLO and Dutch-speaking GROEN, constitute a single bilingual group in the Chamber of Representatives, and have merged their respective pools of university-educated collaborators (as well as their party research centres). There are various patterns of mutualisation in the Flemish and Walloon parliaments too, ranging from pooling all or most personal and group assistants at the level of the group, the party research centre or the party presidency.

In those groups that do use (most of) their university-educated assistants for parliamentary support, most collaborators are specialists in the subject matter of one of the permanent committees. Depending on the size of the group, they can invest two collaborators in important committees such as Justice. In small groups, collaborators are often responsible for two committees.

Most information relevant to policy analysis is produced by the government (bill proposals, budgets, declarations and so on). In most groups, the information from within and outside the government/parliamentary/party nexus is dispatched by the group secretariat, but often outside sources (also) contact directly MPs or collaborators specialised in the topic to which they want to draw attention.

Finally, the rate of turnover among groups' collaborators and coordinators varies. It tends to be larger in parties that participate in the federal and regional governments, as such participation brings opportunities for more interesting jobs in the *cabinets ministériels* (ministerial cabinets, the personal staff of ministers). The parliamentary group may also serve as 'landing spot' for these *cabinetards*. Some group secretaries have held office for 20 years, whereas others have come by their position more recently. Some have a high public profile (for instance, as a former MP), while others manage to stay out of the media entirely.

Policy advice in committee and plenary work

Policy analysis and the formal instruments of committee and plenary work

Federal Chamber of Representatives

Even when the Belgian parliaments fall into the category of 'reactive' or 'non-transformative' legislature (Polsby, 1975; Mezey, 1979), most relevant parliamentary work is done in parliamentary committees, in terms of legislation as well as oversight. The Chamber of Representative's permanent committee structure largely corresponds to the division of labour between ministries. There are currently 11 'permanent committees' with a membership of 17 members (and an equal member of substitutes). While this number falls within the recommended range for committees to be deemed effective (NDIIA, 1996), given the increasing levels of fragmentation in the party system, the groups in the Chamber of Representatives have become 'small' to 'very small' in terms of committee representation. These days it is not uncommon for a single committee member to scrutinise the entire committee policy sector for her or his party.

Committees meet on Tuesdays and Wednesdays (usually only in the morning), and their agenda is often over-full given the short duration of a sitting (usually two to three hours). It is not unusual for dozens of oral questions to the minister (sometimes up to a hundred) to be tabled alongside the discussion of bills referred to the committees. When time runs out, the questions are referred to a future meeting, and hence often lose their topicality ('news value').

Committee meetings have become more frequent over time, from about 300 per year in the 1970s to about 800 in the most recent legislative term (meeting for a total of almost 800 hours a year) (De Winter and Wolfs, 2014).

On the agenda, government bills have priority over PMBs. Hence, many PMBs die in the committee phase, especially those introduced by opposition MPs. Still, since the late 1980s, on average about 50 PMBs have made it into law (against 150 government-initiated bills).

Committee members may bring an accredited collaborator to the meetings. Most of the meetings have – since 1985 – been open to the public, that is, the media. The collaborators serve as the main 'policy analysts' directly to hand. They work most closely with the group's member(s) of the relevant committee(s). They develop their own networks of useful contacts among experts, stakeholders, civil servants and so on. Those university-educated assistants who work for the group and its members rather than the party research centre focus on daily/weekly current matters on the committee and plenary agenda (mostly government bills and oral questions). There is little time for mid- and long-term policy analysis. However, in many groups, the group secretaries require their collaborators to work during the long summer vacation on a number of new dossiers that may become relevant in the upcoming parliamentary year.

Committees in the Flemish and Walloon parliaments

The Flemish parliament currently comprises 12 permanent policy committees, which more or less reflect the 13 different ministries of the Flemish government. These committees usually meet once a week on Tuesday, Wednesday morning or Thursday.

Each committee comprises 15 full members and 15 substitutes, divided among the political groups according to their total number of parliamentary seats. The fragmentation of the party system also has an impact on politics in the parliamentary committees, although not as strongly as in the Chamber of Representatives. The largest political groups count four members in each committee, but most count only two, or even one, member. Some of these committees – such as Economy, Innovation, Research, Employment and Social Economy – have a very broad scope, which is hard to cover with one or two MPs.[6] The number of committee meetings has slightly increased over time from an annual average of 410 in the first parliamentary term (1995-99) to 550 in the most recently completed term (2009-14). The total committee meeting time has also gone up, from an average of 960 hours a year in the first term to almost 1,400 hours in the last term.

The Walloon parliament counts eight permanent policy committees. Committees meet on Monday and Tuesday morning, and the plenary session is on Wednesday morning, leaving the *cumulards* (MPs that are also mayor or local alderman) time to take care of their electoral district. Each permanent committee consists of 12 full members and 12 substitutes. Government bills have priority over PMBs. Hence, many PMBs die in the committee phase, especially those introduced by opposition MPs. Note, however, that unlike the situation in the Chamber of Representatives, government legislative proposals in the Walloon parliament are more numerous than PMBs (379 versus 216 in the last term). However, in the first year of a legislative term the latter tend to be more numerous, as MPs reintroduce proposals that became void at the end of the previous term. The number of committee meetings has gradually grown, from less than 100 in the first term to over 200 in the 2009-14 term. Likewise the total meeting time has more than doubled.

Advisory committees

In addition to standing committees, the three parliaments are equipped with advisory committees that offer some policy analysis information. The Chamber of Representatives counts three permanent advisory committees: for European affairs, equal opportunities, and science and technology. The Federal Advisory Committee for European Affairs comprises 10 members of the Chamber of Representatives, ten members of the Senate and ten Belgian members of the

European Parliament (EP). It is in charge of the coordination of the EP and the Belgian parliament and formulates advice on European affairs. It has its own administrative support unit of five administrators: the European Affairs Service. In contrast to the other collective services of the parliamentary administration, this unit does provide genuine policy advice. For about 10% of the incoming EU documents (797 in 2012), it formulates *fiches de synthèse*.[7] These documents are selected for their capacity to attract the attention of MPs, or their relevance to the seven Belgian legislative assemblies that may call for a subsidiarity check.

There is also the bicameral Committee for Legislative Evaluation (created in 2007), aimed at improving existing legislation in terms of coherence, lacunae, clarity of formulation, internal consistency, topicality and so on. The main triggers of its evaluation initiatives are the petitions of citizens, administrations or companies, the jurisprudence of the Constitutional Court, or direct reports introduced to the committee (by the top judiciary bodies, or by private stakeholders, that is, citizens or companies). The committee can organise hearings with experts, stakeholders, civil servants and so on, and formulate advice for improving laws, which is sent to the relevant minister and committee in the Chamber of Representatives and Senate. In practice, the committee tends to dispatch cases requiring legislative evaluation to the relevant permanent committees and ministers. According to its latest activity report, the committee itself formulated a proposal for a legislative initiative on only three occasions. Hence, in terms of policy advice for improving existing legislation, the committee does not yet play a significant role.

The Flemish parliament does not have a similar system of advisory committees, although it does have a number of control committees. These are not related to specific policy domains, but instead concern procedural and deontological issues. The Walloon parliament has no advisory committees.

Policy advice and the empirical use of oversight instruments

Most policy analysis occurs at the committee stage. Once a bill proposal (often an amended version) has been approved by the committee, the committee's recommendation, in the form of a committee majority report on the bill, is transferred to the plenary assembly for a final debate and vote. Most often debate reiterates (in abridged version) the positions of the parties at the committee stage, and the vote rubberstamps the committee's proposal. During this process, MPs can fall back on a number of instruments to scrutinise the government's position and to obtain additional information on policy issues. Table 6.1 gives an overview of these parliamentary instruments from 1995 to 2014.

Interpellations

Ministerial interpellations represent the classical and the most powerful tool of parliamentary control in Belgium. Interpellations can be used to obtain information from the government, question the policy of a particular minister

Table 6.1: Evolution of the use of parliamentary instruments in the three main Belgian parliaments (1995-2014)

	1995	1995-96	1996-97	1997-98	1998-99	1999	1999-2000	2000-01	2001-02	2002-03	2003-04	2004	2004-05	2005-06	2006-07	2007-08	2008-09	2009	2009-10	2010-11	2011-12	2012-13	2013-14
Written questions																							
Chamber of Representatives	668	3,144	2,874	2,386	1,038	364	1,969	2,210	2,450	905	3,206	3,662		3,369	1,583	6,305	6,537	6,161		5,022	6,386	5,288	2,504
Flemish parliament	364	1,788	2340	2,727	1,298	122	2,188	1,967	2,121	2,053	1,333	150	2,585	2,208	2,211	3,350	2,129	412	5,113	6,004	6,668	8,385	4,057
Walloon parliament	134	694	753	639	282	37	348	350	322	327	248	25	917	1,245	1,674	3,095	1,552	301	3,267	5,482	4,149	4,425	2,426
Interpellations																							
Chamber of Representatives — Plenary	5	44	78	60	15	0	16	46	38	9	10	0	15		7	10	3	0		0	9	4	0
Chamber of Representatives — Committees	3	533	686	286	208	32	228	280	337	159	321	190	202		103	102	154	51	51	0	39	28	17
Flemish parliament — Plenary		62		36	13	0	0	0	4	9	2	2	6		2	6	6	0	1	1	0	0	
Flemish parliament — Committees		111	112	210	228	108	142	148	235	228	116	116			103	79	164	138	112	115	77	70	56
Walloon parliament	2		112	57	34	18	2	17	14	18	11	19	0	127	253	296	295	165	228	145	128	73	31
Oral questions																							
Chamber of Representatives — Plenary	11	448	448	435	483	293	96	487	458	493	293	508	/	464	517	378	461	800	501	488	679	770	432
Chamber of Representatives — Committees					1,008	1,857		2,108	2,276	1,429	3,034	3,653			3,465	2,099	4,268	4,883	3,789	4,180	3,954	3,729	1,955
Flemish parliament		124		219	382	291	602	-	670	1,001	908	662	1176		1,034	766	1,195	677	1,238	1,544	1,328	1,252	778
Walloon parliament	0		15	89	103	67	12	202	174	281	328	298	0	963	1,143	1,047	1,174	566	1,787	1,806	1,816	1,775	1,102
Topical questions																							
Chamber of Representatives																							
Flemish parliament																							
Walloon parliament																							
Hearings																							
Chamber of Representatives		33		199	89	38			76	116	63	60	58		72	55	82	76	52	68	52	46	25
Flemish parliament			49	51	53	45	40		63	64	61	58	36	61		45	46	43	158	275	74	32	37
Walloon parliament	0			51	53	18		87	63	64	61	58	36	193	184	210	188	87	51	39	233	38	14

or criticise general governmental activity. After the speech of the interpellant and the reply of the minister, the debate is opened up and other MPs may join in. In principal, matters of local or special interest are excluded, although in practice they are becoming more numerous.

In light of this, the Chamber of Representatives has begun relegating such interpellations to public committee meetings (permissible since 1985), and only those of general importance are still held in the plenary session. The number of interpellations in the plenary session grew gradually to 80 a year in 1997, but has since declined: in the last term, only 13 interpellations were held in plenary and 135 in committee meetings (against 203 and 1,716 respectively in the 1995-99 term). MPs often compile a thorough file on the issue at stake in their interpellation. Files are prepared with the help of the MP's personal collaborator, group collaborators or the party research centre.

In the Flemish parliament, most interpellations are held during committee meetings. In the first parliamentary term (1995-99) 14% of all interpellations were held in the plenary session, although this number decreased to 2-3% in the following terms. The total number of interpellations has also gradually diminished, from 869 in the 1999-2004 term to only 441 in the last term. Similarly, in the Walloon parliament, most interpellations are held during committee meetings. The total number of interpellations has increased erratically from 225 in the 1995-99 term to 605 in the last term.

Most interpellations are held by opposition MPs, as a majority interpellation would be considered a serious breach of coalition cohesion and could trigger a government crisis. One out of three interpellations is followed by a motion. Members of the opposition usually introduce a motion of censure, while majority members traditionally respond with a motion demanding a 'return to the pure and simple order of the day'. The latter type of motion has voting precedence on motions of censure and annuls all other motions. Thus, majority MPs are not obliged to express an opinion on the political problem raised during the interpellation, a face-saving device in case the government or a minister's reply has failed to satisfy the Chamber of Representatives.

Questions

There are three types of parliamentary question: written, oral and *questions d'actualités* (questions on topical issues). In the Chamber of Representatives, the latter are held in plenary during 'question time' on Thursday afternoons, and are well covered by the media. Oral questions are increasingly posed in public committee meetings, rather than in the plenary assembly. The MP reads the question and the minister answers; there is no subsequent debate and no opportunity to table a motion. Written questions must be answered within 20 working days and are published in the *Bulletin of Questions and Answers*.

The number of questions has increased dramatically but rather erratically: up to the mid-1970s, there were around 2,000 written questions a year; nowadays there are often more than 6,000 a year. Oral questions in the plenary assembly have increased more gradually, to about 700 in recent years. The number of oral questions asked in committee meetings has also increased, to about 4,000 a year.

In the Flemish parliament, the number of topical questions has also gradually increased to a maximum of 406 in 2011-12. The increase in the number of oral questions in the committees is more significant. In the first parliamentary term, only 1,016 oral questions were posed, gradually increasing to 6,195 in the most recent parliamentary term (2009-14). The number of written questions also increased sharply from 8,517 during the first parliamentary term to 30,639 in the most recent.

In the Walloon parliament, the number of oral questions has gradually increased, from 286 in the first term to 8,286 in the most recent term (2009-14). The number of topical questions has also increased gradually, from about 374 in the first term to 945 in the most recent term. The number of written questions peaked in the last term at 19,749 (against only 2,508 in the first term).

Questions typically concern demands for clarification, information or confirmation. They aim to expose neglect, abuse or ill application of the law, and sometimes suggest improvements and reform. They can force a minister to voice an opinion on delicate matters. Yet, in spite of their substantial potential for oversight, most questions concern demands for information and are often inspired by mere electoral and publicity-seeking motives; written questions, for example, can serve as proof that an MP has taken to heart a matter raised by his constituents or a client pressure group, even if ministers fail to give prompt answers, as is often the case. As ministers' answers to oral questions are not followed by a debate, they have limited use as a monitoring tool.

Questions asked during question time are usually inspired by issues that have recently been in the media. Hence, there is often no time to back these questions with serious policy analysis.

Committees of investigation

Each chamber has the power to establish committees of investigation. Such committees have the same powers as examining magistrates, including the authority to use coercion and hear witnesses under oath. Until the 1980s, committees of investigation were quite uncommon to Belgian parliamentary life, as MPs – in solidarity with the government – were reluctant to allow investigations that could embarrass a specific minister or the entire government. Even in some cases where a committee of inquiry suggested that a minister was politically responsible for certain failures, ministers tended not to resign as long they were supported by their party.

Although the Chamber of Representatives established only 10 such committees in the entire 1880-1985 period (Nandrin, 2003), since then the Chamber and the Senate have established a committee of investigation every two years on average. These committees have developed into an alternative instrument of parliamentary oversight, gaining considerable publicity. MPs members of the committees jump at the chance of calling witnesses and experts at will. Still, not a single committee of investigation has yet let to the resignation of a minister responsible for a badly handled dossier. In the Flemish parliament, only one committee of investigation has been established and there is none in the Walloon parliament. In general, committees of investigation provide an opportunity for MPs to collect in-depth information on specific policy issues or problems and to put forward possible solutions or policy alternatives.

External policy expertise through hearings

Hearings are an important source of policy advice, since they bring together a number of experts to give their views and recommendations on a specific policy topic. In the Chamber of Representatives, the number of experts and stakeholders attending committee meeting hearings has traditionally been very low, but since the 1990s committee hearings have become more frequent. The organisation of hearings is often viewed, by the majority or the opposition, as a tool to delay the passage of legislation initiated either by the government or opposition. Calls for hearings made by the opposition are often overruled by majority MPs. Yet, once the decision to hold a hearing has been made, all groups can more or less freely decide which experts they want to invite.

In the Flemish parliament, hearings may be organised by the committees when a legislative proposal, a government memorandum or a motion for resolution is tabled. Most hearings are organised within the framework of a legislative proposal. A hearing can be requested by one third of the members of a committee, which makes it a particular useful tool for opposition parties as a way of gaining policy expertise. On average, the number of hearings here is similar to that in the Chamber of Representatives and varies between 40 and 60 per year, with a significant increase at the beginning of the parliamentary term 2009-14.

External relations of parliamentary policy advisers

Within-party relations and reporting to party principal

For most parliamentary parties, party research centres – especially those that pool their university-educated collaborators – are an important resource for policy analysis (see Chapter Eight). Group collaborators maintain close contact with the thematic working groups of these centres. For instance, the *commissions d'études* of the socialist *Institut Emile Vandevelde* are chaired by an MP. All interested MPs are invited, together with experts and group assistants. The work of these commissions is long term (unrelated to the implementation of the government agreement).

As regards coordination with the central party office, group leaders and most Chamber of Representatives group secretaries are members of the party executive that meets on Monday mornings; they also meet group secretaries of other assemblies on this occasion. In addition, in some parties all MPs (regional and federal) attend the weekly meeting of the party executive. However, multi-level coordination between a party's group in the Chamber of Representatives and the main regional parliaments does not seem to occur in any systematic way, mostly because of the clear distinction between policy competencies between levels. In most parties, the group leader is a member of the national party executive that meets every Monday morning. Several parties hold regular meetings between group secretaries from different assemblies, sometimes assisted by the party's heads of *cabinets ministériels* and the party president's personal advisers.

Ex post control of the party principal over the parliamentary group agent in terms of 'reporting' varies significantly between parties. Until 2009, the annual report of the Chamber of Representatives contained an activity report drafted by each parliamentary group, which often also served as the group's report to its central party offices. Since then, reporting procedures have become more varied. Some groups present activity reports on a weekly, monthly, yearly or longer basis. The 'party principals' they report to also vary enormously: from the party leadership (presidency, executive and board, research centre) to, sometimes, the constituency parties.[8] Groups are also involved, to various degrees, in the preparation of the electoral manifesto of their party,[9] their main programmatic congresses, the electoral campaign, and the thematic working groups set up during the coalition formation negotiations.

Coordination with ministerial cabinets

Parliamentary group collaborators also maintain close and regular contact with their party's ministerial cabinets, especially in the matter of government bills (those upcoming or already being discussed in the Chamber of Representatives). Cabinets have a large information advantage over MPs, as they may draw on the resources of the civil service, experts, law firms and so on. Moreover, each coalition party has a vice-prime minister with a specific cabinet for general policy, responsible for following the initiatives taken by ministers of the coalition partners.

In terms of time, the government parties have another advantage. Majority groups are aware what is being prepared at the cabinet level,[10] and when the government finally introduces a legislative project, they are already well informed. Opposition parties sometimes only receive notice of a proposal the day before it comes up for debate and may have to vote on a bill of 500 pages without prior knowledge of its content.

Coordination with parliamentary groups of other parties: the permanent need for 'majority concertation'

Last but not least, majority parliamentary groups are in quasi-permanent negotiation with their peers (they meet at least several times a week). For every amendment on a bill discussed at the committee stage, or when adding to the agenda a PMB proposal (or even just introducing the idea),[11] groups call a 'majority concertation', where they agree a unified approach in order to avoid open friction between coalition parties in committee meetings and the plenary assembly.[12] For more technical questions, party committee members may act as promoters of the majority consensus, but the more delicate issues are decided by a meeting of the groups' secretaries or group leaders. But most often, a consensus has already been found between the different parties' ministerial cabinets, and once such a consensus exists, it is difficult for majority groups to modify it (even if they reached an alternative consensus).

Note also that half an hour before the Wednesday meeting of the Conference of Presidents that fixes the parliamentary agenda for the following week, the group leaders of the majority parties in the Chamber of Representatives meet in order to pre-decide the conference outcome.

Conclusion

In spite of growing parliamentary activism in terms of legislative initiatives and executive oversight over the past two decades, policy analysis in the Belgian parliaments included in this research (the federal Chamber of Representatives, and the Flemish and Walloon regional parliaments) remains weak in terms of resources and practice as a result of the partitocratic political context in which the assemblies operate.

Belgium is characterised by multi-party government coalitions (comprising four to six parties) that are inherently unstable because of the multitude of policy dimensions involved and the extremely fragmented and volatile party system. Cabinet stability depends crucially on the cohesion of the government parties and leads to the absolute predominance of the executive over the legislature. Government policy is determined by lengthy and detailed coalition agreements – comprehensive policy package deals that cover all policy sectors – that almost completely limit the policy leeway of the parliaments. These agreements define the content of the bills the government will submit for parliamentary approval, and the majority MPs' duty is mainly to facilitate the passage of this government legislation and curtail opposition amendments. In the end, as a result of high levels of party discipline, most government bills are rubberstamped. Consequently, policy analysis by the parliament is politically rather futile.

This structural disempowerment of the parliaments is reflected by the scarce resources available for providing an adequate evidence base in political debates about policy choices. The number of collective parliamentary staff dedicated to policy analysis (judicial services, committee staff and library) is small and mainly offers procedural advice or inventories of existing information. Moreover, the number of staff allocated to parliamentary groups and individual MPs is also comparatively small, and some of these staff members are skimmed off by the party leadership and the party research centres. Only a few (para-)parliamentary bodies provide useful policy analysis: the Court of Audit, committee hearings, the parliamentary ombudsmen, some in-house specialised think tanks and advisory committees, and the occasional committees of investigation.

The dominance of the executive over the parliament not only has an influence on resources, but also on the practice of policy analysis. The incentives for individual MPs to invest in policy analysis or to take individual policy initiatives are limited. Majority MPs are mainly 'agents' of the party 'principal' and employ a wide range of *ex ante* and *ex post* control mechanisms. The most important parliamentary initiatives are, for example, discussed in majority concertation meetings between the majority groups to smooth out conflicts. Opposition MPs make more use of sources of policy analysis, but their input is often rejected. Interestingly, the use of a number of parliamentary instruments – such as oral questions – has increased over time. However, these tools are generally not applied to gain policy expertise, but often have electoral or publicity-seeking motives. Overall, we can conclude that the partitocratic context in which the parliaments operate seriously hampers the development of policy-analytical expertise.

Some regional parliaments have ambitions to modify the partitocratic model that is dominant at the federal level, but in practice, they resort to the same old logic, even though cabinet cohesion is theoretically easier to reach these days, given that there are usually only three coalition partners. Consequently, the disciplining of parliament, for the sake of cohesion of inherently unstable multi-party executives, remains an 'iron law' of Belgian partitocracy and makes parliamentary policy analysis futile. Belgian political culture continues to distrust neutral policy analysis from parliamentary staff, academics, civil servants, stakeholders and the media, as it may disturb the delicate policy compromises reached between coalition parties.

Notes

[1] In most party executives, a majority of members are MPs, but they do not generally consider themselves delegates to be of the parliamentary party (De Winter and Dumont, 2000).

[2] In the Flemish parliament, 25 are employed by the para-parliamentary institutions (discussed later in the chapter).

[3] From 2000 to 2013, the parliament accommodated a third in-house think tank, the Institute for Society and Technology, which had to task of contributing to the development of a long-term vision on innovation through scientific research and analysis. It was dissolved in 2013, mainly due to budgetary reasons.

[4] The ombudsmen send 'general recommendations' (a few per year) to parliament inviting legislative action. In 2014, these recommendations inspired five PMBs and 13 oral and written questions. In 2014, the ombudsmen received nearly 10,000 requests for assistance in dealing with administrative failures.

[5] Five MPs constitute a group, as is the case in the Flemish and Walloon parliaments.

[6] Committee meetings are open to the public, except when two thirds of committee members decide to meet behind closed doors.

[7] A document of about two pages consisting of a summary of the EU legislative proposal, an assessment of the principle of proportionality and subsidiarity, the position of the Belgian government, stakeholders and of other EU national parliaments, and additional relevant information.

[8] Reporting by groups in the Flemish and Walloon parliaments follows similar rules, given the fact that there is no distinction between the national and regional party leadership, as all parties are regional (mentioned earlier in the chapter).

[9] In some parties, groups also participate at the end of the term in drafting a report evaluating their party's achievements in government.

[10] On Wednesday, group political secretaries receive the agenda of the Friday council of ministers meeting.

[11] The introduction of PMBs is free of coalition control, but enrolling it on the agenda of a committee requires majority concertation. The agenda of a committee is also decided through majority concertation with opposition parties. Each party has to indicate the priority for two or three texts.

[12] Majority concertation is also frequent in the Flemish and Walloon parliaments, but is often more informal given the lower number of coalition parties.

References

Depauw, S. and Martin, S. (2008) 'Legislative party discipline and cohesion in comparative perspective', in K. Benoit and D. Gianetti (eds) *Intra-party politics and coalition governments*, London: Routledge, 103-20.

De Winter, L. (1988) 'Belgium: democracy or oligarchy?', in M. Gallagher and M. Marsh (eds) *Candidate selection in comparative perspective*, London: Sage Publications, 20-46.

De Winter, L. and Dumont, P. (2000) 'PPGs in Belgium: subjects of partitocratic dominion', in K. Heidar and R. Koole (eds) *Behind closed doors: parliamentary party groups in European democracies*, London: Routledge, 106-29.

De Winter, L. and Dumont, P (2003) 'Belgium: delegation and accountability under partitocratic rule', in K. Strøm, W. Müller and T. Bergman (eds) *Delegation and accountability in Western Europe*, Oxford: Oxford University Press, 253-81.

De Winter, L. and Wolfs, W. (2014) 'The decline of the Belgian parliament: myth or reality? A preliminary longitudinal analysis', paper presented at the ECPR General Conference Standing Group on Parliaments, Vienna, 26-28 June.

De Winter, L. and Van Wynsberghe, C. (2015) 'Kingdom of Belgium: partitocracy, corporatist society, and dissociative federalism', in W. Rensch and K. Detterbeck (eds) *Political parties and civil society in federal countries*, Oxford: Oxford University Press, 40-69.

Dumont, P. and De Winter, L. (1999) 'La formation et le maintien des gouvernements belges (1946-1999)', *Courrier Hebdomadaire du CRISP*, No. 1664.

Lijphart, A. (1999) *Patterns of democracy*, New Haven, CT: Yale University Press.

Mezey, M. (1979) *Comparative legislatures*, Durham: Duke University Press.

Nandrin, J. (2003) 'Het parlementaire onderzoeksrecht', in E. Gerard, E. Witte, E. Gubin and J. Nandrin (eds) *Geschiedenis van de Belgische Kamer van Volksvertegenwoordigers 1830-2002*, Brussels: Kamer van Volksvertegenwoordigers, 291-308.

NDIIA (National Democratic Institute for International Affairs) (1996) *Committees in legislatures. A division of labor*, Legislative Research Series No. 2, Washington, DC: NDIIA.

Polsby, N. (1975) 'Legislatures', in F. Greenstein and N. Polsby (eds) *Handbook of political science*, Reading: Addison-Wesley, 257-319.

Put, G., Gouglas A. and Maddens B. (2015) 'Candidate selection, intraparty competition and incumbency turnover: analysis of the Belgian lower house elections', paper presented at the Midwest Political Science Association Annual Conference, Chicago, 16-19 April.

Vandeleene, A., Dodeigne, J. and De Winter, L. (2016) 'What Do Selectorates Seek? A Comparative Analysis of Belgian Federal and Regional Candidate Selection Processes in 2014', *American Behavioral Scientist*, 60(7): 889-908.

SEVEN

Policy advisory bodies in Belgium

Ellen Fobé, Benjamin Biard, Nathalie Schiffino and Marleen Brans[1]

In modern democracies, policy advice and policy analysis have a common path. Policy advice helps in analysing policy problems and providing public solutions. One major evolution is that policy advice – solicited by and offered to policymakers – is instrumental (Mayer et al, 2005). It is used to help counter the reduced policy-analytical capacity of governments. Such reduction in capacity results from the increasing complexity of policy problems and their solutions (Jasanoff, 2005; Painter and Pierre, 2005; Howlett, 2008). Advice may be provided by institutionalised advisory bodies. Stakeholder experts may also be solicited for instrumental reasons. When stakeholders hold the key to successful implementation, it is wise for policy formulation to take into account their input. The motives of policymakers to request and receive policy advice from citizens may alternatively be grounded in substantive democratic arguments, favouring legitimisation of decisions thanks to the empowerment of civil society actors, stakeholders and citizens (Brans and Vancoppenolle, 2005; Montpetit, 2008; Schiffino et al, 2013). Therefore, the way policy advice supports policy analysis and policymakers varies in the extent to which it is expert advice, stakeholder advice or a mixture of both.

As a consensus system with neo-corporatist traits, the Belgian advisory system is populated with strongly institutionalised advisory bodies. These bodies play an important role in the policymaking process at all levels of government and hence tend to be highly integrated into the formal policymaking cycle. This chapter discusses the advisory bodies that have been established, supported and regulated by Belgian governments at both national and subnational levels of policy. The aim is primarily to answer three questions on the context and characteristics of policy advice in Belgium in general and policy advisory bodies in particular. The first question pertains to how and why these advisory bodies are established by policymakers. Second, we investigate the role of different types of expertise in these advisory bodies. Third, we discuss their influence on policymaking in Belgium. By reflecting on these questions, we show that the Belgian institutionalised advisory system struggles to meet four important challenges in policymaking, that is, managing growing competition from advisers, blending expert advice with representative opinion, securing societal support for policy interventions from groups other than traditional representative organisations, and ensuring political primacy in the policy process.

The origin and nature of institutionalised advisory bodies in Belgium

This section defines what is meant by institutionalised advisory bodies. It also reveals how they are regulated, and what pressures they face for reform.

Defining institutionalised advisory bodies in Belgium

In general, policymakers around the world obtain policy advice through (semi) permanent advisory bodies (Jasanoff, 1990; Brans et al, 2010; Fobé et al, 2013; Schulz et al, 2015). In Belgium, numerous formal and informal bodies for advice and consultation exist. They have been set up by policymakers to provide both input and support for policies. This chapter focuses on one particular feature of the Belgian advisory system, that is, the presence of highly institutionalised policy advisory bodies. Inspired by Wielemans and Herpelinck (2000), an institutionalised advisory body is defined as follows:

> a (semi-)permanent body which is publically funded, whose principal goal is to provide advice on [a] policy, which is to a certain extent embedded into the policymaking process, and which achieves a certain degree of independence from any single interest through the presence of a range of members from different social groups, political affiliations and/or academic perspectives. (Brans et al, 2010, p 21)

Based on this definition, the chapter will show that the institutionalised advisory bodies in Belgium are characterised most distinctively by the following elements:

- They are formally established, funded and regulated by the government;
- They operate at arm's length from the central public service, while at the same time being formally integrated into the official policymaking cycle;
- They rely more on experience-based expertise that a wide range of societal stakeholders can provide, than on academic expertise;
- They serve as a mechanism for both input to and support for the policymaking process;
- Their influence depends on how these bodies as boundary organisations successfully deliver resources to the various principals they serve.

Until the new millennium, little research had been conducted on the institutionalised advisory bodies in Belgium, although advisory bodies were occasionally a topic of research from a comparative politics perspective (Dewachter, 1995). There is no long-standing policy analytical research tradition on this topic as, for example, in the Netherlands (Halffman and Hoppe, 2004) or the US (Santos and Chess, 2003; Lavertu et al, 2012). It is only recently that empirical evidence has come to shed light on how these bodies are organised (constitution, membership, role), on how advice is produced, and on what the influence of the advice on public policy might be.

Research on the advisory system from a policy science perspective took off with the establishment of a Flemish consortium, the Flemish Policy Research Centre for Governmental Organisation (*Steunpunt Bestuurlijke Organisatie Vlaanderen*), three generations of which dealt with various aspects of advisory bodies.[2] The research started in 2001 with a study of policy capacity in a climate of interactive policymaking (Brans and Vancoppenolle, 2005; Vancoppenolle and Brans, 2005) to move on in 2006 to a study of advisory bodies as part of various forms of citizens' consultation and participation (Van Damme and Brans, 2008; Van Damme et al, 2011; see also Chapter Ten). When the Flemish government and societal organisations sought to evaluate the advisory system that was reformed in the mid-2000s, it was the same research consortium to engage in an evaluation of the operation and outputs of the strategic advisory bodies (Fobé et al, 2009, 2013). The consortium had also executed a comparative study on education councils in Europe, commissioned by the European Union of National Education Councils (EUNEC) in 2008, where, following Halffman and Hoppe (2004), it defined advisory bodies as a type of boundary organisations (Brans et al, 2010; Van Damme et al, 2011). In its third reincarnation as the Policy Research Centre, in 2012, the group investigated the value of Flemish strategic advisory bodies from a policymakers' perspective.

This chapter relies on the empirical evidence these studies brought about. It sheds light on how advisory bodies are organised, on how advice is produced, and on what the influence of the advice on public policy might be (Sakkas and Schiffino, 2013; Fraussen et al, 2014). The decision as such to establish an advisory body may form an important part of a public regulation (Schiffino and Varone, 2005). For instance, in the environmental or the public health sectors, such councils were set up to play a role as experts (Sakkas and Schiffino, 2014). Accordingly, policymakers in other policy domains have sought input and support for their policies via additional formal or informal forums for consultation as well as via institutionalised advisory councils. In the social and economic domains, the creation of advisory bodies was recommended in the mid-nineties by the *Centre de recherches pour la solution nationale des problèmes sociaux, politiques et juridiques en régions wallonne et flamande* (Dumoulin et al, 2006, p 117).

Establishment of institutionalised advisory bodies

There is no consensus on the total number of commissions and committees providing policy advice to policymakers across the different levels of government in Belgium.[3] It is, however, clear that the number of advisory bodies is relatively high compared with neighbouring countries Germany, France and the Netherlands (OECD, 2010a, 2010b; Schulz et al, 2015; Siefken and Schulz, 2015). Institutionalised advisory bodies have for long played an important role in the policymaking process in Belgium, which can be characterised as a consensus-based political system with neo-corporatist traits (Lembruch and Schmitter, 1977; Van den Bulck, 1992; Ongena, 2010). In political systems such as these, key stakeholders are endowed with formal policy formulation and decision-making powers in various policy sectors, such as education, health and economic policies (Ebbinghaus, 2006).[4] Additionally, governments count on stakeholders for input to and support for the policymaking process via the creation of advisory bodies that tend to be highly integrated into the official policymaking cycle (Bulmer, 1993).

Today, the tradition of involving advisory bodies in the policy process is in place in virtually all sectors of government. At the national level in Belgium, advisory bodies are found in various policy sectors, such as justice (for example, High Council of Justice), economics and work, (for example, National Labour Council and Central Economic Council), health (for example, High Council of Health), pensions (for example, Federal Advisory Council for the Elderly), internal affairs (Federal Police Council) and finance (for example, High Council of Finance). Many of these advisory bodies have been in place for decades, being created during the period following the Second World War, some even dating back as far as the 1920s-30s (High Council of Finance). At the subnational level, advisory bodies can be found in sectors related to regional or local competencies such as socioeconomic policies (for example, Socio-Economic Council of Flanders and of Wallonia), science and innovation (for example, Industrial Council in Flanders), mobility (for example, Mobility Council in Flanders), education (for example, Flemish Education Council/Council for Education and Formation of the French-Speaking Community), spatial planning (for example, Regional Commission on Spatial Planning in Wallonia) and environment (Environmental Council in Flanders, Walloon Council for Environment and Sustainable Development). Advisory bodies in Belgium are, in sum, large in number and well established by governments.[5] Their persistent presence in the policy advisory system relies on strong historical legacies, and occasional attempts to abolish them have not been unequivocally successful.

As to the question of how advisory bodies are established by governments in Belgium, there is a general trend from a fragmented legislative set-up toward a stronger incorporation of advisory bodies into the policy process, most notably through the establishment of an encompassing regulatory framework. This development is most pronounced at the Belgian regional level and has equally been identified in France and the Netherlands. In all of these settings, governments have sought to reform their advisory systems during recent decades in light of concerns over a growing number of advisory bodies and decreased transparency and uniformity (Fobé et al, 2013; Schulz et al, 2015). As a result, the Flemish and Walloon governments introduced regional laws to set up a limited number of permanent advisory bodies linked to one or more policy sectors by merging or abolishing pre-existing councils. The regional regulatory framework sets the structure of the advisory system and fixes the number of advisory bodies, thereby attempting to reduce competition between a growing number of advisory bodies. At the Belgian federal level, advisory bodies are also established by the government via laws or royal decrees, but no encompassing framework exists and no significant reforms have yet been implemented.

In more detail, the laws establishing advisory bodies in Belgium – both at the national and subnational levels – determine their general composition and membership characteristics by delineating the number and type of members, assure their formal integration in the policymaking process by defining the specific instance(s) when policymakers are required to solicit advice, and set the main functioning principles for the advisory bodies, such as the allocation of an annual working budget and staff, or the opportunity to provide unsolicited advice. One of the most important principles regulating the functioning of advisory bodies at all levels of government in Belgium is the non-binding nature of policy advice. Governments in Belgium adhere strongly to the primacy of politics in the policymaking process and have sought to ground this principle in legislation. So whereas the establishment of public advisory bodies explicitly recognises them as valuable instruments for input and support via the allocation of public funds and personnel, and most notably through their formal integration in the policymaking process, policymakers themselves are not required to follow the advice provided. Other European countries have also implemented this non-binding characteristic of policy advice (Schulz et al, 2015).

Reform of advisory bodies in Flanders and Wallonia

Over the past decade, Flanders and Wallonia have adopted various reforms invariably aimed at reducing the total number of advisory councils. An important aspect of these reforms has been the implementation of an encompassing regulatory framework embedding advisory bodies into the policy process. Both regional levels of policy (Flanders and Wallonia) have put in place framework laws determining the structure of the advisory system and detailing (in other words limiting) the number of advisory bodies, specifying their membership composition and delineating their main functioning principles.[6] Reforms in Flanders were carried out in light of a variety of concerns: the reduced transparency of the advisory system; the need to increase societal support for policies while at the same time re-establishing political primacy over the policymaking process; and the sheer number of government entities (Stroobants and Victor, 2000; Fobé et al, 2009; Flemish government, 2013). The framework law coined the term 'strategic advisory system' to describe the permanent advisory bodies providing advice on policy issues linked to (in principle) one policy sector.[7] The law was amended at the beginning of the newly established government's legislature in September 2014 following renewed concerns over a growing number of governmental entities. The 12 existing 'permanent' advisory bodies were reduced in mid-2015 to a total of five.[8] By merging and integrating the 'back office' of some of the advisory councils into the Social and Economic Council of Flanders' (SERV's) administrative capacities, some economies of scale will be attained.

In Wallonia, a similar reform of the advisory system was adopted in 2008.[9] As was the case in Flanders, it intended to regulate the advisory bodies' internal procedures and to reduce the total number of bodies (CWEDD, 2006; Walloon government, 2008). Two institutional dynamics may be distinguished. The largest number of advisory councils is linked to Wallonia, but another part of advisory bodies is tied to Federation Wallonia-Brussels (French Community).[10] Federation Wallonia-Brussels is the institution responsible for 'person-related policies', including for the Brussels French-speaking population. Advisory bodies linked with the Federation provide advice notably about culture, youth and teaching.[11] In Wallonia, the framework law that encompass the advisory system formally listed the advisory bodies recognised by the government and described their general functioning and composition. The number of advisory bodies was reduced from a total of 75 councils before the reform to 32 after. These have either been integrated within or are centralised around the Social and Economic Council of Wallonia (CESW), a key advisory body for policymakers providing other advisory bodies with structural and personnel support.

Despite efforts to reduce the number of advisory bodies and produce a stable and transparent advisory structure in Wallonia, the establishment of other advisory bodies continued after the reforms. In 2014, the Walloon government initiated a renewed effort to rationalise its advisory system and make it more effective and efficient by again reducing the number of advisory bodies, by centralising them around thematic issues and by strengthening the central position of its key advisory body.[12] Last but not least, regarding the gender issue, the Walloon parliament adopted a public regulation in 2003 to promote equilibrium between men and women in the advisory councils.[13] The implementation of the regional law was assessed and in 2014, a new law repealed and replaced the initial one. The new regulation states that maximum two thirds of the members of an advisory council can have the same sex.[14] The deadline for the implementation of this law is set for 2016.

The initial reforms in both Flanders and Wallonia have entailed a broad effort to reduce the density of the advisory system and increase its transparency by introducing an encompassing framework (Stroobants and Victor, 2000, 2010; Popelier et al, 2012). The current reforms seem to add much less to these particular efforts, but their impact on advisory bodies' influence has not been assessed. They were at least partly driven by budgetary considerations, and could finally end up being less transparent. This is a risk particularly in Flanders, given that the number of institutionalised, visible, advisory bodies will be further reduced (SERV, 2013; Verhaeghe, 2013) and that hundreds of other councils and committees still exist alongside the institutionalised framework for advice (Popelier et al, 2008; Van Humbeeck, 2010). These informal or ad hoc advisory councils are much less visible and regulated and they often equally serve as forums for consultation, negotiation and cooperation with and among a few privileged stakeholders in a particular policy sector (Vancoppenolle and Brans, 2005). Their existence constitutes a part of the Belgian advisory tradition that is highly opaque and has not yet been subject to any significant reform. Their potential influence still needs to be clarified (see below).

The organisation of the institutionalised advisory bodies in Flanders and Wallonia is quite similar. The framework laws prescribe how advisory bodies should be organised in terms of membership composition and organisation of policy advice. The laws stipulate that ministers are required to solicit advice in certain instances, that advice is (mostly) based on consensus between members and that it is non-binding to the minister. The frameworks also leave room for advisory bodies to produce advice outside of their assigned place in the policymaking process, and include the requirement for the political principal to provide feedback in response to the advice. The advisory bodies are also allocated an annual working budget and personnel by their respective government to ensure their activities. For the Flemish region, this budget totals around €17 million, although there are strong disparities among the councils. A closer look reveals that only three councils in Flanders receive an annual working budget surpassing €1 million. As a consequence, staff size also differs significantly, ranging from less than a handful of people taking up administrative tasks to more than 20 (Fobé et al, 2013). It should be noted that the Social and Economic Councils in both regions are without discussion the most important advisory bodies, in terms of their central position in the system, their budget and personnel size. These councils bring together the traditional neo-corporatist socioeconomic stakeholders (labour unions and employers' organisations); they advise government on socioeconomic policies as well as policies outside of their 'origin' sector such as environment, energy or budget policies. Aside from this, the Social and Economic Councils serve as the tripartite consultation mechanism at the regional level between labour, capital and the government (see www.serv.be). With an annual budget in 2013 surpassing €9 million, SERV is the largest council in Flanders. Its Walloon counterpart, CESW, received a total of €5 million to assure its functioning. A quick scan of the budgetary documents of the federal government indicates that several advisory bodies' budgets surpass €1 million. Several of those can be situated in the policy sector for socio-economic affairs. More precisely, the Central Economic Council (€5.1 million), the National Labour Council (€3.5 million) and the High Council for Independents, and Small and Medium Sized Businesses (€1.3 million) receive about €10 million in subsidies. Similarly, the 'high councils' providing advice about, for example, justice or health policies, receive more than €5 million in public funds. Important to note is that a significant amount of the budget that is allocated to these federal advisory bodies goes to the funding of applied research in the policy sectors concerned (Court of Audit, 2010). The primacy of socioeconomic affairs, both at the federal and regional level, is not aligned with policies within the jurisdiction of Federation Wallonia-Brussels.

It is not yet evident what the precise financial consequences will be of the most recent reforms at the regional level. In both instances, more advisory competencies are assigned to the Social and Economic Councils and administrative support for some advisory bodies is centralised. Subsequent economies of scale could be attained, while the additional abolishment of other advisory bodies could also further reduce spending levels within the advisory system. However, there is a risk that policy advice will be solicited through the establishment of other consultation arrangements, such as, for example, the aforementioned ad hoc and informal advisory committees. The total financial costs of these consultation mechanisms will most likely remain largely hidden. At the federal level, the cost of the advisory system has to date not been subject to discussion or reform.

Role of expertise in institutionalised advisory bodies

The next question addressed in this chapter is the role of expertise in Belgium's institutionalised advisory bodies. Governments seek advice by involving a variety of actors that can provide different types of expertise to the policymaking process based on technical knowledge, scientific analysis or norms and values (Tenbensel, 2006; Wilson, 2006). Advisory bodies, in this rational perspective, are aimed at facing the complexity of policy problems to enhance the policy analytical capacity of governments (Jasanoff, 1990; Painter and Pierre, 2005; Howlett, 2008). However, the establishment of these bodies can also be linked to the legitimisation of policy decisions and the empowerment of civil society actors, stakeholders and citizens alike (Brans and Vancoppenolle, 2005; Montpetit, 2008; Schiffino et al, 2013). As such, policy advisory bodies have been set up by policymakers to provide both input and support for policies.

A key feature of the Belgian institutionalised advisory bodies is that advice is based predominantly on the input of societal stakeholders. The expertise that these societal actors provide is regularly given preference over knowledge that is purely based on academic expert opinion or that is non-representative in nature. This predilection for experience-based advice provided by representative organisations in institutionalised advisory bodies can be seen to be the direct result of Belgium's consensus-based political system with neo-corporatist traits (Lembruch and Schmitter, 1977; Cawson, 1982; OECD, 2010c). Contrary to Westminster systems with a majoritarian tradition wherein effective policies are considered to be supported by facts and objective evidence, consensus-based systems rely more on aspects of legitimisation. They do so not only because decisions are essentially based on the consensus between different political parties in government but equally because the most important societal actors often have a stake in policy implementation (Craft and Howlett, 2013; Fobé et al, 2013). Stakeholders are therefore assumed not only to provide information based on norms and values but also to possess valuable technical expertise that is rooted in their experience with and/or close involvement in the implementation of policy decisions. Another consequence of the role of stakeholders in policy advisory bodies is that this institutionalised system of policy advice can count on broad societal support (Fobé et al, 2009; OECD, 2010c; Fraussen et al, 2014).

Scrutinising the role of different types of actor in more detail, we note that those traditionally few, privileged stakeholders, such as labour unions and employers' organisations, constitute a significant group of actors included in institutionalised policy advisory bodies covering not only socioeconomic areas but a wider range of policy areas (Fraussen et al, 2014). In this sense, these traditional stakeholders are present in the regional councils for mobility, spatial planning and health on top of their historical affiliations with the regional social and economic councils and the federal councils for work and labour policies. In the past two decades, the sourcing of stakeholder input has pluralised to some degree, and several councils expanded their membership to include other stakeholder organisations and interest groups, such as environmentalist, consumers' and users' organisations. The education councils in both Flanders and Wallonia now include representatives from the regional students' and parents' associations; the Flemish and Walloon environmental councils include regional environmental groups; and the federal and regional advisory councils on the elderly include members delegated from federal and regional elderly organisations – to name but a few examples. For most of the less traditional stakeholder organisations, usually characterised by limited budgetary and staff resources, the institutionalised advisory system offers a valuable (and at times sole) entry point into the policymaking process (Fobé et al, 2009; Fraussen et al, 2014). Academic expertise, in turn, is preferred and even considered indispensable in policy sectors relating to matters of risk, safety or ethics in public health (Sakkas and Schiffino, 2013). This pertains to sectors situated mostly at the federal level of government in Belgium. The federal High Council of Health, for example, comprises solely scientific experts from a wide range of sub-disciplines.

In a comparative study of European education councils, a membership typology regarding advisory bodies has been developed (Brans et al, 2010), comprising two dimensions: membership background and membership style (see Figure 7.1). The first dimension considers members' background on the basis of the expertise – be it lay or academic – they bring to the advisory bodies' deliberations. This background has an impact on the way in which the councils operate, the knowledge generated, and the type of advice provided. Academic councillors are expected to contribute more to issue framing and to considerations of the validity of certain policy interventions. Lay advisers are typically more concerned with practical and context-specific considerations, or value-laden perspectives.

The second dimension considers membership styles. Membership styles are distinguished between those based on self-representation on the one hand and those based on delegation on the other. The central aspect here is whether the members of advisory bodies are individuals expressing their own personal views or delegates bound by certain organisational instructions. This distinction may have an important impact on the advisory process and outcome. When the council consists of delegates, its processes are supposed to take longer. This is not the case when members are simply speaking for themselves and out of their own personal expertise or experience. In some cases, one can also expect the advice produced by advisory bodies to carry more weight, when, for example, delegates from large societal organisations have been intensively involved. This kind of advice could then also be expected to have more impact on policy in general. Of course, the latter depends on the level of legitimacy awarded to delegation and to support from societal organisations in the policy process in a specific socio-political context.

Figure 7.1: Membership typology of advisory bodies

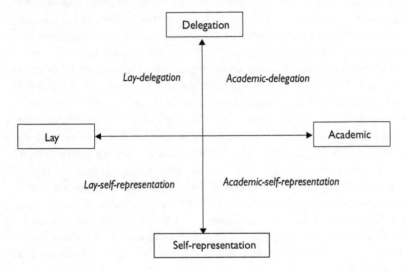

Most institutionalised advisory bodies at the regional level are situated in the first quadrant (lay-delegation), while a limited number of expert bodies at the federal level are placed in the fourth quadrant (academic-self-representation). While this typology is useful for mapping variations in the membership characteristics of advisory bodies, the actual division between representatives' experience-based or lay advice and advice based on scientific expertise is not clear-cut. Advisory bodies in many European countries usually aim to include differing types of expertise in the advisory process when membership composition fails to reflect sufficient breadth of expertise. Representation-based advisory bodies in Belgium regularly consult with outside expertise according to their own needs and requirements. Academic experts may, for example, be consulted on an ad hoc basis, depending on the issue under scrutiny, or they may be co-opted on a more permanent basis (Fobé et al, 2009; Brans et al, 2010). Advisory councils may also commission research from universities.

Finally, most councils produce consensus-based advice. They use consensus as a decision-making rule. This requires a high degree of consultation between their various members and is considered to strengthen the advisory system because it means that policy advice can count on broad societal support (Fobé et al, 2009). If the advice were then embraced by policymakers, it would mean stronger support for policies as well. There is another possible advantage with this mode of deliberation. Members have the opportunity to familiarise themselves with each other's perspectives before presenting a piece of advice to the government. This means they will get to know each other better on a personal level, too, which may engender mutual trust among diverging groups in a certain policy area. The aspect of influence of advisory bodies is treated in more detail in the next section.

The influence of institutionalised advisory bodies

Assessing the influence of advisory bodies on public policies is notoriously difficult to conceptualise as well as to translate in operational terms (Bekkers et al, 2004). One could look at whether the advice of councils is accepted or rejected by the government. Or should one include the long-term effects of advice? Can one consider a piece of advice a failure if its impact is not immediate, or must one wait for a designated length of time to deem a piece of advice ineffective? Assessing this influence is key to understanding the actual role of advisory bodies in a consensus-based political system and in a context characterised by reforms of advisory bodies. In other words, are advisory bodies primarily actors who help legitimise adopted decisions, or do they really take part in framing policies, and if so, at what point?

Some work exists on the evaluation of the influence of advisory bodies. Bekkers and colleagues (2004) have differentiated four kinds of impact of advisory bodies. Their typology is based on the seminal work by Weiss about research utilisation (1979, 1980). First, advice is said to be instrumental when its impact is an immediate change in the actors' behaviour. Second, advice is conceptual where it leads to a change in the knowledge, opinion or argumentation of individuals or organisations. Advice may thus serve an 'enlightenment' function (Weiss, 1980). Third, advice may lead to agenda setting, where a new subject is put on the societal or political agenda. And fourth, advice may have a political-strategic impact if it is used or misused to strengthen the position of one or more players (Bekkers et al, 2004).

Taking a broader perspective, the deliberations and outputs of advisory bodies may also lead to results other than policy impact. On a process level, an important element is the degree of conflict resolution achieved. Intensive processes are often intended to bridge the gap between different perspectives on an issue, or at least increase the understanding of the values and motives of other parties (Kickert et al, 1997). A more long-term result can thus be the development of mutual trust, as insight is gained in the perspectives, values and interests of the different parties involved (Greene, 1988; Patton, 1997).

Some fragmented evidence exists on the influence of institutionalised advisory bodies in Belgium, relating to their self-perception at the regional level in Flanders (Brans et al, 2010; Fobé et al, 2013),[15] and to the appreciation of policy advice solicited or received from advisory bodies by civil servants at Belgium's national and regional levels of policy (for more details on Flemish advisory bodies, see also Bossens et al, 2014). The members of advisory bodies in Flanders found that direct instrumental influence as well as conceptual and agenda-setting influence was relatively low. The results on members' perceptions on influence show some marked differences between the regional advisory bodies, notably between newly established, smaller advisory bodies and those bodies with strong legacies and (often also) a larger membership (Fobé et al, 2013).

At the receiving end, civil servants have a slightly more positive view on the advice that they receive or solicit from advisory bodies. The survey results at the regional level show that on a scale from 1 (completely unsatisfied) to 10 (completely satisfied), the average appreciation of policy advice across the regions is 5.41. The appreciation of policy advice by civil servants is higher in Flanders (5.95) than in the two regional administrations of Francophone Belgium, that is the Walloon Region (5.23) and the French Community (5.04). Only 37% of civil servants in Flanders view the advice produced by advisory bodies negatively, compared with more than half of civil servants engaged in policy work in Francophone Belgium. Civil servants' satisfaction levels seem to rise in accordance with the frequency with which they turn to advisory bodies for advice (Bossens et al, 2014).

Turning then to the estimated quality of the policy advice produced by advisory bodies, there is an agreement across the board, with three characteristics of the policy advice standing out in a positive way: policy workers at the regional and at the national level in Belgium are most satisfied with the fact that the policy advice produced by advisory bodies provides them with a view on the societal support of policies, that it includes practical examples and information, and that it pays attention to future developments and trends. The general levels of appreciation as regards these factors are overall higher in Flanders and at the federal level than in Francophone Belgium. On the other hand, there is overall less appreciation for policy advice grounded in scientific evidence. Respondents also tend to disagree with the statement that policy advice easily allows for reconciliation with the view of the political principal (in Flanders), and that it is concise and to the point (in Francophone Belgium and at the national level).

It is hard to explain the influence of advisory bodies or lack thereof, as well as the way their advice is perceived and appreciated by those who receive it. In general, the strong legal protection of the independence of advisory bodies (Brans et al, 2010; CESW, 2015) should in principle strengthen the status of institutionalised advisory bodies, although their formalisation may at the same time reduce their actual direct, conceptual and agenda-setting influence. As mentioned, there are also notable differences between the respective influences of advisory bodies in Belgium.

The research suggests that three factors are at play for the Flemish advisory bodies. These are the legacy of the advisory councils, with strong legacies increasing the (possibility for) direct influence; the issue of decisions already made by the policymaker before advice is solicited; and the recognition of advisory councils as a valuable mechanism to provide input for policies by the policymaker. In Wallonia, advice A.1210 by the CESW insists on the need for the professionalisation of the advisory bodies.[16] Along with independence, this could matter in terms of influence. Conflicts of interest are highlighted as something that has to be tackled by the Walloon government. As such, government delegates and civil servants should not have voting rights within the advisory bodies. The 2008 regional law on rationalisation of the advisory function already stipulated that such official representatives are non-voting members. However, according to the CESW (2015, p 2) and media outlets, this principle is not respected in practice in several advisory bodies. Intriguingly, the A.1210 advice considers that experts could be members of the public administration or even members of the ministerial cabinets. This is intended to contribute to the continuity of the case files to be investigated. Another element regarding influence, which also plays at the Belgian federal level (OECD, 2010c), is councils' budgetary capacity, which seems to be linked to their legacy, as newly established bodies often have smaller budgets than those that have existed for a longer period of time. Moreover, the interpersonal relationships between the members in the advisory body and policymakers may have a positive effect on the council's position as a valuable mechanism for advice.

Conclusion

This chapter has tackled the Belgian institutionalised advisory bodies. It has discussed the reasons and the way these advisory bodies have been established by policymakers, investigated the role of different types of expertise in these advisory bodies and assessed their influence on policymaking in Belgium. The discussion shows that institutionalised advisory bodies in Belgium are formally established by a law or (framework) decree, as well as being strongly funded, supported and regulated by the government. As public organisations for policy advice, they are formally integrated into the official policymaking cycle, although they operate at arm's length from the central public service. The analysis has focused in particular on the developments at the regional level in Belgium and the reforms that are being implemented. Institutionalised advisory bodies also rely more on experience-based expertise provided by a wide range of societal stakeholders than on input from academic actors. As such, they serve as mechanisms for both input and support for the policy process, although, generally speaking, their influence on the actual content of policies remains rather limited.

By reflecting on the establishment, constellation and influence of the Belgian institutionalised advisory bodies, the chapter has shown that this type of system faces four important challenges in policymaking: managing growing competition in advice provision, blending expert advice with representative opinion, securing societal support for policy interventions from groups other than traditional representative organisations, and ensuring political primacy in the policy process. In theory, institutionalised advisory bodies are well equipped to face these challenges. The extent to which they meet them in practice depends on their relationship with ad hoc advisory committees and on their successful operation as boundary organisations.

Growing competition among advisory actors makes the policy advisory system crowded. The very multiplicity of advisory actors and the complexity of the advisory system (Pitseys, 2015) may contribute to a reduction in institutionalised advisory bodies' influence. Reducing the number of advisory actors, as outlined in recent rationalisation reforms in Flanders and Wallonia, may reduce the potential for competition, and actually be a way of strengthening advisory bodies' influence. However, the extent to which such strengthening actually takes place in part depends on the extent to which advisory bodies get side-tracked by ad hoc advisory committees, which have so far not been the target of rationalisation reforms.

As for blending expert advice with representative opinion, this chapter has shown that – in Flanders as in Wallonia – stakeholders remain the key players in institutionalised advisory bodies, and experts, particularly academic experts – are less prominent. Stakeholders and experts are both considered to contribute to the legitimisation of policy decisions. But there is a third group of actors too, whose input and support is increasingly sought. Involving citizens in the policy process seems to be a new global trend that goes beyond the current neo-corporatist Belgian system and that may contribute to policy legitimisation (Montpetit, 2008). While the Belgian advisory bodies move to include newer interest groups and civil society actors in their ranks, the participation of citizens presents an emerging trend to which advisory bodies have not yet adapted. Combining expertise with the representation and wisdom of crowds is likely to become more important in the future.

Conceptualised as boundary organisation, the success of institutionalised advisory bodies may be judged in terms of the resources they bring to the principals of the organisation. Typical for boundary organisations is that they are accountable to multiple worlds and thus serve multiple masters (from a principal-agent perspective). As Guston (2000) puts it, for such an organisation, its 'dependence is as important as its independence', because its stability is not derived from isolating itself but by being accountable and responsive to opposing, external authorities. This holds for scientific advisory bodies, but possibly even more so for advisory bodies with representatives of stakeholders, as bringing in representatives is a typical bridging strategy.

Multiple lines of accountability ensure that the boundary organisation produces services that participating parties can use for their own purposes. Thus, even though the objectives of parties are not necessarily aligned, the outcome of the work within boundary organisations is useful for multiple 'principals'. In advisory councils, state representatives may stress, for example, the task of generating input and developing policy support and legitimacy, whereas the societal representatives may want to stress their privileged access to the policymaking process and the possibility of influencing policy in a way profitable for their principals. Scientific experts take pride in the objective scientific framing of policy problems and solutions. Guston (2000) refers to Latour's (1987) image of the Janusian visage of science itself, to clarify that the boundary organisation speaks differently to different audiences and clients, which can be further conceptualised as policymakers, the societal rank and file, and the truth (for science). Boundary organisations seem to hold the possibility of delivering positive results for the different parties involved, even though their perspectives and objectives may differ. This 'balancing trick' is what potentially makes permanent advisory bodies successful. The knowledge produced by science and civil society seems indispensable for evidence-based policies (Halffman and Hoppe, 2004), and advisory bodies as boundary organisations seem well placed to blend different types of knowledge into advice useful for policymakers. Here lie the most important challenges to the institutionalised advisory bodies in Belgium. To increase their impact, they would do well to expand their membership to include more academics and make their products useful for their political and societal principals. But the political principals too carry responsibility, in that they should refrain from maintaining the numerous ad hoc scientific and representative committees, the ensuing advisory competition of which potentially leads to a lack of vision as well as legitimacy.

Notes

1   The authors thank Kristian Krieger (Francophone National Research Fund post-doctoral fellow) for editing and reviewing the text, as well as Sébastien Sakkas for a partial listing of some advisory bodies in Wallonia.

2   Policy research centres are financed by the Flemish government to produce long-term and short-term policy-relevant research. Until 2015, the Policy Research Centre Governmental Organisation involved a research consortium established by KU Leuven, the Universities of Antwerp and Ghent, and, since 2011, the University of Hasselt. See Chapter Thirteen for a discussion of Flemish policy research centres.

3   Already in 1977, an inventory at the federal level made reference to 432 institutionalised and ad hoc advisory bodies (Dewachter, 1995) and the OECD (2010c) noted the existence of about 250 advisory bodies at the Belgian federal level and 36 councils in Flanders and Wallonia in 2010. A more recent count placed the total number of councils and committees providing advice to policymakers in Belgium at about 600 (*De Standaard*, 2011).

4   Such as labour and employers' organizations, health insurance funds, and health care or education providers. For more details, see Chapter Ten.

5   This chapter mainly deals with the Flemish and Walloon advisory bodies. Nevertheless, other advisory bodies exist in order to provide advice to other sub-national governments, as in the Brussels-Capital Region, for instance. The Brussels Economic and Social Council is mainly dominated by the social partners, as is the case in Flanders and Wallonia, and it is one of the most important advisory bodies in terms of weight in the policy advisory landscape.

6   Regional law of 6 November 2008 (*Décret-cadre portant rationalisation de la fonction consultative pour les matières réglées en vertu de l'article 138 de la Constitution*), *Moniteur belge*, 19 December, p 67308.

7   Regional law of 18 July 2003, *Decreet tot regeling van strategische adviesraden (Kaderdecreet strategische adviesraden)*. The law was part of a larger reform initiated between 2000 and 2003, aimed at making policymaking more effective and efficient by reshaping the internal organisational structure of the Flemish government (Flemish government, 1999). Concerning the organisation of policy advice, it entailed that existing advisory councils and committees in a policy domain be

merged into one strategic advisory council or be abolished altogether, leading to the creation of new advisory bodies in certain policy fields. It led to the establishment of precisely 12 strategic advisory councils, responsible for advice on policies within the Flemish government's 13 policy domains (Flemish government, 2003).

8   More precisely, three bodies have been abolished, two were integrated into another body and one into a governmental department. Another two bodies merged into one (Flemish government, 2015).

9   Regional framework law of 6 November 2008 (*Décret-cadre portant rationalisation de la fonction consultative pour les matières réglées en vertu de l'article 138 de la Constitution*), *Moniteur belge*, 19 December, p 67308.

10 In comparison with Wallonia and Federation Wallonia-Brussels (or French Community), the situation in Flanders is different, because in the 1980s the competencies of both the Flemish Community and Region were merged.

11 See, for example, regional law of 10 April 2003 (*Décret relatif au fonctionnement des instances d'avis œuvrant dans le secteur culturel)*, *Moniteur belge*, 9 May, p 25338; regional law of 14 November 2008 (*Décret instaurant le Conseil de la Jeunesse en Communauté française*), *Moniteur belge*, 25 February, p 16219, modified by regional law of 4 July 2013, *Moniteur belge*, 2 August, p 48535; regional law of 12 July 1990 (*Décret créant le Conseil de l'éducation et de la formation de la Communauté française*), *Moniteur belge*, 19 October, modified by regional law of 21 June 2001, *Moniteur belge*, 17 July, pp 24362-24365.

12 Advice of 16 March 2015 (*Avis A. 1210 relatif à la rationalisation de la fonction consultative*); see www.cesw.be/index.php?page=avis). See also *Le Soir*, 2015.

13 Regional law of 15 May 2003 (*Décret promouvant la présence équilibrée d'hommes et de femmes dans les organes consultatifs*), abrogated by regional law of 27 March 2014, *Moniteur belge*, 16 April, pp 32635-32636.

14 Regional law of 27 March 2014 (*Décret visant à promouvoir une représentation équilibrée des hommes et des femmes dans les organes consultatifs), Moniteur belge*, 16 April, pp 32635-32636.

15 Assessment based on the self-perception of different types of policy influence by around 200 members of nine advisory bodies in Flanders, carried out in 2009 via survey research (Fobé et al, 2013).

16 See note 12.

References

Bekkers, V., Fenger, M., Homburg, V. and Putters, K. (2004) *Doorwerking van strategische beleidsadvisering*, Rotterdam/Tilburg: Erasmus University Rotterdam/ University of Tilburg.

Bossens, N., Van Damme, J. and Brans M. (2014) *Beleidsadvisering in de Vlaamse overheid. Een analyse van de organisatie van de Vlaamse beleidsadvisering en een verkenning van mogelijkheden voor optimalisering*, Leuven: Steunpunt Bestuurlijke Organisatie.

Brans, M. and Vancoppenolle, D. (2005) 'Policy-making reforms and civil service systems: an exploration of agendas and consequences', in M. Painter and J. Pierre (eds) *Challenges to state policy capacity: global trends and comparative perspectives*, Basingstoke: Palgrave Macmillan, 164-84.

Brans, M., Van Damme, J. and Gaskell, J. (2010) *Balancing expertise, societal input and political control in the production of policy advice. Education councils in Europe*, Brussels: EUNEC.

Bulmer, M. (1993) 'The Royal Commission and Departmental Committee in the British policy-making process', in G. Peters and A. Barker (eds) *Advising West European governments: inquiries, expertise and public policy*, Pittsburgh, PA: University of Pittsburgh Press, 37-49.

Cawson, A. (1982) *Corporatism and welfare: social policy and state intervention in Britain*, London: Heinemann.

CESW (2015) *Avis sur la rationalisation de la fonction consultative*, Liège: CESW.

Court of Audit (2010) *Wetenschappelijke ondersteuning van het federale gezondheidsbeleid*, Brussels: Court of Audit.

Craft, J. and Howlett, M. (2013) 'The dual dynamics of policy advisory systems: the impact of externalization and politicization on policy advice', *Policy and Society*, 32(3): 187-97.

CWEDD (2006) *Réforme et rationalisation de la fonction consultative en matière d'environnement*, Liège: CWEDD.

De Standaard (2011) 'N-VA vraagt einde wildgroei adviesraden', De Standaard, 3 November.

Dewachter, W. (1995) *Besluitvorming in politiek België*, Leuven: Acco.

Dumoulin, M., Gérard, E., Van den Wijngaert M. and V. Dujardin (2006) *Nouvelle histoire de Belgique*, Brussels: Editions Complexe.

Ebbinghaus, B. (2006) 'Reforming Bismarckian corporatism: the changing role of social partnership in continental Europe', paper presented at the conference 'A long good bye to Bismarck? The politics of welfare reform in continental Europe', Harvard, 16-17 June.

Flemish government (1999) *Vlaams Regeerakkoord 1999-2004*, Brussels: Flemish government.

Flemish government (2003) *Decreet tot regeling van strategische adviesraden*, Brussels: Flemish government.

Flemish government (2013) *Conceptnota: beperking van het aantal entiteiten bij de Vlaamse overheid*, Brussels: Flemish government.

Flemish government (2015) *Ontwerp van decreet betreffende de hervorming van de strategische adviesraden*, Brussels: Flemish government.

Fobé, E., Brans, M., Vancoppenolle, D., and Van Damme, J. (2009) *Een verbeteringsgerichte procesevaluatie van het nieuwe strategische adviesstelsel*, Leuven: Steunpunt Bestuurlijke Organisatie Vlaanderen.

Fobé, E., Brans, M., Vancoppenolle, D. and Van Damme J. (2013) 'Institutionalised advisory systems: an analysis of member satisfaction of advice production and use across nine strategic advisory councils in Flanders (Belgium)', *Policy and Society* 32(2): 226-40.

Fraussen, B., Beyers, J. and Donas, T. (2014) 'The expanding core and varying degrees of insiderness: institutionalized interest group involvement through advisory councils', *Political Studies*, 63(3): 569-88.

Greene, J.G. (1988) 'Stakeholder participation and utilization in program evaluation', *Evaluation Review*, 12(2): 91-116.

Guston, D. (2000) *Between politics and science: assuring the integrity and productivity of research*, Cambridge: Cambridge University Press.

Halffman, W. and Hoppe, R. (2004) 'Science/policy boundaries: a changing division of labour in Dutch expert policy advice', in S. Maasse and P. Weingart (eds) *Scientific expertise and political decision making*, Dordrecht: Kluwer.

Howlett, M. (2008) 'Enhanced policy analytical capacity as a prerequisite for effective evidence-based policy-making: theory, concepts and lessons from the Canadian case', paper presented at the International Research Symposium on Public Management XII, Brisbane, 26-28 March.

Jasanoff, S. (1990) *The fifth branch: Science advisors as policymakers*, Cambridge, MA: Harvard University Press.

Jasanoff, S. (2005) *Designs on nature*, Princeton, NJ: Princeton University Press.

Kickert, W.J.M., Klijn, E.H. and Koppenjan, J. (1997) 'Managing networks in the public sector: findings and reflections', in W.J.M Kickert, E.H. Klijn and J. Koppenjan (eds) *Managing complex networks. Strategies for the public sector*, London: Sage Publications, 166-91.

Latour, B. (1987) *Science in action: how to follow scientists and engineers through society*, Cambridge: Harvard University Press.

Lavertu, S., Walters, D. and Weiming, D. (2012) 'Scientific expertise and the balance of political interests: MEDCAC and Medicare coverage decisions', *Journal of Public Administration: Research and Theory*, 22(1): 55-81.

Le Soir (2015) 'Le gouvernement wallon prêt à rationaliser les 135 organismes de consultation', Le Soir, 23 July.

Lembruch, G. and Schmitter, F. (1977) *Patterns of corporatist policy-making*, London: Sage Publications.

Mayer, I., Edelenbos, J. and Monnikhof, R. (2005) 'Interactive policy development: undermining or sustaining democracy?', *Public Administration* 83(1): 179-99.

Montpetit, E. (2008) 'Policy design for legitimacy: expert knowledge, citizens, time and inclusion in the United Kingdom's biotechnology sector', *Public Administration*, 86(1): 259-77.

OECD (2010a) *Better regulation in Europe, France*, Paris: OECD.

OECD (2010b) *Better regulation in Europe, Netherlands*, Paris: OECD.

OECD (2010c) *Better regulation in Europe, Belgium*, Paris: OECD.

Ongena, O. (2010) *Een geschiedenis van het sociaaleconomisch overleg in Vlaanderen (1945–2010), 25 jaar SERV*, Ghent: Academia Press.

Painter, M. and Pierre, J. (eds) (2005) *Challenges to state policy capacity: global trends and comparative perspectives*, Basingstoke: Palgrave Macmillan.

Patton, M. (1997) *Utilization-focused evaluation*, London: Sage Publications.

Pitseys, J. (2015) 'Labourer pour ses enfants: les temps du politique', *En Question*, 112: 8-11.

Popelier, P., Van Gestel, R., Van Aeken, K., Verlinden, V. and Van Humbeeck, P. (2008) *Consultaties in de wetgevingspraktijk*, Brussels: Politeia.

Popelier, P., Van Humbeeck, P., Van Aeken, K. and Meuwese, A. (2012) 'Transparant consulteren in Vlaanderen: de spanning tussen rationeel wetgevingsmodel en besluitvormingspraktijk', *Tijdschrift voor Wetgeving*, 1: 2-12.

Sakkas, S. and Schiffino, N. (2013) 'The use of national ethic committees in the biomedical policymaking process. The case of Belgium', paper presented at the First International Conference on Public Policy, Grenoble, 26-28 June.

Sakkas, S. and Schiffino, N. (2014) 'The framer and the counsellor: providing ethical expertise to policy-makers. Results from a comparison between the national ethics committees in France and Belgium', paper presented at the 23rd World Congress of Political Science, Montreal, 19-24 July.

Santos, S. and Chess, C. (2003) 'Evaluating citizen advisory boards: the importance of theory and participant-based criteria and practical implications', *Risk Analysis*, 23(2): 269-79.

Schiffino, N. and Varone, F. (2005) *Régulation politique des biotechnologies: biomédecine et OGM en Belgique et en France*, Ghent: Academia Press.

Schiffino, N., Garon, F. and Cantelli, F. (2013) 'Visages de la participation et capacités critiques des citoyens', *Politique et Sociétés*, 32(1): 129-42.

Schulz, M., Bressers, D, van der Steen, M. and van Twist, M. (2015) 'International advisory systems in different political-administrative regimes', paper presented at the International Conference on Public Policy, Milan, 1-4 July.

SERV (Social and Economic Council of Flanders) (2013) *Hervorming strategische adviesraden*, Brussel: SERV.

Siefken, S., and Schulz, M. (2015) 'Policy, polity and politics of setting up executive advisory bodies. The cases of Germany and the Netherlands', paper presented at the International Conference on Public Policy, Milan, 1-4 July.

Stroobants, L. and Victor, L. (2000) *Een visie op een transparant organisatiemodel voor de Vlaamse overheid*, Brussels: Ministerie van de Vlaamse Gemeenschap.

Tenbensel, T. (2006) 'Policy knowledge for policy work', in H.K. Colebatch (ed) *The work of policy. An international survey*, Lanham, MD: Lexington Books, 199-215.

Vancoppenolle, D. and Brans, M. (2005) *Een blik op de Vlaamse beleidsarena's: een beschrijvende analyse van de Vlaamse 'state-society'-relatie(s). Resultaten van het survey-onderzoek naar de bestuurlijke organisatie van de Vlaamse beleidsvorming: analyserapport 2*, Leuven: SBOV.

Van Damme, J. and Brans, M. (2008) *Interactief beleid van de Vlaamse overheid. Een internationale verkenning naar visie, beleid and praktijken*, Leuven: SBOV.

Van Damme, J., Brans, M. and Fobé, E. (2011) 'Balancing expertise, societal input and political control in the production of policy advice. A comparative study of education councils in Europe', *Halduskultuur - Administrative Culture*, 12(2): 126-45.

Van den Bulck, K. (1992) 'Pillars and politics: neo-corporatism and policy networks in Belgium', *West European Politics*, 15(2): 35-55.

Van Humbeeck, P. (2010) *Anders en beter consulteren: een prioriteit voor het Vlaamse wetgevingsbeleid*, Antwerp: ICW Working Paper.

Verhaeghe, B. (2013) 'Wat als ... strategische adviesraden niet bestonden?', http://www.dewereldmorgen.be/artikel/2013/04/18/wat-als--strategische-adviesraden-niet-bestonden

Weiss, C. (1979) 'The many meanings of research utilization', *Public Administration Review*, 39(5): 426-31.

Weiss, C. (1980) 'Knowledge creep and decision accretion', *Science Communication*, 1(3): 381.

Wielemans, W. and Herpelinck, R. (2000) *Education councils at national and regional level in the Member States of the European Union*, Brussels: EUNEC.

Wilson, R. (2006) 'Policy analysis as policy advice', in M. Moran, M. Rein, and R.E. Goodin (eds) *The Oxford handbook of public policy*, New York, NY: Oxford University Press.

Part Three
Policy analysis by political parties and interest groups

EIGHT

Ideas as close as possible to power: Belgian political parties and their study centres

Valérie Pattyn, Steven Van Hecke, Pauline Pirlot, Benoît Rihoux
and Marleen Brans

Belgium is often considered a textbook example of partitocracy (De Winter, 1998; Deschouwer, 2012). The dominance of political parties involves many functions and dysfunctions in a polity that is highly fragmented along linguistic and ideological lines. Political parties do not only aggregate citizens' demands and preferences, participate in elections and select personnel for the legislature and the executive office. They also play a dominant role in the policymaking process, by framing problems, promoting ideologically inspired solutions, and negotiating compromises in the cumbersome formation and continuation of coalition governments. However, like other actors involved in the policymaking process, political party organisations are faced with the increasing complexity of problems, and with the demand to back up their proposals with expert-based argumentation.

In Belgium, each party organisation comprises a study centre. Although no scholar denies their importance in the life of a political party, and although they constitute one of the features that denote the professionalisation process of party organisations (Panebianco, 1988), they are generally overlooked in the study of the Belgian political system (Dewachter, 2001; Deschouwer, 2012) as well as in the history writing of particular parties (see, for example, Dewachter et al, 1995). Moreover, in policy-analytical literature, of international or Belgian origin, the party study service as supplier of policy advice is rarely documented. This chapter addresses this empirical void. It is the first attempt to map and to analyse party study centres in Belgium in the period 2010-15, including the effect of the 2014 elections. The central research question is twofold: in which way are these party study centres organised and how do they generate policy advice?

The chapter is structured as follows. The first section briefly situates party study centres situated against the background of the policy analytical literature on alternative sources of policy advice. Next, after a presentation of the authors' fieldwork, the chapter outlines the basic profile of the Belgian study centres, and sequentially discusses their size, relationship and coordination with the party, as well as their advisors' major characteristics. The fourth section describes the nature, process and products of policy advice generated by the party study centres. The conclusion summarises the distinguishing characteristics of the Belgian political parties' study centres.

Political party study centres as alternative source of policy advice

In the policy-analytical literature, political party study centres are rarely documented. One of the scarce sources available that covers the policy function of political party think tanks is the edited volume by Weaver and Stares (2001) about alternative policy advisory organisations (APAOs). APAOs concern 'all organizations outside of line government departments which serve as institutionalized sources of policy expertise for government policymakers' (Weaver and Stares, 2001, p 3). These organisations come in a wide variety of forms. The landscape of APAOs can be represented by a two-dimensional diagram, on which the various organisational types can be plotted. The first dimension concerns the APAO's degree of autonomy from the government. The second one relates to the centrality of policy advice in the organisational mission. Based on the study of political party think tanks in a wide number of countries, Weaver and Stares conclude that political party think tanks generally devote central attention to policy advice production. As for the level of autonomy from the government, political party think tanks are positioned in the middle of the axis, between organisations as central banks (low autonomy) and interest groups or academic think tanks (high autonomy).

The label 'political party think tanks' is a general denominator, however. Internationally, we can observe a wide variety of empirical terms. Take, for instance, the German *Stiftungen*, which, alongside policy advice, support civil education and promote democratic organisations in developing countries (Grunden, 2013, p 184). In Brazil, on the other hand, it is more appropriate to portray political party think tanks as party institutes that serve first and foremost members of parliament and parliamentary work (De Souza, 2001), whereas in Japan, party study centres act as research departments, where policy advice is given a prominent role (Tadashi, 2001).

Method

This chapter concerns the study centres of 12 Belgian political parties. In Belgium, with the obvious exception of the regionalist parties, all political families are split in two parties, which function independently at different sides of the language border. The Belgian Communist Party (*Partij Van De Arbeid/Parti du Travail de Belgique*, or PVDA/PTB) is the only party that operates at the national level. Parties with no study centre, such as *Lijst De Decker*, with one MP in the federal Chamber of Representatives (2010-14), are not included in the research.

The number of party study centres described in this chapter is larger than the number of parties covered, as two parties have two study centres. In 2012, the Flemish Liberal Party decided to split its study service into two separate entities, a federal one and a Flemish one, respectively headed by the Liberal group secretaries of the federal chamber and of the Flemish parliament. The twin structure was only short-lived, however, and in the autumn of 2015, the study centres were again merged. The chapter, however, mainly focuses on the pre-restructuration period of the Flemish Liberal Party, except for those issues for which details about the new structure are already available. In addition to the Flemish Liberal Party, the Francophone Green Party, Ecolo, has worked with two study services since 2004: its Political Department (*Département politique*) and Etopia. The Political Department was created as a political advisory department. Etopia, for its part, has the explicit objective of being further from everyday politics but closer to producing advice in technical fields and carrying out general reflections about the nature of political ecology.

The chapter presents the findings of primary data collection. Our study combined a three-step approach, relying on a complementary range of sources. First, we launched a closed survey, with which we intended to collect basic morphological information on the structure and staff of the party study centres. The morphological data was useful for preparing a series of semi-structured interviews. To get a long-term perspective, we targeted for interview those political staff with a substantial career in the party and/or its study service. Two of the interviews were conducted with ex-directors of the party study centre (in the case of the Flemish Christian Democrats [CD&V] and Flemish Social-Democratic Party [sp.a]). All other interviews involved current staff: the director and/or a policy adviser. For Vlaams Belang, the then party president also attended the interview. The interviews of the Flemish party study centres took place in spring 2013. Those of the Francophone study centres were held in autumn/winter of 2013. Complementary information for the Flemish Green Party (Groen) was obtained via a study visit organised in the framework of the Public Administration Seminar (KU Leuven). Moreover, we were able to draw on data collected for a Master's dissertation, written in spring 2012 under the supervision of one of the authors (Libeer, 2012). Finally, we relaunched our survey in spring 2015, with the ambition of updating the content to reflect the situation after the May 2014 elections. These elections were unique from the Belgian perspective as they concerned all levels of government at once: the federal, subnational and European levels. In light of these concurrent elections, several party study centres decided to restructure their organisation, mainly in terms of personnel numbers, but also in terms of policy fields. We cover these changes throughout the text.

The diverse landscape of Belgian party study centres: key characteristics

The landscape of party study centres in Belgium is very diverse, at least if we consider their basic morphological characteristics. Table 8.1 summarises the major features of the 12 study centres. We respectively discuss the numbers of study centre personnel, their relationship with the party and advisers' profile and background.

Personnel numbers

Table 8.1 lists the number of staff employed at the Belgian party study centres. A distinction is made between the total number of employees (supporting staff included) and those employees with a substantive policy advisory task (in full-time equivalents). The table shows, in descending order, each party's total number of seats in the Flemish and the federal parliaments (Chamber of Representatives and Senate) for the Flemish parties, and the Walloon and federal parliaments (Chamber of Representatives and Senate) for the Francophone parties.

Personnel numbers is the first apparent criterion for which the party study centres show substantial variation. In explaining this diversity, we touch on various key features of the Belgian party study centres.

A first, obvious, explanation concerns the electoral results of political parties. The chapter has already hinted at the importance of such results in reference to recent changes in party study centres' composition since the May 2014 elections. The sudden reductions and increases in staff numbers in several centres are telling. The most striking example is the right-wing Vlaams Belang, which lost no less than 33 parliamentary seats, and had to downsize its study centre by 12.5 full-time equivalents (FTEs). As we explain later, in Belgium study centres do not receive direct subsidies (Göransson and Faniel, 2008). The electoral results of a party determine its finances (Delwit, 2009, pp 330-1). The electoral results of a party are therefore crucial for its study centre, since they affect the budget it receives from its party (the so-called parliamentary handover). Party study centres may therefore suffer from budgetary cuts.

Second, the number of staff highly depends on the party president, and his/her vision regarding the role and need of a party study service. Many study services undergo substantial changes, in size and in content, when a new president comes into office. During the presidency of (former prime minister) Yves Leterme, for instance, the study centre of the Flemish Christian Democrats, CEDER, was downsized substantially, and more importance was given to communication and to parliamentary group work. Inversely, the Francophone Christian Democrat party president Benoît Lutgen decided to revitalise the party's study centre, hiring more new staff to invest in the party's long-term mission.

Third, party history matters. For example, since the FDF (renamed the Francophone Social-Liberal Party, or DéFI, in November 2015) left the Liberal movement in 2011, coordination, cooperation and potential complementarity with the Francophone Liberal Party are no more and the nature of its working staff has changed. To begin with, workload increased, leading to more staff being hired, or at least staff with different skills, to compensate for the gap left by the MR (Mouvement Réformateur). Then, coordination staff disappeared due to fund lacking.

Related to this, and fourth, the age of the study centre can explain its size. On the Flemish side, the Flemish Nationalist Party N-VA constitutes an interesting case. After the June 2010 elections, the party succeeded in gaining 22 extra seats

Table 8.1: Key characteristics of Belgian party study centres

	Acronym	Name	Seats (n) 2013	Seats (n) 2015	FTE (total) 2013	FTE (total) 2015	FTE (policy advisors) 2013	FTE (policy advisors) 2015	Group work	Legal Personality	Separate statutes	Mentioned in party statutes	Representation in party board	Head of centre	Is head politician?
Flemish parties															
Flemish Nationalists	N-VA	–	58	88	9	16	8	11	No	No	No	Yes	Advisory	Political director	No
Christian Democrats	CD&V	CEDER	55	53	9.4	15	7.8	12.2	No	Yes	Yes	Yes	Advisory	Director	No
Socialists	sp.a	–	46	36	21	21.1	18	18	Yes	No	No	No	Advisory	Director	No
Extreme Right	Vlaams Belang	–	44	11	23.5	11	23	9	Yes	No	No	Yes	Yes	Head of department	Yes
Liberals-Flemish Study Service	Open Vld*	–	22		8.8		7.8		Yes	No	No	No	No	Group secretary	No
Liberals-Federal Study Service	Open Vld	–		38		28		27	Yes	No	No	No	Yes	Group secretary	Yes
Greens	Groen	–	14	19	8	7.9	8	7.9	Yes	No	No	No	No	Political director	No

	Acronym	Name	Seats (n)		FTE (total)		FTE (policy advisors)		Group work	Legal Personality	Separate statutes	Mentioned in party statutes	Representation in party board	Head of centre	Is head politician?
			2013	2015	2013	2015	2013	2015							
Francophone parties															
Socialists	PS	Institut Emile vandervelde (IEV)	67	62	23	21	16	14	Yes	Yes	Yes	Yes	Advisory	Director	No
Liberals	MR	Centre Jean Gol (CJG)	42	54					Yes	Yes	Yes	No	Yes	Chief executive	Yes
Greens	Ecolo	Département Politique	27	16	10,5	8	5	11	Yes	No	No	No	Yes	Department manager	No
Greens	Ecolo	Etopia	–	–	11,5	7	11.5	3	Yes	Yes	Yes	No	Yes	Director	No
Christian Democrats	cdH	Centre d'études politiques, économiques et sociales (CEPESS)	26	26	7		6		Yes	No			Yes	Director	
Communautarians	DéFI (ex-FDF)	Centre d'étude Jacques Georgin (CEG)	3	2	–	–	–	–	Yes	No	Yes		Yes	Director	No
National parties															
Communists	PVDA/ PTB		0	4	–	2	–	2		No	No	No	Yes	Director	No

Note: * Reflects the situation of the Flemish Liberal Party Open Vld as of August 2015.

Note: Blank spaces denote a lack of available information.

in the federal Chamber of Representatives. This result was unprecedented for a non-traditional party. Being suddenly the largest Flemish party, N-VA decided to establish a genuine study centre, almost from scratch. Previously, the N-VA study centre was merely 'virtual': there was only one staff member, whose task was to coordinate the work of the political groups and the ministerial cabinets. The young age of the study centre may hence explain the relatively low number of staff, until 2014, in proportion to the number of its parliamentary seats.

A last clarification is related to the type of tasks that each study service conducts. The column 'Group work' in Table 8.1 is illuminating, and highlights a specific characteristic of many Belgian party study centres. A lot, in fact most, of the political parties in Flanders and Wallonia have pooled study service employees with staff working for the political groups. Pooling not only refers to the physical meaning of the term, but also to the pooling of tasks. Vlaams Belang describes the tasks of its study centre as an 'osmosis or amalgamation of group activities and study service activities'. For the parties that operate this way, there is no rigid distinction between staff dealing with day-to-day group support on the one hand, and staff conducting ideal typical study service tasks, such as drafting legal proposals, drafting parliamentary questions and conducting longer-term or ideological studies, on the other hand. In principle, all staff members of this category of study centres can be asked to support the daily work of the party groups.

Relationship with the party

The aforementioned description suggests a close relationship between parties and their study centres. This section examines to what extent this is the case by focusing in turn on legal identity and statutes, financial resources and coordination with the party.

Legal identity and statutes

As Table 8.1 further reveals, the study centres in Wallonia operate under a separate name. Several of them also have a separate legal identity. Of the Flemish study centres, this is only the case for CEDER. In the absence of direct state subsidies for party study centres, the creation of a centre with a self-standing name and separate legal identity is not vital. Nonetheless, a separate name may generate more visibility for the functioning of the study centre. This was one of the particular reasons why the Flemish N-VA decided not to create a separate legal identity or a separate name for its study centre. Not having a separate status allowed the study centre a more low-profile start. Several Flemish parties, however, have included a reference to the study centre in their statutes.

Financial resources

Study centres are primarily financed by their respective political parties, through parliamentary handover and other party means, such as membership fees (Göransson and Faniel, 2008, pp 16-23).

When it comes to parliamentary budget allocated to study centres, electoral results have a huge impact on the financing of study centres, as the latter depends on the former. The same logic applies to membership fees: the bigger the party, the more it gets from membership fees, the more it is likely to invest in its study centre. As a result, for instance, the Francophone Socialist Party receives more financial resources from its members than all other Francophone parties taken together (Göransson and Faniel, 2008, pp 22-3). In the Flemish Christian-Democrat study centre, for example, some MPs used to allocate their allotted personal adviser to the party's study centre. In the past, the Christian Democrats could also rely on resources from other organisations such as the mutualities. This is no longer the case.

In Wallonia, party study centres may also receive subsidies from the Federation Wallonia-Brussels (French Community). To be eligible, the study centres have to report activities relating to popular education to the Belgian Francophone Society. Today, only the Francophone Socialist Party study centre (IEV) and Etopia benefit from these subsidies. CEG (Centre d'Etudes Jacques Georgin) and the study centre of the Francophone Christian Democrats (CEPESS) applied unsuccessfully, and CJG (Centre Jean Gol) stated that it was reluctant to have its autonomy potentially reduced by an external organ. In addition, CJG receives subsidies from the Federation Wallonia-Brussels for its archiving and librarian tasks, as it has a library that complies with scientific criteria. Finally, all political parties receive subsidies for appearances in the media, most often for the public Francophone television channel RTBF. In some cases, these programmes are initiated by the party study centres, which consequently indirectly receive the subsidies. The CJG is particularly proactive in this dynamic.

Etopia is an interesting case with regard to financial autonomy. As stated earlier, the centre was designed to work irrespective of topicality and electoral results. As a result, it has developed its own income strategy. It receives not only financing from the party and as a 'civic education organisation', but also as a private archive centre, accessible to everyone. Last but not least, the Francophone Belgian party study centres generate income by selling publications, but not (yet) the Flemish party study centres.

Coordination with the party

Most study centres do not have fully fledged organisational charts, since their internal structure is overall rather basic. Apart from the Liberal study centres and Vlaams Belang, which are headed by politicians, study centres are steered by party employees. Irrespective of the exact title of study centre heads (director, political director or chief executive), the role of study centres is fairly similar

Table 8.2: Adviser profiles in the Belgian political parties

Party	Name of study centre	% of men employed		Average age		Major professional background		Staff with political function, prior to employment in study centre (%)		Average duration of employment at study centre (years)	
		2013	2015	2013	2015	2013	2015	2013	2015	2013	2015
N-VA	–	55			35.4	Non-profit, government administration	Non-profit, private sector	0	0	2 employees left after establishment in January 2011	5
CD&V	CEDER	87	67	34.5	32	Academia	Academia; other parliamentary faction	0	3 persons (local mandates)	5	Limited turnover. Longest term: 9 years
sp.a	–	64	66	33	37	Academia	Ministerial cabinets		10		5.61
Vlaams Belang	–	92	91	42	45.5	Non-profit, private sector	Non-profit, private sector	42	63 (predominantly local mandates)	3 years, 11 months	14.2
Open Vld (Flemish Study Service)	–	74.4	87	43	35	Ministerial cabinet	Ministerial cabinet, university, academic experience	20	1 person (local mandate)	15	5
Open Vld (Federal Study Service)	–	71.4		36		Ministerial cabinet or first job		0		13	
Groen	–	56	45	35		Academia	No dominant background	11	11	Limited turnover since 2010	
PS	Institut Emile Vandervelde (IEV)	66.5	71	36	36	Ministerial cabinet, government administration, non-profit	Ministerial cabinet, government, non-profit	12.5	14	4.5	6
MR	Centre Jean Gol (CJG)	50									
cdH	Centre d'études politiques, économiques et sociales (CEPESS)	66		29		Ministerial cabinet, private sector		0		16 months	
Ecolo	Département Politique	37	58	38	33	Academia, non-profit, journalism	Academia, non-profit, journalism	6	6	3	5
Ecolo	Etopia	100	80	41	35	Ministerial cabinet, non-profit, journalism	Ministerial cabinet, non-profit, journalism	7	25	7	7.5
DéFI (ex-FDF)	Centre d'étude Jacques Georgin (CEG)	/	0	/	45	n.d.	Parliamentary attaché	/	0	/	/

when it comes to coordination. Study centre heads are invited to the party's weekly meetings to coordinate internal work and tasks. The political director of N-VA and the department manager of Vlaams Belang are each supported by a coordinator. Vlaams Belang describes the role of its coordinator as being the interface between groups, MPs and other employees, and between the national, provincial and local levels. The coordinator of the N-VA study centre is first and foremost a technical manager, who also liaises with other sub-entities of the party secretariat, such as the communication and organisation units. The IEV director is probably the closest to the leader of the Francophone Socialist Party (PS). It is telling that Anne Poutrain, director of the IEV at the time of this research, is currently chief of cabinet of the minister-president of the Walloon government. During her time as IEV director, she gave extensive assistance to the party president during the different government negotiations.

Coordination with external actors, such as labour unions or mutual funds within the same political family, is overall mainly ad hoc, and very limited, according to our interviewees. This is quite surprising, given the strong legacy of 'pillarisation' in the Belgian political system.

Regardless of job title, all study centres heads serve on the party board, sometimes in a personal capacity. Some are full board members, while others have only an advisory vote. However, the formal representation roles should be treated with care as they do not necessarily reflect the actual situation. The head of IEV, for instance, is legally speaking a consultative member of the party board, but in fact her wide knowledge and experience makes her a central key player within the broader party organisation and strategy.

Adviser profiles

The type of advice produced by the party study centres begs the question of advisers' profile. Table 8.2 includes some of the key characteristics of advisers working in the party study centres.

Stereotypically, as the table suggests, advisers are usually men, between the ages 32 and 45. In terms of educational background, all study centres, except Etopia, require its advisers to have a university degree. Generally speaking, party study centres dominantly recruit from the humanities, be it social sciences, economics, law or history. Other disciplines are represented much less frequently. Respondents testified that type of degree is only of minor importance when selecting job candidates. Most of the training is 'on the job' and many staff members combine several thematic fields in their portfolio.

It appears to be difficult for the study centres to find suitable candidates. Finding someone with thematic field expertise who also adheres to the party ideological framework may be problematic. Often, job advertisements do not mention any specific diploma requirement, except in the case of specialised profiles – for legal experts or fiscal experts, for example. Interviewees from the socialist parties stated that it is not always easy to find suitable candidates for the fiscal expert profile. The average wage at party study centres is generally below the standard level of what fiscal specialists earn in the private sector. In addition, public finance and taxation are domains of specialisation, in which not many centre-left people venture. In the case of Ecolo, it is interesting to note that while the organisation's former study and training centre predominantly hired specialised, technical collaborators, the current Political Department and Etopia now favour people who are qualified in the sector and have clear political ecology convictions.

With the exception of a few specialist functions, study centres use mainly generic profiles for their recruitment. This general profile is, according to a former director of the Flemish Christian Democrat study centre, what differentiates staff performing typical study service tasks (for example, providing ideological advice, conducting long-term studies and so on), from staff working for the party groups. In his words:

> "I think that a party study service can work with a relatively limited number of staff, providing that these have a broad profile ... when they can develop a vision, when they can assist in election periods, when they can inform members of parliament, and when they can explain the essence in a comprehensible way.... People working for the groups often have a different profile: too specialised. They sometimes risk getting lost in the detail."

Having an affinity with research is not vital, but in reality, it frequently turns out to be an asset. Staff members are required to understand research that relates to everyone's task portfolio, and should be able to debate with scientists. Political party advisers should have a bridge-building role between both 'worlds': "with scientists they should use scientific language, and with politicians they should use political language" (interview with an ex-director of the sp.a study centre). Having an extensive network with scientists proves to be essential. As mentioned earlier, it can prove challenging to attract top scholars to party's working groups. Having good bilateral contacts with scientists can compensate for this difficulty.

When it comes to political expertise, the picture is diverse. Vlaams Belang, at one extreme, has 63% of staff members occupying a political function before entering the study centre. In most of the other parties, though, advisers do not have an active political background. Yet, experience at a study centre is apparently a trigger for numerous staff members to run as candidate for a political function. On the other hand, party study centres do recruit extensively in ministerial cabinets and parliamentary factions. This is apparent when considering the many former cabinet members who found their way to a party study centre after the 2014 elections.

In most cases, being a party member is not strictly essential. It is self-evident, though, that advisers have an affinity with the ideology of a particular party. In fact, study centre advisers, as reported by interviewees from sp.a and Open Vld, often represent the party's hard core-ideology. Since study centre advisers are expected to deal with party ideology on a day-to-day basis, we can speculate that this also applies to many other parties.

When making the final decision in new staff appointments, the study centre is dependent on the party. While most study centres organise the recruitment process in-house, each new appointment must be approved by the party board or the party president. In 2010, when the N-VA's study centre came into existence, the party hired an independent recruitment bureau. This external procedure was deemed the most efficient way of establishing a large group of capable advisers within a short time frame. In this case, the final selection of candidates still took place in-house.

Policy advice by political parties: nature, process and products

The profile of the staff members working at the party study centres is an indication of what kind of advisory activities the staff members perform. This section addresses the nature of the advice provided by study centres, the topics covered, the type of information concerned, the products of advice and how quality control is organised.

Nature of policy advice

What is the exact nature of the political advice produced/provided by study centres? The objective of study centres is not to practise politics *stricto sensu*. The centres supply information to politicians and have an input into their work. The work of centre advisers is neither political nor technical, and scientific research is left to researchers. The content they create is situated in between: they use scientific statements to find answers to policy problems in accordance with their ideological narrative. These answers, in turn, are used by politicians.

Given the nature of political parties and their role in the policy process, the production of policy advice by party study centres deviates strongly from the ideal-typical rational and strategic policy-analytical process. Rational policy analysis as a strategic process is contingent on the following conditions: the problem at hand is well defined, the information to frame problems and design solutions is perfect, the analytical process is singular, few actors are involved, goals are clearly separated from means, and time is unlimited (Forester, 1984). Admittedly, even the most generous conditions of rational policy analysis will often be compromised by, for instance, the so-called 'wicked' nature of problems, or the lack of complete and accurate information. But in the world of party politics, where time is limited, electoral motives dominate and clients are multiple, rational policy-analytical models fall short both empirically and normatively.

Indeed, political parties' time frames are short, and often do not surpass the timing of the next elections. Up until 2014, elections at different levels of government were non-concurrent, implying that there was hardly any period without elections. Study centres used to be continually under electoral stress, to the detriment of middle- and long-term planning. For these reasons, it seems difficult for political parties, and particularly for their study centres, to build long-term projects.

True to some extent, these first-hand conclusions must be qualified. The director of IEV expressed her doubts about the impossibility of carrying out long-term objectives. Electoral stress is a reality, but it is part of continual day-to-day political stress. Even if long-term objectives seem more difficult to set than short-term objectives, the latter pave the way to the former, in a prospective way. Short-term objectives are not built to respond only to current situations. They follow the party's ideological framework objectives, aiming beyond immediate goals. Study centres mainly agree on the necessity for a balanced ratio between short-term and long-term plans. An exception is the two study centres of Ecolo. Its Political Department tends to respond the fickleness of day-to-day policy work, while Etopia sets long-term goals at arm's length from daily concerns.

Political parties' study centres typically have clients other than their party organisation alone. First of all, study centres typically serve the party's president, as is to be expected when political parties possess a staff of professional experts: those experts constitute a resource that reinforces the power base of those in control of the party apparatus (Panebianco, 1988), that is, the party presidents in the case of Belgian political parties. For example, IEV plays the role of ministerial cabinet for the party president. During pre-electoral phases, the president receives associations and their memoranda together with a political adviser from IEV to back him up. Study centres also provide support to the staff of MPs and their groups. In quite a few parties, there is considerable overlap in the work of MPs' support staff and personnel of the study centres. Bill proposals are often checked against the views of the political advisers of party ministers, or, in some cases (as with PS and sp.a) against ideologically affiliated groups in civil society. Besides, Etopia and IEV organisations of popular education. As a consequence, they are legally bound to produce and publish intellectual content for citizens and militants.

In sum, policy advice in political parties' study centres is generally short term, its goal orientation is dominantly electoral – as such, the study centres reinforce the 'professional-electoral' logic (as defined by Panebianco, 1988) in Belgian party organisations – and it serves several clients, which constrains the centres' activities considerably.

To what extent do party study centres function as think tanks? Clearly, they are too dependent on the daily functioning of MPs, executive ministers and local politicians to assume the role of think tanks. Nearly all Flemish parties experimented with the think-tank model at some point, but all of them abandoned it. On the Francophone side, Etopia comes closest to what scholars would typically call a think tank (Rich, 2004; Boucher and Royo, 2009), first, because of its level of theoretical reflection, and second because Etopia produces intellectual content that is not directly used by Ecolo. Its input is translated by the Political Department before being used by the party.

Production of policy advice: agenda, products and knowledge base

In terms of the production of policy advice itself, what do party study centres produce advice on? What kind of information do they rely on? What are the products of advice and how are these products disseminated?

Agenda setting

As is to be expected, political parties' study centres specialise to a great extent in matters that comply with their ideological and party programmatic profile. Yet, they do not limit their in-house advice to ideological pet projects, but attempt to develop advice on other issues on the agenda. Specialisation on socioeconomic issues is prominent with both the socialists and the N-VA, for instance, but certainly not exclusive.

Who decides, then, about what is and what is not on the study centres' agenda? First of all, the advisers themselves decide, depending on their specialisation and current topical issues. When choices need to be made between different subjects in a thematic area, it is the director of the centre who decides. The study centre prioritises firefighting requests from the party, which often concern ministerial cabinets and MPs featured in contentious media stories. Other potential sources influencing the agenda are pre-electoral memoranda of civil society organisations, although these tend to feed new thoughts rather than directly set topics on the party's agenda.

Products of party study centres

As for the types of product generated by the study centres, some are common to all parties, while others differ. There is also quite some variation in the way they are produced.

Most study centres help formulate parliamentary questions, assist their ministers, contribute to the content of electoral programs, and prepare flash cards for public debates. The latter typically include information on current policy, the position of the party, and the position of the adversaries in the debate. Study centres contribute to these tasks to different degrees. Whereas IEV spends most of its time working closely with the party (assisting with negotiations, writing precise content for MPs notes), other study centres are less committed. For example, they produce content for ministers, but are not physically present at negotiations. They send notes to MPs, but allow them the discretion to use them or not. In terms of formulation of policy advice, Groen produces the largest and most systematic range of policy notes (for example, trajectory notes or concept notes that follow a fixed template).

What has been developed more strongly over the years is input into government negotiations, helping negotiators to formulate on-the-spot policy analysis. When positions need to shift in the direction of a compromise, negotiators have to be well informed about the impact of deviating from the original position. This was definitely important in the consecutive government negotiations on the new financing model of the reformed federal state, during which negotiators had to rely heavily on simulations of effects. The support of government negotiators is extremely demanding for party policy workers, given not only the stakes, but also the ever-increasing time constraints imposed by technological and communication innovation. Producing policy advice to negotiators in an era of email, social media and the internet is quite different from producing advice in times of typewriters and fax machines. More timely information is available from more sources, but the time available to process information decreases. Besides, political advisers are not necessarily part of the negotiations; it depends on organisational structures and on the party's chosen negotiator.

In the face of new technological developments, publishing a party manifesto or convening a congress have survived as rather classic dissemination tools for political parties' policies. Party study centres in Belgium generally play a key role in the organisation of both kinds of 'events'. At congresses, policy advice is typically blended with academic, technical and members' input into texts that are then put the vote as resolutions. These congresses remain one of the major vehicles through which political parties target and disseminate their programmatic vision.

Finally, some parties produce specific studies, or even publish books, for example, Vlaams Belang's book titled *The orderly division of Belgium* (Annemans and Utsi, 2010) and Etopia's review on the philosophy of nature (Etopia, 2010).

Knowledge base

The knowledge base of party study centres comprises both internal and external input. As for the centre's individual staff members, usually everyone has their own thematic portfolio. Interestingly, the number of staff employed does not seem to have substantial impact on the number of themes covered by the various study centres. Yet the smaller the centre, logically, the more themes need to be covered by individual members. Also some coordinators/directors combine their managerial role with a thematic portfolio. The N-VA coordinator, for instance, specialises in migration and institutional issues, and the director of the PVDA/ PTB study centre indicated that he regularly fills thematic voids when there is no expert available.

In-house party analysis is not the only source of policy advice, as parties will turn to external experts when they lack a certain specialisation. Even so, the nationalist N-VA's effort to organise a congress on confederalism is rather exceptional; it hired a consultant for a benchmark exercise. Although in some of the organisations there is some room for in-house independent study work, most study centres seem to make the most out of their networks, especially other knowledge- and advice-producing bodies. As well as following the output of academia, knowledge centres and think tanks, most parties report developing bilateral contacts with academics or technical experts in the administration or civil society organisations, with whom they collect data, carry out research or test ideas. On the initiative of its chief executive, CJG recently convened a scientific committee to inspire the centre and to forge links with academics. Vlaams Belang prizes itself on frequently garnering academic and expert input for its policy work, but highlights the confidentiality of these inputs to avoid fear of ostracisation. The director of CEPESS has a less positive approach of external expertise, even though he does not deny its usefulness. He believes that collaborating with external consultants is a double-edged sword: on the one hand, it brings the expertise that is lacking, and on the other hand, an external expert may not be able to adapt the knowledge to the ideological framework of the party. Consultants may bring expertise, but the study centre has to rework it. On the whole, and in practice, study centres seldom hire external experts, except for volunteers.

Several parties invite external contacts into working groups, or engage them in the activities of their congresses. Parties, however, rely on this method to varying degrees. CEDER and PVDA/PTB represent two sides of a continuum. For the former, working groups only convene for concrete problems relating to government affairs. This is, again, related to the fact that this study centre does not conduct any day-to-day parliamentary group support. For the PVDA/PTB, in contrast, working groups are the most important vehicle for gathering the necessary information on a certain issue, and is a way of compensating for the small size of its centre. Generally, we see a tendency to organise working groups on a more ad hoc basis and from the bottom up, rather than to impose them from the top down. In fact, in most cases, MPs chair the working groups. The success of a working group hence strongly depends on the support of the MP concerned. When the MP leaves the parliament, or when he or she is simply no longer interested, the continuity of a working group can be threatened.

The composition of the working groups, in all parties, is a hybrid affair. The group is usually a forum for MPs, employees from the parliamentary groups, advisers of the political cabinets and other members of the party. In addition, working groups are often an instrument for inviting input from external experts, although N-VA only seldom has external invitees. An ex-director of sp.a highlighted that top scientific experts seldom attend working groups. These experts are better reached through personal bilateral networks, in this way emphasising the crucial importance of individual staff members' contacts.

Another way for study centres to obtain input is to develop links with European foundations. In practice, however, the authors found the institutional collaboration in the European space rather limited. Most parties have international and European contacts, but these are only seldom arranged on a structural basis. The Green parties' study centres, for instance, are part of a network of Green foundations and other Green parties worldwide. Etopia, in its archive and storage role, is an important staging-post for any person interested in political ecology. Moreover, a member of Etopia's permanent staff is the coordinator of the *Green European Journal*. The Liberal parties also have interactions with other Liberal parties worldwide, mostly in Europe and Africa.

Quality control

For party manifestos and congress texts, there is usually a whole machinery to check the quality. As for the daily advice given to MPs and party members, there seems to be a strict quality control system, usually overseen either by the coordinator of the study centre, the president of the party, or both. At N-VA, qualitative coordination is performed by a chief economist, who reads all the reports that the party produces. While most parties do not have formalised quality standards, they usually adhere to scientific criteria. At this point, it is relevant to note that the Francophone study centres take a more science-oriented approach compared with their Flemish counterparts. Although they recruit fewer former university research staff, the Francophone party study centres appear to be more likely than their Flemish counterparts to use scientific criteria in the production of political content. Interviewees considered scientific content to be key to the credibility of their statements. In terms of coherence and scientific veracity, the IEV's director explicitly stated that all of the centre's publications are similar to academic papers.

Conclusion

This chapter maps for the very first time the study centres of the Belgian political parties (the first such exploration of Flemish parties appeared in Pattyn et al, 2014). Study centres are not totally independent of their affiliated political parties but rather enjoy a status of relative autonomy. The degree of independence differs, but none of the study centres is fully part of the party headquarters or operates as a think tank with nothing but ideological ties.

Size and organisation of the study centres largely depend on the party's electoral results, the personal vision of the party president and the party history. Being highly dependent on electoral results, first and foremost with regard to staff numbers, is not without ambiguity, as study centres are expected to be least concerned with elections (and short-term party strategies). Yet, in reality they are highly influenced by elections, as study centres are often easy victims of decreasing party funding. The results of the 2014 elections, however, may prove to be the start of a new phase, as the subsequent introduction of concurrent elections (2014, 2019 and so on) is designed to introduce stability into the Belgian political system. This might also benefit and consolidate the position of study centres, providing more opportunities – in principle – for conducting genuine study service activities, such as long-term 'cold' research and in-depth ideological studies.

Unlike staff numbers, the role of study centres appears to be more stable; every party seems to establish a study centre, therefore implicitly recognising its value for the party organisation, and most study centres follow the same pattern. They operate somewhere between dealing with day-to-day group support on the one hand, and, on the other, performing ideal typical study service tasks, such as drafting legal proposals and parliamentary questions, and conducting longer-term, or ideological studies.

Differences between Flemish and Francophone study centres seem to be fewer, but they do exist in some areas. Francophone study centres, for instance, focus more on popular education, as a result of different financial incentives within the Francophone party system. Francophone study centres also seem to be more 'embedded' in the party structure and strategy compared with their Flemish counterparts, but paradoxically see their output as more explicitly 'scientific'.

Neither do traditional parties seem to differ from newcomers, except that the former have the advantage of relying on their long-established networks with civil society organisations. The effect of this typical Belgian system of 'pillarisation' should not be overestimated, though. The outcome is surprising and therefore needs further research. Organisational and personnel ties may be less strong than in previous periods, but thematic collaboration and networking may still play a role.

In conclusion, time management is critical for study centres, like all political organisations. They have to find the right balance between short-term action and long-term investment, between the electoral emphasis that has been so prominent in recent years within the Belgian political system and the advantages that study centres have over think tanks. Belgian study centres are clearly not think tanks, but instead are relatively close to their parties. Much more than ideas factories, they do not hesitate to be as close to 'power' as they can be.

References

Annemans, G. and Utsi, S. (2010) *De ordelijke opdeling van België*, Brussels: Uitgeverij Egmont.

Boucher, S. and Royo, M. (2009) *Les think tanks. Cerveaux de la guerre des idées* (2nd edn), Paris: Editions du Félin.

Delwit, P. (2009) *La vie politique de Belgique de 1830 à nos jours*, Brussels: Editions de l'Université de Bruxelles.

De Souza, A. (2001) 'Brazil', in R.K. Weaver and P.B. Stares (eds) *Guidance for governance. Comparing alternative sources of public policy advice*, Tokyo: Japan Center for International Exchange.

De Winter, L. (1998) 'Parliament and government in Belgium: prisoners of partitocracy', in P. Norton (ed) *Parliaments and governments in Western Europe*, London: Frank Cass.

Deschouwer, K. (2012) *The politics of Belgium. Governing a divided society*, Basingstoke: Palgrave Macmillan.

Dewachter, W. (2001) *De mythe van de parlementaire democratie*, Leuven: Acco.

Dewachter, W., Dumont, G.H., Dumoulin, M., Gerard, E., Lamberts, E., Mabille, X. and Van den Wijngaert, M. (eds) (1995) *Tussen staat en maatschappij. De Christen-Democratie in België 1945-1995*, Tielt: Lannoo.

Etopia (2010) 'Wallonie et gouvernance/philosophie de la nature', *Revue d'écologie politique*, 7.

Forester, J. (1984) 'Bounded rationality and the politics of muddling through', *Public Administration Review*, 44(1): 23–31.

Göransson, M. and Faniel, J. (2008) 'Le financement et la comptabilité des partis politiques francophones', *Courrier hebdomadaire du CRISP*, no. 1989–1990.

Grunden, T. (2013) 'From hand to mouth. Parties and policy-making in Germany', in S. Blum and K. Schubert (eds) *Policy analysis in Germany*, Bristol: Policy Press.

Libeer, T. (2012) *Beleidsadvies door studiebureaus van politieke partijen. Productie en voorwaarden tot gebruik*, Leuven: Faculteit Sociale Wetenschappen.

Panebianco, A. (1988) *Political parties: organization and power*, Cambridge: Cambridge University Press.

Pattyn, V., Van Hecke, S., Brans, M. and Libeer, T. (2014) 'Tussen politieke partijen en think tanks. Een verkennende analyse van de Vlaamse partijstudiediensten', *Res Publica*, 3: 293–316.

Rich, A. (2004) *Think tanks, public policy, and the politics of expertise*, New York, NY: Cambridge University Press.

Tadashi, Y. (2001) 'Japan', in R.K. Weaver and P.B. Stares (eds) *Guidance for governance. Comparing alternative sources of public policy advice*, Tokyo: Japan Center for International Exchange.

Weaver, R.K. and Stares, P.B. (2001) *Guidance for governance. Comparing alternative sources of public policy advice*, Tokyo: Japan Center for International Exchange.

NINE

Interest groups and policy analysis in Belgium: examining the policy-analytical capacities and practices of prominent citizen and economic groups

Bert Fraussen, Nele Bossens, Alex Wilson and Michael Keating

The interaction between organised interests and public authorities forms a crucial ingredient of policymaking in contemporary democracies. In many countries, policymakers regularly seek advice from organised interests in order to acquire policy expertise, or to gain more insight into the policy preferences of a particular social group. The growing complexity of the policy environment also creates an increasing demand for external knowledge and societal support. As interest groups often have access to valuable information concerning governmental policies, they become important suppliers of policy advice. This chapter focuses on the policy-driven activities of interest groups, and their role as 'service bureaus' or policy advisers to policymakers (Hall and Deardorf, 2006). Policy advice is here defined as an opinion or recommendation offered as a guide for future policy (Brans et al, 2010). While this advice is typically non-binding when shared through informal contacts or consultations, it often has a more binding character when it is channelled via neo-corporatist structures for concertation.

Considering that information is seen as a crucial currency in the interaction between organised interests and public authorities, it seems highly relevant to examine how organised interests acquire and utilise this valuable resource. By specifically highlighting the role of policy expertise, the aim of this chapter is to complement the literature that considers organised interests primarily as advocacy groups, whose main goal is to shape the government's agenda and influence policymaking (for example, Baumgartner et al, 2009; Eising, 2009; Hojnacki et al, 2012). In the past two decades, much scholarly work in this area has focused on strategic matters. Researchers have, for instance, underlined the importance of networks for gaining access to policymakers (for example, Carpenter et al, 1998; Beyers and Braun, 2014), or argued that groups increasingly seek to build and maintain their reputation through regular media appearances or other forms of outside lobbying (Kollman, 1998; Andrews and Caren, 2010; Binderkrantz, 2012). These strategic considerations, however, cover only one aspect of interest group politics. Another key element, one that has been subject to investigation far less frequently, involves the way in which these groups acquire critical and up-to-date information, build policy-analytical capacity, and put this knowledge to use in their interaction with policymakers. While many organised interests play an important role in policy formulation and implementation, research on how groups develop policy-analytical capacity is rather limited (except Halpin et al, 2011). While the supply of information to policymakers is a crucial instrument for organised interests to influence policymaking, not all interest groups are equally capable of providing policy expertise, given that their degree of professionalisation and orientation towards government varies considerably (Bouwen, 2004; Eising, 2007; Klüver, 2012).

This chapter focuses on the policy-analytical capacity of interest groups in Belgium. More precisely, it examines the way in which interest groups are organised in order to acquire policy expertise, as well as the characteristics and dissemination of their policy advice, through a survey of the 30 interest organisations that were most prominent in the news between 2003 and 2010. Interest organisations are commonly defined by four central features: a minimum level of organisation (thus excluding popular movements or waves of public opinion), a specific constituency or membership, political interest, and informality, the latter implying that these organisations do not take part in elections (Beyers et al, 2008). As a result, the label interest group covers a broad variety of organisations, such as labour unions, business associations and citizen groups. Much previous research on policy analysis in neo-corporatist countries exclusively concentrated on neo-corporatist institutions and the functioning of traditional economic interests, such as the umbrella associations of business and labour (van den Bulck, 1992; Jones, 2002; Traxler, 2010; Bouteca et al, 2013). In contrast, this set of organisations includes a mix of economic and citizen groups, the latter referring to associations that have individuals as members and focus on the representation of particular social groups or public interests. By including business associations and labour unions, as well as citizen organisations like consumer groups and environmental non-governmental organisations (NGOs), the aim is to capture the diversity of group types within the Belgian interest group population.

The focus on both economic and citizen groups enables a comparison of groups that all engage in policy work, yet vary in terms of their integration in policy networks and representation in advisory institutions. Hence, one can assess to what extent the privileged status of economic organisations in a neo-corporatist political system shapes their organisation and policy-related activities, compared with the practices of citizen groups. It is expected that, given their higher involvement in policymaking, economic groups will invest more in policy-related activities. Yet citizen groups also frequently seek to shape policy decisions or aim to influence public opinion, and therefore need to develop and acquire policy expertise. Recent research questions the idea that economic groups are generally characterised by a higher degree of professionalisation than citizen groups (see Klüver and Saurugger, 2013). By analysing the organisation of these different groups and their policy-related activities, this chapter aims to examine these matters in greater detail.

The first section of the chapter introduces the Belgian system of interest representation, focusing in particular on how successive state reforms have shaped the organisation of interest groups. Subsequently, the chapter discusses the organisational capacity and policy activities of organised interests in Belgium, mainly distinguishing between economic and citizen groups. The conclusion reflects on the most important findings and suggests some possible avenues for further research.

Interest group politics in Belgium: diversity and fragmentation

In terms of its system of interest representation, Belgium is generally classified as 'moderately neo-corporatist', making it quite similar to countries such as Germany or Denmark, but less corporatist than Austria or Norway (Lijphart and Crepaz, 1991; Siaroff, 1999; Luyten, 2006; Bloodgood et al, 2014; see also Beyers et al, 2014). As a result, the so-called 'social partners', that is, the umbrella labour unions and business associations, are well-represented in a wide range of neo-corporatist institutions, and also play a key role in the administration of social security policies (Deleeck, 2003). Nevertheless, the Belgian interest group population is not confined to traditional business and labour organisations. Many new social movements and NGOs, focusing on issues ranging from environmental protection to development cooperation, emerged in the 1960s and 1970s and some of them have developed into established and professionalised groups (Walgrave, 1994).

The federal nature of Belgium strongly affects the mobilisation and organisation of interest groups, as well as their involvement in policymaking. Since the 1970s, Belgium has moved from a centralised unitary state towards a decentralised federal state. These processes of state reform shaped the supply-and-demand side of interest representation, as existing groups adapted to changed political structures, new regional groups mobilised and regional political elites aimed to facilitate the development of subnational policy communities (Fraussen, 2014). Belgian interest groups have rescaled to very different degrees as successive state reforms have regionalised some policy competencies more than others, leading to an interest group population that encompasses groups organised on a national basis and interest organisations that only represent a regional constituency (Fraussen and Beyers, 2015). Whereas a majority of business associations and labour unions still operate on a Belgian (or nationwide) scale, associations of institutions (for example, local governments, hospitals or universities) or citizen groups are more likely to mobilise constituencies at a regional level. Due to the division of policy responsibilities across different levels of government, many groups face the challenge of linguistic cleavages that have fragmented political parties and civil society into increasingly separate French and Dutch speaking communities (Deschouwer, 2012; see also Caluwaerts and Reuchamps, 2014). In the following paragraphs, more detailed insights are provided on the organisational scale or structure of these organisations, as well as their involvement in policymaking at different levels of government. They draw on the results of a multi-country study on the organisational rescaling of interest groups, which covered the regions of Flanders and Wallonia (Keating and Wilson, 2014). The data for this study includes 22 in-depth interviews with key interest group actors in Belgium: the main employers' associations and trade unions, key environmental groups and some social organisations.

An unusual feature of the interest group system in Belgium is that business associations and trade unions have adopted asymmetrical forms of multi-level organisation. Flanders has two major employers' associations, UNIZO, which represents small and medium-sized businesses, and VOKA for medium-sized and large businesses. UNIZO counts 85,000 individual members alongside 125 affiliated sectoral organisations. Businesses affiliated to VOKA – about 18,000 companies – account for two thirds of business turnover in Flanders. Both associations represent a valuable electoral constituency for Flemish politics and maintain close ties to political parties. UNIZO emerged from the Christian pillar in Belgian society and, while the organisation no longer has structural ties with the Christian Democratic Party in Flanders (CD&V), the latter still is an important political ally. The former minister-president of Flanders, Kris Peeters (2007-14), spent several years as the managing director of UNIZO. UNIZO is a recognised 'social partner' at federal level (as well as at regional level in Flanders), which gives it the right to participate in all collective bargaining processes (Bouteca et al, 2013). UNIZO engages in some competition for influence and membership with VOKA, partly due to the strong presence of medium-sized businesses in Flanders that could potentially join either association. VOKA has never had ancillary ties to a political party, but now maintains a close relationship with liberal and nationalist parties in Flanders. Although influential at the regional level, where it is a recognised social partner, VOKA is not a recognised social partner at the federal level, where the interests of large and medium-sized enterprises are instead represented by VBO-FEB, a Belgian association that comprises over 50 sectoral federations, whose core functions are lobbying and collective bargaining at the federal level. VOKA's exclusion from federal negotiations has encouraged it to push for wage bargaining, labour market policy and social security to become decentralised to the regional level. Such a move faces natural resistance from VBO-FEB but is also strongly opposed by the main business associations in Wallonia, UCM (representing small businesses) and UWE (representing medium and large businesses), both of which insist collective bargaining and social security should remain federal competencies (Bouteca et al, 2013). Although UCM emerged from the same historic national organisation as UNIZO, it has distanced itself from its confessional roots and ancillary ties to Christian Democrats in Wallonia. UCM maintains only loose contacts and no organisational ties with UNIZO. Nevertheless, both organisations are recognised 'social partners' at the federal level and sometimes cooperate in collective bargaining. UWE is a much smaller and less politically influential association than its Flemish counterpart VOKA, and has not pushed to become a recognised social partner at the federal level, being content to delegate decision making on most federal issues to VBO-FEB.

Trade unions in Belgium are significantly more centralised and integrated across organisational levels than the employers' associations they negotiate with in neo-corporatist arrangements. The three main trade unions (Catholic, socialist and liberal) maintain nationwide branch structures reporting to a head office in Brussels.[1] Trade unions are recognised social partners at both the federal level and the regional levels. Their relative centralisation (especially compared with other interest groups or political parties) is partly because the core interests of their membership (such as wage bargaining, labour market policies, social security and healthcare) are still policies largely determined at the federal level. But it also reflects a clear preference among trade union leaders for maintaining an integrated federal state, rather than the looser confederal organisation advocated by Flemish nationalists. The socialist union (FGTB-ABVV) is more decentralised than the others, with an assertive and autonomous Walloon branch, most of whose policy team operates from an office in Namur close to the regional government. This reflects the historic socialist tendencies of Walloon politics, with FGTB-ABVV retaining privileged ties with a Socialist Party that continues to dominate the regional government. FGTB-ABVV is significantly weaker in Flanders, where the Christian Democrat trade union (ACV-CSC) is much larger and retains close ties to the left wing of CD&V but has strained relations with liberal and nationalist parties in the Flemish government. ACV-CSC retains its confessional character and so its political links to Christian Democrats in Wallonia (cdH) have become much looser, especially since cdH moved towards non-confessional positions based on humanism (Deschouwer, 2012). ACV-CSC is technically the largest trade union in Wallonia, but has much less influence in regional policymaking than FGTB-ABVV. The centrist positioning of ACV-CSC means it lacks strong influence in regional governments that tend to lean either towards the right (Flanders) or left (Wallonia) of the political spectrum, but makes it a pivotal actor in federal bargaining, where centrist positions are generally adopted. ACV-CSC maintains a single head office and study service in Brussels, from where it conducts political monitoring and lobbying activities across the whole of Belgium. Its regional branches are allowed to propose policy positions at the regional or federal levels, but their financial autonomy or decision-making power is rather limited.

Devolution in Belgium has been rather uneven across policy competencies. While most economic policies remain the (sole) preserve of the federal level, other policy areas (social, cultural, environmental, agricultural) have been largely transferred to regional governments in Flanders, Wallonia and Brussels. This has resulted in distinct regional policy communities with very little interaction between them. The Flemish agricultural association *Boerenbond* emerged from the Christian pillar in Belgian society and maintains an active presence in Flemish politics, employing around 200 full-time staff and relying on strong financial reserves that compensate for declining membership dues from a shrinking agricultural sector. *Boerenbond* no longer has any organisational links with its Walloon counterpart (*Fédération wallonne de l'agriculture*), which has very limited resources and is rarely able to influence policymakers. The two organisations occasionally lobby the federal government together over issues concerning the residual agricultural competencies at that level, or when EU negotiations on agriculture are taking place.

All Belgian regions include a confederation of environmental associations, whose core objective is to carry out lobbying and political monitoring activities at regional and federal levels. In Flanders and Wallonia these confederations maintain very close working relationships with the main natural heritage associations, which are also regionally organised (*Natuurpunt* in Flanders, *Natagora* in Wallonia). *Natuurpunt* and *Natagora* undertake joint lobbying of the federal government in its few residual environmental competencies: maritime policy, climate change and nuclear energy. On these issues they often find common cause with the international environmental associations, notably WWF and Greenpeace, which adopt a national organisation in Belgium and avoid dividing their resources and splitting their focus along territorial lines. Civil society organisations meanwhile are often entirely regionalised. This includes social associations with ancillary ties to the trade unions, such as the Christian Workers' Movement represented by separate organisations in Flanders (ACW) and Wallonia (MOC). The fragmentation of Belgian society along linguistic lines, combined with the devolution of cultural and social competencies and their funding to regional governments, has removed many incentives to organise on a federal level (see Celis et al, 2013). Interest groups that still organise at the federal level do so because their key policy interests are still determined by the federal government. The territorial fragmentation of interest groups in Belgium is almost unique in the European landscape. Even in highly autonomous regions, such as Scotland or Catalonia, most interest groups still operate as multi-level organisations with national, regional and local structures (Keating and Wilson, 2014).

These complex changes result in an intriguing paradox. The neo-corporatist legacy is generally considered to constrain the number of organised interests and to limit access opportunities. However, other features of the Belgian polity, such as the presence of new groups and its multi-level nature, result in a rather crowded and fragmented interest group landscape, where a diverse set of organised groups interact with policymakers. This diversity is confirmed when one examines the groups that are represented in the strategic advisory councils to the Flemish government (Fraussen et al, 2015).[2] Within this community of policy insiders, many well-established and well-resourced organisations operate, often representing a large constituency. This set of core players, which enjoys high levels of representation in the advisory system, frequently includes traditional economic interests, such as the main trade unions and business associations, as well as other (formerly pillarised) associations with historic links to the Catholic, socialist, or liberal parties. Yet other types of interests are found in the insider community, such as industry associations, consumer organisations and environmental groups, resulting in a rather diverse interest group system. Nevertheless, compared with traditional economic interests, these types of groups (and citizen groups in particular) generally enjoy far fewer instances of representation.

How Belgium's most prominent interest groups acquire, formulate and utilise policy advice

Whereas previous research has mainly focused on the interaction between policymakers and organised interests, this chapter sheds light on how these groups are organised in order to acquire expertise, as well as the specific political activities they undertake in order to shape public policy. To deepen the understanding of these issues, a survey was sent out to a set of interest organisations in Belgium in December 2013. As the authors consciously sought to look beyond traditional economic interests, they based their selection of cases on interest group presence in the media, which is a less institutionalised and possibly more open and dynamic arena compared with the bureaucracy or the parliament. Those 30 groups were selected with the highest number of media appearances in the television news between 2003 and 2010 (Wouters et al, 2011).[3] These are all groups that actively aim to shape political debates and public opinion, although they may do so in different ways. While some focus on providing policy advice, others concentrate on campaigns or protest events. They all aim to get a specific policy message across to the general public and policymakers. For this reason, all these groups are expected to make investments in policy-related capacities, such as well-educated staff, as well as extensive networks with political actors and other organised interests. A total of 25 organisations completed the survey, which means a response rate of 83%. This set encompasses 14 economic groups (business associations and labour unions) and 11 citizen groups (such as environmental and consumer groups). Furthermore, 13 of the groups are organised on a national scale, implying that they have members in both French- and Dutch-speaking parts of the country, whereas 12 groups only have a constituency in one of the Belgian regions: Flanders, Wallonia or Brussels (for more details, see Table A9.1).

This set of groups provides an adequate picture of the organisational diversity in the Belgian interest group population, as it encompasses both economic and citizen groups, as well as nationwide and regional groups. By including only highly prominent groups, however, the analysis is skewed towards more established interest organisations that generally have a larger amount of resources and are among the key players in their policy domain(s) of interest.[4] While the authors believe an emphasis on the top tier of the interest group community is justified given its focus on policy-related activities, this bias should be taken into account when interpreting results.

The following section presents the main survey results. The analysis of the supply side of policy advice first describes the policy-analytical capacity and engagement of the interest groups included in the sample. Then it looks more closely at their policy work by examining the characteristics and dissemination of their policy advice.

Policy-analytical capacity and engagement in policymaking

Considering that the accumulation of policy expertise requires a lot of organisational resources (in terms of staff, budget and time), organisations with a larger number of staff (particularly those with a large number of policy workers) are in principle more likely to build up in-house expertise and maintain networks with a large and broad range of actors, making them more valuable to policymakers. It is often assumed that economic groups dispose of greater financial resources and consequently also employ a greater number of staff. But when considering the respondents, it is noted that in terms of staff the median value is 50, both for economic interests and citizen groups. This similarity does, however, conceal considerable variation. For instance, the set includes two small groups – both citizen groups – that rely on less than 10 staff members, which is in line with the average amount of staff in the broader interest population, where about 75% of groups rely on less than 10 full-time equivalents (Fraussen and Beyers, 2015). In contrast, three organisations – two citizen groups and one economic group – reported they employed more than 1,000 people.[5]

The professional background of the staff of these organisations is rather diverse, in general a mix of people with experience in the private (profit or non-profit) and the public sector, as well as former staff of universities (including researchers and lecturers) and civil society organisations. When considering the distinction between economic and citizen groups, it appears that economic groups mainly employ people with a background in the private *profit* sector or in the public sector, as well as former staff of universities. Citizen groups appear to mainly employ staffs who have experience in the private *non-profit* sector and in civil society organisations. On average, 25% of the staff of these organisations are policy workers, implying that these people are involved in doing research, monitoring policy processes, defining policy positions, and networking with other organised interests and policymakers. Hence, citizen groups generally have fewer policy workers among their staff compared with economic groups, as illustrated in Table 9.1 (the average amount being respectively 15% and 36%).

These differences could relate to the potentially different goals of economic and citizen groups, and the extent to which they prioritise the acquisition of certain 'resources' (Binderkrantz, 2008; Binderkrantz et al, 2014). For instance, whereas citizen groups are often assumed to be more focused on agenda setting

Table 9.1: Policy workers (as % of total staff) and outsourcing of research activities

		Economic group	Citizen group
Policy workers	<20% of total staff	3	8
	>20% of total staff	7	3
Outsourcing of research activities	≤20% of research activities	7	4
	>20% of research activities	4	6

and making broader appeals to the population at large, economic groups are believed to be more concerned with influencing specific (and often more narrow) policy decisions. Following these different priorities, economic groups may invest more in what are called 'insider resources', that is policy-relevant information and expertise, than 'outsider resources', such as the ability to mobilise a rather diffuse set of members and supporters, or the skills to provide journalists with personalised stories.

In spite of the limited number of policy workers these organisations employ, most of them nevertheless focus on building expertise internally. The outsourcing of research activities is rather limited; only two groups indicated that they outsourced the majority of their policy work to external partners. As for the differences between economic and citizen groups, the latter show a greater tendency to outsource their policy work, which could imply that they accumulate less in-house expertise compared with economic groups.

The assumption that economic groups are more concerned with influencing specific policy decisions, whereas citizen groups are more focused on agenda setting or shaping public opinion, may also provide an explanation for the patterns demonstrated in Table 9.2. We asked the respondents how frequently they interacted with policymakers (including elected and non-elected officials) at different levels of government. The great majority of groups indicated that they were active at both the domestic and EU level on a monthly or weekly basis. In addition, policy developments at the local level (local governments and provincial administrations) are monitored closely by some of these organisations, although to a lesser extent. In terms of their policy work, many of these groups appear well adjusted to the dynamics of multi-level governance that characterise contemporary policymaking, where policy responsibilities are spread between public authorities at the European, national and subnational level. This is unusual when compared with most other European democracies, where regional interest groups are rarely active at the EU level, usually delegating this function to the national organisation or their EU-wide representative association (Keating and Wilson, 2014). This difference may be linked to the high degree of overlapping competencies in Belgian policymaking (Bouteca et al, 2013), or simply due to the proximity of the main EU institutions. Nevertheless, there are considerable differences between economic and citizen groups. With the exception of the local level, a much higher percentage of economic groups regularly interact with policymakers. This suggests that economic groups enjoy higher levels of government access, or that they more strongly prioritise insider lobbying strategies involving direct contacts with public authorities (see Dür and Mateo, 2013).

The extent to which groups focus on issues within multiple policy domains (for example, economy, employment, environment or social security) or instead limit their activities to a single policy sector was also assessed. Economic groups generally seem to have a more comprehensive policy portfolio, meaning that they are active in a broader range of policy domains. Whereas citizen groups indicated they were active in an average of five policy domains, economic groups reported they were active in an average of 13 policy domains. The tendency to have a very broad policy portfolio was most noticeable among the social partners (business associations and trade unions), who on average had interests in almost 16 policy domains. This finding is possibly linked to their representation in a wide range of sectoral advisory bodies at the regional level as well as the federal level. Compared with citizen groups, who are often more specialised, the social partners show a rather broad level of policy engagement. Next to being the key (and often sole) representatives in advisory bodies dealing with socioeconomic issues, they often maintain a strong presence in bodies that deal with non-economic issues such as education, culture or the environment.

Table 9.2: Policy focus across levels of government

Level	Percentage of groups active on this level on a monthly or weekly basis	
	Economic group	Citizen group
Local government issues	43%	40%
Provincial themes	29%	9%
Matters concerning other regions and communities	86%	55%
Federal matters	100%	45%
Issues concerning neighbouring countries	36%	30%
European issues	79%	45%
International policy issues	50%	18%

Note: N=25, except for 'local government issues' and 'issues concerning neighbouring countries' (N=24)"

Characteristics of policy advice

The previous section provided some details about the resources that interest groups devote to policy work (in terms of staff), as well as the intensity and scope of their engagement with policymakers. This section deals with the specific features of their policy advice. A first question in this regard involves the extent to which these groups balance activities focused on short-term objectives with those addressing more long-term goals. In other words, it looks at what extent the activities of these groups are driven by the demands of policymakers and issues that currently dominate the political agenda, or rather relate to future objectives. Considering that economic groups interact more regularly with policymakers than citizen groups, and are often strongly represented in various advisory institutions, they might be more focused on short-term objectives related to the current political agenda. As illustrated in Table 9.3, however, this statement cannot be generalised for all economic groups. While some of them strongly prioritise short-term goals, others indicate they engage more frequently in activities geared towards the longer term. For citizen groups the picture is less balanced, as all of them indicate that at least 25% of their activities are linked to long-term objectives.

Table 9.3: Long-term versus short-term issues

Percentage of long-term versus short-term issues	Economic group (N=12)	Citizen group (N=11)
1-25% of activities	33%	0%
26-50% of activities	25%	54%
51-75% of activities	42%	36%
76-100% of activities	0%	10%

Another important question relates to what good policy advice implies. Should advice be based on scientifically valid evidence (epistemic), relate to what works in practice (techne) or reflect on the desirability and legitimacy of a certain policy proposal (phronesis) (Tenbensel, 2008)? From Table 9.4, which gives an overview of the quality criteria the respondents considered *very* important (columns 2, 3 and 4), these three types of knowledge appear to be rather equally valued.[6] Many groups indicated that advice should be supported by both scientific research and examples from best practices, and should also include the formulation of clear and concisely formulated policy initiatives. Close attention to future developments was considered important by the majority of groups, in line with the findings presented in Table 9.3. The results also indicate some interesting differences between the quality criteria used by economic groups and citizen groups. The former attach much more importance to the technical feasibility of policy advice, with 64% of them selecting this criterion compared with 27% for citizen groups. Economic groups find it more important that policy advice should entail a well-considered trade-off of pros and cons, or that it is clearly and concisely formulated. Public legitimacy is seen as crucial to citizen groups, while for economic groups this appears to be of lesser importance (64 % versus 14%).

The second column of Table 9.4 presents a ranking of the expectations of policy officials. It relies on earlier research, where government officials were asked to indicate which three criteria they considered most important (Bossens et al, 2014). While the context of this research was somewhat different (as it related to advice formulated by the strategic advisory councils to the Flemish government), it enables a first assessment of the extent to which quality criteria used by interest groups and policymakers 'match'. Three criteria stand out about the expectations of policy officials towards good policy advice: a well-considered trade-off of pros and cons, attention to future developments, and public legitimacy. The first criterion, a well-considered trade-off of pros and cons, is also an important quality criterion for economic groups, but much less so for citizen groups. The second most selected criterion by policy officials, attention to future developments, is considered an important criterion for both types of groups. The third most selected criterion, public legitimacy, is important to citizen groups, but seems to matter less for economic groups. The data suggests there is a slightly better match between the expectations of government officials and the quality criteria of *economic* groups. However, based on earlier research (Rich and Oh, 2000; Landry et al, 2003; Weimer and Vining, 2005), it is assumed that most of the criteria listed are at least of *some* importance for 'good' policy advice. An alternative inference could be that the advice of economic groups and citizen groups is complementary, as both groups value different quality criteria.

Table 9.4: Relative importance of quality criteria

Criteria	Government officials (ranking)	Economic group (N=14)	Citizen group (N=11)	All (N=25)
Well-considered trade-off of pros and cons	1	57% (8)	9% (1)	9
Attention to future evolutions and trends	2	64% (9)	45% (5)	14
Attention to public legitimacy	3	14% (2)	64% (7)	9
Attention to technical feasibility	4	64% (9)	27% (3)	12
Clear and concisely formulated	5	79% (11)	27% (3)	14
Supported by scientific research	6	50% (7)	73% (8)	15
Formulation of specific policy initiatives	7	50% (7)	64% (7)	14
Supported by examples from best practices	8	50% (7)	73% (8)	15
Responding to a policy need for information	9	21% (3)	9% (1)	4
Well-structured text	10	7% (1)	27% (3)	4
Transparency concerning sources of information	10	7% (1)	36% (4)	5
Aligned with the policy position of the minister	11	21% (3)	0% (0)	3

To be able to provide accurate policy advice, actors that participate in policymaking need to acquire relevant and up-to-date expertise. While these groups mostly focus on accumulating in-house knowledge, they also rely on external contacts to gain more information about specific policy matters. One of the questions focused precisely on this issue and sought to analyse which actors and institutions are consulted by interest groups in order to acquire expertise. Table 9.5 shows that almost all of our respondents indicate that they use information from national or subnational government administrations on a monthly or weekly basis, while they also very frequently rely on articles and reports from the media. Furthermore, reports from the strategic advisory councils are considered a valuable source of information to a majority of economic groups, notwithstanding that these councils are often subject to criticism regarding their effectiveness. Most information sources are more frequently used by economic groups than by citizen groups. Only information from public administrations in other European countries, scientific publications, information from social media networks and information from citizen platforms are more frequently used by citizen groups.

Table 9.5: Interest groups' sources of information

Information source	Percentage using this information on a monthly or weekly basis	
	Economic group	**Citizen group**
Information from federal, Flemish, Walloon or local government administrations	100%	82%
Information from public administrations in other European countries	15%	36%
Information from European and international organisations (such as OECD, International Monetary Fund)	64%	36%
External evaluation reports	57%	18%
Reports and studies from the Court of Audit, the National Bank or the Planning Bureau	71%	18%
Advice of the (strategic) advisory councils	71%	45%
Reports and publications by civil society organisations or NGOs	71%	45%
Reports and publications by think tanks (such as Itinera)	29%	20%
Reports and publications of consultants (such as Deloitte, KPMG)	36%	20%
Reports and publications by foundations (such as Koning Boudewijn Stichting)	8%	10%
Reports and publications by party think tanks	29%	9%
Scientific publications	57%	73%
Contacts with individual academics	57%	40%
Media articles and reports	93%	82%
Information from social media networks (Facebook, Twitter, LinkedIn)	57%	73%
Information from citizen platforms	8%	55%
Information from companies	86%	36%

Note: N varies between 23 and 25 for all items.

Dissemination of policy advice

Interest groups use different strategies to transmit their advice to policymakers. In this regard, researchers frequently distinguish between inside and outside strategies (Binderkrantz, 2008; Dür and Mateo, 2013). The former relate to direct strategies, like contacting the relevant minister or transmitting advice to parliamentary committees. Outside strategies, such as demonstrations, symposia or conferences, contacting news reporters or using social media, are, in contrast, more indirect and seek to communicate a message to the broader public. Table 9.6 shows that the groups in our set use a range of different strategies to influence policy. The vast majority of economic and citizen groups participates on a monthly or weekly basis in consultation or advisory bodies. Most of them maintain frequent contacts with other interest groups and regularly organise media campaigns. As for contacts with policymakers at both the federal and regional level, economic groups appear to engage more frequently with most policy actors than citizen groups do. This high level of direct interaction, however, does not imply less frequent use of outside strategies. Economic groups are also very active in public arenas, through media appearances or social media campaigns. While citizen groups also combine inside and outside strategies, they have much less contact with policymakers compared with economic groups.[7]

Finally, the survey considered to what extent and how interest groups themselves assess their policy work. About 80% of the organisations report that they regularly evaluate their policy activities. Compared with citizen groups, economic groups seem more inclined to evaluate their policy activities (92% versus 73%). When focusing specifically on the social partners, all of them evaluate their policy activities. One important factor in assessing policy work is the degree of policy influence, which 79% of our respondents considers 'very important'. It is therefore no surprise that both access to policymakers and a strong presence in the media are highly valued by a majority of groups.

Table 9.6: Activities of interest groups

Activity	Percentage on a monthly or weekly basis	
	Economic group	**Citizen group**
Federal level: contact with government officials (including cabinets)	93%	36%
Federal level: contact with parliamentarians	64%	45%
Federal level: contact with administration	86%	45%
Regional level: contact with government officials (including cabinets)	71%	45%
Regional level: contact with parliamentarians	43%	36%
Regional level: contact with administration	64%	64%
General: contact with party chairmen	43%	9%
General: participation in consultations or advisory bodies	93%	73%
Organisation of conferences or seminars	50%	9%
Media appearances and press releases	93%	82%
Legal actions	36%	18%
Social media campaigns	46%	55%
Contact with other interest groups	100%	73%

N=25, except for 'social media campaigns' (N=24).

While almost all citizen groups find policy influence an important criterion, only half of them consider this criterion 'rather' to 'very' important, whereas all economic groups indicate this objective to be 'very' important. This finding may relate to more structural differences between these two group types. All organised interests face an inherent trade-off between activities related to shaping public policy and efforts to maintain and secure their membership base (Schmitter and Streeck, 1999; see also Dür and Mateo, 2013). The latter concern might be more critical to citizen groups, which often rely on less stable and more diffuse constituencies compared with economic groups. Following this logic, their high media presence could be regarded not only as a way to shape to shape public policy, but also as an important instrument to demonstrate their value to (current and potential) members or supporters.

Conclusion

This chapter has discussed the Belgian system of interest representation and analysed how interest groups gather policy expertise and put it to use in their lobbying activities. Earlier research on the policy activities and influence of groups in neo-corporatist countries has tended to focus on the functioning of traditional economic interests, such as the social partners. As these groups only represent a minority of the rather diverse and fragmented Belgian interest group population, we opted to examine in this chapter the policy activities and engagement of a more varied set of groups by focusing on 25 prominent interest organisations. In this way, we were able to investigate notable similarities as well as differences between the practices of economic groups and citizen groups.

The results indicate that while most of these organisations consider policy influence a very important objective, their investments in policy-analytical capacity (in terms of staff focused on policy analysis) vary considerably and are sometimes rather low, especially in the case of citizen groups. Nevertheless, these groups manage to monitor policy development at various levels of government and also continue to do most research in-house. Moreover, some interesting differences between the political behaviour of economic and citizen groups emerge. While government officials view a well-considered trade-off of pros and cons as well as attention to public legitimacy as critical to good policy advice, economic groups especially value the former, and citizen groups are much more concerned about the latter.

As regards policy influence, economic groups are slightly more focused on frequent interaction with policymakers, whereas citizen groups attach more importance to regular media appearances. While this could imply that economic groups enjoy higher levels of government access than do citizen groups, it could also be a consequence of different organisational objectives. Whereas economic groups appear more focused on influencing specific policy issues, citizen groups seem more concentrated on agenda setting and shaping public opinion, as well as maintaining and developing a large base of members and/or supporters.

Obviously, conclusions from these findings should be handled with care, as they relate to a small set of interest organisations. Yet, as the sample includes a diverse range of prominent citizen and economic groups, it may provide a balanced image of the policy engagement of interest groups in Belgium. Nevertheless, future research on policy advice would benefit from a more systematic analysis of the policy-analytical capacity of interest groups, as well as a comparison of their perspectives on policy advice with those of policymakers. As demonstrated by the results on the characteristics of good policy advice, these two parties can have quite different expectations, which might impede smooth collaboration as well as the optimal use of policy expertise. In that regard, it would also be valuable to assess how the interaction between organised interests and public authorities varies across policy domains.

There may also be considerable differences across different levels of government, as the style or culture of policymaking differs considerably and many Belgian interest groups are active exclusively (or mainly) in a specific region. While some governments may prefer a consultative approach, others may choose to involve organised interests more closely in decision making and agenda setting, perhaps even granting them co-decision rights. The variation of this interaction across policy domains and levels of government seems a promising avenue for future research on policy analysis and the interplay between organised interests and policymakers.

Notes

[1] The liberal trade union in Belgium is much smaller in terms of membership than its Christian Democrat and socialist counterparts, and lacks developed branch structures. Its decision making is highly centralised and it tends to have very limited influence in policymaking, partly because it no longer has close ties to liberal parties in Flanders or Wallonia, which have adopted more market-driven positions (see Bouteca et al, 2013).

[2] The strategic advisory councils are established by decree and deliver advice to the Flemish government, individual ministers and parliament on strategic matters (see also Chapter Seven).

[3] The selection relies on the Electronic News Archive administered by the University of Antwerp and the KU Leuven, which daily records and codes the 7pm televised news of the biggest public (VRT) and commercial (VTM) broadcasters in Flanders. The period is limited to 2010 as fully coded data was only available until that year. As no data on media appearances of groups in French-speaking media outlets was available, the Walloon counterparts of the Flemish groups were included (when possible) in the set.

[4] Their status can follow from their prominence as an important policy advisor and/or their central role in the provision of specific (public) services.

[5] Yet, the picture is not entirely complete. Of the 25 organisations included, three respondents (all economic groups) did not provide information about the number of staff employed.

[6] Respondents were asked to select the five criteria they considered most important, based on a list of 12 criteria. The percentage (and number) of respondents who selected a criterion is indicated for each criterion.

[7] The finding that media strategies are very important to both types of groups is obviously related to the sample selection.

References

Andrews, K.T. and Caren, N. (2010) 'Making the news: movement organizations, media attention and the public agenda', *American Sociological Review*, 75(6): 841–66.

Baumgartner, F.R., Berry, J.M., Hojnacki, M., Kimball, D.C. and Leech, B.L. (2009) *Lobbying and policy change: who wins, who loses, and why*, Chicago, IL: University of Chicago Press.

Beyers, J. and Braun, C. (2014) 'Ties that count. Explaining interest group access to policymakers', *Journal of Public Policy*, 34(1): 93-121.

Beyers, J., Braun, C. and Haverland, M. (2014) '*Plus ça change, plus c'est pareil*. European integration and interest group politics in the Low Countries', in H. Vollaard, J. Beyers and P. Dumont (eds) *European integration and consensus politics in the Low Countries*, London: Routledge, 134-54.

Beyers, J., Eising, R. and Maloney, W. (2008) 'Researching interest group politics in Europe and elsewhere: much we study, little we know?', *West European Politics*, 31(6): 1103-28.

Binderkrantz, A. (2008) 'Different groups, different strategies: how interest groups pursue their political ambitions', *Scandinavian Political Studies*, 31(2): 173-200.

Binderkrantz, A. (2012) 'Interest groups in the media: bias and diversity over time', *European Journal of Political Research*, 51(1): 1-23.

Binderkrantz, A., Christiansen, P.M. and Pedersen H.H. (2014) 'Interest group access to the bureaucracy, parliament, and the media', *Governance*, 28(1): 95-112.

Bloodgood, E.A., Tremblay-Boire, J. and Prakash, A. (2014) 'National styles of NGO regulation', *Nonprofit and Voluntary Sector Quarterly*, 43(4): 716-36.

Bossens, N., Van Damme, J. and Brans, M. (2014) *Beleidsadvisering in de Vlaamse overheid: een analyse van de organisatie van de Vlaamse beleidsadvisering en een verkenning van mogelijkheden voor optimalisering*, Leuven: Steunpunt Bestuurlijke Organisatie.

Bouteca, N., Devos, C. and Mus, M. (2013) 'The future of Belgian federalism as seen through the eyes of the social partners: a continuing obstacle to social policy decentralization', *Regional and Federal Studies*, 23(3): 293-309.

Bouwen, P. (2004) 'Exchanging access goods for access: a comparative study of business lobbying in the European Union institutions', *European Journal of Political Research*, 43(3): 337-69.

Brans, M., Van Damme, J. and Gaskell, J. (2010) *Education Councils in Europe. Balancing expertise, societal input and political control in the production of policy advice*, Brussels: European Network of Education Councils.

Caluwaerts, D. and Reuchamps, M. (2014) 'Combining federalism with consociationalism: is Belgian consociational federalism digging its own grave?', *Ethnopolitics*, 14(3): 277-95.

Carpenter, D.P., Esterling, K.M. and Lazer, D.M.J. (1998) 'The strength of weak ties in lobbying networks: evidence from health-care politics in the United States', *Journal of Theoretical Politics*, 10(4): 417-44.

Celis, K., Mackay, F. and Meier, P. (2013) 'Social movement organizations and changing state architectures: comparing women's movement organizing in Flanders and Scotland', *Publius: The Journal of Federalism*, 43(1): 44-67.

Deleeck, H. (2003) *De architectuur van de welvaartstaat opnieuw bekeken*, Leuven: Acco.

Deschouwer, K. (2012) *The politics of Belgium: governing a divided society* (2nd edn), Basingstoke: Palgrave Macmillan.

Dür, A. and Mateo, G. (2013) 'Gaining access or going public? Interest group strategies in five European countries', *European Journal of Political Research*, 52(5): 660-86.

Eising, R. (2007) 'The access of business interest to EU institutions: towards elite pluralism', *Journal of European Public Policy*, 14(3): 384-403.

Eising, R. (2009) *The political economy of state-business relations in Europe: interest mediation, capitalism and EU policy-making*, London: Routledge.

Fraussen, B. (2014) 'The visible hand of the state: on the organizational development of interest groups', *Public Administration*, 92(2): 406-21.

Fraussen, B., Beyers, J. and Donas, T. (2015) 'The expanding core and varying degrees of insiderness: institutionalized interest group involvement through advisory councils', *Political Studies*, 63(3): 569-88.

Hall, R.L. and Deardorf, A.V. (2006) 'Lobbying as legislative subsidy', *American Political Science Review*, 100(1): 69-84.

Halpin, D., Daugbjerg, C. and Schvartzman, Y. (2011) 'Interest-group capacities and infant industry development: state-sponsored growth in organic farming', *International Political Science Review*, 32(2): 147-66.

Hojnacki, M., Kimball, D.C., Baumgartner, F., Berry, J.M. and Leech, B.L. (2012) 'Studying organisational advocacy and influence: re-examining interest group research', *Annual Review of Political Science*, 15: 379-99.

Jones, E. (2002). 'Consociationalism, corporatism, and the fate of Belgium', *Acta Politica*, 37(1): 86-103.

Keating, M. and Wilson, A. (2014) 'Regions with regionalism? The rescaling of interest groups in six European states', *European Journal of Political Research*, 53(4): 840-57.

Klüver, H. (2012) 'Informational lobbying in the European Union: the effect of organisational characteristics', *West European Politics*, 35(3): 491-510.

Klüver, H. and Saurugger, S. (2013) 'Opening the black box: the professionalization of interest groups in the European Union', *Interest Groups and Advocacy*, 2(2): 185-205.

Kollman, K. (1998) *Outside lobbying: public opinion and interest group strategies*, Princeton, NJ: Princeton University Press.

Landry, R., Lamari, M. and Amara, N. (2003) 'The extent and determinants of the utilization of university research in government agencies', *Public Administration Review*, 63(2): 192-205.

Lijphart, A. and Crepaz, M.M.L. (1991) 'Corporatism and consensus democracy in 18 countries: conceptual and empirical linkages', *British Journal of Political Science*, 21(2): 235-46.

Luyten, D. (2006) 'Corporatisme, neocorporatisme, competitief corporatisme: sociale regulering sinds 1945', in E. Witte and A. Meynen (eds) *De Geschiedenis van België na 1945*, Antwerp: Standaard Uitgeverij, 365-94.

Rich, R.F. and Oh, C.H. (2000) 'Rationality and use of information in policy decisions: a search for alternatives', *Science Communication*, 22(2): 173-211.

Siaroff, A. (1999) 'Corporatism in 24 industrial democracies: meaning and measurement', *European Journal of Political Research*, 36(2): 175-205.

Schmitter, P.C. and Streeck, W. (1999) *The organisation of business interests. Studying the associative action of business in advanced industrial societies*, Köln: Max-Planck-Institut für Gesellschaftsforschung.

Tenbensel, T. (2008) 'The role of evidence in policy: how the mix matters', paper presented at the 12th Annual Conference of the International Research Society for Public Management, Brisbane, 26-28 March.

Traxler, F. (2010) 'The long-term development of organised business and its implications for corporatism: a cross-national comparison of membership, activities and governing capacities of business interest associations, 1980-2003', *European Journal of Political Research*, 49(2): 151-73.

van den Bulck, J. (1992) 'Pillars and politics: neo-corporatism and policy networks in Belgium', *West European Politics*, 15(2): 35-55.

Walgrave, S. (1994) *Nieuwe sociale bewegingen in Vlaanderen*, Leuven: SOI/KU Leuven.

Weimer, D.L. and Vining, A.R. (2005) *Policy analysis: concepts and practice*, New Jersey, NY: Prentice Hall.

Wouters, R., De Smedt, J., Hooghe, M. and Walgrave, S. (2011) 'Midden in het nieuws? Middenveldorganisaties in het Vlaamse televisienieuws (2003-2010)', *Nieuwsmonitor van het Steunpunt Media*, 10/2011.

Appendix

Table A9.1: List of organisations participating in the survey on interest groups

Organised on a national scale	
ABVV	Labour union
ACV	Labour union
ACLVB	Labour union
Test-Aankoop	Consumer group
Touring	Consumer group
VTB-VAB	Consumer group
VBO	Business association
Artsen zonder Grenzen	Development NGO
Gaia	Environmental NGO
Greenpeace	Environmental NGO
Assuralia	Business association
NSPV (police union)	Labour union
Confederatie Bouw	Business association
Organised on a regional scale	
Unizo	Business association
Rode Kruis Vlaanderen	Development NGO
VOKA	Business association
Boerenbond	Business association
Bond Beter Leefmilieu	Environmental NGO
Horeca Vlaanderen	Business association
Vogelbescherming Vlaanderen	Environmental NGO
Union des Classes Moyenne	Business association
Union Wallonne des Entreprises	Business association
Ligue Royale pour la Protection des Oiseaux	Environmental NGO
Brussels Enterprises Commerce and Industry	Business association
Inter-Environnement Bruxelles	Environmental NGO

Part Four
Policy analysis and the public

TEN

Public consultation and participation in Belgium: directly engaging citizens beyond the ballot box?

Jan Van Damme, Vincent Jacquet, Nathalie Schiffino and Min Reuchamps

This chapter looks into the growth of diverse types of public inquiries and public consultation arrangements in policymaking. These arrangements bring to the table individual members of the public who otherwise have no direct policy – advisory – role, given the predominance of neo-corporatist style advisory bodies in Belgium (Van Damme and Brans, 2012). In some of these new public consultation and participation forms, citizens are not at the end of the delivery process, but are actively engaged in framing policy problems, and selecting and evaluating policy solutions. Nonetheless the rationales behind these consultation and participation processes may differ widely as to perspectives on democracy (Mayer et al, 2005). Some inquiries and consultations are conceived from an instrumental perspective from which it is believed that engaging citizens in policy analysis has something tangible to contribute to policy, by, for instance, enriching knowledge of specific policy problems, or by fostering policy support necessary for implementing solutions. From a more substantive view on democracy, citizen participation is rooted in participatory and deliberative democracy, and expected to contribute to the legitimacy of the decision-making process (Michels and De Graaf, 2010).

This chapter analyses the variety of public consultation and participation arrangements in Belgium at different levels of government in order to clarify the public's role in policymaking and analysis beyond the ballot box. To this end, a framework of analysis in three dimensions is used: Who participates? How do they participate? Why do they participate? This analysis focuses on public consultation and participation forms that are 'arranged' and managed by public authorities, but we also include recent experiments such as the G1000 citizen-led initiative. Such an initiative proposed a bottom-up approach for public participation in the agenda setting of policy problems and even in the formulation of public solutions.

Policymaking and public consultation

The increasing complexity of the policy environment has been critical for the policymaking process. On the one hand, so-called 'wicked problems' combining scientific uncertainty with societal dispute challenge traditional ways of policymaking (Jacob and Schiffino, 2011). Governments are increasingly dependent not only on external information, knowledge and expertise, but also on external support and commitment in order to successfully deliver policies (Barker and Peters, 1993). Governments increasingly feel the need to interact with more actors, and to do so more intensively, as many societal stakeholders often have the power to make or break policy. On the other hand, there is a shift in political attitudes and strategies of citizens and stakeholder groups. Today, citizens mobilise differently, in a more ad hoc and short-lived fashion and at least some groups guard their stakes very actively. Scholars speak of a turn towards more informal and unconventional ways of political interaction (Dekker and Hooghe, 2003). Behind this change in political strategy and behaviour of societal stakeholders, there is a change in their political attitude as more citizens are prepared to resort to strategies of boycott and protest (Van den Brink, 2003). Actions, which many citizens a few decades ago would have labelled as illegitimate, now appear to be acceptable to many. One of the implications of these developments is that the traditional organisations of civil society (at least in a more corporatist democratic system) no longer enjoy their status as privileged channel and access point to government.

In sum, the policy arena is becoming ever more crowded with old and new actors, from well-established lobby groups and new single-issue groups to ad hoc citizen groups, all voicing their opinion and defending their stakes. These groups not only have different ways of interacting with each other and the government, but also often have widely diverging values, stakes and perspectives. In such an environment, it has been observed that policymaking becomes increasingly difficult (Agranoff and McGuire, 1999; Kjaer, 2004)[1] and policy can be, and is being, criticised by actors with different stakes and perspectives. Since being democratically elected no longer constitutes a sufficient basis for policymakers to make legitimate policy choices, 'winning the hearts and minds of the people' on policy itself, becomes almost a daily quest for policymakers (Fung, 2003).

The international development towards more diverse mechanisms of public consultation and participation in the policymaking process (Papadopoulos and Warin, 2007; Van Damme and Brans, 2008; Hendriks, 2010) can be seen in the light of trends towards interactive policymaking, and the quest for policy legitimacy. In consensus democracies such as Belgium and the Netherlands, this means that traditional mechanisms such as permanent advisory bodies with representatives of large stakeholder groups are being joined by more 'recent' and 'innovative' mechanisms such as opinion polls, citizen panels, participatory budgeting and deliberative polling. These mechanisms are often 'borrowed' from other democratic systems and cultures (Hendriks, 2010).

These newly introduced mechanisms aim to contribute to more innovative, more efficient and better supported policy. More actors are being involved, from both within and beyond the governmental system – not only academic experts and big interests, but also individual citizens, specific target groups and so on. Such mechanisms of public consultation and participation are supposed to substantially contribute to both democracy and policy. However, depending on the perspective, the specific targeted goals of such initiatives can be quite different. For example, from a democratic theory perspective, questions of input and throughput legitimacy of policymaking are typically highlighted (Scharpf, 1997; Papadopoulos and Warin, 2007). Input legitimacy deals with questions of increasing public access to the policymaking process ('inclusiveness'), whereas throughput legitimacy focuses on the quality of deliberation preceding the policy decision. The governance literature has more of a managerial and instrumental focus and typically posits questions regarding the efficiency and effectiveness of public consultation (focusing on 'output' legitimacy). To what extent can public consultation and participation contribute to better policy? To what extent can consultation deliver innovative perspectives and ideas?

This chapter starts by defining public consultation and by illustrating the (multiple) possible goals of public consultation and participation. Next it develops a typology of public consultation mechanisms linked to specific democratic regimes as specific consultation mechanisms are typical for a certain democratic system and culture. The following sections illustrate the variety of consultation and participation arrangements in Belgium at different levels of government in order to offer a broad picture of how citizens are directly engaged beyond the ballot box.

Defining public consultation

Public consultation is understood as government-initiated arrangements of interaction on policy with societal parties such as citizens and non-governmental organisations. These can be aggregative systems such as referenda and pollings, integrative systems such as open planning processes and consensus conferences, and complex arrangements combining aggregation and integration/deliberation (Hendriks, 2010; Van Damme and Brans, 2012). The object of the public consultation is a policy of some kind, such as (intended) regulation, legislation or policy plans, to name but a few examples. The subjects of public consultation are societal parties such as citizens, businesses and non-governmental organisations. Public consultation can take place at any stage of the policymaking process: agenda setting, policy formulation, decision making, implementation, monitoring or evaluation.

Public consultation is used here as a broad, umbrella concept. However, this concept can also be used to refer to a specific 'type' of interaction between government and the public. The Organisation for Economic Cooperation and Development (OECD, 2001) differentiates between information, consultation and participation in terms of the nature and direction of the relationship between government and citizens.

First, information is seen as a one-way relationship in which government produces and delivers information for use by citizens. It covers both 'passive' access to information on demand by citizens and 'active' measures to disseminate information to citizens. Second, public consultation has been defined as a two-way relationship in which citizens provide feedback to government. It is based on a prior definition by government of the issue on which citizens' views are being sought and requires the provision of information. Third, active participation is a relationship based on partnership with government, in which citizens actively engage in defining the process and content of policymaking. The OECD stipulates, however, that even though active participation acknowledges equal standing for citizens in setting agendas, proposing policy options and shaping policy dialogue, the responsibility for the final decision rests with government (OECD, 2001). Therefore, the OECD definitions clearly fit an indirect democracy perspective.

This chapter focuses primarily on public consultation and participation. The difference between these concepts in the OECD definition appears to depend mainly on the intensity of the interaction. Although there are clearly differences in the intensity of interaction of specific initiatives (compare, for example, the intensity of an opinion poll with that of an open planning process), the line between consultation and participation is a rather blurred one. Nevertheless, it remains a useful demarcation in describing mechanisms of interaction between government and the public.

Consultation, participation and political regimes

Previous research has mapped different arrangements of public consultation and linked them to specific democratic regimes (Van Damme and Brans, 2008) based on a model by Frank Hendriks (2006). Specific consultation arrangements are indeed typical or dominant for a certain democratic system and culture (see Figure 10.1). For example, in an indirect Westminster style democracy, green papers have commonly been used as a way of gathering written input from organisations (and these days also more often from individual citizens). Government officials have a pivotal role as they collect the reactions to these consultations, use the information gathered and balance the interests of those involved as they see fit. There is no interaction between the societal stakeholders themselves.

A very different system can be found in traditional consensus democracies such as Belgium and the Netherlands where often (semi)permanent advisory bodies have been set up to enable societal stakeholders repeatedly to interact with each other on policy issues, and sometimes with policymakers (see Chapter Seven). These advisory bodies are an institutionalisation of a dominant consensual policymaking culture in which core societal representatives have to be consulted on policy. In many policy fields such as education and welfare these organisations play a central role in policy implementation and their support as well as knowledge is very important in developing potentially successful policies.

Whereas the upper quadrants of the model have indirect democracy at their core, the lower quadrants of the model are based on direct democracy. The central question to differentiate between the upper and the lower quadrants is who decides on policy. In both the voters' and participatory democracies, citizens make the final decisions. Affiliated mechanisms of public consultation are opinion polls and referenda (where the numbers of people in favour of or against a certain policy are a focal point) for the voters' democracy and citizens' panels (where the quality of citizen deliberation is central) for the participatory democracy.

Figure 10.1: Public consultation arrangements[2]

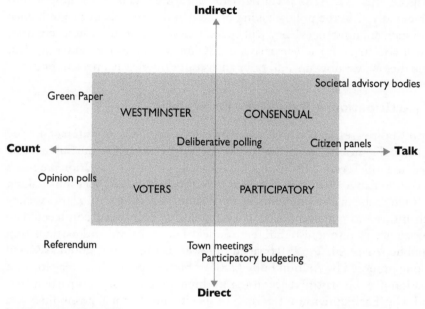

Source: Van Damme and Brans (2008)

In both Westminster-style democracies and consensual democracies (such as the Netherlands and Belgium) there has been an increase in the use and diversity of arrangements used for public consultation (Van Damme and Brans, 2008). Moreover, arrangements that are typically related to direct democratic systems (voters' and participatory democracy) are often also introduced. Accordingly, citizens become somehow more prominent actors in the policymaking process. However, as these mechanisms are introduced in indirect democratic systems, they are often adapted to fit this environment (compare, for example, the binding referendum with the non-binding plebiscite).

As Schudson has observed (1999), even when new institutional arrangements are being introduced, more traditional institutional arrangements – such as in this case (semi-)permanent societal advisory bodies in consensual political systems – are often maintained, although these do come under pressure from different democratic perspectives. In response, more traditional institutional arrangements are often adapted in order to keep their relevance and legitimacy in a changing environment. For example, councils broaden their membership to include lay citizens or experts or they pay more attention to the quality of deliberation (Van Damme et al, 2011).

Involving societal stakeholders in policymaking offers the possibility of increasing the input, process and output legitimacy of policy. If stakeholders or citizens are involved and have a chance to influence policy, and if their contributions are to a certain extent taken into account, their support for the resulting policy decisions will increase and the implementation of the policy will be more effective. Actors will be better informed, gain more insight into the problem as well as the policymaking process, and have a chance to influence policy. In such circumstances, they will be less likely to resort to protest activities, which will also make for fewer delays and swifter policy implementation. But this is the theory; we now need to offer an account of what happens in practice.

Public participation: a framework for analysis

Many possibilities exist for inviting non-elected citizens to interact in the decision-making process. Some are very limited and only enable the public to be informed and offer comments. But other forms of public participation are more intensive and enable citizens to be more fully involved in the decision-making process. One of the major difficulties of this chapter is dealing with a large variety of mechanisms and experiences. Lots of typologies have been constructed in political science to distinguish different modes of consultation and participation of the public (Arnstein, 1969; Rowe and Frewer, 2005; Smith, 2005). We will use the one proposed by Archon Fung (2006).[3] Fung explains that every form of participation may be classified according to three dimensions: who participates, how and why. Each dimension is related to specific institutional possibilities and normative goals, as follows.

Who participates?

This dimension deals with the degree of inclusiveness of the mechanism. Does the public that is invited to participate differ from usual authorised set of decision makers? At one end of the continuum, public authorities can invite professional stakeholders and experts. This is a rather 'closed' environment. At the other end, so-called 'lay' citizens can be invited. This is a more 'open' environment. In order to do this, public authorities can use several communication means to invite citizens (Reuchamps, 2013). First, a general call for volunteers via the media or using the internet can be chosen. This is the most common way to bring together citizens, although it is regularly criticized because there is always a specific segment of the population that participates most. Indeed, in situations of self-selection, those citizens who are already politically active and unrepresentative of the whole population (for instance, older and more educated people) take part in the participatory event (Verba et al, 1995). That is the reason why some organisers try to thwart this phenomenon by means of selective recruitment of the less represented subgroup or by using random selection in order to create a group that is representative of the broader population (Fung, 2003).

Inclusion is central in both a more instrumental and a more democracy-oriented approach. As we have already mentioned, interaction with different actors at the beginning of the policy cycle can improve the acceptance of public policies (Morrell, 1999). Consultation can also help decision makers to govern more efficiently by taking into account citizens' variety of expertise. Citizens indeed possess essential local knowledge that comes from close exposure to the context in which problems occur (Fung, 2006, p 73). But inclusion can also be justified by the will to improve the legitimacy of the governance system. Participatory theory stresses the need for sustained citizen involvement in everyday political life, regardless of the specific mechanisms of participation. Everyday citizen participation is seen as increasing civic competences as well as an objective in itself (Pateman, 2012). For deliberative democrats, inclusion is also central and input legitimacy is a measure of the openness of the deliberative events to the demands and needs of its participants (Barber, 1984; Fiorino, 1990; Pröpper and Steenbeek, 1999; Edelenbos, 2000; Lowndes et al, 2001; Caluwaerts and Reuchamps, 2015). Democratic deliberation can only take place if all concerned actors can expose their point of view and exchange their arguments.

How to participate?

The second dimension deals with the kind of interaction that is being organised. Arnstein (1969) was one of the first scholars to draw a ladder of participation. Again, we can speak of a continuum. At one end of the spectrum, participants are invited to listen as spectator. At the other end, people can extensively deliberate or negotiate on a specific project of public action. Such a more intensive interaction approach is clearly inspired by the development of the deliberative theory of democracy (Manin, 1985; Elster, 1998; Chambers, 2003). For these theorists, democracy is a question of the number of people that participate as well as the quality of the process (Held, 2006). A political process is fair not only if all interested actors are invited, but also if the process is organised on the basis of a fair deliberation among actors who exchange rational arguments in order to find a better solution. In contrast to the classical theory of aggregation at and bargaining after the ballot box, the aim is to base the legitimacy of the political process on defensible argument. Such deliberation also needs to contribute to a transformative process. By opening up to the perspectives of other participants, people can learn from each other and develop a new, richer perspective (Fishkin, 1991; Fung, 2006). For the promoters of a more deliberative democracy, participatory devices should not only give ordinary people access to the policymaking process, but should also offer an arena for meaningful interaction among diverse actors with the possibility to substantially change participants' views and create a common proposition or evaluation.

Why participate?

The third and final dimension is the question of the goal of the participatory mechanism. Is it to ensure that authorities keep citizens informed, or to actively involve citizens in the decision-making process? We have already discussed the difference between information, consultation and participation. These different forms of public involvement lead to different public action goals. It has been argued that involving more diverse actors increases the possibility of developing more insight into different perspectives on the problem, finding common ground (for example, in order to develop a shared problem definition), gaining knowledge about relevant elements of policy implementation, and developing more innovative and/or integrative solutions. The stated purpose of most public hearings and many other public meetings is to enable citizens to contribute to such insights. But the more radical instigators of public participation posit that a consultative role is not sufficient. For them, citizens should have direct power, such as in participatory budgets (Baiocchi, 2005), to counter the authority of elected representatives.

It is clear that public consultation can achieve different goals, depending on the perspective. While the more instrumental or managerial perspective focuses on what public consultation brings to policy, the democratic perspective raises questions of the inclusiveness and the deliberative quality of public consultation. The central question is, then, 'What does public consultation bring to democracy?' The chosen perspective on public consultation, and the desired goals, will inspire the set-up and design of the public consultation.

A diversity of experiences in Belgium

The framework developed in the previous section provides an interesting guide to different forms of public consultation and participation in Belgium. This diversity is twofold. First, there is a wide range of participation mechanisms. The aim of this chapter is not to present a comprehensive overview of every experience but rather to present several emblematic cases of participation along the three dimensions: who, how and why. Second, there is the diversity related to levels of government. Each level of government has developed tools of consultation and participation. Often these tools and mechanisms have been adapted to fit specific perspectives and goals. It is not the aim of this chapter to present all of them, but to shed light on some of them in order to gain a better understanding of the dynamics of public consultation and participation and policymaking in Belgium.

Information

The first possibility – and one that a requirement for public consultation and participation – is to allow citizens to have access to the documents produced by public authorities. Examples include access to public records, official gazettes, government websites, public notice of white papers and other policy documents. At the federal and regional level, there are legal and policy frameworks that impose public information and consultation. First of all, there is legislation that defines citizens' rights of access to government information. During the 1990s at both federal and regional level, freedom of information acts were introduced, providing the legal basis for passive access to information and active measures to disseminate information to citizens, stimulating transparency and openness. Laws that establish rights of access to information are a basic building block for enhancing government transparency and accountability (OECD, 2011). Belgium is, however, a relative laggard in terms of establishing freedom of information legislation.

In Belgium, specific policies have been developed to support active and passive access to information, and institutions are in place to implement and enforce access to information, such as ombudsmen at the federal and regional level.

Consultation

The second possibility is to allow citizens the opportunity to voice their opinions on public policies. Different methods can be used to achieve this goal. Laws and regulations governing public consultation vary considerably among OECD member countries. As in other countries, in Belgium this kind of legislation is more recent than that relating to freedom of information. Consultation covers legislation on complaints and appeals procedures, on consultation during policy impact analysis, and so on.

Comparatively, Belgium scores rather low at the level of public consultation management (OECD, 2009a).[4] This refers mainly to the level of formalisation of public consultation in the policymaking process. In Belgium, unlike in Finland or in Spain, for instance, there is no general administrative procedure law that provides for public hearings, notification periods, appeals procedures and so on. Legislation stipulating public consultation is mostly policy specific. For example, in education policy there is a requirement that educational stakeholders such as teachers, parents and students be consulted, and in health policy that patients be consulted.[5] Alongside legislation, there are several policy documents that support public consultation. Although Belgium as a (moderately) neo-corporatist country has a culture of intensive societal consultation, institutional dialogue and compromise, this consultation is also informal and selective. The same elite stakeholders are those that are consulted, and such consultations are sometimes held behind closed doors (Delwit et al, 1999, pp 7–10). Therefore, more recent legislation and policy documents often stress transparency and inclusiveness in public consultation. In recent years, there have been quite a few innovations that aim to formalise broader and transparent public consultation in policymaking, in line with OECD recommendations (for example, regulatory impact assessment [RIA], consultation codes or the use of green and white papers).

For instance, the previous Flemish government (2009-14) developed an important policy framework document called Pact 2020, committing itself to engaging stakeholders more actively in policy development.[6] Its coalition agreement specified that it would increase the dialogue with stakeholders and integrate this societal involvement into the entire policy cycle.[7] In this document, specific reference is also made to strengthening the involvement of strategic policy advisory bodies, discussed in more detail elsewhere in this volume. Whereas these councils used to function as a neo-corporatist interface between government and elite stakeholders, reform initiatives have been undertaken to broaden their membership so as to increase their inclusiveness and representativeness (Van Damme et al, 2011). Following Fung's typology, these councils have closed membership and they deliberate about policy issues among their members (although it is questionable as to whether discussion is as rational and power-free as deliberative democrats would have it). The primary goal of such councils is to provide high-quality policy advice, but they also have an important role in pacification and bargaining among key stakeholders. The functionality of such councils regarding democracy is limited.

Whereas these advisory bodies are typically permanent consultative bodies with fixed membership, public consultation can also be organised in a more ad hoc manner. Important provisions for public consultation can be found in environmental impact assessment (EIA).[8] EIA laws at federal and regional level include requirements to ensure that information is provided and opportunities are given to the public to express their opinion. Laws on planning and building also offer rights of information and consultation.

A dominant mode of public consultation can be found as an integral part of RIA. RIA as a means of *ex ante* policy evaluation is supposed to contribute to the quality of legislation. In Belgium, developing high-quality legislation and institutionalising standards and systems that need to contribute to high-quality legislation is a relatively new policy goal, and is the responsibility of the Federal Institute for Sustainable Development.[9] Recent years have the seen the introduction not only of RIA, but also a public agenda for new legislation, bodies specifically responsible for legislative quality (called '*cellen wetskwaliteit*' in Flanders), a consultation code, and so on. In the 2009 Inter-Institutional Agreement on the Common Approach of the Regulatory Impact Analysis (IIA-RIA), it was stated that stakeholder consultation should be organised according to minimal EU quality norms. As one of the steps in the process of developing an RIA (which accompanies the legislation), there is an external consultation. Consultation is seen as a criterion of good regulation.[10] However, an important difference between consultation of the strategic advisory bodies and the RIA consultation is that the latter is (usually) not strongly legally entrenched. In other words, the choice whether, whom and how to consult is often made by the administration that initiates new policy depending on their analysis of the relevance of consultation for the specific policy at hand.

Recently, a specific consultation code was developed offering guidance to Flemish administrators in the public consultation process.[11] Several methods and techniques are mentioned in the code, such as notice and comment procedures, hearings, opinion polls, deliberative polls, focus groups and expert panels. Specific attention is paid to e-consultation (by means of, among other tools, e-polls, chat, weblogs and online fora).[12] In Wallonia, the *Code de la démocratie locale et de la décentralisation* centralises several measures about public consultation for guiding administrators as well as citizens.

The increased emphasis on public consultation is driven not only by its role in enhancing the quality of regulation, but also by organisational concerns. All Flemish administrative entities are expected to achieve a 'maturity level 3' in stakeholder management as part of their organisational development.[13] In order to achieve this level, they have to consciously analyse their stakeholders' environment and take appropriate action towards these stakeholders. The different types of public consultation discussed earlier are clearly designed from an instrumental, managerial and/or legal perspective rather than a democratic perspective.

At the local level, consultations can be organised on all kinds of projects and policies. In the field of environment and planning and in line with European directives, various authorisations, permits and plans must be submitted to public inquiries. In Wallonia, for instance, the Walloon Land Planning, Urbanism and Heritage Code (*Code wallon de l'aménagement du territoire, de l'urbanisme et du patrimoine*, CWATUP) organises such procedures. Generally, local authorities allow citizens to consult the documents related to the project and give their comments within a certain time frame. For the most important projects, public information meetings are also organised. All these mechanisms are purely consultative and reactive. There is no possibility for deliberation about the project. The major goal is to enable citizens to give their views and possibly be heard by authorities in charge of the project but not to engage people in the decision-making process itself. In large-scale infrastructure projects, a project logic dominates, and public consultation offers citizens a formal opportunity to express their views and give comments. It is a minimal, formal guarantee to have a say. However, such consultation typically takes place late in the decision-making process and has little impact on the decision.

Another typical example of consultation, although less legally formalised, concerns city strategic planning. In the *projet de ville* (city project) in Liège, the fifth largest city in Belgium, local authorities sent every household a questionnaire with a mix of open and closed questions, which was also distributed in public spaces (March to April 2012). It was thus a form of non-representative opinion poll. According to the final report, 5,741 citizens responded to this consultation, 2,593 by post and 3,156 via the municipality website (Ville de Liège, 2012). After a meeting with the stakeholders of the city, the municipality analysed the responses and determined the city priorities for the next 10 years. This can be considered as a typical consultative and aggregative form of participation, whereby the public is invited to respond to a survey but the realisation of the project remains in the hands of elected representatives and their staff.

Generally speaking, this kind of public consultation is used frequently. A consultation document is developed and published, with a call for comments. The media is encouraged to attract public attention to the consultation. Although this kind of consultation can potentially attract a large audience, in some cases it fails to produce sufficient reaction. Moreover, it may only interest a specific segment of the public, meaning that any engagement will be unrepresentative. This form of public participation is defined by some scholars as 'selective listening' (Sintomer et al, 2008). There is the possibility of participation, but there is no real obligation for elected politicians to take this into account. In other words, the autonomy of the public is very limited as they are not involved in the policymaking process and do not have the opportunity to start an open debate on the subject.

This form of project-based, ad hoc public consultation is quite different from that practised by the more traditional permanent consultative bodies that are also quite prominent at the local level in Belgium. In these councils, non-elected citizens with expertise in a specific policy field (environment, mobility, and so on) regularly meet to discuss specific project or policy issues and deliver collective advice to policymakers. Although members need to be re-elected or reappointed every four or five years, membership is typically quite stable over longer periods of time, which helps build up expertise and capacity. There are, however, criticisms that such councils are not innovative enough and merely promote the status quo. The main feature of the more individual forms of consultation concerns the second dimension of our framework of analysis. Indeed, the idea is to gather not only a series of individual opinions but also the collective advice of a delineated group of citizens, following a period of good quality deliberation.

The first dimension (the 'who') may vary, of course. For instance, municipalities in Wallonia are invited to organise a consultative commission for town planning and mobility (*Commission consultative communale d'aménagement du territoire et de mobilité*, CCATM).[14] The CCATM comprises 12 members for municipalities of less than 20,000 inhabitants and 16 members for municipalities over 20,000. Inhabitants are chosen by the city council on the basis of an application submitted after a public call in the local media and through posters. It also respects the age profile of the municipality. We can see that even though this mode of selection is open to every citizen, the bias of *self-selection* plus selection by the city council limits the inclusive potential of this consultative body. Other consultative bodies are specifically dedicated to a segment of the population: youths, seniors, and so on.

At higher levels of governance (regional, community and federal), these permanent bodies are less open to so-called 'ordinary' citizens but welcome stakeholders (representatives) and experts. The Belgian Advisory Committee on Bioethics, for example, is composed of university professors, doctors, lawyers, magistrates and representatives of the different governments of the country. The strategic advisory councils of the Flemish government, meanwhile, are mainly populated by societal representatives, and some councils have lay and/or academic experts (Fobé et al, 2013).

Consultation and direct democracy

One very specific form of direct democracy is citizens' consultation. While plebiscites or referenda are binding, popular consultation as it is practised in Belgium is not. A binding referendum is not permitted in Belgium, but a popular consultation is possible at different levels of government.[15] What is the link with policy analysis? The rationale of a consultation, be it binding or not, is to ask the population a specific question, possibly in a very inclusive way. But the consultation is not a deliberative process. Policymakers do not receive arguments from citizens in favour or against the issue at hand, only a 'yes' or 'no' to the question asked. The formulation of policy problems or solutions is thus not enhanced by such a process.

Moreover, this type of consultation can yield strong opposition within the political community. At the Belgian national level, the only instance of direct public consultation – that is, consultative referendum – is known as the 'royal question' in 1950, concerning the return of Leopold III to the throne in light of his conduct during the Second World War when he retained close ties – too close, for some – with Germany. This event has an important place in the collective memory because it revealed strong divisions between the north and the south of the country, as well as some strong intra-community divisions (Mabille, 2011). This rather negative experience is therefore regularly used by politicians and citizens to reject the use of this kind of public consultation at the federal level. In any case, Belgium's Constitution does not allow this type of public consultation at the federal level.

At the other levels of government, the possibility for consultative referenda does exist. Since the sixth reform of state in 2012, regions can now organise such referenda in their jurisdiction except for issues related to the budget (article 39bis of the Constitution). Each regional parliament must determine the organisational aspects of the process. Non-binding referenda are also possible at the local and provincial levels. In Wallonia, consultation is initiated by the municipal council or a group of citizens on a subject within the jurisdiction of the municipalities. The Walloon parliament established a special commission in 2015. Called 'democratic renewal', it aims to fine tune the use of petitions and popular consultations.[16] In both regions, even though innovative types of public consultation are now legally entrenched at the local level, they are not used very widely (Hennau and Ackaert, 2014).

Participation and participatory budgeting

Throughout the world, the mechanism of participatory budgeting is often presented as best practice in the field of public participation because it scores highly in every dimension of the framework of analysis. Generally speaking, a participatory budget is a procedure that allows non-elected citizens to participate in the design or distribution of public finances (Sintomer et al, 2008). By a complex mechanism of meetings in districts and semi-delegation to citizens at the level of the whole city, citizens are invited to exercise power directly by allocating a part of the budget of the municipality. There is nevertheless much diversity: in South America, for example, procedures are often characterised by a radical reversal of political priorities, while in Europe they tend to reflect a more managerial perspective (Sintomer et al, 2008).

Some Belgian cities have also experimented with this type of participation. In Mons, the mayor and president of the Socialist Party at the time, Elio Di Rupo, visited Porto Alegre, the birthplace of the participatory budget in Brazil (Damay, 2013) and decided to implement a similar system in his city. Two districts duly developed a participatory budget. The procedures were institutionalised in 2002 and organised according to pyramid design, where citizens of districts were elected by the population. According to Damay (2013), there were some difficulties regarding the lack of transparency and clarity about the source of fundraising, the difficult relationship with the public administration and the ambiguous role of the municipal council in the final decision. There was also a disconnect between the general purpose and the actual implementation of the project. Nevertheless, the project has been upheld as an example, and in 2012 the Walloon government introduced in communal law the option for every municipality to organise a participatory budget, with generous autonomy concerning the practical organisation and design of the process.[17] In Flanders, there has also been some cautious experimentation with participatory budgets. In Antwerp, for example, one of the district councils set up a participatory budgeting exercise in 2014. About 10% of the budget of the district (€1.1 million) was allocated by citizens over 12 policy themes. However, the district council still decides on the specific projects that will be developed with this budget.

Towards deliberative democracy?

While public consultation and participation has increased over the years, there is also a move towards more deliberative democracy. In Belgium, the King Baudouin Foundation has played an important role in initiating and supporting deliberative debates on policy issues. One example concerns a unique exercise conducted by the King Baudouin Foundation and Rathenau Institute in 2005/2006 involving the general public in a discussion on cutting-edge brain science (Raeymaekers et al, 2014). In Flanders, the para-parliamentary institute VIWTA (now part of the Flemish parliament) has experimented quite widely with deliberative citizen fora, such as the Citizen Consultation on Health and Mobility in 2008, which involved convening a representative sample of almost 300 citizens to discuss in small groups issues relating to mobility and health, during a one-day intensive exercise in the Flemish parliament in Brussels. These kinds of initiative have been called, among other things, citizens' juries, citizens' panels and open fora. The aim is to gather together a group of experts and citizens, generally selected at random from the population as a whole, to discuss and arrive at an informed public opinion on a specific policy issue, sometimes accompanied by policy recommendations (Smith, 2012).

One such recent exercise, G1000, has had particularly marked effect on public opinion in Belgium (Caluwaerts and Reuchamps, 2012). During the 2010-11 political crisis, when it took more than 500 days to install a new government, citizens' mistrust of government increased dramatically. Against this backdrop, a group of citizens sought to bring the people back into the political arena. Their reading of the situation was that it was not only a Belgian crisis, but also a crisis of the model of representative democracy. The aim was as follows:

> ... to be a citizen initiative that is capable of innovating democracy, a project which attempts not to overthrow the representative system, but to complement it and to breathe new life into it. Its aim is to gather ordinary citizens in a setting, which is conducive to open and uncoercive deliberation on possibly contentious political issues, and to let citizens themselves experience democracy and thus the difficulty of building bridges over highly polarizing issues. (Caluwaerts and Reuchamps, 2012, p 4)

As a consequence, G1000 was more than a one-day deliberative event. It comprised three distinct – but interrelated – phases: first, a broad public consultation (via an online tool to collect ideas and votes in order to set the agenda of the following phase); second, an intensive one-day citizen summit involving 1,000 citizens (for large-scale deliberation); and third, a citizen panel (for an in-depth deliberation of the issues selected during the citizen summit).

This experiment is interesting in terms of the three dimensions under study here. G1000 tried to be very inclusive and to have a strong deliberative character. To this end, participants were selected at random (Caluwaerts and Reuchamps, 2015). Random selection is a classical method used in different forms of democratic innovation, as it gives everyone an equal chance to be picked for participation. Even in Ancient Greece, random selection was seen as the most democratic way to select public authorities (Manin, 1997; Van Reybrouck, 2013). Today, this ideal relates to the statistical aim to convene a mini-public, in other words, miniature demos by random selection (Gastil, 2000; Fishkin, 2003; Sintomer, 2010). But the major criticism directed at the G1000 concerned its output, focusing on its lack of impact on actual politics and policies. Then again, albeit G1000 did not have an impact on the content of public policies, its impact on the public sphere has been progressively growing (Jacquet et al, 2016). Indeed, the exercise was extensively discussed in the media and put the issue of democratic innovation on the political agenda. In the 2014 elections, a large majority of party manifestoes stressed the need to develop fora to integrate citizens' participation at different stages of the policy process. The French-speaking green party (Ecolo), for example, stated in its manifesto that G1000 should upheld as an example and that such exercises in deliberative democracy should be organised more regularly. Indeed, the G1000 inspired current initiatives around the country, such as the G360 in Genk (Flanders) and the G100 in Grez-Doiceau (Wallonia).

Conclusion

This chapter has discussed the different public consultation and participation arrangements in Belgium at different levels of government. Belgium has been a relative laggard in terms of establishing freedom of information legislation and formalising public consultation processes. In Belgium, unlike in countries such as Finland and Spain, there is no general administrative procedural law that provides for public hearings, notification periods, appeals procedures and so on. Legislation stipulating public consultation is mostly policy-specific. In the field of environment and planning, more formal public 'notice and comment' consultation is legally entrenched.

In Belgium, as in other countries, we can observe a growth in various types of public inquiry and public consultation arrangements in policymaking. More traditional institutional arrangements, such as (semi-)permanent societal advisory bodies common in a country with a neo-corporatist background, are being joined by public consultation initiatives inspired by democratic theory. Recently there have been developments aimed at formalising public consultation in policymaking (for example, RIA and consultation codes) in order to increase the quality of regulation and fall in line with OECD recommendations. There have also been exercises inspired by participatory and deliberative democracy at different levels of government (for example, G360 and participatory budgets). The recent G1000 initiative was an important part of these developments.

However, whereas legislation allows for novel means of public consultation (for example, plebiscites or rights to petition), the actual use of these mechanisms is limited. It appears that the current state of affairs in Belgium regarding public consultation and participation is still firmly embedded in an indirect democratic framework, and that experiments with broader and more deliberative citizen participation are adapted to fit rather than challenge the status quo.

It we look at the goals that guide public consultation practice in Belgium, it appears that a legal and instrumental perspective dominates. Consultation is set up because it is required by law or because it is alleged that it may contribute to better supported policies, as mentioned in the introduction. Democratising policies (that is, using consultation or participation to inject more democracy into policymaking or even policy analysis) is clearly a secondary goal. Nevertheless, in recent years such a democratic perspective appears to be on the rise.

In the coming years, there is a need to systematically evaluate both more traditional and more innovative types of public consultation. What do they contribute to policies and to policy analysis? What do they contribute to democracy? How do they contribute to citizens' attitudes towards the public decision-making process? In the future, discussion could move towards a more optimal organisation of different types of consultation, so that the different perspectives on, and expectations of, consultation can be combined.

Notes

1   This aspect is not further detailed here as it is discussed in other chapters of this volume, but new public management trends, with their tendency to break up governmental units, have also contributed to this evolution.

2   The different public consultation mechanisms have been situated indicatively in the model, according to their democratic 'roots'. Clearly, the specific use of the mechanism will decide its position in the model.

3   This typology is more analytical than that of the OECD (2001).

4   In the OECD 'better life index', Belgium scored 4.5 on the consultation on rule-making, a weighted average of yes/no answers to various questions on formal consultation procedures enabling the general public, business and civil society organisations to influence legislation and governmental actions, and on whether citizens' views on such consultation procedures should be made public. The US scored 8.3 and the UK 11.5 (OECD, 2009b).

5   The 1998 Aarhus convention was particularly important as it was a forerunner in stimulating federal and regional legislation regarding access to information, public consultation and justice in environmental matters.

6   www.vlaandereninactie.be/over/pact-2020.

7   www.vlaanderen.be/nl/publicaties/detail/het-regeerakkoord-van-de-vlaamse-regering-2014-2019.

8   European directive 85/337/EG. In Wallonia, the regional government produced a decree entitled 'Arrêté du Gouvernement wallon organisant l'évaluation des incidences sur l'environnement dans la Région wallonne' (*Moniteur Belge*, 21 September 2002) that was modified two years later (*Moniteur Belge*, 23 February 2004). The so-called 'CWATUP' and the situation in Flanders are further developed later in the chapter.

9   http://ifdd.belgium.be/fr/content/l-eidd-devient-l-air.

10   The Flemish government decided on eight criteria of high-quality regulation, one of which relates to evidence-based regulation resulting from consultation and institutional dialogue at administrative, societal and political level (Flemish application decree of 7 November 2003).

11   This also relatively late when compared for example with the UK Code of Practice on Written Consultation, which dates from 2000.

12   The consultation code can be found at www.bestuurszaken.be/sites/bz.vlaanderen.be/files/Consultatiecode_LR.pdf.

13   www.bestuurszaken.be/leidraad-ic-ob.

14   Article 7 of CWATUP of 19 April 2007.

15   Article 39bis of the Belgian Constitution for the regional level and article 41 for the municipal level.

16   *Proposition de résolution portant création d'une commission spéciale relative au renouveau démocratique*, 130 (2014-2015) – No. 7.

17   Article L1321-3 of the *Code de la démocratie locale et de la décentralisation* (Walloon law of 26 April 2012).

References

Agranoff, R. and McGuire, M. (1999) 'Managing in network settings', *Policy Studies Review*, 16(1): 18-41.

Arnstein, S. (1969) 'A ladder of citizen participation', *Journal of the American Institute of Planners*, 35(4): 216-24.

Baiocchi, G. (ed) (2005) *Militants and citizens: the politics of participatory democracy in Porto Alegre*, Princeton, NJ: Princeton University Press.

Barber, B. (ed) (1984) *Strong democracy, participatory politics for a new age*, Los Angeles, CA: University of California Press.

Barker, A. and Peters, B.G. (eds) (1993) *Advising West European Governments: Inquiries, expertise and public policy*, Pittsburgh, PA: University of Pittsburgh Press.

Caluwaerts, D. and Reuchamps, M. (2012) *The G1000: facts, figures and some lessons from an experience of deliberative democracy in Belgium*, Brussels: Re-Bel.

Caluwaerts, D. and Reuchamps, M. (2015) 'Strengthening democracy through bottom-up deliberation: an assessment of the internal legitimacy of the G1000 project', *Acta Politica*, 50(2): 151-70.

Chambers, S. (2003) 'Deliberative democratic theory', *Annual Review of Political Science*, 6: 307-26.

Damay, L. (2013) 'Le budget participatif de la ville de Mons: compétence des citoyens et procédures d'action publique', in F. Claisse, C. Laviolette, M. Reuchamps and C. Ruyters (eds) *La participation en action*, Brussels: P.I.E. Peter Lang.

Dekker, P. and Hooghe, M. (2003) 'De burger-nachtwaker. Naar een informalisering van de politieke participatie van de Nederlandse en Vlaamse bevolking', *Sociologische Gids*, 50(2): 156-81.

Delwit, P., De Waele, J.-M. and Magnette, P. (1999) *Gouverner la Belgique. Clivages et compromis dans une société complexe*, Paris: Presses universitaires de France.

Edelenbos, J. (ed) (2000) *Proces in vorm. Procesbegeleiding van interactieve beleidsvorming over lokale ruimtelijke projecten*, Utrecht: Lemma.

Elster, J. (ed) (1998) *Deliberative democracy*, New York, NY: Cambridge University Press.

Fiorino, D.J. (1990) 'Citizen participation and environmental risk: a survey of institutional mechanisms', *Science, Technology and Human Values*, 15(2): 226.

Fishkin, J.S. (1991) *Democracy and deliberation: New directions for democracy*, New Haven, CT: Yale University Press.

Fishkin, J.S. (2003) 'Consulting the public through deliberative polling', *Journal of Policy Analysis and Management*, 22(1): 128-33.

Fobé, E., Brans, M., Vancoppenolle, D. and Van Damme, J. (2013) 'Institutionalized advisory systems: an analysis of member satisfaction of advice production and use across nine strategic advisory councils in Flanders (Belgium)', *Policy & Society*, 32(3): 225-40.

Fung, A. (2003) 'Survey articles: recipes for public spheres: eight institutional design choices and their consequences', *Journal of Political Philosophy*, 11(3): 338-67.

Fung, A. (2006) 'Varieties of participation in complex governance', *Public Administration Review*, 66(S1): 66–75. doi:10.1111/j.1540-6210.2006.00667.x.

Gastil, J. (ed) (2000) *By popular demand*, Berkeley, CA: University of Berkeley Press.

Held, D. (ed) (2006) *Models of democracy*, Stanford, CA: Stanford University Press.

Hendriks, F. (ed) (2006) *Vitale democratie. Theorie van democratie in actie*, Amsterdam: Amsterdam University Press.

Hendriks, F. (ed) (2010) *Vital democracy. A theory of democracy in action*, Oxford: Oxford University Press.

Hennau, S. and Ackaert, J. (eds) (2004) *De implementatie van het gemeentedecreet anno 2012*, Leuven: Steunpunt Bestuurlijke Organisatie- Slagkrachtige Overheid.

Jacob, S., and Schiffino, N. (2011) 'Risk, democracy and schizophrenia: the changing roles of citizens in risk policy-making. Putting GMO policy to the test', *Journal of Risk Research*, 14(8): 983–93.

Jacquet, V., Moskovic, J., Caluwaerts, D., and Reuchamps, M. (2016) 'The macro political uptake of the G1000 in Belgium', in M. Reuchamps and J. Suiter (eds) *Constitutional deliberative democracy in Europe*, Colchester: ECPR Press.

Kjaer, A.M. (ed) (2004) *Governance*, Cambridge: Polity Press.

Lowndes, V., Pratchett, L. and Stoker, G. (2001) 'Trends in public participation: Part 1. Local government perspectives', *Public Administration*, 49(1): 205–22.

Mabille, X. (2011) *Nouvelle histoire de la Belgique*, Brussels: CRISP.

Manin, B. (1985) 'Volonté générale ou délibération? Esquisse d'une théorie de la délibération politique', *Le Débat*, 33: 72–94.

Manin, B. (1997) *The principles of representative government*, Cambridge: Cambridge University Press.

Mayer, I., Edelenbos, J. and Monnikhof, R. (2005) 'Interactive policy development: undermining or sustaining democracy?' *Public Administration*, 83(1): 179–99.

Michels, A. and De Graaf, L. (2010) 'Examining citizen participation: local participatory policy making and democracy', *Local Government Studies*, 36(4): 477–91.

Morrell, M.E. (1999) 'Citizens' evaluations of participatory democratic procedures: normative theory meets empirical science', *Political Research Quarterly*, 52(2): 293–322.

OECD (Organisation for Economic Co-operation and Development) (2001) *Citizens as partners. Information, consultation and public participation in policy-making*, Paris: OECD.

OECD (2009a) *Focus on citizens: public engagement for better policy and services*, Paris: OECD.

OECD (2009b) *Indicators of regulatory Management*, Paris: OECD.

Papadopoulos, Y. and Warin, P. (2007) 'Are innovative, participatory and deliberative procedures in policy making democratic and effective?', *European Journal of Political Research*, 36(4): 445–72.

Pateman, C. (2012) 'Participatory democracy revisited', *Perspectives on Politics*, 10(1): 7–19.

Pröpper, I. and Steenbeek, D. (eds) (1999) *De aanpak van interactief beleid: elke situatie is anders*, Bussum: Coutinho.

Raeymaekers, P., Rondia, K. and Slob, M. (eds) (2014) *Connecting brains and society. The present and future of brain science: what is possible, what is desirable?*, Amsterdam: King Baudouin Foundation and Rathenau Institute.

Reuchamps, M. (2013) 'Les expériences délibératives. Essai de typologie des pratiques', in S. Brunet, F. Claisse and C. Fallon (eds) *La participation à l'épreuve*, Brussels: P.I.E. Peter Lang.

Rowe, G. and Frewer, L.J. (2005) 'A typology of public engagement mechanisms', *Science, Technology and Human Values*, 30(2): 251-90.

Scharpf, F. (1997) *Games real actors play: Actor-centered institutionalism in policy research*, Boulder, CO: Westview.

Schudson, M. (ed) (1999) *The good citizen: a history of American civic life*, Cambridge: Harvard University Press.

Sintomer, Y. (2010) 'Random selection, republican self-government, and deliberative democracy', *Constellations* 17(3): 472-87.

Sintomer, Y., Herzberg, C. and Röcke, A. (eds) (2008) *Les budgets participatifs en Europe. Des services publics au service du public*, Paris: La découverte.

Smith, G. (ed) (2005) *Beyond the Ballot: 57 Democratic Innovations From Around the World*, London: Power Inquiry.

Smith, G. (2012) 'Deliberative democracy and mini-public', in B. Geissel and K. Newton (eds) *Evaluationg democractic innovations. Curing the democratic malaise?*, London: Routledge.

Van Damme, J. and Brans, M. (eds) (2008) *Interactief beleid van de Vlaamse overheid. Een internationale verkenning naar visie, beleid en praktijken*, Leuven: Steunpunt Bestuurlijke Organisatie Vlaanderen.

Van Damme, J. and Brans, M. (2012) 'The design and management of public consultation in policymaking: a conceptual framework and empirical findings from Belgian case studies', *Public Administration*, 90(4): 1047-66.

Van Damme, J., Brans, M. and Fobé, E. (2011) 'Balancing expertise, societal input and political control in the production of policy advice. A comparative study of educational councils in Europe', *Halduskultuur- Administrative Culture*, 12(2): 126-45.

Van den Brink, G. (ed) (2003) *Mondiger of moeilijker? Een studie naar de politieke habitus van de hedendaagse burgers*, Den Haag: Sdu Uitgevers.

Van Reybrouck, D. (2013) *Tegen verkiezingen*, Brussels: De Bezige Bij.

Verba, S., Schlozman, K.L. and Brady, H.E. (eds) (1995) *Voice and equality: civic voluntarism in American politics*, Cambridge: Harvard University Press.

Ville de Liège (2012) *Projet de ville*, Liège.

ELEVEN

The role of news media in the policy process in Belgium

Baldwin Van Gorp and Dave Sinardet

The interactions between politicians, the public and the media form a triangle that is discussed frequently, not least by political scientists and communications scholars (for example, Esser and Strömbäck, 2014). The influence of the media on voting behaviour, in particular, is a recurring topic on the research agenda (for example, Walgrave et al, 2008b; Hooghe et al, 2011). Conversely, if policy, and any decision that goes with it, forms the research focus, the *explanandum* is all the more complex, with the result that the media are not included in the research design. Wolfe and colleagues (2013) deplore this approach, and argue that the public agenda, the news media and the policy agenda should all be taken into account within the same study. However, patterns within these relationships are difficult to determine unambiguously, especially because the news media shape both the input (for example, the salience and definition of issues to be dealt with) and the output (for example, communicating policy decisions to the general public) of the political system. As a result, there is plenty to explore within this underdeveloped area of research. This chapter aims to offer an overview of the state of the art in the research literature on the complex relationship between media and policy in Belgium.

The chapter starts with a description of the media landscape in Belgium. Just as in most other countries, it is increasingly characterised by media concentration in the private sector, whereby progressively fewer individuals or organisations control increasing shares of the mass media. A second, more unique, feature is the prevalence of public broadcasting in Belgium, especially in Flanders. However, the most unique characteristic is that these government-funded public broadcasters have generally been conceived to play a key role in the construction of the Dutch-speaking (Flanders) and French-speaking (Wallonia and French-speaking Brussels) communities' identities and public spheres in Belgium, and have less effect on national identity and public sphere than one might expect (Sinardet, 2012). Against this backdrop, the chapter looks at the impact of private sector media concentration on the diversity of news reporting (for example, on policy topics) the depiction of ethnic minority people in the media and their representation in media organisations. Media concentration also evidently underlies the gradual depoliticisation and 'depillarisation' of the Belgian press. Finally, the chapter discusses the relationship between journalism and politics in more detail. Agenda-setting research explores the relationship between topics on the policy agenda and the attention they receive in the press.

Again, the specificity of the Belgian media system plays a significant role. Belgium is a small country with a limited number of media, which results in a high degree of interdependence between journalists and politicians. Although the press has been depillarised, many journalists maintain close ties with politicians, who often act as their privileged sources. We argue that the way news media in Belgium are structured and organised results in a policy process in which they play a role, on the one hand, as a *conduit* for policy actors, distributing information about policy solutions and alternatives, and on the other hand, as a *contributor* to the political and the policy process (see Shanahan et al, 2008).

The Belgian media landscape

The media landscape in Belgium has an almost unique structure, originating from its division on the basis of language. Broadcasting led by the public sector is the other specific characteristic of the Belgian media landscape. Media concentration in the private sector is an additional and increasingly common characteristic.

Language territoriality

First of all, the role that news media plays in the policy process is specified and even determined by Belgium's unique structure (Sinardet, 2012). Its trilingual status results in an administrative division of the territory (see Chapter Eight). This also has implications for the (news) media, which usually target a specific language community. This is a key feature of the Belgian media landscape, in addition to the strong position of public broadcasting in Flanders and increasing media concentration in the private media sector.

The country is characterised by a system of official language territoriality: the north is Dutch-speaking, the south French-speaking and the capital, Brussels, is bilingual. There is a small population of German speakers in the east of the country. News media that cover the complete territory are a rarity in Belgium, mainly because it is no easy feat to report the news in several languages.

Broadcasting led by the public sector

The language barrier is even stricter in the audiovisual media sector, where the big players focus on either the Dutch- or the French-speaking public, although the nationwide distribution and reception of TV signals is assured by law (the 'must-carry' regulation for cable providers). This brings us to another special feature of the Belgian media landscape, namely that public broadcasters have a large market share within the audiovisual sector: *Vlaamse Radio- en Televisieomroep* (VRT) in Flanders and *Radio-télévision belge de la Communauté française* (RTBF) in the French-speaking part of the country. The domination of public broadcasting is the most striking in Flanders: in 2015, VRT realised a 38.5% market share with two TV channels (CIM TV, 2015). In French-speaking Belgium, channels from neighbouring France take the largest share (35.4%). RTBF's three TV channels still hold a considerable market share of 21.9% (CIM TV, 2015).

Both parts of Belgium have had a major private broadcaster since 1989: Medialaan in Flanders (26.1% market share for three TV channels) and RTL in French-speaking Belgium (25.2% market share for three TV channels). International RTL Group is the leading private player in the audiovisual market in French-speaking Belgium. The Luxembourgian TV station *RTL Télévision* had already implicitly acquired a share of the Belgian TV market in the early 1980s and became a commercial competitor of monopolist RTBF. This position was made official in 1987 when RTL-TVI (*Radio télévision luxembourgeoise-Télévision indépendante*) launched a commercial broadcaster for the French Community, in which French newspaper owners also participated through the AudioPresse holding. In the meantime, the broadcast company once again operates under a Luxembourg license.

Concentration in the press

In Belgium, the print media are under great pressure, magazines even more than newspapers. One of the consequences of shrinking readership is, as in many other countries, an increasing level of media concentration. In the 1950s, there were 18 Dutch-language newspaper titles from 14 publishers, 29 French-language newspaper titles from 19 publishers, and one German newspaper (De Bens and Raeymaeckers, 2010). Currently, there are a handful of media groups, which are also intertwined.

At the moment, and as far as the traditional news media, that is newspapers and news broadcasts on radio and TV, in Flanders are concerned, there remain just three major private players (De Persgroep, Mediahuis and Roularta) in addition to the public broadcaster VRT. Two media groups, De Persgroep and Mediahuis, own the entire market of Flemish daily newspapers. In French-speaking Belgium, there is a clear trend towards concentration, with three players on the newspaper market (IPM, Rossel and Publifin) and two on the audiovisual market (RTL and AB Productions). Looking ahead, it seems that telecoms companies will increasingly engage in producing media content, although not specifically news content. The main actors here are Tecteo (an energy and telecoms holding renamed to Publifin as of June 2014), Belgacom (originally a telephone company) and Telenet (originally a cable company).

The media's role in Belgium's multilingual federal system

As a result of structuring and language territoriality, the news media do not provide an actual forum at the national level discussing federal policy issues. As they do not offer a linkage mechanism that reflects diverse political viewpoints, particularly on linguistic issues, the media have contributed to the polarisation of political conflicts between the language communities.

Subnational identity construction

While Belgium follows an international trend concerning increasing media concentration, it is quite unique with regard to the position of the public broadcasting companies and, more specifically, the absence of national broadcasting structures. Like in many other countries, Belgian media have played a role in – and have been used as instruments for – the construction of a national identity. In Belgium, however, the two public broadcasting companies have mostly been seen as instruments for *subnational* identity construction.

There are very few structural ties between RTBF and VRT, with the exception of a joint central office building in Brussels. Linked to this, and also quite unique internationally, is the fact that, in Belgium, the agreement between the regional governments and the broadcasters, enumerating the obligations of the latter, contains explicit references to stimulating the cultural identity of the concerned language community but none relating to the federal context.

The 1960 broadcasting law split the unitary public broadcasting organisation NIR-INR (*Belgisch Nationaal Instituut voor Radio-Omroep/Institut national belge de radiodiffusion*), which had existed since 1930 and had started television broadcasting in 1953, into two quasi-autonomous companies: BRT (*Belgische Radio en Televisie*, Dutch-language broadcasting) and RTB *(Radio-télévision belge*, French-language broadcasting). Having been granted a monopoly for their language community, their programmes were aimed specifically at, respectively, a Dutch-speaking and a French-speaking public. The splitting of public broadcasting was the first policy act that can be considered an implicit announcement of the existence of two large language communities in Belgium, which would only be inscribed in the Constitution 10 years later.

The Catholic and Flemish-nationalist elite who ran public broadcasting considered the creation of a Dutch-language television channel within the still unitary NIR-INR as an opportunity for Flemish nation building in 1953. Not only was this Flemish broadcaster aimed specifically at the Dutch-speaking part of the population, thus contributing to the construction of a Flemish *imagined community* (Anderson, 1991), it also introduced an explicit policy aimed at developing and promoting a Flemish identity and culture (Van den Bulck, 2001). This use of television in a nation-building project was, however, largely absent in the case of the Francophone broadcaster (Sinardet, 2012).

Still, as this all happened within the Belgian context, the media of course also contributed to the representation of a Belgian identity, through the broadcasting of, for example, football matches featuring the Belgian national team, ceremonies of the national holiday, the King's Royal Messages and so on, albeit this was not the reflection of a clear political project. However, it is striking that despite explicit Flemish nation-building policies, in the media and elsewhere, public opinion research continuously shows that among Flemish citizens, the Belgian identity remains substantially stronger than the Flemish identity (Deschouwer and Sinardet, 2010).

The media's role in Belgium's multilingual federal system

The fact that media in both parts of the country are oriented towards their own community raises questions as to whether they report in a similar way on federal policy, and whether regional policy in one part of the country is also discussed in the media in the other part. A systematic study of the correlations between policy issues dealt with in television news and in newspapers on the two sides of the linguistic border between 1993 and 2000 showed that they run remarkably parallel, though the correlation with the direct competitor in their own language is stronger (Dandoy and Nuytemans, 2007). From another study, focusing on a comparison of television broadcasts in the same time period, it appears that RTBF was more oriented towards 'hard news' (Sinardet et al, 2004). For example, 10% of the items on this channel dealt with domestic politics, foreign news accounts for about 25.6%, of which 2.3% covered Europe. The Flemish counterpart, VRT, reported more 'soft news'; in that respect, it leans more towards the commercial channels VTM and RTL-TVI than the French-language public broadcaster.

Coverage of federal politics in Belgium is still high, substantially higher in fact than coverage of regional politics. Nevertheless, research by Sinardet (2012) showed that the far-reaching division between Dutch and French-language media also means that media do not contribute to the existence of a genuine federal *public sphere* (to be discussed later), where the same actors under the same premise discuss nationally relevant topics across the linguistic border. While Belgium's federal government reflects linguistic parity and while decisions made by any federal minister are applicable to the entire Belgian population, this is not reflected in political reporting. For instance, on Dutch-speaking television's main news programmes (public as well as commercial), 80% of the federal ministers interviewed are Dutch-speaking, while on French-speaking television news, 70% to 80% are French-speaking. The news value of a federal minister thus seems to depend on his or her belonging to a particular language group. This also leads to certain topics not being covered when a minister from the 'other' language group is concerned. This media dynamic is clearly interwoven with political dynamics, as Flemish- and French-speaking federal ministers in Belgium have a tendency to communicate their decisions primarily through their 'own' media. This can in turn be linked to the fact that political parties are split along language lines in Belgium and electoral districts do not cross the language border, so that parties and politicians only have an electorate in one of both large language communities and voters can only choose between parties in their language community. Therefore, national elections could be considered not to be truly 'national'.

Media also tend to frame political information according to the political consensus within their own community, particularly on linguistic matters. Research by Sinardet (2013) on political reporting on the controversial matter of the electoral district of Brussels–Halle–Vilvoorde,[1] about which politicians in both communities were divided, showed that the number of political representatives from the 'other' language community is very limited, their position thus receiving much less attention. Also, the premise, which is the starting point of most debates, corresponds with the political consensus in the own community, which means that there is no discussion on the heart of the matter. Even factual elements are emphasised or omitted depending on whether or not they fit into this political consensus. Moreover, the consensus is sometimes reinforced by journalists' use of deictic references (such as 'us' or 'them'), which would undoubtedly be considered a serious breach of deontology if used in the context of debates on other than linguistic issues. The linguistic segmentation of the media landscape thus further contributes to a democratic deficit, as consumers are not fully informed about all actions and policies of the federal government and cannot witness debates on these issues where all relevant viewpoints and arguments are exchanged.

Paradoxically, the long-running political crisis that began in 2007, while exacerbating political tensions between representatives of the two large language communities and spawning speculation on a split of the country, may also be seen as the trigger for the opposite dynamic of more interaction and exchange between the communities: news media tend to feature more politicians, journalists and experts from across the language border. Newspapers from both communities have also begun to collaborate more in recent years, especially on federal politics. In general, the debate on the relationship between both communities has been much stronger and also more conflicting during the years of political crisis. However, this also means that indifference among one community towards the other has diminished to some extent. Nevertheless, despite these recent evolutions, the structural segmentation on political and media levels remains and continues to have a dominant influence. The focus of media on only one part of the country ultimately also affects the policy process and how news media report on it.

From depillarisation to guaranteed pluralism

Belgian media has been going through a process of depoliticisation and depillarisation, mainly since the 1980s. However, this has not resulted in a significantly higher degree of active and passive diversity and pluralism of media content.

Depoliticisation and depillarisation of the press

Most newspapers in Belgium originated at the end of the 19th century as election newspapers (De Bens and Raeymaeckers, 2010). From the very beginning, they could be linked to a specific pillar (Catholic, socialist or liberal), consistent with the societal segmentation along religious and socioeconomic lines (Deschouwer, 2009). *Le Soir* is the only neutral newspaper that confirms the rule: newspapers were spokespersons (advocates) of the party. More so, many editors were political appointees (De Winter, 1981). And if no structural link existed, there was a clear political preference that guided coverage (Van Aelst, 2006).

The process of media concentration is the main reason why the political ties between newspapers and political parties first loosened and were then abandoned. In Flanders, the most striking example was when De Persgroep, which has typically liberal newspapers in its portfolio, acquired *De Morgen*, which was owned by the Socialist Party until 1986. As soon as the marketing people got all the more involved, new target groups where sought and news outlets tried to reach readers with different political affiliations. As a result, the scope of the newspapers broadened and converged.

This process of depoliticisation and depillarisation manifested itself mainly from the 1980s onwards. A key moment that fuelled both public and political debates was the resignation of Daniel Buyle. As a journalist for the VRT news, he conducted a particularly critical interview in December 1981 with Wilfried Martens, a Christian Democrat who led the negotiations in forming a new government at that time. The two Flemish parties that were going to form the new coalition were very angry about the interview. The Catholic newspaper *De Standaard* openly requested sanctions against the TV journalist, who even claimed in an interview that direct telephone calls had been made to the former broadcasting chief Paul Van de Bussche asking him to intervene (Pander, 2001). Because the journalist involved had tenured status as a public servant, the dismissal procedure dragged on for a very long time. Resignation, however, seemed inevitable. Meanwhile, there was a debate going on about interference from politics in news reporting. Surprisingly, Cas Goossens, the administrator-general who approved the dismissal, denied in his memoirs that he had experienced any political pressure in this particular case (Goossens, 1998). In the same sentence, however, he stated that political pressure at that time was indeed a fact:

> ... In other cases, the political pressure was sometimes heavy, sometimes even very blatant. I have letters lying in front of me in which politicians ... who gave me a proposal barely concealed to revoke an appointment because they wanted to see a candidate, another one than the one who I considered most appropriate, promoted.[2] (Goossens, 1998, p161)

More than 30 years later, the Belgian news media are no longer spokespersons of one political ideology. Interviews may be evaluative and possibly even more critical for politicians and policymakers than ever. Direct political interference in editorial policy belongs to the past, despite some rare informal testimonials from editors with anecdotes of incoming phone calls from angry politicians.

Pluralism in media content

Do depillarisation and media concentration have an effect on media content? Although the political roots of the Belgian dailies are no longer unambiguously empirically observable, for instance by means of a content analysis, a line of demarcation still exists between the Flemish and the French-speaking press. An explanation for this could be that the editorial line of the respective newspapers corresponds with the dominating political orientation in the region, with French-speaking Belgium more leftist than Flanders. European value research, however, seems to contradict this, as it concludes that such differences are not so clearly reflected in attitudes among the population: Flemish people turn out to be less ethnocentrically outspoken than Francophones. Neither does the political orientation of both groups of journalists offer a clear explanation because the political views of Dutch-speaking and French-speaking journalists in Belgium are practically the same: 56% left, 27% centre, and 17% right (Raeymaeckers et al, 2013). This distribution holds for all journalists, not specifically for political journalists; however, what we can conclude is that Belgian journalists tend to be more progressive than the general population.

According to publishers, increasing press concentration is necessary for cost-efficiency reasons. It is a regularly formulated criticism that commercialisation, the 'fight' for an audience and convergence result in a gradual increase of soft news to the detriment of hard, policy-oriented news, a trend that can be characterised as the 'tabloidisation' of the news media (Hauttekeete, 2005).

One area that features regularly in research on tabloidisation is the extent to which the media pay attention to foreign news. A systematic analysis of Flemish television demonstrated that the proportion of foreign news fluctuates. At about 26% (De Smedt, 2014), there has been no clear downward trend in recent years (2012-13). However, the news value of proximity turned out to be important for journalists.

Political interference in the public media sector as a guarantee of pluralism

Within a democratic system, the media form a public sphere in which different ideas and opinions circulate, challenge each other and are subject to discussion (Habermas, 1962/1999). This leads at least to citizens who are better informed and who, in free elections, base their opinion on knowledge about current issues and the positions of the electoral candidates. If a limited number of conglomerates owns and controls the news media, there is a corresponding risk of a decrease in *political* pluralism. Political pluralism in the media implies that there is a fair and diverse representation in news coverage of the various political and ideological groups, and of their opinions and beliefs, including the positions and the interests of minority ethnic groups (ICRI, 2009). This form of pluralism is achievable by granting all groups both *passive* and *active* access to the media. Progressive media concentration puts great pressure on both forms of pluralism.

Passive access means, among other things, introducing members of minority ethnic groups as sources in news coverage, which is one of the key issues in the diversity debate (Van Gorp, 2004). There are no reliable statistics available, mainly because many people from an ethnic minority background have Belgian citizenship and ethnicity is not an indicator in official statistics. In Belgium, however, Moroccan and Turkish people constitute the largest groups of minorities

(Vanduynslager et al, 2013). The sources quoted in this paragraph estimate that about 15% of the Belgian inhabitants could be counted as belonging to an ethnic minority.

Although it is a delicate matter for scientific research validly to assign ethnicity based on a name or appearance, a mere 3.3% of all sources quoted or paraphrased in the Flemish press in 2012 were counted as people from an ethnic minority background (Vandenberghe et al, 2013). In 2013, 4.3% of people visible in Flemish news broadcasts, public and private combined, had a (seemingly) ethnic minority background; this percentage was 7.7% in broadcasts for the French-speaking part of the country (Jacobs and Hooghe, 2014).

Granting active access implies that people from minority ethnic groups have the ability to act as news producers and disseminators themselves. No indication can be given on how many journalists from these groups are active in the Belgian media. From the recent survey among Belgian journalists mentioned earlier (Raeymaeckers et al, 2013), however, we learn that 94% of the journalists are born in Belgium, and 4% of the Dutch-speaking journalists and 7% of the French-speaking journalists have at least one parent who was born outside the European Union. This implies that both the passive and active diversity of Belgian news media is limited.

An ideal situation would be for the news media not only to inform the public about policy issues but also to raise awareness about the processes behind them. As a consequence, members of the public themselves could actively participate in governance or hold those in power accountable (Strömbäck, 2005). In that respect, the news media form the fourth power in a democracy.

The role of the public broadcaster also has to be evaluated in the light of the pluralistic ideal and the optimal functioning of democracy. However, this role is more paradoxical. On the one hand, public broadcasters in Belgium are almost fully subsidised by the taxpayer, apart from some sponsorship (VRT) and commercial advertising (RTBF), and dominate the audiovisual sector, which may lead to market distortions viewed from a free market perspective. On the other hand, most stakeholders opt for a *full-portfolio* model for public service broadcasting in Belgium, which means that organisations are expected to take the lead in the development and implementation of new media technologies in such a way that they become public service *media* and not just broadcasting companies (Jakubowicz, 2007; Bardoel and d'Haenens, 2008; Donders and Raats, 2012). The idea is that private companies could also benefit from the pioneering role of the subsidised initiatives of the public broadcasters and that there should be plenty of room for collaboration with the private sector.

A major reason why, despite some objections, the position of public broadcasting remains unaffected at the moment is that it is seen as a *guarantee* of media pluralism. In Flanders, the public broadcaster VRT operates under the tutelage of the Minister of Media, who obviously has a political bias. The broadcaster and the government sign a five-year management agreement that stipulates the tasks the broadcaster has to fulfil if it wants to secure its €290.9 million government grant

(VRT, 2014). For instance, the 2012-16 agreement stipulates that the VRT has to ensure that, on average per day, 60% of viewers who watch its TV channels also tune into its news broadcasts or current affairs programmes. The seats on the board of directors of public service broadcasters are allocated according to the political balance of power in the Belgian parliament. The largest government party appoints the broadcaster's administrator-general. This is also the case for RTBF, for which the board plays an equally important role, in particular when it comes to respecting political balance in current affairs programmes and election manifestos.

The interdependence between the news media and politics

Belgian politics has been undergoing a process of 'mediatisation' for some time. There is an ever-changing dynamic in the relationship between the media and coverage of policy issues, but – again – the small size of the country, and the relatively few players in both government and media, results in mutual dependency.

The mediatisation of politics

As daily newspapers abandon direct links with their founding ideologies and embark on their own editorial course, and as strong public broadcasters are simultaneously obliged to run news broadcasts with impartiality and neutralism, the question arises as to how to typify the relationship between journalists and politics in Belgium.

The point at which media start to function more independently of political institutions is in fact just one step in the ongoing process of the 'mediatisation' of politics (Strömbäck, 2008). After a first step of 'mediation', in which the media become the main source of political information for citizens, the news media start to operate according to their own 'media logic' (Altheide and Snow, 1979). It is crucial, in the process of mediation, that political actors adhere to that same media logic. They will organise their activities to align with the way media operate, for example, by foregrounding individuals rather than policies. So politicians will try to anticipate that logic, for instance, by sending out a 'test balloon' with the expectation that the media will pick it up and some potentially useful controversy will arise. Political parties may also seek to involve the news media in their quest for legislative influence. By exchanging information and opinions with the media, politicians may bring issues to the attention of policymakers and other authorities. In that respect, the news media operate as a public relations tool for politicians, increasing the number of ways in which they communicate with the electorate. It's no different in Belgium than elsewhere.

Van Aelst (2006) confirmed the trend towards mediatisation in research that demonstrated that in 2003 politicians received more coverage in the news media than political parties. However, he also immediately qualified this finding. Personalisation does not necessarily mean that there is no room for party positions, especially as politicians try to be at the centre of attention when expressing an opinion or clarifying a policy decision. Furthermore, this practice does not necessarily mean that it is inspired by media logic. Parties may choose to pay more attention to personalities than to policy issues so that the party logic is decisive or at least plays a significant role (Van Aelst et al, 2008).

When typifying the relationship between politics and the media, Strömbäck and Van Aelst (2013, pp 347-51) also refer to 'issue ownership', which means that voters perceive certain policy issues as belonging to specific political parties. This is relevant because when certain issues touch citizens very strongly, they will be more inclined to vote for the party that 'owns' the issue. Walgrave and De Swert (2004) described a notable example of issue ownership, whereby the far-right party Vlaams Belang put so much emphasis on security and migration that people thought it was the only party dealing with these policy topics. However, issue ownership is not a given, so it is important for political parties to keep claiming issues by communicating about them (Walgrave et al, 2009).

Conversely, the dependency relationship is at least as inevitable because the news media are interwoven with the many aspects of the political sphere. For news reporters, this interdependence implies specifically that they have to take care of their political sources because reporting on local and national politics is part of the core business of most of the news media. Governments are important or even very important sources for 60% of the Belgian journalists and 55% say the same for politicians as a journalistic source (Raeymaeckers et al, 2013). Therefore, journalists' contact with political actors is indispensable and, ideally, of consistently high quality. This contact is based on mutual understanding, and is essential for conducting interviews, including on sensitive topics and in times of crisis, and for obtaining first-hand, breaking news, or at least for confirming rumours.

Furthermore, politicians and policymakers communicate strategically with the news media, for instance when deliberately leaking news to a 'preferred' medium or a journalist 'friend' in exchange for positive coverage or an interview. Informal contact cannot be ruled out either; in fact, this is considered to be essential to political journalists performing their job well.

Agenda setting

The interplay between media and policy issues, that is, the preferred topics of politicians, becomes all the more clear from research into agenda setting. The focus here is on the relationship between the ranking of issues on the agenda of respective actors. For example, when politicians pay a lot of attention to a particular policy issue, the question is whether the media's coverage of the issue is proportionate, and vice versa. McCombs and Shaw described this relationship in 1972, and it is still considered a source of inspiration for a great deal of research, not in the least in Belgium.

The content analyses conducted within the agenda-setting tradition do not always show a clear-cut perspective on the agenda-setting power of the media (for example, Van Aelst, 2006). According to one study (Walgrave et al, 2008a), which analysed longitudinal data over a large part of the 1990s, the news media in Belgium played a relatively *independent* role in determining to what extent certain issues received the attention of policymakers. However, these effects were more pronounced for parliamentary questions and interventions in parliament than for the real decisions taken by the government. This agenda-setting effect was stronger for newspapers than for television; after all, newspapers are still the main fora for public and political debate in Belgium.

The study by Walgrave et al (2008a) also showed that the effects varied depending on the subject. News media were more decisive for the agenda of policymakers in terms of issues relating to justice, crime and the environment than to foreign policy or financial affairs. A survey of journalists and politicians confirmed the role of the Belgian media as major agenda setters, and the politicians consider that role to be more important than journalists do. Walgrave (2008, p 457) concluded that Belgian politicians are 'obsessed' by the power of the media. He found, however, differences depending on the function that a politician fulfilled and on the type of issue at stake. The media influenced one third of the policy initiatives of opposition MPs, compared with one fifth of those among MPs from the ruling party. Politicians proved to be driven more by the media on occasions when they supposed that they could influence other politicians, and, second, on occasions where there was a correlation between how the media covered an issue and how public opinion perceived it.

A survey of political journalists, known as *Wetstraatjournalisten* in Dutch, made clear that, with regard to agenda setting, Belgium differs from other northern European countries such as the Netherlands, Norway, Denmark and Sweden (Van Dalen and Van Aelst, 2014). In Belgium, the political parties and the news media are considered to have an equally major agenda-setting effect. After all, Belgium is characterised as a partitocracy, in which many parties and their presidents are by far the most important political actors (De Winter et al, 1996; Deschouwer, 2009). Belgian journalists perceive this in the same way.

The 'objective' measures of different agendas deliver a less consistent picture than the 'subjective' studies in which the involved actors are asked to assess the influence of the news media on the political policy agenda. Through detailed content analyses and longitudinal studies, it is possible to determine the direction of the effect and exactly when it occurs. Remarkably, the researchers involved are inclined to attach more weight to 'objective' measurements and to minimise the 'subjective' assessment of politicians' own experiences as dictated by a 'media power syndrome' (Van Aelst and Walgrave, 2011, p 303). Politicians who believe in the agenda-setting function of the news media adhere to the view that the media can make or break a politician's career. What politicians overlook, however, is that their response to political news does not necessarily reflect that of the public or their constituents (Walgrave and Van Aelst, 2006).

Punctuated equilibrium

Other research from the political communication tradition focuses on different types of policy issues and compares them in order to reveal underlying patterns (Van Aelst and Walgrave, 2011). From this research, it has become clear that the focus on policy topics does not follow a fixed pattern, but shows remarkable highs and lows, referred to as a 'punctuated equilibrium' (Baumgartner and Jones, 1993). This phenomenon has been demonstrated in cross-national comparisons, including for Belgium (Baumgartner et al, 2009). On the political agenda side, the determining mechanism is termed 'friction', while on the media side it is known as 'cascading' (Walgrave and Vliegenthart, 2010).

Policymakers are confronted with many topics that could be turned into problematic issues that need their attention. In fact, there are so many potential issues that most of them are simply ignored until the moment at which the resistance (friction) in the political system reaches a point where intervention can no longer be postponed. When further barriers are overcome, certain policy options receive collective attention. Causes of resistance might be that political leaders stubbornly cling to ideological principles (cognitive friction) or that institutional structures refuse to cooperate (institutional friction) (Baumgartner et al, 2006).

Friction plays a role in the news media, too, but the process is relatively different from that in politics, mainly because the news media can decide independently whether or not to pay attention to a particular issue. However, because they are still competitors, competing for the attention of much of the same audience, they keep an eye on each other, imitate their competitors and tend to elaborate on the same news topics, albeit from a different angle. Cascading originates in this way, a kind of snowball effect in which a particular news topic succeeds in dominating the news over a long period of time.

For example, euthanasia as a policy issue remained on the policy agenda much longer in Belgium and in the Netherlands than in Denmark (Green-Pedersen, 2007). In Belgium, at least, opposition parties politicised the issue as a way to break the repeated inclusion of the Christian Democrats (CD&V) in the coalition government. In this process of friction, the opposition parties fought to keep the issue on the agenda. Once they were able to send the CD&V to the opposition benches, the ruling parties were forced to deal with the issue and consequently legalise euthanasia. In Denmark, such an 'accidental' positioning between competing parties never occurred and the issue was not put on the policy agenda.

The Dutroux affair as a case in point

Suppose that the media manage to put a policy issue on the political agenda. In such a case, it is not known how this issue will be dealt with in the political arena. Conversely, the same is also true when a politician manages to get a policy topic picked up by the news media; in such a case, it is far from certain whether the journalists involved will opt for the interpretation that the politician had in mind; more often than not, the (electoral) loot will be seized by competing parties. In-depth studies that focus on specific cases provide us with additional insight into agenda-setting mechanisms and into how policy change occurs. One such example arises from studies on the arrest of child rapist and murderer Marc Dutroux in 1996.[3] These show that major policy changes are not just the result of scandals and media hype, but of lengthy consultation among political actors – of which political parties have proved to play a decisive role in the Belgian context – and a willingness to engage in compromise and effective leadership.

At the time of the Dutroux case, the news media were not only filled with follow-up stories concerning Belgium's national trauma. The scandal also had an impact on the topics covered by Belgian journalists, to the extent that similar incidents and related issues, such as child pornography, sex tourism and child abuse, ranked high on the media agenda. Vasterman (1996) called this phenomenon media 'hype'. The hype could evoke the impression that these issues were much more prevalent during and after the Dutroux case than they were before. However, according to Vasterman, the main lesson learned from this media hype was that the issues would henceforth more easily be defined and perceived as problematic, regardless of what could be deduced from real-life statistics.

The scandal brought about so much social agitation that an estimated 300,000 Belgians took part in the White March, a peaceful demonstration that advocated for change. Walgrave and Manssens (2000) described how the news media succeeded in mobilising such a huge group of people. Eventually these dramatic events led to some major policy decisions, including the much-debated formation of an integrated police force. One of the reasons why Dutroux got away with committing his crimes over such a long period of time was because of the lack of information exchanged between the local police, the judicial police and the national *gendarmerie*. Maesschalck (2002) delved deeper into this policy change, taking a long-term perspective. He argued that the Dutroux case and the White March led to this policy decision only because some other conditions were also valid. After all, police reform had been on the policy agenda since the 1980s, well before the Dutroux affair shook the country. However, the parallel police structures provided too much institutional friction, which explains why quite a number of changes were not implemented, even when the mass media succeeded in mobilising thousands of people.

It took Marc Dutroux's escape in April 1998 to prompt the eight parties of the majority and the opposition finally to debate the issue, with prime minister Jean-Luc Dehaene as chair. A month later, the debate resulted in the Octopus Agreement, 'octopus' being a metaphor for the eight parties involved. The policy process, which had come to an impasse, could only be reinvigorated when political parties were given full control over the policy process (Walgrave and Varone, 2008).

Conclusion

The relationship between media and politics is far from a new area of research for Belgian scholars. The literature review in this chapter intends to demonstrate that. The direct impact of the media on the policy process is difficult to determine, but for Belgium at least, there is quite some empirical data available. In conclusion, it can be stated that the role of the news media in Belgium is not limited to that of a conduit for policy actors, as they also act as a contributor to the political and the policy process, both indirectly and directly.

First, there is mutual interdependence, partly boosted by the mediatisation of politics and the increasing media concentration. News media and politicians are intertwined with one another, so they cannot function entirely independently. Politicians and policymakers anticipate the media logic, and this logic is dictated by fewer and fewer players in a media landscape characterised by a high level of convergence. Indeed, fewer players mean fewer alternatives to get one's message across.

Second, direct influence stems mainly from agenda setting: the media help to determine which issues are on the policy agenda. Belgium is a small country, so the journalistic and political elites are no strangers to each other. Although the direct link between newspapers and political parties may have disappeared several decades ago, it is a form of professionalism and even a requirement that a journalist rely on an extensive network of informants and (exclusive) sources. This does not imply that there is undue pressure on, or direct manipulation in, the editorial process, but there is always some degree of influence and negotiation at play.

A final conclusion, which characterises the relationship between media and policy in Belgium, derives from the country's division along linguistic lines. The public media sector has been used to strengthen the subnational identity of both large language communities and to inhibit social cohesion within the national territory. News media exclusively address one language community, resulting in remarkably limited coverage of the other. In both communities, there is a distinct lack of coverage of the many regionalised policy domains (including economy, energy, education, media and scientific research). Notwithstanding the many remaining federal policy domains (such as foreign policy, defence, finance, social security and justice), there is still a remarkable imbalance in the amount of coverage of such issues by the media in both communities. Language forms a potential barrier, yet perfectly bilingual federal ministers are rarely featured in media on both sides of the language border. Here, the broader political system in Belgium – where politicians only attract votes in their own language community – also comes into play. As a consequence, Belgian news media lack the ability to structurally link and integrate the various (policy) debates in the different parts of the country and do not contribute to the development of a genuine national public sphere in Belgium. Also, by making the political consensus of their own language community seem obvious and natural, Flemish and Francophone media have helped reinforce political conflicts between the language communities.

Notes

1 Brussel-Halle-Vilvoorde (B-H-V) was an electoral district that covered the bilingual region of Brussels as well as 35 municipalities in the unilingual Flemish Region. Flemish politicians wanted to split this district in the name of the linguistic territoriality principle; Francophone politicians were opposed to this. This strongly symbolic issue (in which strategic party politics also played a role) came to the forefront of political debate in 2004 to become one of the main topics in the political crisis in Belgium (2007-11), when an agreement on how to split the district was finally reached (for more details, see Sinardet, 2010).

2 Original text: '... in andere gevallen is de politieke druk soms zwaar, soms zelfs heel flagrant geweest. Ik heb hier brieven voor me liggen van politici ... die mij het nauwelijks verholen bevel gaven een voorstel tot benoeming in te trekken omdat zij een andere kandidaat dan degene die ik het meest geschikt achtte, bevorderd wilden zien' (authors' own translation).

3 Marc Dutroux is Belgium's most notorious serial killer and child molester. His deeds, arrest, trial and escape caused much commotion, fuelled by conspiracy theories and the malfunctioning of the police and judicial systems at that time.

References

Altheide, D. L. and Snow, R.P. (1979) *Media logic*, Beverly Hills, CA: Sage.

Anderson, B. (1991) *Imagined communities: reflections on the origin and spread of nationalism* (2nd edn), London: Verso.

Bardoel, J. and d'Haenens, L. (2008) 'Reinventing public service broadcasting in Europe: prospects, promises and problems', *Media, Culture & Society*, 30(3): 337-55.

Baumgartner, F.R., Breunig, C., Green-Pedersen, C., Jones, B.D., Mortensen, P.B., Nuytemans, M. and Walgrave, S. (2009) 'Punctuated equilibrium in comparative perspective', *American Journal of Political Science*, 53(3): 603-20.

Baumgartner, F.R., Green-Pedersen, C. and Jones, B.D. (2006) 'Comparative studies of policy agendas', *Journal of European Public Policy*, 13(7): 959-74.

CIM TV (2015) 'Sud/Nord, 1/1 - 31/12/2015, 02-26h, groupe cible & invités', Brussels: GfK Belgium, available at www.cim.be (accessed 1 July 2016).

Dandoy, R. and Nuytemans, M. (2007) 'Media and public policy in Belgium: empirical evidence from quantitative thematic analysis', paper presented at the ECPR Joint Sessions of Workshops, Helsinki, 7-12 May.

De Bens, E. and Raeymaeckers, K. (2010) *De Pers in België: het verhaal van de Belgische dagbladpers, gisteren, vandaag en morgen* (4th edn), Leuven: Lannoo Campus.

Deschouwer, K. (2009) *The politics of Belgium: governing a divided society*, New York, NY: Palgrave Macmillan.

Deschouwer, K. and Sinardet D. (2010) 'Identiteiten, communautaire standpunten en stemgedrag', in K. Deschouwer, P. Delwit, M. Hooghe and S. Walgrave (eds) *De stemmen van het volk: een analyse van het kiesgedrag in Vlaanderen en Wallonië op 7 juni 2009*, Brussels: VUBPress, 75-98.

De Smedt, J. (2014) *Het binnenlandse en buitenlandse nieuws verweven*, Belgium: Steunpunt Media, available at www.steunpuntmedia.be/wp-content/uploads/2014/02/Nieuwsmonitor-Flash_buitenlandberichtgeving.pdf (accesed 3 June 2014).

De Winter, L. (1981) 'De partijpolitisering als instrument van de particratie: een overzicht van de ontwikkeling sinds de Tweede Wereldoorlog', *Res Publica*, 23(1): 53–107.

De Winter, L., Della Porta, D. and Deschouwer, K. (1996) 'Partitocracies between crises and reforms: comparing similar countries Italy and Belgium', *Res Publica*, 38(2): 215–35.

Donders, K. and Raats, T. (2012) 'Analysing national practices after European state aid control: are multi-stakeholder negotiations beneficial for public service broadcasting?', *Media, Culture & Society*, 34(2): 162–80.

Esser, F. and Strömbäck, J. (eds) (2014) *Mediatization of politics: understanding the transformation of Western democracies*, Basingstoke: Palgrave MacMillan.

Goossens, C. (1998) *Radio en televisie in Vlaanderen: een geschiedenis*, Leuven: Davidsfonds.

Green-Pedersen, C. (2007), 'The conflict of conflicts in comparative perspective: euthanasia as a political issue in Denmark, Belgium, and the Netherlands', *Comparative Politics*, 39(3): 273–91.

Habermas, J. (1962/1999) *Strukturwandel der öffentlichkeit: Untersuchungen zu einer Kategorie der bürgerlichen Gesellschaft*, Frankfurt am Main: Suhrkamp.

Hauttekeete, L. (2005) 'De tabloidisering van kranten: mythe of feit? De ontwikkeling van een meetinstrument en een onderzoek naar de tabloidisering van Vlaamse kranten', unpublished PhD thesis, University of Ghent.

Hooghe, M., Marien, S. and Pauwels, T. (2011) 'Where do distrusting voters turn if there is no viable exit or voice option? The impact of political trust on electoral behaviour in the Belgian regional elections of June 2009', *Government and Opposition*, 46(2): 245–73.

ICRI (Interdisciplinary Centre for Law and ICT) (2009) *Independent study on indicators for media pluralism in the member states – towards a risk-based approach*, Leuven: KU Leuven, available at http://ec.europa.eu/information_society/media_taskforce/doc/pluralism/pfr_report.pdf (accessed 3 June 2014).

Jacobs, L. and Hooghe, M. (2014) *Roldiversiteit op de Vlaamse en Franstalige televisie*, Antwerp: Steunpunt Media, available at www.steunpuntmedia.be/wp-content/uploads/2014/04/Roldiversiteit-op-de-Vlaamse-en-Franstalige-Televisie.pdf (accessed 13 June 2015).

Jacubowicz, K. (2007) 'Public service broadcasting: a new beginning, or the beginning of the end?', available at http://www.coe.int/t/dghl/standardsetting/media/doc/PSB_Anewbeginning_KJ_en.pdf (accessed 2 June 2014).

Maesschalck, J. (2002) 'When do scandals have an impact on policy making? A case study of the police reform following the Dutroux scandal in Belgium', *International Public Management Journal*, 5(2): 169–93.

McCombs, M. and Shaw, D.L. (1972) 'The agenda-setting function of mass media', *Public Opinion Quarterly*, 36(2): 176–87.

Pander, I. (2001) 'Journalisten en de Wetstraat: de verhouding tussen de journalistiek en de politiek in Vlaanderen', unpublished Master's thesis, University of Amsterdam.

Raeymaeckers, K., Heinderyckx, F., De Vuyst, S., Libert, M., De Maeyer, J., De Dobbelaer, R., Le Cam, F., Deprez, A. and De Keyser, J. (2013) *De Belgische journalist in 2013: een zelfportret*, Ghent: Academia Press.

Shanahan, E.A., McBeth, M.K., Hathaway, P.L. and Arnell, R.J. (2008) 'Conduit or contributor? The role of media in policy change theory', *Policy Sciences*, 41(2): 115-38.

Sinardet, D. (2010) 'From consociational consciousness to majoritarian myth. Consociational democracy, multi-level politics and the Belgian case of Brussels-Halle-Vilvoorde', *Acta Politica*, 45(3): 346-69.

Sinardet, D. (2012) 'Is there a Belgian public sphere? What the case of a federal multilingual country can contribute to the debate on transnational public spheres. And vice versa', in M. Seymour and A.G. Gagnon (eds) *Multinational federalism: problems and Prospects*, New-York, NY: Palgrave MacMillan, 172-204.

Sinardet, D. (2013) 'How linguistically divided media represent linguistically divisive issues: Belgian political TV-debates on Brussels-Halle-Vilvoorde', *Regional and Federal Studies*, 23(3): 311-33.

Sinardet, D., De Swert, K. and Dandoy, R. (2004) 'Les sujets des journaux télévisés francophones et flamands: une comparaison longitudinale', *Courrier Hebdomadaire du CRISP*, no. 1864.

Strömbäck, J. (2005) 'In search of a standard: four models of democracy and their normative implications for journalism', *Journalism Studies*, 3(3): 331-45.

Strömbäck, J. (2008) 'Four phases of mediatization: an analysis of the mediatization of politics', *The International Journal of Press/Politics*, 13(3): 228-46.

Strömbäck, J. and Van Aelst, P. (2013) 'Why political parties adapt to the media: exploring the fourth dimension of mediatization', *International Communication Gazette*, 75(4): 341-58.

Van Aelst, P. (2006) 'Toeschouwer, speler of scheidsrechter? Een empirische studie over de rol van de media in de verkiezingscampagne van 2003', unpublished PhD thesis, University of Antwerp, available at www.m2p.be/publications/00110832. pdf (accessed 3 June 2014).

Van Aelst, P., Maddens, B., Noppe, J. and Fiers, S. (2008) 'Politicians in the news: media or party logic,' *European Journal of Communication*, 23(2): 193-210.

Van Dalen, A. and Van Aelst, P. (2014) 'The media as political agenda-setters: journalists' perceptions of media power in eight West European countries', *West European Politics*, 37(1): 42-64.

Vandenberghe, H., d'Haenens, L. and Van Gorp, B. (2013) *Hoe divers is de Vlaamse pers? Leeftijd, gender en etniciteit in het Vlaamse krantennieuws*, Antwerp: Steunpunt Media, available at www.steunpuntmedia.be/wp-content/uploads/2013/10/ Nieuwsmonitor-15.pdf (accessed 3 June 2014).

Van den Bulck, H. (2001) 'Public service broadcasting and national identity as a project of modernity', *Media, Culture and Society*, 23(1): 53-69.

Vanduynslager, L., Wets, J., Noppe, J. and Doyen G. (2013) *Vlaamse Migratie-en Integratiemonitor 2013*, Antwerp: Steunpunt Inburgering en Integratie, available at www.vlaanderen.be/nl/publicaties/detail/vlaamse-migratie-en-integratiemonitor-2013 (accessed 12 June 2015).

Van Gorp, B. (2004) 'De massamedia als factor voor sociale cohesie', in C. Timmerman, I. Lodewyckx, D. Vanheule and J. Wets (eds) *Wanneer wordt vreemd, vreemd?*, Leuven: Acco, 241-57.

Vasterman, P. (1996) 'De echo van de Belgische beerput in de Nederlandse media', *De Journalist*, available at http://vasterman.blogspot.be/1996_10_01_archive.html (accessed 3 June 2014).

VRT (Vlaamse Radio en Televisie) (2014) *Jaarverslag 2014*, Brussels: VRT, available at www.vrt.be/sites/default/files/attachments/VRT_jaarverslag_2014.pdf (accessed 1 July 2016).

Walgrave, S. (2008) 'Again, the almighty mass media? The media's political agenda-setting power according to politicians and journalists in Belgium', *Political Communication*, 25(4): 445-59.

Walgrave, S. and De Swert, K. (2004) 'The making of the (issues of the) Vlaams Blok', *Political Communication*, 21(4): 479-500.

Walgrave, S. and Manssens, J. (2000) 'The making of the White March: the mass media as a mobilizing alternative to movement organizations', *Mobilization: An International Journal*, 5(2): 217-39.

Walgrave, S. and Van Aelst, P. (2006) 'The contingency of the mass media's political agenda setting power: toward a preliminary theory', *Journal of Communication*, 56(1): 88-109.

Walgrave, S., Soroka, S. and Nuytemans, M. (2008a) 'The mass media's political agenda-setting power: a longitudinal analysis of media, parliament, and government in Belgium (1993 to 2000)', *Comparative Political Studies*, 41(6): 814-36.

Walgrave, S., Van Aelst, P. and Nuytemans, M. (2008b) 'Do the vote test: the electoral effects of a popular vote advice application at the 2004 Belgian elections', *Acta Politica*, 43(1): 50-70.

Walgrave, S. and Vliegenthart, R. (2010) 'Why are policy agendas punctuated? Friction and cascading in parliament and mass media in Belgium', *Journal of European Public Policy*, 17(8): 1147-80.

Wolfe, M., Jones, B.D. and Baumgartner, F.R. (2013) 'A failure to communicate: agenda setting in media and policy studies', *Political Communication*, 30(2): 175-92.

Part Five
Policy analysis by advocates and academics

Thinking in splendid isolation? The organisation and policy engagement of think tanks in Belgium

Bert Fraussen, Valérie Pattyn and Justin Lawarée

During the last two decades of the 20th century, think thanks proliferated dramatically in various countries. Once a predominantly American and British phenomenon, think tanks are now dispersed throughout the world (Stone, 2007; Pautz, 2011; McGann, 2014). The most recent overview of the Think Tanks and Civil Societies Programme (TTCSP, 2013) covers 6,826 think tanks in 182 countries. This report indicates that 1,984 think tanks are based in North America, of which 1,828 are in the United States, while Western Europe is home to 1,267 think tanks, of which 52 are based in Belgium. The majority of these 'Belgian' think tanks have an exclusively European or, to a lesser degree, international focus. Well-known examples are Bruegel, the Centre for European Policy Studies and the International Crisis Group. The strong presence of these think tanks is not so surprising, considering the large presence of EU institutions in Brussels (Boucher et al, 2004; Nichelson, 2009; Blockx, 2011).

While various scholars have studied think-tank activity at the EU level (for example, Sherrington 2000; Boucher et al, 2004), the nature and work of domestic think tanks in Europe – without an exclusive EU focus – has rarely been documented. Furthermore, the little work on domestic think tanks that does exist focuses mainly on pluralist polities, such as the UK. As a result, we have much less knowledge of the internal organisation and activities of think tanks in a neo-corporatist setting. This chapter constitutes one of the first attempts to cover this empirical void by focusing on domestic think tanks in Belgium.

Defining what a think tank is (or, and especially, what it is not), represents a challenging undertaking. Think tanks appear in great diversity, varying in size, legal form, policy ambit, organisational structure and political significance. As a result, researchers tend to observe many hybrid forms, rather than one dominant model. Furthermore, the national context, including elements such as constitutional architecture and political culture, also plays an important part in determining the particular features of think tanks (Stone, 2007, p 261; Campbell and Pedersen, 2014, p 27). In the case of Belgium, one should pay special attention to three particular characteristics of its political system: the neo-corporatist nature of interest intermediation, the consociational legacy and the federal state structure.

Each of these characteristics can be assumed to influence the nature of the Belgian think tank landscape. First, the neo-corporatist mode of policymaking implies that in several policy domains (mostly economic affairs, but also education and healthcare) a select number of interest groups have strong representational monopolies and enjoy institutionally privileged access to policymakers. Considering that practices of consultation of societal interests are generally strongly institutionalised, it may be difficult for new political actors, including think tanks, to get a foot in the door.

Second, Belgium's consociational legacy should shape the think-tank landscape. Consociationalism relates to the legacy of pillarisation, referring to strong and dense networks among organisations from the same subcultures. These subcultures were based on religious, ideological and economic cleavages (Deschouwer, 2009). While pillars were distinguished according to whether they had a Catholic, socialist or liberal worldview, those in the former two categories in particular represented large networks of well-established organisations. While pillarisation reached its peak in the 1960s and 1970s (Huyse, 2003), many pillar organisations are still pivotal political players with close affiliations to one of the traditional parties (see Brans and Maes, 2001). This chapter explores whether similar party linkages still exist among think tanks.

Finally, following the development from a unitary towards a federal state, political actors (such as parties and interest groups) needed to adapt to the evolving political structures. While all political parties are currently organised on a regional (Flemish, Brussels or Walloon) basis, the interest group population contains a mix of national and regional organisations. These developments have resulted in the fragmentation of policy communities (see Chapter Nine). As think tanks are subject to similar challenges resulting from Belgium's changed institutional architecture, we question how they deal with this multi-level landscape. Are most of them organised at a national scale, or are they also split along regional lines? Related to this, the chapter investigates whether think tanks prioritise interaction with regional policymakers, or whether they distribute their attention and efforts equally across different levels of government.

The first section of this chapter reviews the relevant literature on think tanks, discusses their hybrid and diverse nature, and presents the definition that we applied in our research. Next, it clarifies the data collection strategy, which relied on a survey completed by 15 domestic think tanks between December 2013 and May 2014. The chapter subsequently presents the results of the research, focusing on the organisational features of these think tanks and their policy activities. Overall, the chapter demonstrates that think tanks in Belgium are rather new political players, with very limited resources, that appear not to be strongly connected to policymakers. Furthermore, while Flanders is home to several think tanks, such organisations are rather scarce in Wallonia.

One size does not fit all

Compared with other political organisations such as political parties and interest groups, think tanks are a relatively new phenomenon. In many countries, they only became prominent in the 1980s (Sherrington, 2000; Stone, 2000). Until that time, most think tanks were predominantly 'low-profile actors seeking to inform policy in a detached non-partisan scholarly fashion.... They operated behind the scenes and could be discounted by social scientists as private academic associations of no political importance' (Stone, 2000, p 150). This raises the question why the 'think tank' is currently an emerging organisational form. The academic literature commonly refers to two possible explanations. First, as expertise increasingly becomes a crucial currency in contemporary policymaking, organisations that specifically focus on recruiting the brightest minds and accumulating expertise in specific policy domains are more and more valued by policymakers (and journalists for that matter) in need of information and advice (see, for example, Hall and Deardorf, 2006; Maloney, 2012). Think tanks do not merely transmit research to government officials, but also 'help to provide the conceptual language, the ruling paradigms, the empirical examples, that then become accepted assumptions for those making policy' (Stone, 2007, p 276; see also Pautz, 2010, 2013). Stone thus considers think tanks as a manifestation of the knowledge/power nexus, rather than a bridge between knowledge and power.

Second, while think tanks often engage in policy debates from a specific angle or ideology, their analyses do not result from the preferences of their membership, but instead from the collection and analysis of information. Rather than representing the voice of a constituency, they try to shape policymaking by spelling out solutions to policy problems (although their neutrality is often subject to debate, as discussed shortly). They tend to do this through a wide range of activities, including framing policy issues, publishing research, conducting policy evaluations, and organising conferences and networking opportunities (McGann, 2007, p 6).

As a result of their organisational diversity, think tanks are hard to define. Rich provides the perhaps most encompassing definition, conceiving them as 'independent, non-interest based, non-profit organisations that produce and principally rely on expertise and ideas to obtain support and to influence the policymaking process' (2004, p 11). In the literature, this point of view is shared by many others. Pautz, for instance, states that 'think tanks are non-governmental institutions; intellectually, organisationally and financially autonomous from government, political parties or organised interests, and set up with the aim of influencing policy' (2011, p 419). Their basic activities consequently involve doing research and disseminating their findings and ideas. Furthermore, according to Rich, they aim to maximise their public credibility and political access by detaching themselves from specific constituencies and by avoiding financial dependence from narrow groups of supporters (2004).

The extent to which think tanks are truly 'independent', however, is a critical issue about which opinions strongly diverge. As argued by Pautz, 'they lay claim to political neutrality while often not making a secret of their ideological standpoint' (2010, p 276). Some definitions add that 'think tanks may be affiliated *or* independent institutions' (McGann and Sabatini, 2011, p 23, emphasis added), as these types of organisations *are* frequently linked to parties, government, private companies or universities (see also McGann, 2007, p 11; the TTCSP takes a similar approach). Obviously, such affiliations might limit think tanks' credibility in the eyes of policymakers. Rich (2004), whose research focuses on the US, finds that the current think-tank landscape is characterised by the recommitment of the business community, as many think tanks have linkages to business associations and companies, or include representatives from the latter on their own board of directors (a similar observation is made for EU-focused think tanks by Sherrington, 2000, p 188).

Stone (2007) makes a similar point when she questions the extent to which think tanks serve the public interest. In her view, many think tanks pursue private interests, as they mainly formulate concerns that resonate with the economically and politically literate. Likewise, Rich notes a development from objective research towards a more ideological agenda and an increased emphasis on marketing activities (Rich, 2004). The most elaborated account of this argument can probably be found in the work of Smith (2000), who demonstrates how business increasingly considers the funding of likeminded think tanks as an effective way to shape public opinion: policymakers often attribute more legitimacy to analyses of think tanks than to policy reports from business or professional associations. If this trend intensifies, it might become harder to distinguish think tanks from other players such as organised interests and commercial firms, who display very similar behaviour (for example, Boucher et al, 2004, p 97, cited by Stone, 2007).

Within the scope of this chapter, the intention is not to re-examine the 'independence debate'. Hence, we adopt the perspective of Sherrington who considers think tanks as '*relatively* independent organisations, engaged in research on a broad scope of interests' (Sherrington, 2000, p 174, emphasis added; see also Boucher and Royo, 2009, p 34). This chapter excludes think tanks with particular members such as individuals and companies, as well as think tanks with formal affiliations with interest groups, or study centres of political parties (these actors are discussed separately in Chapters Eight and Nine).

To determine whether organisations can be classified as think tanks, the think tank conceptualisation of Boucher and colleagues is applied (Boucher et al, 2004, pp 2-3; Boucher and Royo, 2009, p 35), but translated in nine clear-cut criteria, which read as a checklist. All of these criteria implicitly or explicitly feature in the think-tank definitions of other authors, and organisations should meet these criteria to classify as a think tank. To this end, think tanks:

- are permanent organisations;
- specialise in the production of public policy solutions;
- rely on staff dedicated to research;
- produce ideas, analysis and advice;
- invest in the communication of their ideas to policymakers and public opinion;
- are not responsible for government operations;
- aim to maintain their intellectual freedom, and are not beholden to any specific interests;

- do not confer degrees or carry out training as a primary activity; and
- seek to act in the public interest.

This checklist therefore excludes foundations and organisations with a primarily academic function.[1] While foundations may occasionally engage in research activities, this is generally not their core function. Furthermore, foundations tend to provide funding for research, rather than embark on these activities themselves. The next section discusses the use of this checklist as a guide for the case selection and clarifies the means of data collection.

Research design

To arrive at a comprehensive list of think tanks that match the abovementioned criteria, we used a snowball sample strategy. Starting with an initial selection, we approached academics, journalists and other chosen informants and asked them whether they could add other think tanks. In addition, we systematically asked the think tanks themselves whether they knew of others in Belgium. This strategy yielded a result of 24 domestic think tanks. All think tanks were sent a written questionnaire that included a mixture of open and closed questions, in either Dutch or French, the two main national languages. For purposes of consistency throughout the book, a substantial share of the questions was similar to those used for the chapters on policy advice by other political actors, such as political parties (Chapter Eight), interest groups (Chapter Nine) and in-house policy workers (Chapter Four).

Of the 24 contacted think tanks that initially agreed to participate, 15 completed the survey (60% response rate). Some organisations provided rather general arguments for not participating (such as 'most questions do not seem applicable to our situation') or claimed that 'they were an interest organisation or citizen group rather than a think tank'. Others argued that the policy-oriented nature of the questions did not really fit with their core activities. To be precise, while the authors used a definition that represents the common scholarly view on think tanks, this definition did not always match the way in which some of the organisations that were expected to classify as think tanks perceived themselves.

Most of these organisations are rather informal groups that mainly provide platforms for reflection and discussion. The *Gravensteengroep* and *Re-Bel* are two such organisations: they unite (mostly academic) experts with the aim of discussing the process of state reform in Belgium. Whereas these organisations are often classified as think tanks in the media, their main objective does not directly involve providing policy advice and seeking influence. Instead, they primarily aim to contribute to the public debate through collective reflection on current and future societal challenges. Such organisations, despite their popular classification as think tanks, are not included in the analysis. To be clear, some of the organisations that did agree to participate emphasised that their main goal involved providing a forum for discussion, rather than shaping public policy, yet this did not prevent them from considering themselves as think tanks. These organisations are therefore included in the analysis.

Interestingly, and importantly, some organisations were rather averse to considering themselves as think tanks, although we expected them to match most of our nine-item checklist. The concept of 'think tank', at least in Belgium, still appears to have a somewhat negative connotation. This supposedly relates to the abovementioned claim of think tanks' (financial and ideological) dependence on certain interests. For the purpose of this research, where organisations were requested to complete a survey, the authors proceeded only with those that considered themselves as think tank, no matter how they are classified by the media or in public. The scholarly definition of think tanks and the definition applied by organisations themselves apparently do not always match. Future research should reveal whether this observation is unique for Belgium, or whether this is a universal phenomenon.

A closer look at the policy focus of think tanks and the nature of their policy advice

This section first describes the Belgian think-tank landscape based on the survey results. Next, it discusses some of the think tanks' key features, including their mission, and their capacity and engagement in policymaking. The last two sections focus on the characteristics and dissemination of policy advice.

The think-tank culture is relatively new in Belgium, especially if one considers those think tanks that do not exclusively focus on the EU. While not claiming to paint an exhaustive picture, we nonetheless believe that the research represents an important first step in gaining a better understanding of the organisation and functioning of domestic think tanks in Belgium. Table 12.1 lists the organisations finally included, with their year of establishment. It makes a distinction between think tanks organised on a national scale, and those organised on a regional basis. All the think tanks surveyed were established after 2000, their median age being eight years. Compared with political parties and interest groups, think tanks are newcomers on the policy advisory scene.

From this overview, it appears that the think-tank culture is much more vibrant in Flanders than in Wallonia. Eleven of the 13 think tanks organised on a regional scale are Flemish. Importantly, only two of the think tanks are organised on a national scale: the *Vrijdaggroep* and Itinera Institute. The scarcity of nationally organised think tanks may reflect the devolution of powers to the regions (discussed later in the chapter).

Table 12.1: Overview of think tanks and their years of establishment (N=15)

Organised on a national scale			
Itinera Institute			2006
De Vrijdaggroep			2013
Organised on a regional scale			
Aula Magna	2005	Pro Flandria	2003
iD	2006	VKW Metena	2004
Libera!	2009	Vooruitgroep	2008
Liberales	2002	WeCitizens	2012
Logia	2010	Werkgroep Taal en Onderwijs VVA	2002
Oikos	2010	WorkForAll	2004
Poliargus	2010		

A variety of missions and policy domains

Departing from a literature-based definition of think tanks, it is important to verify how the organisations themselves conceptualise a think tank. Comparing the respondents' answers to the nine criteria checklist of Boucher and colleagues (2004), two criteria are frequently mentioned: the production of policy advice or public policy solutions based on expertise, and the communication of these ideas to policymakers and the public.

Despite consensus on the core activities of think tanks, there is much diversity in their *raison d'être*. This is illustrated in Table 12.2, which mentions the mission of the various think tanks. Whereas some think tanks focus on very specific issues, such as education or the future of Brussels, many adhere to a specific political philosophy, such as conservatism, liberalism or ecology, or a specific religion. When looking at the interaction of these think tanks with political parties and organised interests, the pillarised landscape described earlier is still evident. This confirms earlier findings on the interaction between organised interests and policymakers in Belgium (Fraussen and Beyers, 2016). Data about these interactions being limited (not all respondents were willing to answer this question), the tentative evidence indicates that think tanks promoting a liberal, socialist or Christian perspective are not only more likely to interact with like-minded political parties, but also frequently to engage with interest organisations that were formerly important allies in the same pillars. For instance, a liberal-leaning think tank still appears more likely to liaise with liberal parties and with liberal–minded interest groups, such as liberal trade unions or health organisations with equally close links to this party.

While these mission statements clarify the central objectives of the think tanks, they do not reveal much about the policy domains these organisations focus on in their actual policy work. The 'policy portfolio' of think tanks varies considerably. Rich (2004), for instance, distinguished three types of think tanks, based on their policy portfolio: full-service, spanning the broadest array of issue domains; multi-issue, with an interest in various topics in more than one policy domain; and single-issue, focusing on one category of issues. In the Belgian case, some think tanks clearly have a more specialist profile and limit their attention to two to five policy domains (see Table 12.3). In Rich's terms, they can be

Table 12.2: Overview of think tank missions

Name	Mission
Aula Magna	Aims to create an open, well-informed debate on all aspects of the future of *Brussels*.
De Vrijdaggroep	Aims to be a pluralist and multidisciplinary think tank for *Generation Y*, providing specific policy solutions for the most important challenges of present and future generations
iD	Aims to contribute to a social and coherent society, conscious about the past and open for challenges in the future, by providing sophisticated conservative insights that take into account cultural history and complex social reality
Itinera Institute	Aims to '*pave new ways*' by providing quality independent expertise, strategic vision, concrete solutions, open debate and collaboration
Libera!	Aims to promote classical-*liberal* ideas by conducting studies and organising events
Liberales	Disseminates *liberal* philosophical ideas
Logia	Aims to promote *Christian*-inspired opinions in general media by engaging Christian-inspired experts in the public debate, in print and audiovisual media
Oikos	Independent think tank working on socio-ecological change by contributing to the public debate from an *ecological* perspective
Poliargus	Independent think tank within the broader *progressive* movement that advocates for freedom, equality, democracy, solidarity, decommodification and sustainability
Pro Flandria	Network of Flemish entrepreneurs and academics that strives to ensure and increase the Flemish and European well-being, based on three principles: *entrepreneurship*, *values* and *autonomy*
VKW Metena	The association promotes social entrepreneurship, inspired by *Christian* values, and seeks to provide a unique meeting venue, to conduct groundbreaking research and to launch innovative initiatives
Vooruitgroep	Analyses how the current *Flemish nationalism* represents a neo-conservative and neoliberal perspective on society
WeCitizens	Represents the interests of *citizens and voters* by generating more transparency
Werkgroep Taal en Onderwijs van het Verbond der Vlaamse Academic	Focuses on *academic education*, permanent training, future possibilities and responsibilities of academics, scientific research, and the position of Dutch in education and science. To accomplish these objectives, the association acts as an *actively flamingant* pressure group, a cultural association in the broadest sense and an association of academics
WorkForAll	Independent *socioeconomic* think tank focused in particular on recreating the conditions whereby all people can exercise the right to work and the right to self-determination

Note: Authors' own translation; emphasis added.

considered single- or multi-issue players. Others, in contrast take a more generalist orientation, with four think tanks that focus on more than 20 policy domains (fitting the full-service category). The extent to which think tanks can monitor developments in all these areas on a daily basis is questionable, considering their limited workforce. This broad orientation may rather imply that these think tanks do not *a priori* limit their attention to a specific policy domain. They may deploy policy-oriented actions on a wide range of societal and political issues, depending on the governmental agenda, current events and organisational priorities. When asked about the top priority policy domains, economics, education and training, employment, general government affairs, and budget and finance are most frequently mentioned. In terms of time and resources spent per domain, the broad field of economics surpasses the others.

Table 12.3: Policy portfolio breadth of think tanks (by number of policy domains)

Number of policy domains	N
1-5	27%
5-10	27%
10-15	0%
15-20	20%
20-25	27%

Note: Percentages may not total 100 due to rounding.

Policy capacity and engagement in policymaking

As the think tanks' staff members monitor multiple policy domains and liaise with a diverse set of (political) actors, they might be expected to have considerable resources and a critical mass for the production, collection and diffusion of policy expertise. Yet, the organisational capacity of the studied think tanks is rather limited. Let us first consider capacity in terms of the number of staff. While this admittedly is a rough proxy, it nonetheless provides a relevant indication about the overall resources of think tanks. Almost 50% of the surveyed organisations work exclusively with volunteers. Most of the organisations with paid staff have a limited number of employees, generally ranging from one to four full-time equivalents, with the great majority of think tanks only employing one or two staffers. The only think tank that does not fit this picture is Itinera, which employs 10 full-time equivalents. Given its high level of resources (especially compared with the other organisations included in our analysis), it is no surprise that Itinera is generally considered one of Belgium's most prominent think tanks. It not only frequently produces policy dossiers on various topics, but is also widely covered in the media, whereas most other think tanks have barely any media exposure (see also Lamotte, 2012; Markey, 2013).

Organisational capacity can also be approached from a financial point of view. The survey collected information about the diversity of think tanks' financial resources. Half of the think tanks work with volunteers, and several rely exclusively on resources contributed by these individuals (be it time or modest financial contributions). A second important source of finance is provided by foundations; this accounts for the full budget of five think tanks. The combination of these two sources is quite rare; only one organisation has a 50:50 balance between support from foundations and individuals. Two of the surveyed think tanks rely on contributions from firms, in addition to support from foundations or individuals. Yet, the contribution from firms only represents a small share (10%) of those think tanks' budgets. This finding suggests that most of the think tanks either depend on the labour and contribution of volunteers (often academics), or survive thanks to support from foundations. Future research would obviously benefit from a more comprehensive insight into the financial resources of these organisations. A survey is perhaps not the most appropriate tool for collecting evidence on these matters, as finance is still a very sensitive issue for most think tanks.

Generally, it is rather uncommon for think tanks in Belgium to outsource their research activities (see Table 12.4). The limited financial resources of think tanks explain a lot in this regard. As organisations' own staff members (paid or volunteers) conduct most policy research, one may wonder where they acquired their research background. Of the 14 think tanks that provided information on the professional experience of staff members, no less than 10 indicated that they employed people with an academic background, previously or currently employed by universities as researchers and/or lecturers. Next, albeit to a lesser degree, five of 13 think tanks frequently employ people with experience in the private sector. People leaving think tanks also often return to one of these two sectors. Think tanks only rarely employ staff with any other type of professional background.

The multi-level structure of the Belgian political system is a feature that is also reflected in the orientation of the think tanks across different levels of government (see Table 12.5). A first interesting observation is the scarce attention to the local level, with only a few think tanks engaging in activities at this level. Local politics are clearly not a strategic priority for most think tanks. In contrast, most think tanks are active at both the regional and the federal levels. This is an interesting observation, in light of the abovementioned fact that only two think tanks are organised on a national basis. The federalisation process of Belgium may have

Table 12.4: Outsourcing of policy research (N=13)

Percentage of research activities outsourced	Percentage of think tanks
20% or less	61%
21-40%	0%
41-60%	23%
61-80%	8%
More than 80%	8%

affected the territorial scale at which think tanks are organised, but not so much their policy portfolio. The surveyed think tanks also demonstrate a high level of activity at the supranational, that is, EU level. The proximity of Brussels is definitely a factor here. Besides, the long-term orientation of most think tanks is presumably associated with greater attentiveness to policy developments at the European and international level.

Having provided an initial description of the think-tank landscape in Belgium, the next section turns to the policy advisory activities of think tanks, the primary focus of this book.

Table 12.5: Think tank activities across different levels of government (N=11)

Level of government	Percentage of think tanks active at this level at least a few times a year
Municipal	36%
Provincial	18%
Regional	81%
Federal	81%
Neighbouring countries	45%
European	81%
International	54%

Characteristics of policy advice

The way in which organisations providing policy advice, such as interest groups and think tanks, frame topics greatly influences the way in which policymakers understand issues (Baumgartner, 2009, pp 521-4). Organisations frame their messages in different ways. For instance, they may choose to highlight financial issues or instead focus on the extent to which certain policy measures have broad societal support. Two criteria were considered central to the provision of high-quality advice by all the think tanks in the survey sample. First, the advice should integrate all relevant research about a particular topic. Second, it should focus on the formulation of long-term objectives. The latter element is of utmost importance. Think tanks, unlike political party study centres and interest groups, are primarily focused on long-term objectives and on shaping eventual public policy. This is apparent from the answers to the question about the proportion of activities devoted to the current political agenda versus those focusing on long-term objectives. More than 70% of the activities of 10 of the 14 think tanks in the survey are devoted to issues with long-term goals.

Other important elements of best practice involve attention to the financial implications of public policies and a focus beyond specific organisational interests (see Table 12.6). Considering the policy position of the minister, or taking into account the current government agenda or existing policy programmes, are considered to be less important. Think tanks are free to take a position irrespective of current policies or ministerial preferences. When one conceives of think tanks primarily as providers of policy advice, one may find these results rather surprising. However, as discussed earlier, many of these organisations explicitly mention that they do not aim to have an impact on policymaking, but rather seek to contribute to the public debate. In that sense, the results once more confirm that seeing think tanks as mere policy advisers is too narrow a conceptualisation of their nature and objectives.

Table 12.6: Elements of good policy advice (N=13)

Good policy advice is characterised by	Percentage of think tanks agreeing with this statement
Scientific knowhow	100%
Long-term vision	100%
Financial implications	92%
Looking beyond the specific interests of your organisation	92%
Technical feasibility	85%
Specific recommendations	85%
General recommendations	77%
Social legitimacy	69%
As little jargon as possible	54%
Concise	38%
Alignment with current government policy	38%
Alignment with current government agenda	31%
Alignment with preferences minister responsible for the issue	15%

Given their low staff numbers, think tanks necessarily rely on other actors and organisations for acquiring information and policy expertise. What are their most important sources of information? For a majority of think tanks, individual academics are a popular source of knowledge. Scientific publications are also frequently consulted (see Table 12.7). This reflects the research-driven nature of think tanks and the profile of many of their staff members. According to Pautz, think tanks (and especially so-called academic think tanks) highly value interaction with researchers, who not only provide them with objective information and valuable inspiration, but also give their output additional legitimacy and credibility (2014, p 349). News articles and information acquired through social media are another useful source of information. Both sources are equally important. Furthermore, unsurprisingly, think-tank staff regularly consult official governmental sources (such as documents from public administrations). Although one out of three think tanks relies on reports and publications of organised interests on a monthly or weekly basis, staff only rarely seek input from other think tanks and even less frequently from the study centres of political parties.

Table 12.7: External sources of knowledge and information (N=12)

Information source	% of think tanks using this information on a monthly or weekly basis
Contacts with individual academics	67%
Articles and reports from the media	58%
Information from public administrations: government organisations, National Bank, Court of Audit, Planning Bureau	50%
Scientific publications	50%
Information from social media networks (Facebook, Twitter, LinkedIn)	42%
Reports and publications by civil society organisations, NGOs or foundations	42%
Information from European and international organisations (such as OECD, International Monetary Fund)	33%
Reports and publications by other think tanks	25%
Advice of the (strategic) advisory councils	17%
Reports and publications of consultants (such as Deloitte, KPMG) or companies	17%
Information from public administrations in other European countries	17%
Reports and publications by study centres of political parties	8%

Dissemination of policy advice

As influencing policy and shaping the public debate are generally considered key objectives of think tanks, it is interesting to investigate to what extent think tanks are actively consulted by other actors. While think tanks frequently rely on other organisations to acquire policy information, they are surprisingly rarely consulted by others, be it government organisations, organised interests, advisory councils or companies. Considering the objective of policy influence, this is a remarkable observation, which indicates that the majority of think tanks in Belgium are not really strongly connected to other key political players, especially compared with interest groups (see Chapter Nine). The only notable exception is the category 'individual citizens', as six think tanks indicate that they are consulted by citizens on a monthly or weekly basis. This is puzzling, although the citizens' category may include ordinary citizens who request information on a specific policy issue and (perhaps more likely) individual journalists. The questionnaire mentioned individual academics as a separate category, but they tend also to avoid actively consulting think tanks. Third parties do not very often approach Belgian think tanks, at least generally speaking, a finding that is presumably related to their relatively young age. The establishment of a solid reputation, as well as close ties with third-party actors, is likely to require more time.

The observation that third parties only rarely approach think tanks for input does not mean that there is no contact at all with political players or other societal actors, as think tanks may initiate these contacts themselves. Table 12.8 shows that about 40% of think tanks interact with members of parliament (both at a federal and regional level), on (at least) a three-monthly basis. Contacts with members of the federal government, including their personal advisers, are less common, although they are more frequent at the regional level. With ministerial cabinets having considerable impact on Belgian policy (see Chapter Three), more direct interaction between think tanks and ministerial advisers would have been expected. Further research should verify why members of parliament (MPs) are targeted more frequently than other government members. It would also be interesting to examine the profile of these MPs. Do they belong to the government parties or to the opposition? Alternatively, do think tanks merely contact actors that share the same ideological orientation? Civil servants are seldom directly approached. This observation is generally in line with the primacy of politics principle along which the politico-administrative landscape in Belgium is modelled (Brans et al, 2006).

Table 12.8: Type and frequency of contact with political actors (N=15)

Level and type of contact	Frequency: every three months	monthly or weekly
Federal level: contact with government officials (including cabinets)	13%	13%
Federal level: contact with parliamentarians	40%	13%
Federal level: contact with administration	8%	8%
Regional level: contact with government officials (including cabinets)	40%	0%
Regional level: contact with parliamentarians	40%	23%
Regional level: contact with administration	8%	8%
General: contact with party chairmen	13%	0

Besides face-to-face contacts with political actors, there are a number of other ways of gaining policy influence. Half of the think tanks engage from time to time in the organisation of conferences or seminars, which are seen as important networking events and dissemination channels, while a minority also occasionally participate in consultation or advisory bodies (see Table 12.9). Legal actions, by contrast, are an exceptional practice for Belgian think tanks. Furthermore, half of the think tanks surveyed frequently send out press releases or engage in social media campaigns. Yet, despite these efforts, actual media exposure seems to be the privilege of only a very limited number of think tanks, as hinted at earlier in the chapter.

Table 12.9: Type and frequency of other activities (N=15)

Activity	Frequency: every three months	monthly or weekly
General: participation in consultations or advisory bodies	20%	0%
Organisation of conferences or seminars	27%	20%
Media appearances and press releases	7%	47%
Legal actions	0 %	0%
Social media campaigns	7%	53%

Conclusion

This chapter has examined the organisational features and policy activities of think tanks in Belgium, in light of three defining characteristics of its political system: neo-corporatist culture, consociational legacy and the federal structure of the state. Given the absence of available research on domestic think tanks in Belgium, the primary objective of the survey was to collect information on the basic organisational and structural features of think tanks, as well as to map elementary characteristics of their policy work. Rather than to examine the activities and influence related to specific policy issues, the aim was thus to provide a first systematic outlook on the hitherto unexplored landscape of domestic think tanks in Belgium, and in this way encourage more in-depth research on the precise policy engagement of these organisations in the future.

In Belgium, practices of consultation are strongly institutionalised, with a bias towards a privileged pool of interest groups with strong access to policymakers. This study confirms the assumption that think tanks are having a hard time getting a foot in the door. Interest groups have more primacy in neo-corporatist countries, which may hinder the integration of think tanks in policy networks. Generally speaking, think tanks are relatively new players in the political arena in Belgium: all of those surveyed were established after 2000. Their number is also small, compared with other European countries, and their resources are rather limited. Obviously, differences exist across think tanks. Not all think tanks aim to influence policy or to provide advice to policymakers. Some emphasise instead their contribution to the general public debate. These diverging missions and objectives should be taken into account when analysing and evaluating their activities. Time will reveal how the think-tank landscape will evolve in the country. Most think tanks in Belgium are still in a stage of infancy, seeking their position in the political and advisory landscape. The recent restructuring of Itinera, Belgium's most well-resourced think tank and the one that is featured most often in the media, is a case in point. Having quickly expanded in recent years, the organisation decided to restructure its internal operations. This may have been an attempt to evolve from a semi-professional to a professional organisation.

The impact of pillarisation is ambiguous. When considering think-tank missions and their prioritised policy domains, the legacy of pillarisation is evident. On the other hand, think tanks are not strongly connected to political actors and other institutions. The level of structural interaction is lower than might have been expected at the outset of the study, which raises questions about the political role of most of these organisations. In a way, they display the features of a more traditional generation of think tanks, which Stone has described as 'low-profile actors seeking to inform policy in a detached non-partisan scholarly fashion', with several of them 'not overly seeking media attention' or being 'highly visible actors in policy debates' (2000, p 150). It will be interesting to see whether these organisations follow trends seen in other countries, and gradually become more advocacy-oriented and therefore more important contributors to public policy.

Finally, the Belgian federalisation process is reflected in the organisation of Belgian think tanks. Only a limited number of think tanks are organised at the national level. Yet, although predominantly organised at the regional level, most organisations are active at all government levels. When comparing Flanders and Wallonia, think-tank activity in the former region is much more vibrant than in the latter. Does this relate to differences in political culture (such as a less assertive attitude among policy entrepreneurs, or a less strongly developed regional identity), the economic fabric (the greater dominance of the public sector) or to party-political factors (for example, the continued dominance of one single party, the Socialist Party, which also has a quite large and strongly professionalised party study centre, the *Institut Emile Vandervelde*)? Further research is required to gain a better understanding of these regional differences.

Note

[1] An example of the latter organisation is Vives, affiliated to the Faculty of Economics at the University of Leuven. While Vives considers itself exclusively as a university research unit, it is often portrayed as a think tank by the media.

References

Baumgartner, F.R. and Leech, B.L. (2001) 'Interest niches and policy bandwagons: patterns of interest group involvement in national politics', *Journal of Politics*, 63(4): 1191–213.

Blockx, K. (2011) 'EU think tanks in Brussels: a mapping exercise revealing their nature', unpublished Master's dissertation, KU Leuven.

Boucher, S. and Royo, M. (2009) *Les think tanks. Cerveaux de la guerre des idées* (2nd edn), Paris: Editions du Félin.

Boucher, S., Cattaneo, D. and Ebélé, J. (2004) *Europe and its think tanks: a promise to be fulfilled. An analysis of think tanks specialised in European policy issues in the enlarged European Union*, Paris: Notre Europe.

Brans, M., De Visscher, C. and Vancoppenolle, D. (2006) 'Administrative reform in Belgium: maintenance or modernisation?', *West European Politics*, 29(5): 979-98.

Campbell, J.L. and Pedersen, O.K. (2014) *The national origins of policy ideas: knowledge regimes in the United States, France, Germany, and Denmark*, Princeton, NJ: Princeton University Press.

Deschouwer, K. (2009) *The politics of Belgium: governing a divided society*, Basingstoke and New York: Palgrave Macmillan.

Fraussen, B. and Beyers, J. (2016) 'Who's in and who's out? Explaining access to policymakers in Belgium', *Acta Politica*, 51(2): 214-36.

Hall, R.L. and Deardorf, A.V. (2006) 'Lobbying as legislative subsidy', *American Political Science Review*, 100(1): 69-84.

Huyse, L. (2003) *Over politiek*, Leuven: Uitgeverij Van Halewyck.

Lamotte, G. (2012) 'Think tanks in Belgium', unpublished Master's dissertation, KU Leuven.

Maloney, W. (2012) 'The democratic contribution of professionalized representation', in J.W. Van Deth and W. Maloney (eds) *New participatory dimension in civil society. Professionalization and individualized collective action*, New York, NY: Routledge, 84-96.

Markey, B. (2013) 'Itinera, the media and public policy influence. A newspaper content analysis', unpublished Master's dissertation, KU Leuven.

McGann, J.G. (2007) *Think tanks and policy advice in the US: academics, advisors and advocates*, New York, NY: Routledge.

McGann, J.G. (2014) *2013 Global go to think tank index report*, Think tanks and civil societies program, Philadelphia: University of Pennsylvania.

McGann, J.G. and Sabatini, R. (2011) *Global think tanks: policy networks and governance*, New York, NY: Routledge.

Nichelson, S. (2009) 'EU think tanks in Brussels: policy-making roles, functions and influence', unpublished Master's dissertation, KU Leuven.

Parsons, D.W. (1995) *Public policy*, Aldershot: Edward Elgar.

Pautz, H. (2010) 'Think tanks in the United Kingdom and Germany: actors in the modernisation of social democracy', *British Journal of Politics & International Relations*, 12(2): 274-94.

Pautz, H. (2011) 'Revisiting the think-tank phenomenon', *Public Policy and Administration*, 26(4): 419-35.

Pautz, H. (2013) 'The think tanks behind "Cameronism"', *British Journal of Politics & International Relations*, 15(3): 362-77.

Pautz, H. (2014) 'British think-tanks and their collaborative and communicative networks', *Politics*, 34(4): 345-61.

Rich, A. (2004) *Think tanks, public policy, and the politics of expertise*, Cambridge: Cambridge University Press.

Sherrington, P. (2000) 'Shaping the policy agenda: think tank activity in the European Union', *Global Society*, 14(2): 173-89.

Smith, M.A. (2000) *American business and political power: public opinion, elections, and democracy*, Chicago, IL: University of Chicago Press.

Stone, D. (2000) 'Introduction to the symposium: the changing think tank landscape', *Global Society*, 14(2): 149-52.

Stone, D. (2007) 'Recycling bins, garbage cans or think tanks? Three myths regarding policy analysis institutes', *Public Administration*, 85(2): 259-78.

TTCSP (Think Tanks and Civil Society Programme) (2013) *2013 Global go think tank index report*, Philadelphia, PA: TTCSP.

THIRTEEN

Policy analysis by academics

Marleen Brans, David Aubin and Valérie Smet

Through their policy-relevant research outputs and integration in policy networks, Belgian academics aim to 'speak truth to power' (Wildavsky, 1979) and 'make sense together' (Hoppe, 1999) in political and public debates about policy problems and options. Gradually they are also becoming involved in evaluating policies. At the turn of the millennium, the federal and regional governments began to move towards institutionalising policy-relevant research in the so-called inter-university research pillars and in middle- to long-term research programmes thematically organised to reflect the priorities decided by respective governments. Besides the structural interfaces that are typical for institutionalised research programmes, there are many other access points for academics to bring their expertise to policymaking. Sectoral academic experts maintain multiple relationships with knowledge brokers. They are welcome contributors to the opinion sections of written and spoken media and some hold positions in the many advisory bodies of the various governments. Several of them are also active in think tanks, or themselves act as consultants in commercial university spin-offs. This chapter analyses the ways in which academics access policymaking in Belgium. The empirical material is based on documents analysis, on a study of knowledge utilisation in labour market and education policies in Belgium (Brans et al, 2004; Florence et al, 2005), and on survey research on knowledge utilisation, focusing on individual perceptions of social science researchers and policymakers (Smet, 2013). The data is supplemented with information on the utilisation of academic research provided by the survey organised for this book.

This chapter is composed of the following sections. In a first section, we demonstrate the importance of research dissemination strategies and structural interfaces for the utilisation of research on the position of immigrant children in education and labour market participation. This section will at the same time reveal the power of divergent policy paradigms in facilitating or blocking knowledge utilisation. The second section draws on the results of survey research, focusing on the perceptions of individual policymakers and academics, about the role of social sciences in policymaking and the obstacles and enablers of knowledge utilisation. Since structural interfaces between communities of researchers and policymakers seem to an important enabler of knowledge transfer in Belgium, the third section engages in a description of the organisation of policy research by the different Belgian governments.

Knowledge utilisation in immigration policies: a comparative case study

This section presents the research questions and method, and the results of the single most comprehensive case study on knowledge utilisation in Belgium (Brans et al, 2004; Florence at al, 2005). Although the study was finalised more than a decade ago, its conclusions on the value of research dissemination and structural interfaces between policymaking and research still hold today.

Research questions and method

In the early 2000s, the Belgian Federal Science Policy Office financed a project to evaluate the impact of research on public policies in the field of migration. The funded project addressed two major questions. The first question was empirical: to what extent have policies in the field of migration rested on the results of scientific research? Put differently, have policymakers in Belgium been inspired by research on migration to formulate, implement or evaluate policies? The second question was normative, and sought an answer to how knowledge utilisation between academia, policymakers and stakeholders can be improved.

The research followed a framework of inquiry suggested by UNESCO. This was very much based on Carol Weiss' work (1979, 1999). Following Weiss, the funded research approached knowledge utilisation from three perspectives: instrumental utilisation, conceptual utilisation and strategic utilisation. In terms of explaining utilisation, the research focused on the supply-and demand-side features of the research and policymaker communities, but supplemented these with an exploration of the role of Lindquist's (1990) third community, that is civil society actors.

Two subjects were selected for in-depth case study: the education of pupils of foreign origin and labour market discrimination. These subjects covered the greatest relative number of studies over the period 1989-2002.

The research team in charge of the study constructed a database that connected research with policy documents related to education and the labour market. All research projects and policy documents were analysed using the same grid, with a policy-analytical focus on similarities and differences in the definition of policy problems and proposed solutions. This was complemented by a series of semi-structured interviews with policymakers, researchers and members of the third community (that is, business associations, trade unions) and by a network analysis of research collaboration.

Belgian scientific research on immigration and integration (1989-2002)

The database comprised a total of 420 research projects in the studied period, 239 on the Flemish side (57%) and 181 on the French-speaking side (43%). In 1991, the demand for research gained momentum when a royal commissioner for migrant policy took office and introduced a blueprint for integration policy with new policy interventions.

The network analysis of research collaborators revealed a significant degree of joint working across universities and disciplines on the Flemish and French-speaking sides alike. Furthermore, a number of joint projects cutting across the language divide were financed with federal money.

On both sides of the language border, education and labour market participation were the most popular research topics, making up 35% of all research in the domain in Flanders, and 32% on the Francophone side. By the late 1990s, research into labour market participation by people of foreign origin increased on the Flemish side. It was also increasingly financed by the Flemish government, while on the Francophone side, the federal government remained the prime sponsor for this kind of research. For education research, the source of financing is more consistent with the devolution of competencies. On both sides of the language border, education research was thus financed solely by the communities.

Findings on the role of research dissemination and interfaces

The dissemination of research results proved crucial to the utilisation of research. A case study into the renowned International Labour Organisation (ILO) research on ethnic discrimination in the labour market (Feld and Castelain-Kinet, 1997) was a particularly good example of the importance of dissemination strategies. The way the ILO study was disseminated largely contributed to its influence on policymakers. It was made clear from the outset that the ILO study should involve stakeholders other than research institutes in disseminating the results. While the ILO disseminated results at the international level, the Belgian Centre for Equal Opportunities and the Fight against Racism helped publicise the study at the national level. The research results were thus circulated by policy entrepreneurs – the potential users of the research – rather than by researchers themselves. The dissemination process was further facilitated by what Head would call insider academics (2015) who had been consecutively, even at times concurrently, active as both researchers and policymakers. This insider role facilitated the transfer of research to policymakers in the area of education of children of immigrant origin in Flanders.

The research also showed the impact of structural interfaces between the communities of researchers, policymakers and third-party actors. Flemish policies regarding pupils of foreign origin are a case in point. In Flanders, structural links between policies aimed at teaching pupils of foreign origin and social science research had already been established in the early 1990s. The government had financed two policy research centres for a number of years, and had commissioned a number of research projects on the position of children of immigrant origin in the education system.

Several of these studies had an immediate instrumental impact and contributed to specific changes in the working procedures of schools and practical educational support. The policy research centres created continuity, thus facilitating the accumulation of expertise in the scientific community, irrespective of government turnover and changing political priorities. They also fostered relationships of trust and positive perceptions among policymakers of the credibility and value of research, thus providing more favourable conditions for research utilisation than would have been the case with the linear dissemination associated with so-called independent research.

Knowledge utilisation in the policymaking process: survey results for Flemish policymakers

Research questions and method

To gain empirical evidence on factors influencing knowledge utilisation at the individual level, a survey on the relationship between social science and policy was conducted among Flemish social scientists (universities) and policymakers in 2010 (Smet, 2013). This survey focused on the use and possible impact of science on policy, as well as on the policy roles of science, seen from both scientists' and policymakers' points of view. Topics addressed were grouped into the following categories of conventional knowledge utilisation research:

* features of the information involved, for example scientific quality of research, relevance of research, adaptations of research aimed at enhancing impact thereof or types of incoming information policymakers are confronted with;
* characteristics of the researcher/research groups involved, such as expertise, attitudes towards adaptation of research or reputation of the scientist;
* qualifications of the interaction between social science and policy, that is linking mechanisms, shared problem definition or available scientific expertise;
* knowledge user characteristics, for example involvement in the research process, or receptiveness regarding outside information or scientific research;
* political–ideological context, for example supportive policy environment, particularities of the policymaking process or actors involved.

All social scientists of the Flemish universities were addressed, irrespective of their experience of policy-relevant research. Researchers with expertise on policy-relevant research were presented with additional questions. In total, 641 social scientists responded, 41% of whom had had previous experience with policy-oriented research.

Ninety-seven policymakers in the Flemish ministerial cabinets and administrations responded to the survey, 38% of whom were ministerial cabinet members. The rest of the respondents were spread over departments (16%), external agencies (21%) and internal agencies (20%).

Role of social science research in the different policy phases and documents

Of the different groups surveyed, civil servants reported the highest levels of utilisation of social science research, followed by ministerial cabinet members. However, none of the respondent policymakers considered the role of social science in the policy process to be highly significant. Respondents were also asked about the role of social science research in the preparation of specific policy documents (such as policy plans, annual action plans, ministerial speeches, press announcements, and so on). The use of social science research in such documents was mainly occasional. Annual ministerial policy action plans (64%) and ministerial speeches (55%) scored highest in the group of policy documents for which social science was used/consulted.

In terms of the role of social science researchers, respondents mainly valued functions that corresponded with instrumental knowledge utilisation and to a lesser extent conceptual knowledge utilisation (see Table 13.1). The roles most valued by policymakers varied over the different stages of the policy process. Strategic (or political) knowledge utilisation scored low, which may hide a social desirability effect given that the term has a negative connotation.

Given the pressures for evidence-based policymaking, one would expect social sciences research to be of greatest use to policymakers in the areas of policy formulation and policy evaluation. While the 2010 survey confirmed that policymakers indeed value social science for its input at the policy formulation stage, it also found that they deem it less useful at the policy evaluation stage. Half of the respondents found the input of social scientists useful at the evaluation stage, while the other half did not. Moreover, the social scientists themselves deemed their role in policy evaluation to be of limited use. These findings thus confirm those of other studies on evaluation practices in the Flemish government, where both the demand and supply of policy evaluation is underdeveloped and where practices of outsourcing evaluations to social scientists at universities are not well institutionalised and are unevenly distributed (Pattyn, 2014). The role of social science research in agenda setting ranks remarkably low with policymakers, while social scientists on the contrary deem this to be one of its most important functions. This is further evidence of a mismatch between policymakers' and social scientists' expectations. The closer social science researchers get to producing evidence for instrumental use in the policy cycle, the lower they rank their contributions. Social scientists much prefer to see themselves contributing to conceptual use by scientifically framing the determinants of policy problems, and by setting the agenda.

Table 13.1: Roles of social scientific research according to policymakers and researchers

Policymakers		Researchers	
Role	N	Role	N
Investigating potential explanations/ causes for a problem	25	Providing a different way of thinking	108
Choosing between potential policy alternatives	22	Providing potential determinants for a specific problem	101
Evaluating policy measures	21	Making policymakers aware of new or existing issues so that they can become part of the political agenda	85
Mapping out policy options	17	Making policy recommendations	70
Legitimising current policy	14	Aiding in defining problems	41
Arguments for policy change and feeding the discussion thereon	14	Aiding in developing policy	28
Gaining attention for a specific issue	4	Evaluating policy	22

Knowledge utilisation: obstacles and enablers

There is a common perception in the field of knowledge utilisation that neither the quality nor the availability of social sciences research can guarantee its use in the policy process. Many authors do agree that knowledge is underused (Devroe and Ponsaers, 2008; Lampinen, 1992; Ritter and Lancaster, 2013). Some of this underuse can be attributed to the nature of social science research itself and to the features of the organisational context in which researchers operate. In general, social science is not neutral. It always involves specific viewpoints, underlying theoretical assumptions and paradigms. Furthermore, social science does not cover the entire social world, but presents only fragmentary views on certain aspects of social reality. As is the case in all science, discussion is the core of scientific discourse, but social sciences risk a greater lack of consensus and uncertainty than do 'hard' sciences. Another obstacle to policymakers' use of social science research is the frequent lack of action-orientation or applied problem-solving conclusions, which sometimes leads policymakers to complain that they know less and have even more questions with than without research evidence.

Table 13.2 shows what policymakers perceive as the main obstacles to knowledge utilisation. Table 13.3, in turn, points to the conditions under which research might more easily get picked up or taken into account in the policy process.

It is interesting to note that political-ideological factors are considered smaller obstacles to the use of research than features of the information and of the users involved. Adaptation of the information to the needs of the users as well as relevance for the policy domain seem beneficial for the use of scientific knowledge, whereas the absence of policy recommendations, researchers' alleged limited knowledge of the nuts and bolts of the policy cycle, and policymakers' lack of time to dedicate to research are considered the main obstacles. Policymakers prefer operative, unambiguous and adapted products. At the same time, the 2010 survey showed that those researchers who are active in policy-oriented research take

Table 13.2: Policymakers' priority ranking of knowledge utilisation obstacles

Obstacles	N
Absence of policy recommendations	25
Contradiction between different studies	24
Researchers' knowledge on policy and decision making is too limited	24
Lack of time for analysing or studying existing research	20
Research is not specific enough for the policy domain involved	19
Results are politically unacceptable	5
Too big an offer of available research	3

Table 13.3: Policymakers' priority ranking of knowledge utilisation enablers

Enhancing factors	N
Relevance for the policy domain involved	34
Quality of the research involved	32
Adaptation to the policy domain and user	25
Credibility/reliability of the research results	14
Research involving quantitative research	9
Ideological orientation of the researcher	2
Presence of opportune political and media climate	3

these obstacles and enablers into account when producing their evidence. The first interesting finding deconstructs a common prejudice against policy-oriented researchers in Flanders. Such researchers do in the first place disseminate their results to the academic world (83%) and to a lesser degree to stakeholders and target groups (54%). Policy-oriented research by academics is hence not isolated from scientific control. At the same time, it is true that those social scientists with little self-reported policy experience score very low on dissemination efforts to policymakers (12%). Dissemination to the press, in turn, is rare for both researchers with experience in policy-oriented research (28%) and those without (15%).

Results from surveys on policy analysis in Belgium's federal and regional government[1]

The survey developed for this book inquired about the frequency with which civil servants engaged in policy work acquire scientific knowledge, and where they put research to use.

Table 13.4 shows different sources of scientific information and the extent to which these are regularly consulted by civil servants engaged in policy analysis in Belgium. Overall, about a third of the respondents regularly consult scientific articles, whereas a similar number of respondents at the regional level indicate regular use of reports produced by government research centres. Such reports are consulted less frequently at the federal level, however, which may be explained by the relative scarcity of government research centres in federal Belgium.

Table 13.4: Regular consultation of scientific documents

	Federal (N=380)	Flanders (N=450)	French Belgium (N=777)
Scientific articles	26%	32%	29%
Reports from government research centres	8%	28%	23%

Although information produced by scientific actors is regularly consulted by a substantial number of respondents, only a small group actively seeks out policy advice from these scientific actors. Specifically, as shown in Table 13.5, the results indicate that 10% of respondents or less regularly solicit policy advice from research centres carrying out applied research, from scientific research groups or from individual scientists.[2] Overall, civil servants are more likely to solicit advice from government research centres than from external sources.

Researchers sometimes provide advice on policy issues to civil servants on their own initiative, without it being requested. Overall, it appears that policy advice is received more often than it is actively solicited by Belgium's policy analysts, and advice from external scientific actors is received and solicited less often than advice produced by policy research centres. The results of the regional surveys also indicate that civil servants are not overly satisfied with the quality of the advice that is provided by such centres. On a satisfaction scale from 1 to 10, the average scores range from 5.54 to 5.62.

The survey at the federal level produced a number of further insights relating to the perceived usefulness of scientific knowledge in policy-analytical work. First, 15% of federal civil servants do not feel the need to access scientific research or expertise with regard to their policy-analytical work, while 20% indicate that they never apply scientific arguments (see Figure 13.1). However, 36% of respondents apply scientific arguments in their work at least a few times per month.

Similarly, scientific arguments are perceived as *useful* by about 30% of federal civil servants (Figure 13.2). In more detail, almost half of respondents (47%) find that scientific research and expertise are directly applicable to various components of

Table 13.5: Policy advice solicited or received by civil servants in Belgium

	Federal		Flanders		French Belgium	
	Solicit	Receive	Solicit	Receive	Solicit	Receive
Government research centres	5%	16%	10%	7%	10%	8%
Scientific research groups	2%	1%	7%	6%	2%	6%
Individual scientists	2%	2%	N/A	N/A	3%	8%

their policy-analytical work. About a third, then, (somewhat) agree that scientific research can help to develop a common framework fostering better cooperation with others, and a further quarter of respondents find scientific research useful for providing theoretical backing to their work.

In sum, the findings from the surveys at the federal and the regional policy levels reveal that scientific expertise produced by various types of actor is taken up in policy-analytical work in Belgium by a substantial number of civil servants on a fairly regular basis, and that this type of information is also considered useful for a variety of policy-related purposes. Whether this is a comparatively high or low degree of research utilisation requires further research.

Figure 13.1: Frequency of application of scientific arguments in policy analysis at the federal level (N=366)

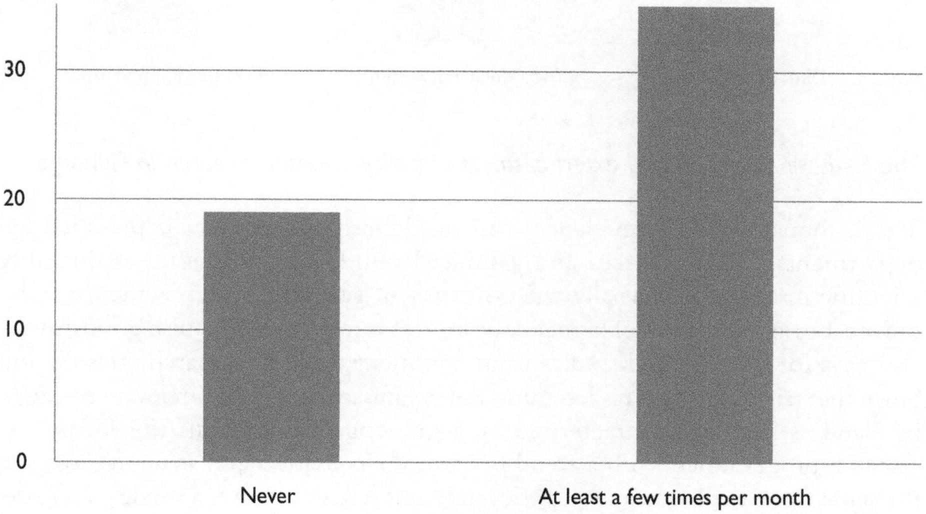

Policy research in Belgium

The case study on research and policymaking in the context of immigration revealed the importance of structural interfaces between research and policymaking. These interfaces have the potential to facilitate knowledge utilisation as well as create a source of academic accumulation of policy-relevant expertise. This section gives an overview of the landscape of policy-relevant research, financed by both the federal and regional authorities, and assesses whether there are divergent or convergent trends towards institutionalising and externalising policy-relevant research.

Figure 13.2: Scientific arguments' perceived usefulness (N=357-359)

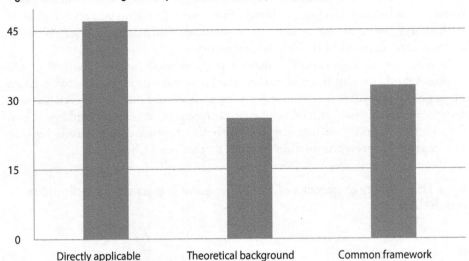

The institutionalisation and externalisation of policy-relevant research in Flanders

The in-house scientific evidence base of Flemish government is provided by departmental study services and a limited number of autonomised Flemish scientific institutes. Externally, the government garners research evidence from universities and institutes of higher education. Moreover, the Flemish government also pays for analyses and studies from commercial policy research consultants. Since the start of the new millennium, the organisation of policy-relevant research in Flanders has been characterised by a growing institutionalisation of policy research programmes, with a trend towards formalisation and structuration. At the same time, the landscape of policy-relevant research shows a modest increase in the number of commercial research bureaus.

The institutionalisation of policy research made a start in 1997, when the Policy-Oriented Research (PBO) programme took effect. The programme was mainly targeted at research groups from social sciences, and cultural and behavioural sciences, in both universities and polytechnics. The programme achieved a number of goals relating to professionalisation, the objective selection of research proposals, and the sensitisation of researchers to policy-relevant subjects. Soon, however, the demands of annual research themes turned the PBO into a complex, bureaucratic and fragmented programme with a plethora of short-term projects on a wide variety of themes. Subsequently, a number of advisory bodies, including the then Flemish Council for Science Policy, started pushing for a new approach with a view to better quality control, greater focus on impact and evaluation of outputs, and a longer-term perspective.

In 2001, the Flemish government responded with a call for policy research centres (*Steunpunten Beleidsgericht Onderzoek*); at the time of writing, the third generation had expired and a fourth was being negotiated. The aim of the policy research centres is to provide scientific support to the Flemish government on government-prioritised themes considered to be relevant to policy formulation and evaluation. The fragmented project approach was hence replaced by a thematic approach, based on structural financing that allowed for both long-term PhD research, and shorter-term research projects. Policy research centres aim to disclose knowledge about important societal developments and amass specialised data for analysis. In their third-generation incarnation, policy research centres were also expected to engage more frequently in policy evaluation. This is not a formal requirement, but a practice derived from the growing demand for evaluation from departments and ministerial advisers who have identified policy research centres as a potential supplier in this regard.

As demonstrated in Box 13.1, nearly all policy domains are thematically covered by the policy research centres. The annual budget per centre (on the basis of the indicative budget of the call in 2011) varies from €400,000 to €1.4 million. The selection of centres was made on the basis of matching the demands of ministers and departments with the offers of research consortia of institutes of higher education.

An analysis of the 2011 call shows great variation in direction of content. Some ministers have chosen strictly to demarcate the requested research themes, while others leave more room for the discretionary input of participating research consortia. In a few cases, it seems that the call was a way to remedy ills revealed by the evaluation of the previous research outputs, or the missed opportunity of departments to encourage policy-relevant outputs.

The policy research centres are held to focus specifically on policy relevance and use. The policy impact is further supported by the interfaces between producers and users of research, such as steering committees and feedback groups, as well as by science communication in conferences and symposia. Consecutive evaluations of policy research centres in terms of research output and usefulness have been positive. Some actors, such as the Social and Economic Council Flanders, have pushed for greater emphasis on impact and short-term research. In its third generation, the balance between long-term and short-term research has not suffered, except perhaps from the reduction of the duration from 5 to 4 years, which had consequences for the completion of PhD research. How this balance will play out in the next generation is too early to tell.

Despite the trend towards institutionalising policy-relevant research, policy research centres are not the only providers of research-based policy recommendations. There are in-house suppliers of policy research, and the external market is characterised by growing numbers of commercial players. In-house policy research takes place in the study services or knowledge centres of government departments. The Study Service of the Flemish Government, for example, conducts scientific research on demographic, social and macro-economic developments. The Monitoring and Study Unit of the Department of Agriculture and Fisheries, and the Knowledge Centre for Well-Being, Public

> **Box 13.1: Overview of research centre policy domains (2012-15)**
>
> | | |
> |---|---|
> | Poverty | Spatial planning |
> | Equal opportunities | Road security |
> | Youth | Entrepreneurship and regional economics |
> | Well-being, public health and family | Work and social economics |
> | Study and school trajectories | Transport of goods and services |
> | Culture | Administrative organisation |
> | Sports | Taxation and budget |
> | Environment and health | Citizens integration |
> | Transitions to sustainable development | Foreign Policy, international entrepreneurship, and development co-operation |
> | Sustainable materials | Media |
> | Housing | |

Health and Family, are examples of in-house services that engage in research themselves, and also steer and disclose policy research that takes place elsewhere. In addition, there are four autonomous Flemish scientific institutions that engage in both fundamental and applied research for the Flemish government and other users. These are the Institute for Agriculture and Fisheries, the Royal Museum for Fine Arts, the Flemish Heritage Institute, and the Institute for Nature and Forest Research.

Finally, it is important to note that departments, as well as being catered for by the research centres, have other means of financing research. Departments put their resources to use in more than one way. Some engage in ad hoc financing of research projects, while others finance more structural research programmes. In 2012, for instance, the Department of Education invested, €576,647 in education scientific policy- and practice-oriented research, while the Department of Work and Social Economy spent €373,000 on the VIONA programme, the Flemish Interuniversity Research Network on Labour Market Monitoring.

In 2000, there were only a handful of commercial players in the policy research market in Flanders. These included a limited number of local niche bureaus such as Tempura (city planning and labour) and the West-Flemish Economic Study Bureau (regional economics and tourism). In addition, there were a small number of dependencies of Dutch companies. Iris Consulting, for instance, was part of the Dutch DHV group, one of the bigger international engineering and advisory companies. Meanwhile, other dependencies of Dutch research companies (Grontmij, Arcadis, TNO) have gained terrain in a variety of policy domains. Flemish companies such as Idea Consult and Technum (formerly named Resource Analysis) have also increased their market share, and finally, bigger consultancy groups, such as Deloitte, have also expanded their activities targeting the public sector in Flanders.

The extent to which commercial research bureaus can access policy research financing from the Flemish government depends on the nature of programmes and the outsourcing traditions of the Flemish departments. The policy research centres are meant solely to involve academic consortia, while private consultant Idea Consult, for example, has carried out policy-analytical tasks for the Department of Work and Social Economy's VIONA programme. Evaluation research seems to be relatively more accessible for private groups, albeit often in combination with academic evaluators. Idea Consult, for example, evaluated inter-municipal and city planning with the academic Public Governance Institute. The latter also collaborated with private consultant SUM in evaluating the Flemish Spatial Structure Plan. With regard to outsourcing traditions of the Flemish government, the Flemish Department of Education stands out as having a strong preference for academic policy research.

Policy research in Francophone Belgium

Policy-oriented research is fragmented in Francophone Belgium along a series of lines. First, the political landscape is fragmented. Responsibility for financing and monitoring research institutes and projects is divided between three federated entities, namely the Federation Wallonia-Brussels (French Community), Wallonia and the Brussels-Capital Region. The Federation Wallonia-Brussels finances and evaluates higher/university education and scientific research. Like the Flemish Community in Flanders, the Federation Wallonia-Brussels has a research budget that is distributed through a tendering process by the universities' own research councils and finances the Francophone National Research Fund (F.R.S.-FNRS), which allocates grants to individual researchers hosted in the universities (PhD students, post-docs and permanent researchers) and funds research projects. Both funding streams prioritise fundamental research. One exception is the Francophone National Research Fund's FRESH programme (*Fonds pour la recherche en sciences humaines*), which was developed by the French Community in 2012 along new budgetary lines for projects that focus on 'societal impacts'.

Other types of policy-oriented research in the French Community are conducted within the administration's single ministry or its government agencies, or are contracted out to university research institutes. Policy-oriented research within the ministry focuses mainly on (compulsory) education. The General Unit for Supervision of the Education System (*Service général du pilotage du système éducatif*) at the Department of Education evaluates the performance of the education system. It manages pedagogical reforms and defines learning objectives. In particular, it supervises the participation of Francophone Belgium in the Organisation of Economic Co-operation and Development's Programme for International Student Assessment (PISA), a triennial survey that aims to evaluate education systems worldwide by testing the skills and knowledge of 15-year-old students. These surveys are contracted out to university departments of educational science. The unit also implements the research plan drawn up by the Committee for the Monitoring of the Education System (*Commission du pilotage du système éducatif*). The committee comprises seven university faculty members, together with representatives of the administration and the relevant research sector. The research is conducted in the universities, but is monitored by the unit, which also disseminates the outcomes. In all others areas, the *Direction de la recherche*, which is part of the general secretariat, has responsibility for coordinating policy-oriented research within the ministry. It supervises statistical functions in several departments (Task Force Statistics) and occasionally conducts in-house research. Ministers may also request specific policy-oriented research or policy evaluations, which are usually contracted out to universities or consulting firms.

Two government agencies of the Federation Wallonia-Brussels are specifically involved in policy-oriented research in culture and youth policies. The Observatory of Cultural Policy (*Observatoire des politiques culturelles*, OPC) and the Observatory of Childhood, Youth and Youth Assistance (*Observatoire de l'enfance, de la jeunesse et de l'aide à la jeunesse*) both conduct research on matters of importance for the government. OPC conducts in-house research in certain areas (for example, on the history of the cultural policy), but also contracts out specific research projects and evaluations to universities (for example, the evaluation of the literacy policy or the qualitative analysis of cultural practices). The budget for external research is about €160,000 per year. OPC has a scientific advisory body comprising six academics and sets up ad hoc groups with university scholars around specific research projects. Each year, it distributes prizes for best Master's and PhD thesis projects.

The two regional authorities, Wallonia and the Brussels-Capital Region, do not formally evaluate scientific research, but finance two aspects of it: innovation and technological development on the one hand, and policy-oriented research on the other. In Wallonia, most policy-oriented research is conducted by the Walloon Institute for Evaluation, Foresight and Statistics (*Institut wallon de l'évaluation, de la prospective et de la statistique*, IWEPS). This agency also contracts out policy oriented research projects. IWEPS (2013) has 53 employees and a budget of €6.4 million (2013 figures). Its three main areas of interest are employment policy, regional development and policy evaluation. With regard to policy evaluation, its core task is to evaluate regional strategic plans and, in particular, the Marshall Plan for the Redeployment of the Walloon Economy. These policy evaluations are prepared by IWEPS but monitored by a steering committee, composed partly of scholars.

Like the rest of Belgium, Wallonia has neo-corporatist traits. Consultation with interest groups is considered to be of outmost importance. By law, new bills must undergo three readings by the government before being presented to parliament. After the first reading, the bill is sent for consultation to sector-based advisory bodies, which deliver non-binding advice to the government (see Chapter Seven). There are around 30 such bodies (for example, the Regional Commission for Land-Use Planning, the Science Policy Council and the Walloon Environmental

Council for Sustainable Development); each has around 20 to 40 members, usually including some representatives of the universities.

Wallonia also uses observatories in a variety of sectors, notably health, mobility, regional development and employment. Often composed of small teams of researchers, their aim is to compile information to support the policy process in their fields. They manage databases and disseminate research results, but also conduct policy-oriented research projects in-house or contract out research to universities. These observatories usually have an accompanying committee that provides advice on the direction of their activities. Academics usually have a seat on the committee as representatives of the universities. Both the statistics offices and the sector-based observatories of Wallonia and Federation Wallonia-Brussels cooperate with each other.

In the Brussels-Capital Region, the government has created a research agency, Innoviris, to support innovation and research. Among its activities, Innoviris finances policy-oriented research carried out by academics of all disciplines within the Brussels universities. As part of the Anticipate programme (with funding of €2.7 million in 2013), a call for projects on selected issues (for example, urban economic development and public cleanliness) is launched once a year, while the parallel Attract programme finances post-doctoral students from abroad (€1.3 million in 2013) (Innoviris, 2013). The Brussels Institute for Statistics and Analysis, meanwhile, provides decision-making support to the government. It collects and analyses statistics, conducts socioeconomic analyses, and supports policy evaluations.

In sum, the landscape of policy-oriented research by academics is very fragmented in Francophone Belgium. Policy analysis and advice is organised along sectoral lines and often results from individual academics' contacts in the government or the administration. Moreover, the financing of policy-oriented research is divided between numerous small-scale programmes with their own objectives and operating rules. Finally, the involvement of academics in advisory bodies serves mainly to legitimate organisations' research activities. The science–policy interface is not organised at government level and results from individual contacts between academics and the stakeholders.

Policy research in Federal Belgium

Policy-oriented research at the federal level is overseen by the Belgian Federal Science Policy Office (BELSPO). BELSPO manages several research programmes and Belgium's participation in the European Spatial Agency, and supervises the federal museums and scientific institutions. In 2015, it had about 2,800 employees. In the late 1990s, the Society and Future programme organised calls for funding multi-university research programmes related to the federal government's areas of responsibility. This programme no longer functions and has been partly replaced by streams four and five of the BRAIN programme – Federal Public Strategies and Major Societal Challenges (€35 million) – which aims 'to finance the activities and support of the competencies of the federal authorities, from a perspective that is historical, contemporary and prospective'. Two examples of projects financed through this programme are BCC ('Measuring cost and impact of cybercrime in Belgium', coordinated by Jos Dumortier at KU Leuven) and INCh ('Integrated networks to combat child poverty: a mixed methods research on network governance and perspectives of policymakers, social workers and families in poverty', coordinated by Danielle Dierckx at the University of Antwerp). BELSPO also manages the Interuniversity Attraction Poles, which finance fundamental joint research between the Belgian universities. It had a budget of €156.5 million for the 2012-17 period and granted awards to 47 networks each bringing together four to eleven research teams, eight of which conduct research in the human sciences. After 2017, this programme will be regionalised and co-managed by the FNRS and FWO (Fund for Fundamental Research – Flanders) with funding from the communities (€31.6 million).

Some government agencies are also committed to policy-oriented research, providing information and analysis to the federal government, mainly on economic issues. One such agency, the National Bank of Belgium, is not only the country's central bank, but also a reputable and prolific research institute. It publishes a series of studies about monetary policy in the Eurozone, economic activity in Belgium and abroad, labour, prices, wages, public finances and financial markets, as well as more specific studies by sectors and branches. It also publishes public reports and notes, as well as documents specifically for the federal government or the prime minister. It maintains relationships with the universities, notably through joint workshops on subjects such as macroeconomics or company analysis, and finances short-term scholarships for PhD students.

The Federal Planning Bureau is another agency that provides policy-related analysis to the federal government. It studies major current policy themes such as demography, ageing, energy provision, prices and consumption, and sustainable development. The studies have a mainly economic focus. Members of the Federal Planning Bureau maintain strong contacts with the academic world. The bureau collaborates with universities on regional, national and European joint research projects, hosts trainees, and solicits expertise from scholars.

Once again, the policy–science interface appears rather fragmented at the federal level. Federal agencies operate on their own but liaise with individual academics, who are in a position to influence policies through the advice they provide.

Conclusion

Study on research utilisation in Belgian immigration policies confirms the findings of the knowledge utilisation literature on the importance of the interface between the research community and the world of policymakers, and the dissemination of science. It seems that over the past 20 years governments in Belgium have come to see the advantages of creating such links, in which academics interested in policy issues produce reports and briefings on themes that not only reflect the priorities of the government of the day, but also address long-term policy challenges. In Flanders, these interfaces have taken the shape of policy research centres where academic consortia engage, at least up until the most recent generation, in short and long term policy relevant research. At the federal level too, multi-university consortia produce research to support federal policies, although the institutional interfaces between policymakers and academics are more loosely organised. In Francophone Belgium, policy-oriented research is mainly the domain of the government, with a number of agencies being active in the monitoring and evaluation of certain policies and the production of statistics. But these agencies also invest in relations with academia, albeit in a different way, by appointing academics to their advisory panels and boards, and occasionally commissioning applied research from university groups. As for science dissemination, the individual-level data presented in this chapter shows that there is still a substantive number of social scientists who do not invest much in disseminating research to policymakers, and who, as mainstream academics or policy critics, prefer not to get their hands dirty helping policymakers to formulate or evaluate policies (Head, 2015). Those social scientists who self-reportedly engage in policy-relevant research also treat the scientific community as their prime interlocutor, but they do invest substantially in dissemination strategies for policy impact. They thus appear to facilitate knowledge utilisation. However, there remains a number of mismatches between the expectations of academics and policymakers, which seems endemic to their relationship. Contributions such as evaluations or policy recommendations do not traditionally sit well with the way academics are (increasingly) rewarded in their academic careers, and with the reluctance of the Belgian Fundamental Research Foundations to specify impact as a condition for funding projects.

At the demand side, too, there remain a number of obstacles that prevent policy-relevant research from being utilised. While it appears from the data presented in this chapter that a good number of civil servants use scientific research in their policy work, it also transpires that they are reluctant to seek input, and have reservations about the quality of research. Moreover, as shown in Chapter Four, civil servants indicate that they do not have much time for study and following up on research results. It will take systematic comparative research to evaluate whether or not the practices of and prospects for knowledge utilisation are better or worse than can be expected from the naturally cumbersome relationship between science and policymaking. Yet, there are reasons to assume that the epistemological culture of Belgium is such that what counts as evidence and expertise depends to a great extent on the political rules of conduct and the nature of governance (Straßheim and Kettunen, 2014).

In countries with neo-corporatist traits such as Belgium, and with the strong presence of political advisers in the shadow of ministers, the necessary policy compromises cannot primarily reflect academic evidence, with its uncompromising claims to the truth. In such a system, social scientists must indeed be weary of political manoeuvres behind the instrumentalisation of policy analysis. Yet, this healthy scepticism should not blind them for seeing the benefits of emerging practices where seemingly conflicting pressures are reconciled in procedures and practices that comply with interaction models of research utilisation.

Notes

[1] The authors wish to thank Ellen Fobé for providing the data in this section.
[2] The survey for Flanders did not include a question on the advice produced by or received from individual scientists.

References

Brans, M., Eric, F., Jacobs, D., Martiniello, M., Rea, A., Swyngedouw, M. and Van der Straeten, T. (2004) *Onderzoek en beleid: de gevalstudie van immigratie in België*, Ghent: Academia Press.

Devroe, E. and Ponsaers, P. (2008) 'Veel beleidsinformatie, weinig gebruik: over het informatiedeficit van verborgen tendensen', *Orde van de dag. Criminaliteit en samenleving*, 41: 161-74.

Feld, S. and Castelain-Kinet, F. (1997) 'Pratiques de formation antidiscriminatoires en Wallonie et à Bruxelles', in ILO (ed) *La discrimination à l'embauche en raison de l'origine étrangère*, Geneva: International Labour Organisation.

Florence, E., Martiniello, M., Adam, I., Balancier, P., Brans, M., Jacobs, D., Rea, A., Swyngedouw, M. and Van der Straeten, T. (2005) 'Social science research and public policies: the case of immigration in Belgium', *International Journal on Multicultural Societies*, 7(1): 49-67.

Head, B. (2015), 'Relationships between policy academics and public servants: learning at a distance?', *Australian Journal of Public Administration*, 74(1): 5-12.

Hoppe, R. (1999) 'Policy analysis, science and politics: from "speaking truth to power" to "making sense together"', *Science and Public Policy*, 26(3): 201-10.

Innoviris (2013) *Rapport annuel*, Brussels: Innoviris.

IWEPS (Walloon Institute for Evaluation, Foresight and Statistics) (2013) *Rapport annuel*, Namur: IWEPS.

Lampinen, O. (1992) *Utilization of social science research in public policy*, Helsinki: VAPK Publishing.

Landry, R., Amara, N. and Lamary, M. (2001) 'Utilization of social science research knowledge in Canada', *Research Policy*, 30(2): 333-49.

Lindquist, E.A. (1990) 'The third communicy, policy inquiry, and social scientists', in S. Brooks and A.G. Gagnon (eds) *Social scientists, policy, and the state*, New York, NY: Praeger, 21-51.

Pattyn, V. (2014) 'Why organisations (do not) evaluate? Explaining evaluation activity through the lens of configurational comparative methods', *Evaluation*, 20(3): 348-67.

Rich, R.F. (1997) 'Measuring knowledge utilization: processes and outcomes', *Knowledge, Technology and Policy*, 10(1): 11-23.

Ritter, A. and Lancaster, K. (2013) 'Measuring research influence on drug policy: a case example of two epidemiological monitoring systems', *International Journal of Drug Policy*, 24(1): 30-7.

Smet, V. (2013) *Sociaalwetenschappelijk onderzoek en beleid. Een analyse van de interactie, kennisgebruik en doorwerking in België en Vlaanderen*, The Hague: Boom Lemma.

Straßheim, H. and Kettunen, P. (2014) 'When does evidence-based policy turn into policy-based evidence? Configurations, contexts and mechanisms', *Evidence & Policy*, 10(2): 259-77.

Weiss, C.H. (1979) 'The many meanings of research utilization', *Public Administration Review*, 39(5): 426-31.

Weiss, C.H. (1999) 'Research-policy linkages: how much influence does social science research have?', in UNESCO (ed) *World social science report 1999*, Paris: Elsevier, 194-205.

Wildavsky, A.B. (1979) *Speaking truth to power*, New Jersey, NJ: Transaction Publishers.

FOURTEEN

Policy analysis instruction in Belgium

Marleen Brans, David Aubin and Silke Ruebens

In Belgium, policy analysis is relatively young as an academic discipline. It found its way into the academic curricula of universities only towards the end of the last century (De Winter et al, 2007). This is surprising given that policy-analytical models were being disseminated in Belgium in the late 1960s, and only a little later in the Netherlands. While this sparked the policy analysis movement in the Dutch government and academia, policy analysis education in Belgium remained subsequently underdeveloped, and policy-analytical knowledge was taught in a fragmented fashion. The concept of the policy cycle was, for instance, taught on general political science courses, or as a section in a course on public administration. Other policy-analytical knowledge, such as – for example – policy instruments or policy-analytical methods, appeared as part of public management courses, while substantive policy courses such as social policy, socioeconomic policy, and urban planning would touch mainly on the content of policies, rather than their policy scientific understanding or their design. On the basis of document analysis (including the regional university accreditation reports), and a limited number of interviews, this chapter describes the development of policy analysis instruction from a fragmented into a more autonomous discipline. The chapter also touches on two more questions: whether official professional training curricula have come to embrace policy-analytical knowledge, and whether divergences in policy analysis instruction across the language border reflect different practices in government.

Policy analysis as a discipline in Belgium

Policy analysis is a young discipline in both the Flemish and the French Communities of Belgium, dating back to the late 1990s. In order to understand its emergence better, it is useful briefly to trace the development of political science in Belgium. Political science would become one of the main hosts for the development of policy-analytical instruction and unitary Belgian legislation regulated higher education until the country became a federal state. Part of the story told is indeed national, as political science appeared in Belgium before the country split into a federal state, and before higher education became an exclusive competency of the language communities.

The first School of Political and Social Sciences was founded in 1889 in Brussels by Ernest Solvay, a well-known local industrialist in the chemical sector. This school joined the Free University of Brussels in 1897.[1] Shortly after, the

Catholic University of Louvain created its own school in 1892 and political science programmes were offered in the law faculties of Ghent and Liège the year after. These events were in line with developments in Western Europe and North America (Balzacq et al, 2014).

However, the emergence of modern political science dates back to the 1950s (Balzacq et al, 2014), with the foundation of a political science association, an official journal, and an outreach to the international community of political scientists. The Belgian Political Science Association (*Institut belge de science politique*) was established in 1951, and its journal *Res Publica* in 1959 (initially bilingual in Dutch and French). In 1967, the seventh congress of the International Political Science Association was organised in Brussels.

In the early 1970s, the regionalisation process provoked a split of the former bilingual universities of Brussels and Louvain, and a division of the Political Science Association in 1979, to form the *Politologische Instituut* and the *Institut de science politique*, which was replaced by the *Association belge de science politique – Communauté française* in 1996 (Balzacq et al, 2014). *Res Publica* is still published quarterly in Dutch by the *Politologische Instituut* in collaboration with the Dutch Political Science Association and the Dutch-speaking Belgian Association for Political Sciences (*Vereniging voor de Politieke Wetenschappen*). At the Université catholique de Louvain (UCL), political science emancipated itself both from law and sociology and was recognised as a distinct discipline among the social sciences under the authority of Jean Buchmann, who was the founder of the Department of Political Science in the 1960s (Rihoux et al, 2015, p 23). At KU Leuven, political sciences remain integrated in the Faculty of Social Sciences, which separated from the Faculty of Economics in 1973.

Before the regionalisation of universities, there are no records of distinct policy-analytical courses being taught in political science curricula. It seems that, just like in France (Hassenteufel and Le Galès, forthcoming), policy analysis developed at the margin of political science departments, to be progressively integrated into political science curricula.

Two areas became a focus for modern policy analysis, prior to its integration into political science curricula. One pertains to what is now called applied policy analysis, while the other involves an understanding of actual policymaking, and, more specifically, processes of political decision making. The former found its origin in the Belgian Productivity Centre, which was established under the Marshall Plan. The centre was the driving force behind the Industry-University Foundation that initiated the first management programmes for private sector managers. When it was felt that the public sector should not lag behind, a successful round of training sessions for top civil servants was held in 1960, after which the Administration-University Institute was established (in 1962). Key figures in this institute were much influenced by cybernetics, rational planning and, among others, the works of Yehezkel Dror (1968) and Jay Forrester (1968). This group helped introduce the planning-programming-budgeting system in the mid-1960s, and promoted applied policy-analytical methods. They would later find a home in the political science department of KU Leuven and contribute substantively to policy-analytical curriculum components (as discussed later).

Another early record of policy analysis in the post-war era is the Socio-Political Research and Information Centre (*Centre de recherche et d'information socio-politiques*, CRISP). CRISP was created as an independent research institute in 1958 by Jules-Gérard Libois, a researcher and former journalist. Close to the Social-Christian movement, the aim of the CRISP was, and is, to study political decision making in Belgium. In partnership with CRISP, Jean Meynaud, Jean Ladrière and François Périn, who were themselves affiliated to the universities of Louvain and Liège, published an influential book entitled *La décision politique en Belgique* (*Political decision in Belgium*) in 1965, in which they conduct an empirical analysis of the policy process in Belgium around a series of cases, implicitly referring to the American literature of policy sciences to build up their theoretical framework (Meynaud et al, 1965). They initiated a tradition of empirical descriptive research on policy analysis, which distanced itself to some extent from theoretical endeavour (see CRISP's *Courrier hebdomadaire* publication series at www.cairn. info/revue-courrier-hebdomadaire-du-crisp.htm). Despite the fact that CRISP is not a teaching organisation, its publications promoted the theories of decision making in political science courses (for example, see de Bruyne, 1995).

Policy instruction in academic curricula in the Flemish Community universities

As mentioned above, the transformation of Belgium from a unitary into a federal state entailed that policy competencies for education were regionalised to the language communities. The following two sections describe how policy analysis developed at Flemish universities, and what kind of policy analysis current curricula comprise.

The development of policy analysis in the Flemish Community

It is only since the turn of the millennium that policy analysis courses (known either by that name, or as policy sciences or policy craft) acquired a place in academic curricula. The trajectory of the institutionalisation of policy-analytical instruction is, however, not the same at all Flemish universities. At KU Leuven, policy-analytical content and courses developed under the auspices of public management and public administration, within the Department of Political Sciences of the Faculty of Social Sciences. To be sure, political decision making and the policy cycle also featured in introductory political science courses, operational research and planning was found in economics courses, and sociology and urban policy classes covered some policy content. Yet it was the management research and training at the Perfection Centre for Government Policy and Management, and the transformation of public administration research and instruction, that shaped future policy analysis education. The Perfection Centre was primarily involved with post-academic training in public management and with management research, but its professors Roger Depré and Hugo Van Hassel, and later also Geert Bouckaert, also provided courses with policy-analytical content to the political science curriculum, such as socioeconomic policymaking, and policy and management techniques.

The Public Administration Unit originally provided public administration classes from an administrative law perspective. Its chair, Rudolf Maes (Maes and Jochmans 1996), did much to transform PA (public administration) teaching at Leuven, moving it away from descriptive analysis, and incorporating policy sciences, inspired by the booming field of Dutch policy sciences (see Brans, 1996). In 1997, the Perfection Centre and the Public Administration Unit merged into what is now called the Public Governance Institute. This merger created momentum for the expansion of academic and post-academic programmes in public administration as well as the space to create a new chair in public policy, which was occupied by Marleen Brans. In 1999, the first ever stand-alone course 'Beleidsanalyse' (policy analysis) was added to the curriculum of political science, and comprised both academic policy analysis and applied policy analysis. When half a decade later, the political science curricula adapted to the Bachelor/Master's degree structure, policy analysis instruction expanded once more, with academic policy analysis taught at the Bachelor level, client-oriented applied policy analysis at Master's level, and comparative public policy analysis at the postgraduate level.

Other universities in Flanders also incorporated policy analysis instruction in their curriculum, albeit later on, with the exception of Ghent University, and to a less extensive and less binding degree. In Ghent, public administration was again the adopter of policy analysis. While the curriculum of political sciences introduced a single optional course on policy analysis only in the mid-2000s, it was Ghent Polytechnic that had developed and diversified policy-analytical instruction in the 1990s. Under the leadership of Filip De Rynck, the polytechnic developed a course on public administration and policy craft, and applied policy analysis also found its way into the curriculum in a seminar on policy design and formulation. When the polytechnic merged with the University of Ghent, one of its former lecturers, Ellen Wayenberg, taught a range of policy-analytical courses at the Bachelor and Master's level – policy craft (changed to policy analysis in 2012) and policy evaluation (2014) – as well as a seminar on policy craft. In Ghent, building on the tradition of the polytechnic, policy analysis instruction is now mainly hosted by the Faculty of Economics and Business Administration, within the Bachelor and Master's programmes in public administration and management. It is there that the discipline began to mature through a growing number of policy-analytical courses and increased subject differentiation. At the same time, policy analysis acquired a modest place in the Bachelor degree in political sciences, and gained a firmer foothold as a pre-entry course required for admission into the more specialised Master's programmes on policy craft and management, and on political sciences (national politics).

At the Universiteit Antwerpen, where there is a strong tradition in social policy research, policy courses are found in sociology curricula, for instance, policy sciences. There is no single policy-analytical course in the Bachelor of political sciences, and the one optional course on public policy at Master's level is shared with the Vrije Universiteit Brussel. Yet, content relating to academic policy analysis is also found in political sciences courses, albeit more confined to the study of elites, agenda setting, lobbying and decision making. As for applied policy analysis, the post-executive Master's programme at Antwerp Management School (AMS) offers a skills lab on policy planning and documents.

Social policy analysis has been traditionally strong at the Universiteit Antwerpen, but also, since the late 1990s, at KU Leuven. The late Jos Berghman (educated in Antwerp) established an international Master's programme in social policy analysis (IMPALLA, 2014), run by an international consortium of KU Leuven and CEPS (Centre for Population, Poverty and Public Policy Studies) (Belval, Luxembourg) as host institutions, with Tilburg University (the Netherlands), Université de Lorraine (France) and the University of Luxembourg as associate institutes. For more than a decade, the programme trained advanced Master's students in the analysis of comparative social policy and ran courses devoted to applied and academic policy analysis and policy evaluation.

Policy instruction in the Flemish Community today

As the previous section has shown, there are no specific academic programmes or policy schools in the Flemish Community. Topics of policy analysis are most often addressed as part of political science, sociology or public administration programmes. Master's programmes in public administration in particular feature policy-analytical courses as compulsory components, and so does the Bachelor's degree programme on public administration and management at Universiteit Gent. Most other political science Bachelor programmes, with the exception of that at the Vrije Universiteit Brussel, now have introductory policy-analytical courses on offer or, as at KU Leuven, as part of the compulsory programme. At the KU Leuven, the policy analysis course is opened up as an elective to students from law, economics and arts faculties, as part of the pre-entry requirements for Master's programmes in public administration and political science. Another development of note in the past decade is the growth in substantive policy-analytical courses focusing on a particular domain, such as environmental policy, economic policy, social policy or educational policy. These courses focus on the content of certain public policies but do not study policy analysis as a specific academic field. These courses are therefore not included in this overview.

Policy analysis in Flemish academic instruction clearly represents two complementary perspectives of analysis of policy and analysis for policy (Lasswell, 1951). On the one hand, policy-analytical courses instruct students on theoretical and academic policy analysis. This perspective derives from the science *of* policy, which provides an understanding of the policy process and the actors therein. All four of the Flemish universities that instruct students in social and political science have such a general policy analysis course in their programme. At the Bachelor level, this is mostly a single introductory course. Most of these general courses start from the stages approach, and present meta-analytical and meso-analytical concepts and theories to understand agenda-setting and policy formulation processes, decision making, implementation, evaluation and feedback. Policy analysis in the Master's programmes with a public administration focus more often use an applied perspective to policy analysis and focus mostly on the science *for* policy. This means that students are instructed in methods that focus on the improvement of policies in the real world. While this focus first comprised policy design only, it later expanded to include policy evaluation. At each university, there is also a number of courses with a more singular focus on policymaking. Courses on European policymaking or on pressure groups are cases in point.

It is interesting to note that the term 'policy analysis' retains a certain ambiguousness (Enserink et al, 2013), given that it sometimes refers to the analysis of public policy, sometimes to the analysis for public policy, and sometimes to both. In Dutch, it would make sense to create more clarity if courses on analysis of policy were called '*beleidswetenschap*' or policy science, and courses on analysis for policy '*beleidskunde*' or policy craft.

Policy instruction in academic curricula in the French Community universities

This section shows how policy analysis instruction in French-speaking universities developed from rather empirical descriptive studies of policy, to include more theoretical perspective on policymaking in the 1990s, and, later on, more applied policy-analytical components.

The development of policy analysis in the French Community

The history of policy analysis instruction in the French Community has its origin in CRISP. CRISP's tradition of empirical research on policy analysis was revived in the 1990s, with the creation of policy-analytical chairs and research projects. After a very quiet period in the 1980s, policy analysis was revitalised in the late 1990s. At UCL, Frédéric Varone was hired in 1999 as the first full-time professor in policy analysis at a Francophone university. He set up research projects with theoretical ambitions about policy design in environmental and morality policies, as well as about policy evaluation. This trend continued as UCL increased its staff to three full-time professors in policy analysis. The Université de Liège followed the trend by hiring Catherine Fallon in 2011. At Université libre de Bruxelles (ULB), the focus on sociology and political science was different, and the Department of Political Science here did not consider the option of creating a full-time academic position in policy analysis, even if the discipline was represented and taught at the university.

In parallel, a tradition developed in sociology around the study of public policy (*sociologie de l'action publique*), both at ULB and UCL, where scholars have mainly focused on health and urban policies. Also in sociology, research and related teaching activities developed in the three universities of the French Community about other substantive policies (for example, in the field of immigration and education policy).

Table 14.1: Policy analysis courses in the Flemish Community (2015-16)

	Bachelor	**Master's**
KU Leuven	Policy Analysis (Political Science)	Policy Design and Strategy (Public Administration) Policy Evaluation (Public Administration) Policy Implementation (Public Administration) Comparative Public Policy in Europe (Public Administration) European Policy- and Decision Making (Public Administration) Pressure Groups in the European Union (Public Administration) The Policy Cycle (Sociology) Evaluation Techniques and Tools (Sociology)
Universiteit Gent	Policy Craft (Public Administration) Policy Analysis (Political Science; Public Administration) Seminar Policy Areas (Public Administration) Micro-Economic Analysis of Policy Issues (Public Administration)	Strategic Management and Policy (Public Administration) Scientific Approaches to Public Administration and Policy (Public Administration) Policy Evaluation (Public Administration) Policy Informatics (Public Administration) EU Decision Making (Public Administration)
Universiteit Antwerpen	Policy Sciences (Sociology)	Society, Policy and Evaluation (Political Science) Interest Groups (Political Science) Public Policy Analysis (Political Science) Politics, Policy and Society (Post Executive Management School) Lab Policy, Planning and Documents (Post Executive Management School)
Vrije Universiteit Brussel		Policy Evaluation (Political Science) Discourse Analysis (Political Science) Public Policy Analysis (Political Science)

Note: the information in brackets indicates in which curriculum a course is located.

Policy instruction in the French Community today

In terms of teaching, policy analysis courses follow two objectives: they provide basic policy analysis instruction to multidisciplinary audiences (for example, in law, economics, political and social sciences), and present theories of the policy process. On the one hand, general policy analysis courses provide a toolbox to enable students to conduct policy analyses in a professional environment. They usually start from the stages approach, and develop a policy design perspective, with a view on the actors' interactions at each stage of the policy process. They aim to train future civil servants and introduce students to policy analysis research. Specialised courses in policy evaluation belong to this category. Other specialised courses present the theories of the policy process with a research orientation. In this case, students gain an understanding of the theories with a view to applying them to specific cases. Universities also offer substantive policy courses (for example, social and labour policy, industrial policy or cultural policy), but they usually present the content of specific public policies in a descriptive fashion, and without mobilising the tools of policy analysis. These courses remain outside of the scope of this chapter.

The tradition in the French Community is to have multidisciplinary programmes in social sciences, with a mix of law, economics and history courses. These provide students with the tools to analyse society as well as government activities. It is important to note at this stage that the term 'public policy' is not widely recognised and used in Francophone Belgium. Although this term is used more often in France, the French Community politicians and civil servants almost never refer to '*politique publique*' when presenting a public programme or policy. In fact, in the French Community, the Bachelor degree in political science remains general, and the most specialised courses in policy analysis are located in the Master's programme in public administration, which combines the two sub-disciplines, namely public administration and policy analysis, in a single programme.

With some exceptions, courses on policy analysis remain limited to the portfolios of political science departments. Most are introductory courses, taught in a variety of programmes. There are no schools of public policy in the French Community (they exist in North America and elsewhere) and the policy analysis courses are mainly proposed in the Bachelor degree in political science and the Master's in public administration (see Table 14.2). At the Bachelor level, the offer is broadly limited to a single introductory course over three years, except at ULG, where three courses are on offer. As at KU Leuven, these introductory courses are not limited to the Bachelor in political science (for example, UCL and ULB), and are offered as optional courses in related disciplines in humanities.

More specific courses are proposed in the Master's in public administration (mainly at UCL and ULB), such as policy analysis (or *sociologie de l'action publique*), policy evaluation and comparative public policies. Most of these courses are also accessible to Master's students in political science and sociology. The Master's programmes in environmental management and sciences borrow from policy analysis courses too.

There is no specific PhD programme in public policy, this being recognised as a sub-field of political science and not a discipline in itself. One or two students a year gain a PhD in policy analysis. Most of the students trained in public administration become professionals in the public sector (federal, regional and local administrations, advisers to ministers or MPs, consultants), and very few embark on a scientific career.

Table 14.2: Policy analysis courses in the French Community (2015-16)

	Bachelor	Master's
Université de Namur	Political Analysis of Public Policy (Political Science)	
Université Saint-Louis Bruxelles	Policy Analysis (Political science)	Actors in the European Political System (European Studies) Europeanisation (European Studies)
Université catholique de Louvain	Public Administration and Policy (Political Science) Theories of the Policy Process (Political Science)	Policy Analysis (Public Administration) Comparative Public Policy in Europe (Public Administration) Policy Evaluation (Public Administration) Public Policies of Sustainability (Public Administration) Governance and Public Policy (Public Administration) Public policy (Public Administration)
Université de Liège	Policy Evaluation (Political Science) Policy Analysis (Theory) (Political Science) Methodology and Analysis of Public Policies (Practice) (Political Science)	Comparative Analysis of Public Policy (Political Science) Public Policy (Environmental Studies) Political Science and the Environment (Political Science)
Université Libre de Bruxelles	Introduction to Policy Analysis (Political Science)	Policy Analysis (Public Administration) Sociology of Public Policy (Sociology) European Integration and Public Policy (European Studies) Advocacy and Lobbying in European and Global Affairs (European Studies)

Note: the information in brackets indicates in which curriculum a course is located.

In conclusion, policy analysis courses are more often part of multidisciplinary training programmes than specific training programmes in policy analysis.

Policy instruction in continuous training

This section illustrates some of the rather limited initiatives in policy-analytical training of civil servants at the federal and regional levels. At the federal level, most training programmes are heavily management-oriented, and the single comprehensive policy analysis certificate did not survive the controversy that originated from its content. At the regional level too, management training tends to prevail, although policy-analytical content has started to gain ground.

Policy instruction in federal training programmes

At the turn of the millennium, when the federal government sought to modernise its administration, the minister advocating the reform wanted to create a pool of experts who were capable of supporting the administration's modernisation (De Visscher, 2005; De Visscher et al, 2011). He introduced the Public Management Programme (PUMP), which ran from 2001 to 2009. This intensive programme in public management was tailored to 'promising' middle-range officials (level

A, that is, those with a university degree). Two separate versions of PUMP were developed for Dutch- and French-speaking officials respectively, managed by KU Leuven and ULB. The programme involved public administration and management scholars from the whole country. Eight programmes were organised, with a total of 351 participants (SPF P&O, 2012).

PUMP comprised a two-year, part-time programme, and included 30 days of courses, a traineeship in Belgium or abroad, and consultancy exercises. The aim was to train participants in the processes of public sector modernisation, giving them the vision, knowledge and skills to deal with them. PUMP comprised a series of modules: motivations and social competences; strategic public management; management reforms and management of public policies; budget and management control; Europeanisation of public policies; human resources management; and e-government. Policy-analytical content included themes of policy design, policy evaluation, regulatory governance and Europeanisation. Training took place over a total of five days for each module.

In 2010, PUMP ceased, notably for budgetary reasons, but also because managers complained that their staff took too much time off work to attend the training, and that there was little immediate transfer from the training to the running of their units. The programme was replaced by a two-year development path for managers, including 15 days of training per year. The programme was no longer run by the universities and did not include policy analysis courses.

Current professional training in the federal administration consists of separate courses that are selected individually. In 2007, a single module was offered on policy analysis. Its short history is interesting in that the content of the course was not welcomed equally by participants. The content was very much inspired by client-oriented policy analysis, as promoted in classic handbooks such as that by Weimer and Vining (1989). This did not go down well with a number of participants, who feared that the alleged Anglo-Saxon orientation of the class would create a bias in examinations, and hence also jeopardise the substantial premium that was to be granted on successful completion of the training. Numerous discussions arose on key concepts and particularly on multi-criteria policy analysis. After threats of trade union action on behalf of a number of participants, the course was removed from certified training.

While policy analysis is no longer part of centrally organised certified training, lower federal public officials preparing for promotion to level A can still follow policy-analytical courses as single courses at university, and level A officials can negotiate educational leave to enrol in Master's programmes with policy-analytical content.

Policy instruction and training in the Flemish Community

The first government-wide policy-analytical training of note in the Flemish administration was a course on effectiveness analysis. With the publication of a manual by Geert Bouckaert on effectiveness analysis in 1996, a new set of training objectives was established around the capacity and tools needed to analyse and integrate goal attainment and public service costs (Bouckaert and Vankeirsbilck, 1996). This was organised in close cooperation with the Flemish government, and involved numerous departments and skills labs. While this experience no doubt left its mark on the Flemish civil service, it clashed with an equally short-lived rival training programme that focused on strategic management. Since the 2000s, no other new comprehensive training programmes have been launched. Flemish government executive training initiatives are rather fragmented and bottom-up, tailored to the needs of different agencies and sub-units (Hondeghem et al, 2014). Internal training programmes are heavily management-focused with little focus on policy analysis. Yet, many civil servants have participated in policy-analytical training sessions offered by external private companies, or more often, universities. The Public Governance Institute has been particularly active in offering policy-analytical courses over the past 10 years, covering such content as policy evaluation, policy design, policy instruments and drafting policy documents.

The drafting of policy papers has been a popular training module since it was first introduced in the earlier 2000s. This module focuses on three classical policy-analytical activities – problem analysis, solution analysis and implementation analysis – and on the communication of policy advice in policy papers. Policy evaluation is a more recent module, which has consistently attracted policy workers seeking an introduction to techniques for *ex ante* evaluation, mid-term or *ex post* evaluations.

AMS also offers training modules with policy-analytical content. Its skills lab on policy planning and policy papers now also features more firmly in its post-executive Master's in public management (Antwerp Management School, 2015).

Policy instruction and training in French Community

The first intensive training programme in the French Community was a certificate in management (*Brevet de management de la Communauté française*), which was introduced as part of an administrative reform introducing a mandated qualifications regime for top officials of the French Community (Göransson, 2010). The core courses in the programme covered the various dimensions of public management (for example, human resources, leadership, change management and public marketing), but 10 hours were dedicated to policy evaluation. In 2003, this two-year training programme for public officials with a university diploma was outsourced to ULB. But a few months after courses began, training was suspended for the 60 course participants. In fact, trade unions mounted a legal challenge in the Public Court (*Conseil d'Etat*) to suspend the regional law that had introduced the mandated system in public organisations. It was decided that the *brevet* should no longer be a prerequisite for senior appointments. The certificate subsequently lost its *raison d'être*, and the programme was suspended.

A new initiative for an intensive training programme for level A public officials was introduced by the Francophone governments of Wallonia and Federation

Wallonia-Brussels in the government coalition agreement at the beginning of the 2009-14 legislature. Both governments' coalitions shared not only the same political parties but also a number of ministers. At a time when many mandates for top positions were to be renewed, the Green Party proposed introducing a compulsory qualification for candidates seeking senior appointments in the public administration. The aim of this programme was to constrain political appointments, or at least ensure that candidates were competent in management.

A school of public administration was established (*Ecole d'administration publique Wallonie-Bruxelles*) to administer the Certificate of Public Management (Petit Jean, 2013). There are three stages in the process of gaining certification. First, a competition is organised to recruit candidates. Second, selected students attend a year-long programme – the Executive Master's in Public Management – for one day per week (240 hours of training), sit two exams and write a thesis. The programme is led by ULB and involves almost all of the professors of public administration in the French Community universities. Third, candidates take an oral test organised by the federal selection office, during which they must prove their ability to hold a managerial position.

In the first year, 413 persons entered the competition, and 70 were selected. Of these, 53 passed the Executive Master's programme, and 40 were finally certified after passing the oral test. The results for the second cycle are equivalent.[2] Budgetary constraints and a change of government coalition after the 2014 elections, which put the Greens in the opposition, resulted in the programme being suspended. However, a third and fourth round were still planned in 2016.

In terms of content, the Executive Master's is mainly a management programme. The aim is to make future managers immediately effective in their new position and ensure that they contribute to 'good public governance'.[3] The programme contributes to the development of transversal competences: know the institutional structure of Belgium and the distribution of competences; understand the role of the EU in the policymaking process; create a positive culture in the public service that puts the users at the centre; understand the political objectives and turn them into operational objectives; promote performance and quality, notably with personnel and policy evaluation; manage resources, including human resources; and pilot managerial change.

As a matter of fact, the courses are mainly focused on management issues and tools. There is a strong emphasis on the ability of students to design operational plans that will translate the political objectives of the ministers in concrete measures. It provides the management tools for succeeding in this exercise. The only real policy-analytical course consists of six hours on policy evaluation.

Alternative professional training is provided by the universities of the French Community. In the field of policy analysis, several certificates have been developed, a certificate being a university diploma of 20 credits (where the standard number of credits for a one-year Master's programme is 60). The Francophone universities have joined together to organise a certificate in policy evaluation. This provides students, professionals and public sector officials with an introduction to policy analysis, evaluation process and analytical techniques, and competes with other certificates in public finance and foresight. The supply of alternative training courses is an expanding area and is a topical issue for the Francophone universities.

Conclusion

In this chapter, we have shown how by the turn of the millennium policy analysis instruction at Belgian universities converged to reflect two complementary perspectives on policy analysis: academic policy analysis and applied policy analysis. These perspectives developed at the margin of university education in the 1960s and gradually developed into Bachelor and Master's programmes, mainly in public administration, and particularly at those universities that by the end of 1990s had expanded their faculty with policy scholars. KU Leuven and Universiteit Gent are cases in point, along with UCL and the Université de Liège, where the number and diversification of courses with policy-analytical content increased and diversified. It is mainly public administration programmes that have embraced policy-analytical knowledge and skills as learning outcomes, while there are still a number of political science Bachelor programmes to have only half-heartedly acknowledged policy analysis as a 'must-have' learning outcome for political scientists. As around 20% of civil servants who are engaged in policy-analytical work across the Belgian administrations hold a degree in political and social sciences (see Chapter One), the absence of policy analysis from some political and social science curricula is problematic. The critical mass of policy scholars has increased in Belgium, but the maturation of the policy-analytical discipline at universities is still hampered by the relatively small size of faculty overall. Compared with the Netherlands, for instance, where there are many kinds of policy scholars teaching many kinds of policy analysis, the policy-analytical courses in Belgium remain rather mainstream. For Belgian policy scholars, this is not so much a matter of choice, but rather of necessity. Having said this, low numbers have not kept certain universities from building high-quality internationally accredited programmes that prepare students for policy work and research.

As for continuous training, executive courses for public officials have traditionally been heavily management-oriented. In our view, this still reflects the rather weak institutionalisation of policy analysis as a professional practice, and of a politico-administrative culture that constrains the policy advisory role of civil servants. Moreover, the results of the survey developed for this book confirm that there is room for improving policy-analytical training still further. Between 25% and 40% of civil servants engaged in policy-analytical work are not overly satisfied with the current opportunities for training. There are signs of change, though. The survey results show that substantive numbers have occasionally participated in training programmes related to their policy-analytical work. Increasingly, civil servants have been signing up for external courses. In Flanders, this is most notably the case for courses that train civil servants in drafting policy briefs and papers. In the past decade, the policy cycle in Flanders has come to rely substantively on all kinds of policy briefs and notes with civil service input. Another area that has gained popularity is policy evaluation. While the reliance on policy documents in the policy cycle is less engrained in Wallonia, policy evaluation has received equal if not more attention there, possibly accelerated by that region's higher dependence on European funds, and with it on European evaluation demands.

Notes

1 When referring to bilingual universities, the name of the university in English is used, but when referring to unilingual universities, the names in Dutch and French are used. For example, the Catholic University of Louvain refers to the bilingual university. KU Leuven and the UCL refer respectively to the Dutch-speaking university and the French-speaking university that originated from the split of the bilingual one.

2 See www.eap-wb.be/eap/certificat-de-management-public/les-resultats-du-cmp/ (consulted 16 February 2016).

3 See www.eap-wb.be (consulted 16 February 2016).

References

Antwerp Management School (2015) 'Executive Master in het Publieke Management', available at www.antwerpmanagementschool.be/nl/onze-programmas/masters-voor-professionals/executive-master-in-het-publiek-management-%28mpm%29 (accessed 11 December 2015).

Balzacq, T., Baudewyns, P., Jamin, J., Legrand, V., Paye, O. and Schiffino, N. (2014) *Fondements de science politique*, Brussels: De Boeck.

Bouckaert, G. and Vankeirsbilck, D. (1996) *Doelmatigheidsanalyse van de gemeentelijke dienstverlening: een handleiding*, Leuven: KU Leuven.

Brans, M. (1996) 'De beleidswetenschappelijke benadering in de bestuurskunde', in R. Maes and K. Jochmans (1996) *Inleiding tot de bestuurskunde. Deel 1*, Leuven: StOHO.

De Bruyne, P. (1995) *La décision politique*, Leuven: Peeters.

De Visscher, C. (2005) 'Le coup dans l'eau de Copernic: réforme de la haute fonction publique, nouvelle gestion publique et particratie en Belgique', *Politiques et Management Public*, 23(4): 33-52.

De Visscher, C., Hondeghem, A., Montuelle, C. and Van Dorpe, K. (2011) 'The changing public service bargain in the federal administration in Belgium', *Public Policy and Administration*, 26(2): 167-88.

De Winter, L., Frognier, A., Dezeure, K., Berck, A. and Brans, M. (2007) 'Belgium: from one to two political sciences?', in H. Klingemann (ed) *The state of political science in Western Europe*, Ridgebrook: Barbara Budrich Publishers, 57-72.

Dror, Y. (1968) *Public policymaking reexamined*, Somerset: Transaction Publishers.

Enserink, B., Koppenjan, J.F.M. and Mayer, I.S. (2013) 'A policy sciences view on policy analysis', in W.A.H. Thissen and W.E. Walker (eds) *Public policy analysis: new developments*, New York, NY: Springer, 11-40.

Forrester, J. (1968) *Principles of systems*, Walthan, MA: Pegasus Communications.

Göransson, M. (2010) 'La responsabilisation des hauts fonctionnaires aux différents niveaux de pouvoir', *Courrier hebdomadaire du CRISP*, no. 2056-2057.

Hassenteufel, P. and Le Galès, P. (forthcoming) 'The academic world of French policy analysis', in C. Halpern, P. Hassenteufel and P. Zittoun (eds) *Policy analysis in France*, Bristol: Policy Press.

Hondeghem, A., de Visscher, C., Petit Jean, M. and Ruebens, S. (2014) 'Belgium', in M. Van Wart, A. Hondeghem and E. Schwella (eds) *Leadership and culture. Comparative models of top civil servant training*, New York, NY: Palgrave Macmillan, 137-52.

IMPALLA (2014) *Master of Science in Social Policy Analysis (IMPALLA): self-evaluation report*, Leuven: KU Leuven.

Instituut voor de Overheid (2015) 'Historiek', available at https://soc.kuleuven.be/io/over-het-instituut/historiek (accessed 2 December 2015).

Lasswell, H.D. (1951) 'The policy orientation', in D. Lerner and H.D. Lasswell (eds) *The policy sciences: recent developments in scope and method*, Stanford, CA: Stanford University Press, 3-15.

Maes, R. and Jochmans, K. (1996) *Inleiding tot de bestuurskunde. Deel 1*, Leuven: STOHO.

Meynaud, J., Ladrière, J. and Périn, F. (1965) *La décision politique en Belgique: le pouvoir et les groupes*, Paris: Armand Colin.

Petit Jean, M. (2013) 'Le régime des mandats dans l'administration wallonne', *Courrier hebdomadaire du CRISP*, no. 2166-2167.

Rihoux, B., Van Ingelgom, V. and Defacqz, S. (2015) (eds) *La légitimité de la science politique. Construire une discipline, au-delà des clivages*, Louvain-la-Neuve: Presses de l'Université de Louvain.

SPF P&O (2012) *10 ans SPF P&O 2001-2011*, Brussels: P&O.

Vakgroep Publieke Governance (2015) 'Over de vakgroep', available at www.ugent.be/eb/publiek-management/nl/over-ons (accessed 9 December 2015).

Weimer, D L. and A.R. Vining (1989) *Policy analysis: concepts and practice*, Englewood Cliffs, NJ: Prentice-Hall.

Index

Note: Page numbers in *italics* indicate figures and tables.